I0625764

BEFORE I FORGET

BEFORE I FORGET

An Adventure Story

JEFFREY M. PURYEAR

Yuba Books
Washington, DC

Copyright © 2024 by Jeffrey Puryear
Yuba Books
Washington D.C.
All rights reserved.

ISBN: 979-8-9921741-0-6 eBook
ISBN: 979-8-9921741-1-3 Paperback

ACKNOWLEDGMENTS

I offer a special thanks to my parents—Oscar and Lucille—whose love, discipline, and encouragement helped me go places they couldn't have imagined.

I thank five institutions that fundamentally changed my life: Michigan State University for placing the world in front of me; the Peace Corps for introducing me to Latin America and giving me a second culture; the University of Chicago for connecting me to academic elites and excellence; the Ford Foundation for providing seventeen years of the most challenging and stimulating work—and colleagues—I could imagine; and the Inter-American Dialogue for thrusting me into the policy game.

I thank my simply wonderful wife, Myriam, for her love, patience and inspired suggestions.

I thank our daughter, Milena, for expanding my world, making me laugh, and keeping my feet on the ground.

I thank my copy editor, Regina Higgins, for making a manuscript I thought was perfect, perfecter.

And I thank the many friends and colleagues who read and commented on drafts of the manuscript, or simply provided advice: Abe Lowenthal, Peter Hakim, Jim Himes, Steve Heyneman, Marcela Gajardo, Michael Shifter, John Dinges, Jim Sterba, Peter Osnos, Shep Forman, Gary Theisen, Paul and Amanda Brink, Scott Durschlag, David and Penny VanDam, Eduardo Vélez, Frank Fukuyama, Gary Horlick, Michael Lisman, Karen Neva Bell, Peter Cleaves, Alan Flusser, and Patricia Arregui.

ACKNOWLEDGMENTS

TABLE OF CONTENTS

PROLOGUE

WHAT AND WHY

I STARTED OUT just wanting to write. Anything, really, and see how it turned out. I opted for memoir because nothing else seemed to make sense. So I've focused on remembering. But it all started with wanting to write.

Remembering turns out to be fertile ground. I've got a good story—about how a kid from rural Michigan grew up, got out, and did good. At least that's what he thinks. And at the end of his life tried his hand at real writing, something he finally realized he also wanted to do. An adventure story for sure. Perhaps a success story. Maybe even a love story.

But writing is what got me going. I'm driven by the mad idea that maybe I can write well. Better than I've ever written before. Just thinking about it excites me. Memory is my vehicle.

Still, writing well isn't much if you don't have something to say. And saying implies that there's someone out there—a reader—you're saying it to. That means it's not just stream of consciousness and it's not just about me. It's also about my reader (who may be more than a little mysterious). I'm not just documenting and interpreting, I'm also sharing. It's got to be good and it's got to be interesting.

It is, and that's surprising. I was born to parents of modest means who grew up even more modestly in the Great North Woods of Michigan's lower peninsula and moved to the state capital, Lansing, as soon as they got married, seeking better prospects. Both had been raised in warm, loving families and graduated from high school. But that's pretty much all they had. My father was an Army medic in Europe during World War II and then managed a gas station on the west side of Lansing. Eventually he moved up to an executive position in the company that owned the gas station. My mother stayed at home until my brother and I started junior high, when she began work as a secretary. Lots of people, including many of my aunts and uncles, were like them, leaving behind the rural communities they'd been raised in up north for jobs downstate, often in the big city.

And their timing was good. The automobile had replaced lumber as Michigan's major source of wealth and Lansing was well-positioned. R.E. Olds had founded Oldsmobile there in 1897. A Fisher Body plant began operations in 1935. The city was already a budding industrial powerhouse. And the post-war boom was about to start. My parents would catch a small piece of that.

I grew up on a 20-acre "farm" a few miles south of Lansing in surroundings that started out rural and then, when I went off to high school, became small-town. I lived a normal life so far as I can tell: a little crazy, occasionally rebellious, reasonably happy, and largely unconnected to the world of ideas, money, and power—or to anything beyond Michigan. There was nothing uncommon about that. Lots of kids grew up like I did.

But what I did after was not so common—getting my hands dirty helping *campesinos* with the Peace Corps in Colombia, studying with giants at the University of Chicago, working with luminaries at the world's largest private foundation—Ford—in Latin America, and thinking with really smart people at a Washington think tank. I gave away money. I wrote an academic book. I met amazing people. I saw the world—or at least enough of it. I even saw, a few times I'm pretty sure, history being made. That was uncommon—a genuine adventure. How it happened, what it was like, and what I think I learned are what this memoir is about.

A note about what's in and what's out: I'm writing about what I find interesting and important (and can remember reasonably well—no small task). Some of that is about work, some about play, and some about growing up. The rest I'm leaving out. Most memoirs I've read do that. They chronicle what their authors feel strongly about and have the vision and courage to put into words. They're personal. When they show us something important about the author's world, and that we can relate to—which is what I'm trying to do—they can be delightful.

What I'm not doing is confessing. Several memoirs I've read are filled with poverty, trauma, pain, and family dysfunction (Mary Karr's *Liar's Club* and Frank McCourt's *Angela's Ashes* are high-profile examples). Their authors document vividly how and why they suffered when they were young—how it was tough, and how, nonetheless, they managed to make it. Their stories are painful and inspirational, but when I compared them with what I was writing I found myself wondering why my story wasn't more fraught. How come I hadn't suffered like they did? What dark past was I leaving out but ought to be putting in? What was I ignoring, or even hiding?

I couldn't come up with much. I didn't feel seriously disadvantaged or traumatized or neglected while growing up. I could complain about this or that, of course, but basically life was pretty good. And I say that after having done nearly three years of psychotherapy where the objective was to shine light into dark corners, see what was there, and get it out. I found some stuff and I benefited from confronting it. But it didn't seem anywhere near the trauma the authors whose memoirs I was reading had experienced. I just didn't have a lot of angst. Woe is not me.

I may be deluding myself, of course. It's tempting, when you write a memoir, to indulge in pleasant and long-held convictions about who you are, where you came from, and what shaped you—and to make yourself look good. I'm aware of that. I've tried to avoid it. But it's hard. And the past is often dark and fuzzy. I can only hope I've gotten it reasonably right. You are, at least, getting my best effort.

So I didn't grow up in pain and privation. Nor did I grow up in money and privilege. Winston Churchill has an observation in his first memoir, *My Early Life*, that makes you realize how different he was from you, me, and just about everybody: "My father and mother had always been able to live near the summit of the London world, and on a modest scale to have the best of everything." (I especially like the "modest scale" part.)

I didn't grow up with the best of everything. But I grew up with the best, or near-best, of a few things: love, values, discipline, and the conviction that I mattered. I got an especially strong sense of right and wrong from my family and my church and probably from the Boy Scouts. I was told I had things to do, even though it wasn't clear what they were. I wasn't always comfortable or in agreement with what I was getting, but that combination had a tremendous impact. It explains much of any success and happiness I've had. I was lucky. I may even have been blessed.

So this is a making sense of my life—or at least those parts that I think deserve setting down. I was driven from the beginning by three big urges: get out of rural Michigan, become an intellectual, and make the world a better place. I don't know where those urges came from, exactly. I first remember feeling them in high school. They never went away. I've tried to make good on all three. They explain much of what I did—the Peace Corps, the PhD, the Ford Foundation, the think tank, the academic book I wrote, and the book you're reading now. They add up. Those urges have guided my life.

The story I'm telling is uncommon in various ways. I went to a one-room country school, which a few still did back then, although today almost no one does. I spent two years in the Peace Corps, and in the process acquired a second culture—almost a second identity—that enriched my life and fundamentally shaped my career. I studied at one of the world's great universities and was amazed by how much it demanded, and how much it gave in return. I practiced a rare and little-understood profession—international philanthropy—and developed strong views on what it's like to give away millions and how to do it. I spent a couple of decades at a Washington think tank trying to influence Latin American policy and policymakers and discovered how hard that is, but how rewarding as well. I met extraordinary people and did a lot that was not only extraordinary but just plain fun.

What these exploits have in common is that they're not things a kid from rural Michigan could reasonably expect to do. I regularly had to operate in terrain very different from the terrain I grew up in, and for which I had little preparation. So my experience might offer lessons (or at least encouragement) to others starting from similarly humble backgrounds and wondering where and how far they might go. It demonstrates, I think, the merits of aiming high and working hard—and of being lucky. Few have been as fortunate as I. Fewer write about it.

Because the simple urge to write was so fundamental to my decision to write a memoir, you'll see that at the end of some chapters I stop and ask myself how the writing's going. Those sections chronicle the journey within my journey: trying to figure out how to write well. I find that fascinating, of course, but I'm biased. Feel free to skip over them. There's plenty more to read.

Finally, a word on structure. This book follows the sequence of my life: growing up, school, career. That's because I'm trying to make sense not only of what I did but of how I came to do it. That, I think, requires describing how I got to be who I am and what I learned on the way. And, frankly, no other organizing principle came to mind. I also jump around a bit, usually when what I'm saying reminds me of something more distant that is connected in a way I find interesting. When I do I hope you'll find it interesting too.

That goes for the entire book, of course.

I

GETTING STARTED

Very few writers really know what they're doing until they've done it.

—ANNE LAMOTT, *BIRD BY BIRD*

AFTER FOUR DECADES, and with real reluctance, I decided to retire. It wasn't easy. Retiring was like returning a book to the library. It was a good book. I'd enjoyed reading it. I didn't really want to take it back. But it was dog-eared and overdue. It was time.

I was satisfied—delighted, really—with my career. I'd spent nearly forty years working on Latin America and the Caribbean, mostly with two institutions, the Ford Foundation and the Inter-American Dialogue. I'd lived in East Lansing, Durham, Granada (a small village in the mountains of Colombia), Medellín (the capital of Colombia's Antioquia province), Chicago, Bogotá, Santiago, Lima, San Francisco, New York, and Washington DC, and studied or done research at five excellent universities—Michigan State, Duke, Chicago, Stanford, and NYU.

In the process I'd become fluent in Spanish, gotten to know some of Latin America's best and brightest intellectuals and politicians (along with a bunch of artists), met several Nobel prize-winners, and several presidents, and worked with some of the smartest and funniest colleagues anyone could imagine. I also learned first-hand about military dictatorships, development economics, human rights, ceviche, North

Beach, the Shining Path insurgency, Tribeca, and a lot more. I gave good people real money, did some policy analysis, wrote an academic book and a bunch of articles, and published Op-Eds in two of the *Times* (*New York* and *Los Angeles*). I hiked and skied in the Andes. I became a husband, stepfather, and serial dog owner. I made good friends in the U.S. and Latin America. I traveled a lot.

That seemed pretty good for a kid from rural Michigan.

So, retire? I wasn't ready to do that. I had always defined myself in terms of work, and for the most part enjoyed working. Now that I could do what I wanted, I wanted to work. But what kind of work? I wasn't sure. I wasn't enthusiastic about doing more of the same, and I wanted to have control over my time. I wasn't looking to earn money. Something inside was urging me to think different.

Pretty quickly I realized that I wanted to write. I enjoyed writing and had written throughout my career. But it was always part of my broader professional responsibilities—recommending that the Ford Foundation do this or that or outlining the prospects for democracy in Chile. For a couple of years, I did more of that kind of stuff.

But in the back of my mind there was always another notion—more accurately an urge—to write something completely different. I had no idea what. Something was in there—a mysterious figure under a black cloth, rocking back and forth, and waiting to come out. A muse, perhaps, who could take me to new heights of creativity and delight. At least that's how I felt. And you don't ignore a muse.

It made me nervous—the idea of sitting down to write without a clear objective, just to see what might come out—fact, fiction, my life, life on Mars. I had never given myself that kind of freedom. What would I say? What if nothing came out? What if something awful came out? Or boring? Why did I think I had anything worth saying? How much of this was vanity? Self-deception?

So I started looking around see how others had responded to the "Why write?" question. I found a good answer almost immediately in Stephen King's memoir (*On Writing*). King is a prolific writer (over fifty books) who started when he was a little boy. He takes writing seriously.

In fact, he's a little nuts about it (in a nice way—he sees writing as an "act of telepathy"). Looking back on his experience, he argues that writing is "about enriching the lives of those who will read your work, and enriching your own life, as well." Writing is "...magic, as much the water of life as any other creative art."

Magic. Great. Enrich my life. And the lives of my readers (Please Lord, let me have readers!). That was all the encouragement I needed. I would write. I would write about whatever I wanted. I was all in.

But what did I want to write? On the one hand, I was reluctant to try writing a memoir. It seemed tedious to revisit the details of my life— how I had thought this and wanted that and overcome something else. I already knew this stuff. Why rehash it? Albert Hirschman, one of the twentieth century's most distinguished social scientists, resisted writing about his past: "I tend to think of it as the ultimate admission of having run out of ideas." That's how I felt. I had often criticized people who keep talking over and over about some meaningful experience they had years ago, instead of letting go and moving on. Too much of that and you stop growing, it seemed to me.

Plus I had reservations about putting my life down in print. Maybe I'd have plenty to say and enjoy saying it. But, so far as I could tell, I had no strong urge to share it with the world. It was personal. When it came to my inner feelings, I had never been a show-and-tell kind of guy. I was raised Lutheran, after all.

On the other hand, the standard dictum is "write what you know," so writing about your life probably shouldn't be taken off the table too quickly. After all, what else do you have? Maybe I could offer some lessons to others.

I went back to Stephen King's memoir (which, by the way, is great). He urged writers to write about "Anything you damn well want...as long as you tell the truth." Further, he interpreted the "write what you know" dictum broadly to include what your heart knows and what your imagination knows. Otherwise, he noted, no one would write science fiction. Good point. Follow your nose, write about what moves you, and don't get too hung up over it.

So I sat down at my desk to see what would happen. That was interesting. I can't say that nothing happened. But I did not suddenly see, in all its glory, the magic that King said was there. No topic appeared in floodlights, demanding I write about it. No outline for a wonderful book scrolled across my screen. My muse, if he existed, remained under his black cloth.

What did happen was that a few thoughts floated by, like goldfish in a tank. I grabbed one and began to write. You have to start somewhere.

The thought turned out to be a place: Michigan State University. I had done my BA there, just ten miles from home in rural Michigan. For a small-town kid (rural, really) to enroll in a large, modern university was a big deal—welcome to the world. This seemed to have dramatic potential. I could write about a callow youth facing challenges and choices for which he had little preparation, and that would mark him for the rest of his life. A promising theme. Kind of a sequel to *American Graffiti*.

Instead I wrote humor. To my utter surprise, what came out were a couple of humorous sketches. At least I thought they were humorous. The kind of thing a standup comic might do. Here they are:

> I went to school at Michigan State University, which was the original land-grant college, so you met all kinds of people. I remember it had a lot of fraternities and sororities. And because of the university's <u>roots</u> in agriculture (get it?) some of them <u>catered</u> to people who wanted careers in the food service industry (get it again?).
>
> For example, there was a sorority exclusively for food service majors. I think it was called Pita Pita Pi. The sorority house was shaped like an eggplant. Or maybe it was the sorority sisters…could have been a requirement for pledging (bada bum!). I don't quite remember. But they were a fun bunch.
>
> Michigan State was also a big football school. You would stumble across these All-American football players with names like "Sherm" and "Bubba" walking—lumbering—around campus

munching on cheeseburgers. There was even a fraternity for football players. It was called Wham Bama Slama. Everybody said they had really good food, but I never got invited to their parties. Probably just as well because I was pretty small and could easily have been mistaken for an appetizer.

Where did that come from? My inner Woody Allen? What happened to serious? What should I make of this?

I decided: a) that this was genuine, so I should accept it; b) that I liked it; and c) that writing is more mysterious than I thought. Not a bad start.

I sat down again. This time what showed up was very empirical: I wrote about retiring and deciding that I should write, and what it was like to write after deciding to write. I wrote what you're reading right now. It was fun at first, but pretty quickly I got worried. Writing about deciding to write? How far would that take me? Wasn't that an infinite loop? At some point wouldn't I have to write about something more than deciding to write?

Anyway, I kept at it. I took heart from another of King's observations: "Sometimes you have to go on when you don't feel like it, and sometimes you're doing good work when it feels like all you're managing is to shovel shit from a sitting position." There must be something worthwhile here.

I noticed also that I was having fun. And I realized that fun was part of what attracted me to writing. I was feeling playful. Taking a topic, finding its essence, and expressing that well in words was like solving a puzzle. I had gotten involved and didn't want to stop until I got it right. It put me in the here and now, and it felt good.

That was big. As long as I was having fun, I didn't have to worry about whether what I wrote was any good, or even what good meant, or whether anybody else would read it. It was like spending a couple of hours on the golf course all by yourself. Play is its own reward.

OK, but what next? A novel? I had no idea, so I decided to pick my earliest memory and write about it. Here goes:

II

UP NORTH

When does one first begin to remember? When do the waving lights and shadows of dawning consciousness cast their imprint upon the mind of a child?

—Winston Churchill,
My Early Life 1874-1904

The great, dark trees of the Big Woods stood all around, and beyond them were other trees and beyond them were more trees. As far as a man could go to the north in a day, or a week, or a whole month, there was nothing but woods.

—Laura Ingalls Wilder,
The Little House in the Big Woods

I **WAS THREE** years old and standing outside the pump house on my grandparents' farm near the village of Freesoil in northern Michigan on a hot summer day watching cold water pour onto the ground from a tall cast-iron pump. That's why they called it the pump house. There was something mesmerizing about watching ice-cold water gush from God's good earth into the summer heat. You just had to wet your hands and splash it on your face.

Polio had driven my brother, Gary, and me to our grandparents' farm for the summer. Normally we lived downstate, in Lansing, but a major polio outbreak frightened our parents with images of crippled children, leg braces, and iron lungs. So they sent us to the farm, to avoid contagion. My mother also spent one of those summers in a sanatorium, recovering from tuberculosis, and someone needed to care for us while my father worked. Disease loomed large in our lives back then.

The upside was that we got to live on a real family farm. My grandparents, Frank and Anna Battige, farmed 40 acres the old-fashioned way—with a team of draft horses, a herd of cows, and a flock of chickens. They had a red-brick farmhouse, white wooden barn, granary, chicken coop, corn crib, garage, and (of course) the pump house. The farm was largely self-sufficient and a little like something out of Laura Ingalls Wilder (whom of course I hadn't read yet).

My grandfather milked cows, tended chickens, plowed, disked, dragged, cultivated, hauled manure, made hay, planted and harvested grain, and repaired what needed repairing. He did all that with horses and hands. He never owned a tractor.

My grandmother cooked on a wood-burning stove, tended a large garden, gathered eggs, slaughtered and plucked chickens, washed clothes, cleaned house, and sewed. She regularly took the farm's produce (eggs, chickens, sweet corn, tomatoes, lettuce, cucumbers, green beans, strawberries, rhubarb, and more) "to market"' in Manistee, the nearest decent-sized town, to sell from a stand. Their kids—my mother, aunt Helen and uncle Bill (plus my "aunt" Carol who'd joined the family after her mother, my grandmother's sister, died)—helped out.

They did that successfully. My aunt Helen, decades later, would say "We were poor but we didn't know it." I'm more inclined to say that, while they didn't have much money, they met their needs, had good values, raised good kids, and were upstanding members of the local community. Not bad.

I was, of course, too young to remember much. Until you're six or seven, you mostly remember images and feelings. Remembering activities is hard, and dialogue is impossible.

I loved the horses—massive, quiet, and powerful in their leather harnesses, smelling of sweat and manure. They pulled the plow, disk, drag, cultivator, mower, side and back rakes, hay-loader, dray, and wagons that were needed to plant, raise, and harvest crops in those days. My grandfather walked or rode behind them holding the long leather reins and shouting "giddyup," "gee," "haw," and "whoa"—a general in bib overalls. The noise, dust, energy and movement were exciting. I was delighted when I was occasionally allowed to take the reins, even if only for a few seconds—a little boy driving big horses. For the first time I had power and responsibility.

My grandfather made hay. Hay was indispensable—the food that would keep the horses and cows alive during northern Michigan's long, cold winters—so it got high priority. But once you started to make it, you couldn't stop. You had to get the cut hay dry and under cover before it rained, or it might turn moldy. "Make hay while the sun shines" was no joke. You worked long and hard.

The process was elaborate. You cut the hay with a mowing machine, let it dry a bit, used a side rake to shape the swaths into windrows that would dry it more, and that the loader could pick up and drop onto a wagon. Then you hauled the wagon to the barn, where a set of large steel forks descended by pulleys from a rail inside the roof, lifted a huge pile of loose hay to the ceiling, carried it across the gloomy interior, and dropped it into the loft. There was something deeply satisfying about getting the hay safely into the barn—as if you'd taken one more step in protecting the farm from northern Michigan's brutal winters. And watching those big loads of dry hay land with a "whomp" in the loft was high entertainment—the nearest thing we had to fireworks. It also smelled great. Making hay was my favorite part of summer.

Another thing I remember is manure. Kids learned about manure at an early age on the farm. You saw it, smelled it, and stepped in it. We had three kinds: horse, cow, and chicken. They were all different. Horse manure, AKA "horse apples," was a collection of round, dark spheres that smelled a little bit sweet. They dried out quickly and got hard, and sometimes my brother and I threw them at each other. Cow manure, AKA "cow pies," were slightly rounded khaki-colored discs, the outsides of which dried in the hot sun, leaving a brittle crust over a squishy mess. Barefoot kids were always stepping in them. I can't explain what they smelled like, but it wasn't good. Chicken manure, AKA "chicken-poop," was entirely different, gray or white squiggles like fat worms, that smelled awful and were the worst to step in. I still remember that smelly, greasy stuff between my toes. We avoided it at all costs.

Manure had to be removed. The stuff accumulated quickly in the stalls, barnyard, and chicken coop, and you couldn't leave it there. Among other things, it smelled bad. Fortunately it was good fertilizer. So you shoveled it onto a manure pile outside the barn and later onto a dray to be dragged out and scattered on the fields. (So far as I can remember, my grandfather didn't have a manure spreader.) Much of the time you didn't really shovel manure, you pitched it, with a manure fork that was wider than a hay fork and had tines that were closer together. In the stalls, manure usually fell on top of straw, which held it together so the fork could handle it. If the manure was not lying on straw, or if it was urine-soaked (often the case), you needed a shovel.

What I never understood, and still seems mysterious, is why manure inspires so much feeling. "Horseshit," for example, is slang for "non-sense," and "chickenshit" is slang for "coward." People use these words with emotion. How did that happen? And why isn't "cowshit" slang for anything? What does that say about horses, chickens, and cows?

The farm also had an outhouse. Most farms still had them back then, even after installing indoor toilets (which my grandparents had done only recently). For a while, at least, people continued to use outhouses out of habit. In the summer you were outside, so the outhouse was more convenient (which I guess was why they called it an outhouse). There was something relaxing about entering that cool dark space, closing the door and sitting on the round hole worn smooth and shiny by countless backsides. Theirs was a "two-holer," so you might sit side-by-side with someone—usually someone you knew. Mostly it was my brother, Gary. I don't remember talking much. It was quiet, peaceful and the smell wasn't bad. There was usually toilet paper, and if not, there were always pages from an old *Sears and Roebuck* catalogue.

There were neighbors. The rural community my grandparents lived in was populated substantially by migrants from northern Europe. Their parents (named Battige and Woebbeking) had migrated from Germany. But the community also included Poles, Swedes, and Lithuanians with names like Kranaskas, Yanusv, Eganeski, Lindquist, Shereda, Larsen, Stoppenhagen, Vitucki, Pieczynski, Bigge and Kepulviac. There were home-made sausage, sauerkraut, dill pickles, and cake. There was a tiny Lutheran church. People danced the polka.

The nearest town (a village, really) was named Free Soil, after the political party that had opposed the expansion of slavery into the western territories during the mid-1850s. Choosing that name for their village probably said a lot about their anti-slavery sentiments. Just as interesting, my father grew up in a tiny village a few miles away that was founded as a colony of the German Baptist Brethren Church. They called it Brethren, naturally. These were new settlements, and people put their stamp on them. I guess most people I met were either immigrants or the children of immigrants. But I never thought of them as anything but Americans.

Two more thoughts about my grandparents:

First, they were connected to nature in ways that today we can barely imagine or appreciate. Their money and food came almost entirely from the soil they worked and the animals they raised. They tilled, planted, weeded, harvested, stored, tended, butchered, fished, hunted, and gathered. They made their own bread, soup, pies, cookies, sauerkraut, pickles, and sausage. They canned and otherwise stored what they raised in the garden to help them get through the long Michigan winter. That was what farmers did. And even if they did it well, they had to worry about the weather. Nature was their serious and unruly partner. They grappled with it every day, often in ways that were not only economic but also intimate (imagine slaughtering a chicken or milking a cow).

That was true despite the fact that they'd managed to get further from the clutches of nature than had their parents. By the time I was spending summers on the farm (the late 1940s), my grandparents had central heating (downstairs, at least), indoor plumbing, electricity, a radio, and an automobile. Their parents (my great-grandparents) did without running water, central heating, or electricity, and traveled largely on foot or on horseback. Life was a lot tougher. They dealt with nature routinely in ways none of us, or anyone we know, does today.

Second, my grandparents were deeply connected to their neighbors. It was hard to be anonymous in Free Soil. The community was small. There wasn't much to do beyond farming and churchgoing, except deer-hunting in the fall and ice-fishing in the winter. And maybe on a summer evening driving the mile or so into Free Soil proper for an ice cream cone. All that put you in contact with neighbors. Everybody pretty much knew everybody else.

And neighbors helped each other out. Threshing was one example. Any farmer who raised wheat or oats had to hire a threshing machine for a day or two each summer to beat the dried shocks, separate the grain from the straw and chaff, and funnel it into bags so it could be stored or sold. ("Combines," which combined these processes with cutting and gathering the grain in the field had not yet become common up north.) Threshing required lots of hands, so neighbors would come for the day to help. My grandmother would prepare a huge lunch of fried chicken, boiled potatoes, home-baked bread, coleslaw, sweet corn, lettuce, dill pickles, sliced tomatoes, cake, and pie, and serve it on a table outdoors, under the big tree beside the pump house. It was festive and social. It brought people together. It helped build community.

Church was an important part of social life. Since most people had roots in northern Europe, they tended to be Lutheran and attend church every Sunday (or so it seemed to my little-boy eyes). We certainly did. Church was firmly religious, of course, combining the spiritual majesty of Jesus with the moral authority of His teachings. It was a rock on which neighbors relied in the face of a world that often seemed arbitrary and precarious.

But it was also social. This began with arrival at church on Sunday morning—everyone dressed in their best and greeted inside by an usher (also a neighbor dressed in his best) who showed them politely to a pew where more neighbors (dressed in their best) silently nodded in greeting. These were good people signaling to each other that they shared important beliefs and values, and intended to get along.

When the service ended the social side ramped up. People filed out the door at the back of the church, paid their respects to Pastor Hessler and started talking. They didn't talk about religion. They talked about each other—what they'd done, seen, thought, and felt during the past week. It was a catching up and a comparing of notes on topics as diverse as family, politics, crops, and the weather—an oral version of a local newspaper. They enjoyed It. I especially remember, during one of those post-church chitchats, the light in my Grampa Frank's eyes and the smile on his face as he talked with neighbors. This met a need. It was important.

The result, despite distance, rudimentary transportation and very few telephones, was a community that provided identity, conversation, entertainment, assistance, and meaning, all contained within a few square miles. People had their differences, of course, and life was hard, but they shared geography, heritage, and livelihood, and they felt (so far as I could tell) connected in ways that were vital and positive. It was pretty good, as Garrison Keillor might say. Today communities like that are difficult even to imagine.

Perhaps the most important thing I got from those summers was Northern Michigan. Basically, I fell in love with the place. My grandparents' farm was in the blessed northern third of Michigan's mitten-shaped lower peninsula—an area marked by rugged forests, pristine lakes and cold weather. Northern Michigan is geologically and ecologically distinct from the southern part of the state. That's why locals refer to it as "Up North."

Downstate the land is relatively flat, dominated by farms and towns, with the occasional lake or rivers. Fields outnumber forests, giving a sense of space and openness. Cities are common. Many are large. Roads are generally paved. Life is about people and civilization, order and control. You think about the future. Winters are cold, but no worse than in Chicago or Cleveland. You could just as well be in Illinois, Indiana, or Ohio.

Northern Michigan is different. As you drive north, cities give way to towns and villages. Farms give way to forest. Flat land gives way to hills, hollows, lakes and ponds. The sense of space, so common downstate, gives way to a sense of confinement—of being surrounded by trees. You begin to notice ferns growing in the woods. The occasional white-barked paper birch is silhouetted against dark pines. The soil becomes sandy. You see deer. Maybe wild turkeys. Maybe even a porcupine. One-lane dirt roads disappear mysteriously into the woods. Northern Michigan's past—the Indians, fur traders, missionaries, lumberjacks, and farmers who wrested a life from this dark and difficult terrain—creeps into your mind. You begin to suspect that the great Laurentide Ice Sheet (which Bruce Catton—Pulitzer laureate and northern Michigander—famously described in *Waiting for the Morning Train* as "two miles high, hundreds of miles wide and many centuries deep") and which only relaxed its frigid grip 10,000 years ago, is lurking on the other side of Lake Superior, and planning its return. A sense of wildness takes over. Civilization recedes and the ghosts of Hiawatha emerge from the gloomy forest.

Northern Michigan's woods are part of something bigger—the Great North Woods that also cover New England, upstate New York, upstate Wisconsin, eastern Minnesota and much of northern Canada. Dense and mysterious, they sprang up many centuries ago, blanketing the moraines, gullies and lakes the glacier left as it melted its way back north. Pretty much all land that wasn't covered by water was covered by trees—mostly beech, sugar maple, oak, hemlock, and white pine. The early European explorers encountered the deep shade and magical shadows of trackless, seemingly endless, forest. This was, as Henry Wadsworth Longfellow declared, "the forest primeval."

But the lumber boom of the 1850s changed all that, causing most of the first-growth forest to be cut down, sawed into boards and shipped to the cities flourishing further south, and making Michigan temporarily rich. The exploding demand for lumber so near Michigan's (seemingly inexhaustible) supply probably made the deforestation inevitable. But it was intensified by two inventions. The narrow-gauge railroad made it possible to harvest logs that were nowhere near rivers, suddenly opening the entire forest to lumbering. And the steam sawmill dramatically increased the speed at which logs could be cut into planks, turning what had been handicraft into industry. So over the next sixty years, the woods were pretty much clear-cut. The land was exposed. The forest primeval became stumps.

My grandfather was part of that lumber boom, working as a cook in a lumber camp while a youngster. Decades later my father, who grew up near-poor, spent part of his teenage years working in a Civilian Conservation Corps camp near Cadillac replanting forests that had been decimated by the lumber boom. They'd experienced the woods from opposite sides, but for both my grandfather and my father it was the source of much-needed money. Anyone, it seemed, who grew up in those times in Northern Michigan was touched by timber.

The miracle is that, a century or more later, the forest has crept back. Its return has followed the classic ecological succession model—from aspens and poplars to conifers to hardwoods. We're well into the conifer stage. Second-growth pine forests, typically 80-100 years of age, predominate, but are dotted with sugar maples, oaks, beech, and other hardwoods—the trees of the future. That's the forest I fell in love with as a kid.

Why? Part of it was the wildness. There was nothing like it downstate. Entering the forest was like leaving civilization. I was a visitor in a land populated by deer, bears, and snakes. The only humans who belonged here were Indians, and they'd pretty much gone. I was surrounded by trees, ferns, rocks, and grasses. A huge glacier had ground through years ago. The rules were different. Nature was in charge. Rain, snow, wind, heat, and cold were decisive. I could only observe and keep out of the way.

The wildness changed how I saw the world. It pulled me back a bit from the creeping civilization and urbanity I'd grown up in downstate. It put me in touch with something different and elemental—something that was part of me and maybe where I'd come from. And, like the glacier, it marked me. Perhaps in ways I didn't realize. I'm probably not the only one. Ernest Hemingway, let's remember, spent the first twenty-one summers of his life in a 20- by 40-foot clapboard cottage that his parents had built on Walloon Lake in the woods of Northern Michigan. And he wrote a number of short stories set in Michigan's woods, the most famous of which is probably "Big Two-Hearted River."

Another part of it was the mystery. There was something unknowable about the woods. It was profoundly silent, except for the wind rustling through the trees. It was at least a little gloomy. You could only see short distances—after that it was all trees. What was out there? An old Indian path? A deep pond scraped out by the glacier? Owls? Bear? Ancient white pines that lumberjacks somehow missed? You wanted to walk in and find out. But no matter how far you walked, you never really knew. The woods held its secrets close.

Maybe part of the attraction was its similarity to the Wild West. Bruce Catton, writing about the North Woods in *Michigan: A History*, asserts that "the magnet that drew men…was that it offered escape; here, at the least, a man was not forced into a mold, his life constricted by the nearness and prejudices of innumerable neighbors, and if he wanted to he could move out to the realm of the wholly lawless and live as he chose—with, to be sure, the penalty of absolute death if he chose unwisely. Here…was absolute freedom, and no European had been offered anything like this before." Catton argues that "the profound and subtle lure of the wilderness…in the land of blowing trees, unbroken shade, and the huge lakes that lay empty beyond the horizon…" was the first incarnation of the fascination evoked by the Wild West a century or more later.

I don't remember hearing the siren call of absolute freedom. But all that spoke to me. I wanted to be in that gloomy forest, walking the hills and streams, smelling the leaves and ferns, and getting closer to their silent mystery. It was an elemental feeling. Whenever my family made the long drive from Lansing to my grandparents' farm just south of Manistee in our four-door Hudson there was always a moment, usually around the town of Clare on US 127, where we declared ourselves officially "Up North." That's when we left downstate behind and entered the North Woods. To this little kid it was magic.

I also fell in love with Lake Michigan. Its dazzling openness contrasted with the murky profusion of the woods. Arriving at the beach and looking out over the water—you can't see the other side—was like reaching the edge of the world. The lake opened up before me. The blue sky, clear water, and crisp sand felt great. I wanted to jump in.

Lake Michigan connected me to pure nature—a marvel that seemed way beyond anything humans could do. The basic facts make that clear:

- It was formed nearly 15,000 years ago by huge ice sheets that dug basins into the ground and filled them with meltwater.
- It is one of five Great Lakes that together form the largest group of fresh-water lakes in the world, and hold over 20 percent of the world's fresh surface-water.
- It is the world's fifth largest lake, and the largest that is entirely within one country.
- It has the world's largest collection of fresh-water sand dunes, many of them rising more than 100 feet above the surface.
- Its rolling waves, strong currents, fierce storms and great depth make it more like a sea than a lake.
- It has hosted Indians, fur-traders, and great boats carrying lumber, iron, and copper.
- It gave the state of Michigan its name, based on the Ojibwa word mishigami, which means "great water."

Of course, I didn't know any of that the first time I stood on a Lake Michigan beach. My eyes simply got big, and I've been filling out the picture ever since.

The beach was my vantage point. Beautiful, broad, sandy, washed by waves, it invited play. I remember my grandmother taking my brother and me to the beach after finishing up at the farmers' market in Manistee. There were two beaches—at First Street and at Fifth Street. Both felt sunny and open. Running across the sand and into the water was a dash into nature. Those waves were waving at me. I've loved beaches ever since.

OK. So that's how I started out. Writing about my earliest memories. It was fun. But looking at it, I think I see a few lessons—or at least patterns.

One was that as soon as I started writing about life on the farm I began to move away from writing about me and towards writing about something else (the farm or the woods or whatever). "I" gave way to "it." I began to describe things I had seen and to provide a little history. Nothing wrong with that, I guess, but I had the gnawing feeling that I was moving away from a memoir and towards travel writing or history or something that was less me. In the process some of the life came out of my writing. So I found myself consciously going back to each paragraph and looking for a way to add myself and my reactions into it. That seemed more interesting. If this was to be a memoir, how I felt probably needed to be part of what I said.

Another thing I noticed was that I had quite a bit to say—much of it unexpected. I enjoyed figuring out why I had liked the farm and loved Northern Michigan. Reflecting on manure was an unexpected treat. Like stumbling across something rich and colorful I'd nearly forgotten. I didn't know what I was going to say until I sat down and wrote. Writing was discovering.

I also realized how totally impossible it is to write about all you know, and therefore how much of writing is about choosing. Most of what you've seen and heard and learned will remain unwritten. You must select that less than one percent that you remember and can say. And that you think, for some mysterious reason, is worth saying.

And I noticed how easy it is to write poorly, cranking out phrases that are imprecise, wordy, weak, or trite. Much of what I wrote I threw out. It was just the first step on the road to what mattered. Good writing is about correcting bad writing. You have to sift through the stuff that comes up and find the gold. The rest you dump back into the creek.

So I was on my way. Where to next? I decided to write about Dimondale.

III

DIMONDALE

When I was seven, or maybe six, we moved from Lansing to a 20-acre farm a few miles south, near the village of Dimondale, and stayed there until I left for college. Dimondale was hardly more than the proverbial wide spot in the road—a place nearby we seldom set foot in or thought about. Much later I was surprised to discover that Dimondale—at least according to Wikipedia—became a "recognized hotspot for championship horseshoe pitching." Not much was happening back when we lived there.

The farm wasn't exactly a farm. It was more a collection of woods, old apple orchards, swamp, and a couple of open fields. But my parents immediately tapped their farming instincts, buying a small bright-red *Farmall* tractor and putting in a large garden. They bought a cow, which we milked by hand. They built a chicken coop and stocked it with a dozen or so egg-laying hens. They bought a couple of quarter horses (my Dad loved to ride). And a dog. Pretty soon they got rid of the cow. But I was back on the farm—sort of.

It was in Dimondale that I began noticing my parents. They were, of course, hugely important. Both came from rural and relatively humble northern Michigan backgrounds. Both knew about life under highly straitened circumstances. Both knew about love, hard work, self-sufficiency, honesty, and getting along with others. For whatever reason, both cared a lot about principles of right and wrong. They made it clear that they loved me. And that I'd better behave.

My father, Oscar, was a special guy—smart, thoughtful, and enterprising. He managed to be successful despite starting out with no money and little education. He was born in a tiny village—Brethren—in Northern Michigan. He grew up in a family of 11. His father died when he was around nine. I don't know how they survived. After high school he spent several years planting trees in the Civilian Conservation Corps and somehow managed to spend a year at Indiana University. Then it was marriage and the Army (where he was a medic in Europe). And after that managing a gas station in Lansing, where he did well and eventually got promoted to manager of wholesale accounts at the company (*Drake's Refinery Stations*) that owned the gas station. He read a lot but was also a people person. He was mostly positive and often funny. He was also an intellectual in that he read and thought and speculated about the world more often and in a way that no one else in my family did. I always wondered what might have happened had he been able to complete his degree at Indiana.

What I think my father did really well was taking me seriously. He talked to me. I remember particularly his effort to make me understand that I must be self-reliant, and not expect others to take care of me. He gave me several books to read about "life." The message I remember was that life is not fair, that you can't expect others to solve your problems, and that you must take responsibility for finding the best way to live. It seemed a little bleak, but he was adamant and appeared to know what he was talking about. And he was clearly trying to help me. So I bought it.

At the same time, he taught me something quite different—that other people are important, and that I should pay attention to them. He gave me a copy of Dale Carnegie's *How to Win Friends and Influence People*, which of course is about understanding what others want and need, and developing successful relationships based on that understanding. Since I was already well on my way to becoming a bookish introvert, Carnegie's people-centered ideas did not come naturally. But my father was equally adamant, and appeared to be speaking from experience. So I bought that too.

Those two ideas—self-reliance and paying attention to what others want—are in some sense opposites, of course. But they're also complementary. They've been pretty good guides for navigating the serpentine curves my life has taken.

Dad also pushed positivity, giving me a copy of Norman Vincent Peale's *The Power of Positive Thinking* (then a best-seller) to read, and recommending a mantra: "Every day, in every way, I am getting better and better." I read at least part of the book and have never forgotten the mantra. Years later, when I was in the Peace Corps, a fellow volunteer expressed amazement at my gut-level positivity and pointed out that "The world isn't that nice." He was right on both counts.

Two other memories of my dad that persist: The first was listening to him play the ukulele and sing "You Are My Sunshine." I always thought he was singing to my brother, Gary, and me. Second was him declaring "That's horse manure" when we said something stupid, which was often. We had to consider that maybe he was right.

My mother, Lucille, was different—less a seeker and more a manager. She had her values and goals pretty clearly in mind and concentrated on getting things done. She brought order to our lives. Where my father was generally ahead of me, inspiring, my mother was generally behind, pushing. She was about execution. My aunt Helen always called her "Sarge."

My mother pushed me a lot—to get up, brush my teeth, work hard, go to Sunday school, behave. She taught me to cook, starting simply enough with heating up a can of Campbell's tomato soup, but moving quickly on to frying eggs and making grilled cheese sandwiches. She enrolled me and my brother in a 4H cooking class without even asking whether we were interested. (We learned to make muffins, and later won red ribbons at the county fair). She also signed us up for tap dance lessons at a school in Lansing run by a Black guy who clearly knew what he was doing. The highlight was performing in a recital at the end of the year. (I can still do a pretty good "hop, stamp, shuffle.")

One summer she signed Gary and me up for a week of Vacation Bible School at a little church on M-99 a couple of miles from our house. This might sound boring, but it was a great social opportunity for little kids who, out of school for the summer and confined to the farm, didn't have many playmates. Religion, for us, was secondary. We sang hymns and prayed, but what I remember most was a competition to see who could find Bible verses the fastest. The pastor would announce the verse (e.g. Matthew, chapter 14, verse 26) and then say something like "Draw swords…Charge!" and we began thumbing frantically through our bibles to find that verse. The first to start reading won. It was great fun and spoke to my competitive spirit. And we got to hang out with other kids.

My mother introduced me to the public library in Lansing, which I visited every week and came to love. She bought me and my brother our first jazz and classical LP albums (Duke Ellington, Ahmad Jamal, and Peter Tchaikovsky).

She took us skiing, which she'd never done herself and in which we'd never shown any interest—and gave us skis and boots for Christmas. That turned into a lifetime passion for me. She got me my first paid job, planting tree seedlings and ground cover for a neighbor. Mom was a can-do person. But she was also a must-do person. We were expected to do things. Lots of things.

There was a "Let's go" quality to our relationship that I don't remember resenting or rebelling against. I signed on to the general idea of doing things, even though I might disagree at times with what she wanted me to do. The idea of getting things done, and sooner rather than later, got drummed into me. Mom kept us busy.

That's probably why I've always felt at least a little bit driven—or even compulsive. I'm a Type-A guy who goes to the office early every morning, tends to finish work before it's due, and jealously guards his time. I remember once working my tail off at the University of Chicago to get a paper done by the end of winter quarter so I could go skiing in Colorado with a bunch of students from the Business School—and drawing looks of surprise from my classmates, who had elected instead to wait and finish their papers during spring break. It seemed normal to me to meet the deadline. That was how you did things. First you got it done, then you went out and had fun. That attitude came, I suspect, substantially from my mother and her marching orders.

(How I financed that ski trip was interesting, since I didn't have money for that kind of thing. When I heard about the Business School's ski trip, which cost $350, I took out a student loan for the full amount—the only student loan I ever had—and paid it back after I graduated and finally got a job. It was money very well spent.)

It's worth noting, however, that my mother's marching orders didn't turn me into a yes man. I've always been skeptical of authority, and have tended to resist and question the views of my superiors. I'm particularly allergic to bureaucracy and to rules—which has occasionally gotten me into trouble. I want to make my own decisions. That aversion (and often hostility) to authority probably explains why I've avoided military service, and never seriously considered working for the government. (I got my fill of Sarge at an early age.) Perhaps that's my rebellion.

And Mom wasn't perfect. Sometimes she overdid it. For example, once I started high school and began driving—and dating—she started worrying (with good reason, of course) about the trouble I could get into. Her advice was "Don't do anything you wouldn't do if your Mom and Dad were there." I rolled my eyes. "Thanks, Mom."

But I drank quite a bit of her Kool-Aid. I'm still at the office early every morning despite having "retired," and am finding more to do than I have time for. I love to cook (and make soup from scratch rather than from a can), read lots of books, and ski as much as I can. And I still listen to Duke Ellington, Ahmad Jamal, and Tchaikovsky. In case you're interested the albums were *Masterpieces by Ellington* (his first LP), *Ahmad Jamal at the Pershing: But Not for Me* (his first live recording), and a Tchaikovsky collection that included *Capriccio Italien*. I've downloaded and still listen to the first two, and light up whenever I hear *Capriccio Italien*.) Few regrets, frankly.

Most of what I remember about my parents took place on the farm in Dimondale, which turned out to be a nice rural life. We lived on Burke Highway, a one-mile-long gravel road named after the Burke family who lived on a farm at one end and, I presume, had been the first settlers. The road ("Highway" always sounded pretentious to me) was lined in places by ancient maples and piles of stones cleared long ago from the adjoining fields so people could farm them. Clambering along the tops of those stone piles on our way to and from school was fun, and made you think a little bit about the past.

Twenty acres is plenty if you're a little kid. My brother, Gary, and I spent immense amounts of time outdoors, following paths made by the horses, climbing our favorite trees, and getting wet feet tromping through swampy woods. We picked berries, skinny-dipped in Grand River, and rode our bikes on gravel roads. We watched tadpoles turn into polliwogs and then into frogs. We got to know staghorn sumac, shagbark hickory, catnip, and poison ivy. We ate sweetcorn, rhubarb, and black raspberries (AKA "black-caps"). We carved our initials in the trunks of trees (are they still there?) and dreamt of animals and Indians. We skated on black ice in the woods and threw ourselves on sleds down snow-covered hills. We went on hayrides and watched the harvest moon. We played with neighbor kids. We were Cub Scouts, Boy Scouts, and Explorers. We learned to camp.

We also learned to work. First in our garden, pulling weeds and picking whatever was ripe, and in our "barn" feeding the animals and cleaning up. Then on a neighbor's farm (a real farm) where we drove tractor and helped bale hay. And finally, once we reached sixteen, the legal working age, pumping gas in the gas station my father managed. Work was what you did.

The fact that I was expected to work from an early age (any ten-year-old can pull weeds) gave me some discipline and at least a little responsibility. And in some vague way it gave me a positive role. I had something to offer.

Not that I liked it. Working in the garden was hot, dirty, and boring if you don't count eating the strawberries. Pulling weeds got old quick. I did it because I had to.

On the other hand, once I started getting paid, I liked work a lot more. When a neighbor offered to pay my brother and me a dollar an hour to plant some trees and shrubs, I was delighted. I even said he didn't have to pay us so much—which got funny looks not only from my neighbor, but also from my brother. But for me just getting paid was enough. I was valued, and it put real money in my pocket. That's a big deal for a young kid.

I also went to church. A Lutheran Church (Missouri Synod) in Lansing. Since my mother's entire family was German Lutheran, Lutheranism came naturally. It was not something you chose. I was a faithful Sunday Schooler, and later did two years of Confirmation classes that led, at age 15, to formal membership in the Lutheran Church.

I took Church about as seriously I did working in the garden. It was what you did and you tried to do it well. Church was different, of course. I studied the Small Catechism in weekly Confirmation classes and tried to understand the concepts of original sin, salvation by grace alone, the Holy Trinity, the two natures of Christ, and consubstantiation. My approach was more intellectual than spiritual. I wanted to figure it out. Of course, you don't really "figure out" religion—which is probably why I moved away from Lutheranism, and from religion in general, once I got to college. Had I begun with a more spiritual perspective and understood that the religious experience is essentially unknowable (at least to humans), I might have expected less and gotten more. Today I see that.

But the Lutheran Church was a central part of my young life. I went to church most Sundays, participated in a youth group (the Junior Walther League!), and identified in some general way with church values. The experience was probably more social than spiritual. I adored Christmas—those candlelit Christmas Eve services singing "O Come All Ye Faithful" were an entree into the wonder and mystery of the spiritual. But I was lukewarm about Easter and found communion to be only vaguely mysterious. Baptism I couldn't relate to at all. Spirituality never really captured my imagination. But through church I met kids my age (no small attraction when you live on a farm) and got to practice some social skills—which met a deep need welling up in my adolescent heart. Confirmation classes got me into Lansing every Saturday. It was a step toward the bigger world, where I was determined to go.

Mostly I identify my Lutheran upbringing with values. There was always something fundamentally good about being a Lutheran. You were expected to be positive, kind, humble, and reliable. You respected others and helped them out. You weren't greedy and didn't need to be the center of attention. You tried to be a good person.

Garrison Keillor has a great skit entitled "The Young Lutheran's Guide to the Orchestra" (a spoof, or course, of Benjamin Britten's *The Young Person's Guide to the Orchestra*) that appears in *We Are Still Married: Stories and Letters*. Keillor meditates on which orchestral instrument is appropriate for a Lutheran, rejecting most because they don't embody Lutheran values. The clarinet, for example, is "too clever, sarcastic, and snooty"; the flute is "the show-off of the wind section; a big shot"; the oboe is vaguely naughty "in movie soundtracks you tend to hear the oboe when the woman is taking her clothes off"; the piccolo is unfitting: "all you can play with it is the blues which, being Lutheran, we don't have"; the first violin is "a solo virtuoso instrument; not a place for a Lutheran to be." He settles on two instruments: percussion, which requires endless patience because in most orchestras percussionists hardly ever get to play; and the harp, which is so large and unwieldy that it keeps its players home—"you can't run around with a harp." Sounds Lutheran to me.

Of course, you never know for sure where you got your values. My parents (and grandparents) held most of these same values and made it pretty clear I should too. And the Boy Scouts preached values. I learned by heart, and can still recite, the Scout Law (Want to hear it? "A Scout is trustworthy, loyal, helpful, friendly, courteous, kind, obedient, cheerful, thrifty, brave, clean and reverent") and the Scout Oath ("On my honor, I will do my best, to do my duty, to God and my country, and to obey the Scout Law, to help others at all times, to keep myself physically strong, mentally awake, and morally straight"). Sounds like something Martin Luther would proclaim, and my parents would endorse. I got it from all sides.

Whatever their origin, these values stuck with me. I've always identified with them, even when I haven't lived up to them. They've shown up in the personal and professional decisions I've made. And I've always thought of them as Lutheran.

I also went to school. Skinner School. Named presumably for the Skinner family that lived nearby, on Skinner Road. Leota Skinner was a classmate. For years I assumed her family had donated the land for the school many years earlier, and that's why it was called Skinner School. But I saw her at a high school class reunion a few years back and she said it wasn't true. They were just the first settlers in the community.

Skinner School was right out of a storybook—a one-room country schoolhouse built of white clapboard and topped by a cupola with a big iron bell that the teacher rang by hauling on a twisted hemp rope that hung from a hole in the ceiling. It had blackboards with dusty white chalk and felt erasers, boys' and girls' "cloakrooms" (we actually called them that), a sandbox, swings, a slide, a teeter-totter, a merry-go-round, and out back a softball diamond. All the basics.

It was a remnant of the past—when rural schools were established and run by neighbors looking to educate their kids. There were only a few students in each grade (kindergarten through 6th), and fewer than 30 in total, so one teacher had to teach them all. A school board composed mostly (maybe entirely) of parents managed the finances and hired the teacher. Pretty much everything was local.

Having to teach all grades and subjects was a challenge, of course. The teacher sat at the front, facing a small semicircle of folding chairs. Behind the chairs were the students, at their desks. The teacher would call a class—say, "third grade arithmetic"—to come forward with their workbooks and sit in the folding chairs while she quizzed them, explained the next lesson, and assigned tasks. The third graders would then return to their desks, and she would call the next class. Students not up front were supposed to be working on their lessons. And older students often had to help younger students—which was probably good for both.

The only subjects I recall were reading, arithmetic, phonics, and penmanship (the Palmer Method). Maybe there was a class on spelling. It was basic stuff. The teacher had to teach these to six different grades, answer questions and make sure that kids were working rather than causing trouble. Getting all those pieces moving simultaneously must have been like staging an opera. The teacher had to compose, direct, and sing. It was a performing art.

The school also had a library—just a corner with shelves, a table, and chairs, but lots of books and a collection of old *National Geographics*. Once you got your lessons done you could go back there and read. To me the library was magic—a rabbit hole that led out of Dimondale and into the big broad world. I spent hours exploring the books and dreaming. My favorites—or at least, the only ones I specifically remember—were the novels of Laura Ingalls Wilder (*The Little House on the Prairie*) and of L.M. Montgomery (*Anne of Green Gables*). I loved them. They chronicled the hopes and fears of growing up rural. They had happy endings. I read them all.

Within a few years I became a voracious reader, checking four or five books a week out of the Lansing Public Library—where my mother took me once a week to hang out. It was like dog finding a bone. I couldn't put them down. I don't remember a single book, but I loved reading them. I even got written up (with a photo!) in the local newspaper—the *Lansing State Journal*. The article said I was an amazing kid who reads six books a week, or something like that. All that started at the Skinner School library.

Recess was another joy. Mostly it was about the games we played. Kick-the-can was a favorite, combining intensity, strategy, and yelling into a single package. There was also a game in which one group of kids defended the sandbox from another group trying to invade (sounds like pirates, and maybe we called it that). It was my favorite, but tended to deteriorate into hand-to-hand combat and get us into trouble with the teacher—who as I recall banned the game entirely. There's probably a lesson here—about people or teachers or both. We love to fight and it gets us into trouble.

In the winter, play was mostly about snowball fights and their time-honored variant—stuffing snow down the back of someone's neck. Sometimes we built snow forts and pelted each other with snowballs from within and without. Hard, really, to find anything wrong with those. They injected heat and excitement into cold, dark winter afternoons, and we hardly ever got hurt.

Softball was king in the spring. We went through the daily ritual of using a bat to choose sides and somehow we determined who would play which position—decisions that never made much difference to me. What I loved was stepping up to the plate with bat in hand, and trying to make something happen. Getting into my crouch, waving my bat and looking to see what the pitcher might throw was grand. Feeling the ball explode off my bat and curve toward the outfield was like setting off my own private rocket. I have no idea whether I was any good. I just loved playing. The game was the thing.

Softball always culminated during the last week of classes when we played a school located a few miles down the road. The game seemed to concentrate all the effort and emotion of the entire school year into a single event, causing excitement to run high. Maybe it was because this was the only time all year we played against our neighbors rather than against each other. But I think we also saw it as our final big activity of the year—one last chance to do something meaningful before the languor of summer set in.

Curiously I don't remember whether we won or lost any of those games. The excitement   that bubbled up so fiercely was almost entirely about anticipation. We played the game and then it was over. And we were happy. Maybe there's a lesson here too. For some things it's the doing that counts. Winning or losing is secondary.

Another thing I really liked about school was lunch. We carried our lunch to school in metal "lunchpails" which included a thermos (usually filled with some kind of Campbell's soup) held in place by a metal bracket, sandwiches and dessert. My favorite lunch was the fried-egg sandwiches my mother made with Cheez Whiz (a spreadable cheese "food") and sandwich spread (a mayonnaise-like dressing with chopped pickles). Dessert was often Hostess Twinkles or Cupcakes (I loved them both). On nice days we'd sit on the ground behind the schoolhouse, eating and talking. Delightful.

Another important part of Skinner School was getting there. The school was located more than a mile from our house and there weren't any buses. Our parents drove us or we walked. My brother and I walked a lot.

It was a trudge, and we didn't like it much. It took close to an hour. We tried to make it interesting by climbing the ancient maples that lined the gravel road we lived on or walking along the top of the big rock piles that farmers had thrown up long ago when clearing their fields. Sometimes we took a shortcut across the farmers' fields and through the dim and swampy woods—which were splendid in the spring when they erupted with life. Especially the frogs.

The big challenge, though, was walking to or from school in the winter. It was cold, windy and our gravel road was often blocked by three-foot-high snowdrifts. You had to walk through deep snow with head down into the wind for what seemed like forever. You worried about your fingers, your toes, and your nose. Other kids did it, though, and you learned that you could do it, too. Ever since I've enjoyed—well, at least appreciated—walking into a cold winter wind. The trick is to dress for it, and to focus on the exhilaration. It sounds perverse, but has its charms.

I don't know how good Skinner School was at preparing kids for high school or college. Nobody worried much about achievement tests back then. Most people assumed that the local school was good enough. The goal was to finish sixth grade.

It certainly worked for me. I had no difficulty continuing on to secondary school, and then to college. It may be that having to do so much work on our own made us take more responsibility for learning. And the fact that we had to help younger students—explaining lessons and drilling—may have helped us as much as it did them.

But I don't think that many of my classmates at Skinner School went to college. It could be that the education they got wasn't good enough. But I'm more inclined to think it was just rural Michigan in the fifties. High school was far enough. College was still largely beyond the horizon.

One final part of growing up in Dimondale: horses. Once he bought the farm, my father indulged a long-standing desire by purchasing a quarter-horse, along with saddle, bridle, and a horse trailer. Then he bought a second horse. The horses roamed the farm, creating trails that criss-crossed the woods and orchards, and sprinkling them with horse manure. My brother and I didn't ride them much—I have no idea why not. But we began to spend summer weekends at rodeos organized in small towns throughout central Michigan (amazingly, there were quite a few) where I learned about barrel racing, calf roping, and bronc riding—but almost never rode in the events. I guess I was too young. Mostly I remember being there, caring for the horses, and sleeping in the back of our pick-up truck. At the time, going to a rodeo seemed natural; today it seems like a quaint anachronism—and a vivid demonstration of the grip the frontier still had on American life.

There was one horse-related trauma. My father once insisted I ride a horse that I didn't want to ride and turned out to be too much for me. He hoisted me on. The horse bolted. I clung terrified to the saddle horn, and then fell off. My parents took me to the doctor. I wasn't seriously hurt—just some bruises. I had the vague impression that my Dad was trying to teach me something important—that I needed to have courage and to face challenges head-on. That's what I remember, at least, and probably what I got out of it.

My rural upbringing was long on family, church, and nature, and short on money and sophistication. That was fine. Later I found ways on to make up for what was lacking. It was in some ways a standard, almost storybook, American upbringing. I got love, warmth, belonging, values, demands, hard work, discipline, and responsibility. I realize now what a big deal that was, and what a leg up it gave me for the rest of my life—a kind of operating system that would serve me well in other contexts. If you don't start with that core, you've got a lot to overcome.

⋙

That's Dimondale. I enjoyed writing about it, but it doesn't seem like I said much. Five or six years in just a few pages. These were presumably formative years. Is that all there is? No anxiety, yearnings, trauma or rejection? Did I dislike anything? How did I feel about my brother, sister and playmates? Didn't I feel isolated living on the farm? What about my best friends—Les Gibson, Jon Eddy, and Ronnie Kitchen?

The fact is that this is pretty much all that comes to mind, emotion-wise. I'm not working from a map (except that, at least so far, I'm proceeding chronologically). My approach has been to sit down and see what happens. I look at what floats by and grab what seems worth saying. I follow my nose—trying to sniff out the good stuff and say it well. The mystery is determining what's good. The challenge is saying it well.

And in fact life in Dimondale seemed pretty tranquil. I don't remember worrying much about who I was or where I was going. It was a small rural community and everybody was like everybody else—sort of. You were thankful to have kids to play with. You got along.

One thing I've realized, though, is that I want an audience for what I write. Readers are important to me. I don't want to be the tree that, when it falls in the woods, doesn't get heard because no one's listening. So my decisions about what's worth saying depend in part on what I think my readers will find interesting—or what I think is important. It's a mix.

That raises the question, of course, of who my readers are (or will be, when that wonderful day comes). So far, I don't have an answer. Another mystery. But they're out there, and I care about them.

But it raises another question that's probably more important—whether wanting an audience is good or bad. Writing, after all, is its own reward. It opens your eyes and ushers you into a world that is magical and mysterious. It's a way of setting the world straight. You do it because it's good for you. Publishing—which is how you reach your audience—comes after you've written well. It's posterior. In her great book on writing, *Bird by Bird*, Anne Lamott captures the secondary character of publishing nicely, arguing that "…publishing is not all it's cracked up to be. But writing is."

My ego doesn't always see it that way, of course. But I'd like to think that what's really going on is that my imaginary audience is pushing me to write well. I remember that, while at the Ford Foundation and having trouble writing, I would sometimes imagine I was writing a letter to one of my mentors (the great thing about Ford back then was that there were first-rate mentors—intimidating sometimes, but first-rate). Almost always the words would immediately start to flow and I would begin to make sense. I could not write poorly in front of those people. They made me raise my game—which meant concentrating on what was worth saying (which of course is the mysterious part), writing clearly and telling the truth. I think that's at least part of what's happening with my desire for an audience. I need them to make me be at my best.

I'm also noticing that my prose is usually short and seldom flowery. I don't seem to have much to say, and when I say it, it comes out short and simple. Then I edit. Then I edit again. By that time there isn't much left. Having read Hemingway over the years, perhaps I've been influenced by his style. (Who can forget his marvelous six-word story: "For sale: Baby shoes. Never worn.")

But mostly I think it's just me. I've never had a lot to say. It seems to me that only a few things are worth saying, so I spend most of my time trying to figure out what they are. Maybe worthy thoughts are like the morel mushrooms we used to hunt in the Michigan woods—tasty but rare. You can't grow them. You have to find them. So the question is whether your nose is good enough to sniff them out.

Mine is only so-so. And even when I find something worth saying I seldom get it right the first time, so I'm constantly editing. Writing is successive approximation. Sometimes I wonder whether I should have been an editor rather than a writer (assuming, of course, that I am a writer). Another mystery.

Finally, I may be noticing a pattern here: Kid growing up in rural Michigan wants to get out into the big world but has no idea where to go or what to do. That's pretty much how I felt. Something of a blank canvas. How's that going to turn out?

IV

EATON RAPIDS

OK. OUR NEXT stop is Eaton Rapids, where I went to school (grades 7-12) for the next six years. For me, the jump from rural to small town was big. And it included high school, which we all know marks you for life. No one ever gets over high school (as Meg Greenfield, former Editorial Page Editor of the *Washington Post*, famously pointed out). So what happened?

Eaton Rapids was also like something out of a storybook—a sleepy town of 4,000 located in south-central Michigan on an island in the middle of the Grand River (hence the "Rapids") and surrounded by farms.

It was different from my grandparents' community in Northern Michigan. It had been a mill town (wool, grist, and lumber) and a mineral-water spa. It had the boosterism that was common to small towns in the Midwest, with slogans like "The Only Eaton Rapids on Earth," "The Saratoga of the West," and "The Ice Cream Capital of the World." Even today, the Chamber of Commerce promotes the—much less colorful—slogan "We are ER."

Lots of people had British names—Miller, Davidson, Banfield, Stewart, Anderson, Downing, Henderson, Richardson, Whitlock, Bristol, Brown, Booth, Buckley, Clark, and Ackley—in contrast to the German, Lithuanian, Polish, and Swedish names so common where my grandparents lived up north. The main church was Methodist rather than Lutheran. I don't remember ever hearing a polka.

Eaton Rapids was pretty much what you would expect a small town to be—quiet, self-contained, and a little rural. It had a drug store, bakery, soda fountain, "dime" store, bowling alley, movie theater, and pool hall, along with bars, restaurants, and at least one drive-in. There was an island park with band concerts on Sundays. Teen-agers attended dances at the school, or at the "Canteen"—a social center organized by parents trying to keep kids busy and out of trouble on Saturday nights. Quite a few kids were active in 4-H and the Future Farmers of America. The county fair was a big event each fall. So were high school football and basketball (Go Greyhounds!). There were pep rallies, assemblies, and sock hops. The main street was named Main Street. The center of town was the center of activity. Everybody seemed to know everybody else.

You could almost imagine Eaton Rapids being home—a century earlier—to Tom Sawyer (although the river was too small). Or being the setting—a decade later—for *American Graffiti* (but it certainly wasn't California). Or the inspiration for *The Music Man* (which debuted on Broadway while we were in high school). And in fact, we sometimes called it "River City." It was 1950s small-town America.

We hung out a lot, mostly in the center of town, which was just a few blocks from the high school. We would wander downtown during lunch or after classes to sip lime phosphates at Collizi's, listen to music (doo-wop was big, rock & roll was sending up green shoots) on the jukebox, buy chocolate eclairs at the Taylor-Made Bakery, or just walk around and check each other out. A prime hangout was a burger joint just off Main Street called Bentley's, which would fill with teenagers during lunch, after school and at night. I loved the food—grilled cheese sandwiches, hamburgers, cheeseburgers, french fries, and milkshakes— even though I seldom had much money to spend, and usually carried my lunch.

Sometimes we would stop by Pick's Pool Hall to shoot some pool. Pick's always seemed a little shady, which was probably part of its appeal. Kids were smoking cigarettes, men were playing cards (sometimes for money), and it had a functioning spittoon. There weren't any girls. You could relax at Pick's. It was kind of a refuge from the demands of school and family.

There was also a bowling alley near Main Street that was wildly popular after school, mainly because it was a good place for guys and girls to get together. On weekend nights, kids with cars cruised up and down Main Street looking for excitement. You moved around a lot and were always doing something.

But what we did wasn't all that important. Hanging out was mostly about seeing and being seen. And learning how you fit in. You looked at how other kids dressed, talked, and acted, compared that with yourself, drew some conclusions, and maybe made some adjustments. That was important for teenagers who were disengaging from their families, figuring out who they were, and learning to deal with the big wide world.

For me, Eaton Rapids was where things got complicated. It was small-town society instead of rural solitude. I was delighted to be there, but uneasy. Where did I fit in? There were lots of kids and they sorted themselves out into different groups. At first, I didn't belong to any of them. That bothered me. A lot. I had run into a question for which I had no answer.

Pretty quickly I spotted a group I wanted to belong to. It included kids that, it seemed to me, were from the town's leading families. I don't know what I meant by "leading" or why it was important, but I wanted those kids to accept me.

Fortunately, they did. Right away. I got invited to a birthday party (perhaps at Sheila Brown's house) that included most of the kids on my wish list. I have no idea why they decided to invite me, or what (if anything) I did to court them. But something must have worked. I'd passed a test. I was in. I was relieved. The rest of my years in Eaton Rapids included plenty of anxiety, but none of it was about being accepted by the kids I wanted to be accepted by. It was a milestone.

Now, there's nothing uncommon about a kid wanting to be accepted. But one aspect of my (otherwise ordinary) drama strikes me as interesting. Targeting the "best" or the "top" and finding a way to get there turned out to be something I'd repeat throughout my life. I have always been drawn—almost mysteriously—to talent, or intelligence, or quality, or some variation of "best." I don't ever remember deciding or thinking much about it. It just seemed natural. That was where I was supposed to be.

It happened again in college, when I somehow fell into campus politics (remember, I'm a kid from rural Michigan with no background or contacts, or even clear aspirations) and ended up holding a number of high-level positions in student government. I gravitated naturally toward student leaders.

It happened in graduate school when I decided that where you studied was more important than what you studied, and so accepted a fellowship to study international education at the University of Chicago—even though I had no interest or background in education— rather than studying international affairs at less-prestigious schools. (My first choices, Princeton's Woodrow Wilson School of Public and International Affairs, and the Johns Hopkins School for Advanced International Studies, turned me down). My priority was to sit at the feet of the best minds and I wasn't too fussy about what we studied, as long as it was in the social sciences.

Frank Fukuyama, by the way, has a great story about getting into graduate school at Harvard. He originally wanted to study political theory but was told that specialty was oversubscribed and to apply to national security studies instead, which he did and got accepted. The important thing was getting into Harvard. The rest was history.

It happened again as I was finishing my PhD, when I applied for a job only at the Ford Foundation. Several years earlier I had decided that Ford was the best institution working on international development, at least in Latin America, and that it was the place for me. So I didn't apply anywhere else. I would have taken any job they offered.

And once at the Ford Foundation, I found it almost natural to deal with the distinguished academics, government officials and political leaders that Ford regularly talked to. That's not to say it was easy. I struggled a great deal to learn how to behave and impress. But I was happy to take on the challenge. It seemed like I was doing what I was supposed to do.

Curiously, however, I've never much wanted to be in charge or in the spotlight. Getting ahead, in the sense of rising to a position of power and prominence, was never a priority for me. I've generally been happy to let someone else make the speeches and run the show while I operated behind the scenes. I'm an introvert, after all. What mattered most was working alongside first-rate people and doing good things. That has generally made me happy. Anything more was gravy.

I realize that I risk sounding like some kind of snob here—associating with the "best" people and all that. I can only say that I'm reporting on what I've lived and trying to understand it. For reasons that seem mysterious, I've always been drawn to people who were smart, worked hard, and did well. I don't remember deciding that; it came from within. In fact, my affinity with talent and achievement has been so strong and visceral that I've come to take seriously the concept of samsāra in the religions of India, which posits the transmigration of souls from one life to another. I have the distinct feeling that I had a previous life in Eastern Europe (why there I don't know) in which I was accustomed to power, responsibility, and leadership. That's why I've gravitated naturally toward the best and the brightest in my current life. I was predestined. It sounds goofy, of course. But there it is.

My six years at Eaton Rapids high school were pretty much what you would expect high school to be—intense, emotional, and a little crazy. I'm amazed by how much I learned, how much fun I had, and how many dumb things I did. The change was major. I had to make new friends, adapt to new teachers and courses, and figure out a small town. Plus I was starting to pay a lot more attention to girls. And I was an outsider seeking to get into a community that was doing just fine without me. It was a shock. The stakes were high.

My first major challenge had nothing to do with classwork (which seldom worried me) and everything to do with social life (which always worried me). Initially I didn't know any of the town kids, and I desperately wanted to be accepted. But we lived five miles out of town and I couldn't yet drive, so participating in after-school activities, which in my view was crucial to becoming a kid-in-good-standing, was a huge problem. I needed to be there, but I wasn't.

Week-days weren't so bad, since the school bus took me into town each morning, and I could always hitchhike home in the afternoon (I did a lot of hitchhiking). But on weekends, at least until I could drive, whether my life was to be happy or ruined depended entirely on whether my parents would take me into town and pick me up. I lived in fear.

Fortunately, my parents were pretty good about it. And eventually some older kids in the neighborhood got their licenses and started giving me rides. But during those early years of high school, my chief source of anxiety was getting into town so I could be part of the social life. Not much else mattered.

Most of what I did in high school was unsurprising. I took the standard academic courses and got good (but not great) grades. Several first-rate teachers, particularly in English and science, got me to pay attention and work hard. I played football and golf, and participated in lots of extracurricular activities. I had a high school sweetheart, and plenty of friends. Once I turned sixteen I also had a part-time job that paid for life's basics—a car, gas, cheeseburgers. I was pretty happy. For a teen-ager.

I enjoyed my courses. Since I was doing college prep (there was also a vocational track) I took English, social studies, language (only Spanish was offered), algebra, geometry, trigonometry, biology, chemistry, and physics. Everybody had to take a few vocational courses as well, so we brandished tools in shop class, learned to type in typing class (easily one of the most useful skills I acquired in high school), and drafted blueprints in mechanical drawing class. At Skinner School we had con- centrated on learning basic skills—reading, writing, and arithmetic. At Eaton Rapids we applied those skills to new subjects. I was happy to try them all.

It was a pretty good introduction. I got basic math and science, discovered literature, and learned the rudiments of Spanish. I may have been starting from a low base, but I found most of the courses challenging, and many stimulating. It was only in social studies where nothing much happened. I don't remember a single class or anything I learned (did we study history, politics?). That's ironic for someone who later became a dedicated social scientist. Maybe the courses weren't that good. Or maybe I just wasn't ready for to appreciate them. But they have disappeared from my memory. The lesson, if there is one, may be that cause seldom produces immediate and direct effect. You shouldn't demand an immediate payoff. Just study what you can and let it play out.

There was, however, one interesting exception to the forgettability of my social studies classes. Recently I came across, in a box of high school documents my mother put aside long ago, an elaborate report I had written on Chile (entitled "Chile: The String-bean Country") that had earned a grade of A+. Since several decades later I would live and work in Chile, write a book about Chile, and marry a woman from Chile, finding that report written while I was probably 13 or 14 was, frankly, spooky. Why Chile? Did I foresee that I would go there? Was fate beginning to weigh in? I don't know. But you can see why I take predestination seriously.

I also liked my teachers. They seemed to know what they were talking about. Mrs. Horn was one of my favorites largely because she so effectively combined enthusiasm with discipline. I don't remember anything about the class (seventh-grade English and history), but I always felt she was talking to me. Another favorite was Earl Rich, who taught chemistry and physics with authority, and with a twinkle in his eye.

His silver-haired wife, Dorothy Rich, taught senior English and introduced me to American writers like Hawthorne, London, and Hemingway. I wrote my senior paper on Steinbeck and did most of the research at the Michigan State University library several miles away. That made me feel grown-up. The only thing I remember about the paper is that I got an A+. In retrospect I wish I had chosen Twain. He's the one I'm still reading. But you learn by doing. Just trying to say something intelligent about *The Grapes of Wrath* was plenty. At a minimum, I discovered the power and majesty of literature. I was inspired to read more.

And it was in Mrs. Rich's class that I first recall feeling like an intellectual. The feeling was vague, but a door had opened. A very different world began to beckon.

I also began to think maybe I was smart. We were required to take the National Merit Exam (I think that's what it was called), perhaps in our junior year, and I did very well. I know that only because my mother told me. I don't recall being informed officially of my score. Much later my good friend Jamie Davidson told me that the school principal, Mr. Fransted, told him that I'd scored in the top one percent. Perhaps Mr. Fransted told me too and I've simply forgotten (although you'd think I'd remember something like that). Regardless, doing well on that exam was important. It probably put me on the road to wanting to become an intellectual.

One of the surprises of my high school years was being elected president of the senior class. It was a surprise because I don't remember aspiring to the office. The idea of becoming any kind of a leader hadn't entered my mind—at least not consciously.

What I recall is that a couple of teachers decided, without consulting me, to put my name on the ballot. Somehow I won. And I was happy to serve. It was a good push in the right direction. But I've always wondered what moved them to do that. Were they trying to tell me something? Did they just think I was the lesser evil? I don't remember asking them. I just accepted it. It's typical of how clueless I was about some things (and have continued to be over the years, frankly). So it's one more mystery. I'll forgo arguing for predestination in this case. After all, I haven't been elected president of anything since. But I certainly was an accidental president.

Curiously (at least to me), I got mediocre grades in citizenship while at Eaton Rapids. Mostly I got a steady drumbeat of C's, along with comments like "Jeff's attitude is not as good as it was at the beginning of the year…" and "needs to practice better self-control." (One teacher charged me with chewing gum in class, which I thought was excessive.) I find my underperformance in citizenship hard to explain, but suspect it had something to do with my instinctive distrust of authority. I've always been touchy about people telling me what to do. "Don't Tread on Me" is my idea of a good motto. It's not that I rejected all authority, but rather that I was fussy about the kind of authority I would accept. In some vague way, I wanted authority to justify itself and to make sense.

Sometimes that led me to act up in class. Spitballs were an early favorite, along with talking back to the teacher and arriving late. Other times it led to rebellious behavior outside of school, like drinking, smoking, and hanging out with kids who were trouble-prone. I tended to have a foot in several camps, rather than confining myself to the straight and narrow. Some of that was curiosity and excitement, but some of it was rebellion.

The most common example was drinking—mostly beer—with my buddies, even though we were well under the legal age of 21. Buying beer wasn't hard. You could usually find someone who was old enough to buy and willing to buy yours, if you bought them a six-pack as well. And I don't remember drinking a lot. It was more about excitement. But it was dumb because it was illegal and could get you picked up by the police—something that would have been devastating for me (not to mention my parents). I had no desire to become an outlaw. It was also dumb because it was dangerous. Since we didn't have a secure place to drink our beer, we usually did it while driving around in somebody's car. That could get you killed. We were lucky.

Another example occurred at the end of my senior year when, along with several classmates, I got suspended from all extra-curricular activities for skipping school (on a beautiful spring afternoon) and hanging out instead at the Michigan State University library. It may have been a case of collective spring fever. We got carried away with the fact that graduation was upon us and we would soon be starting college, and—like young birds—take flight. But it was a scandal. I was the class president, one my co-offenders was the class salutatorian, another was our Foreign Exchange student and the rest were honors students. Playing hooky was prohibited. We had to pay. We did. We were prohibited from participating in any extracurricular activities until graduation. It was embarrassing, and certainly rebellious. (I must point out, however, that we had a great time at the library.)

But I didn't always resist authority. I was perfectly capable of being the kid with a halo floating over his head, particularly with teachers I liked, or when it served my interests. I generally accepted the authority of people and institutions I respected. (That may help explain why I've been so drawn to smart, talented people over the years.) And sometimes (often, in fact) resistance just wasn't practical. I learned to pick my battles, and that kept me out of trouble—mostly.

An example of avoiding a battle occurred a couple of decades later during a visit to Cuba with my boss (and Ford Foundation vice president), Bill Carmichael. At the time (the early 1980s), Ford was viewed with distrust by Cuban officials, and I had invested a good deal of time and effort in convincing the government to trust us and even organize formal visits, complete with meetings, car, driver, and "minder" (whose job was to take care of—and keep tabs on—us). But when we had an unscheduled half-day, Bill (who had his own doubts about authority, and was often irrepressible) suggested we go to the Havana airport by ourselves and try to get on a plane to the Isle of Youth, where the government had built numerous boarding schools for students from poor (mostly African) countries to study free of charge. "It would be fun to see the schools," he mused, "and interesting to see how the government reacts to our little adventure." I was aghast. I had no love for the Castro regime, but wasn't about to see my careful efforts to establish a working relationship with the government go up in smoke. There are times and places to exercise your distrust of authority. This wasn't one of them. I refused to go, and he backed off. Maybe he was just testing me.

My resistance to authority—skepticism is probably the better word—caused me some problems, but having less might have caused more. I might have accepted more bad thinking, wasted more time, learned less and grown more slowly—not to mention having had less fun. Always doing what you're told is seldom the best policy.

One great thing about challenging authority is that it helps clarify where you stand. You ask for an explanation. Hopefully you'll see the arguments for and against. You may prevail. Or you may discover you're wrong. But it's a powerful learning process. And you'll build backbone, which is no small blessing.

The question, of course, is how much resistance—or skepticism—is healthy. There's no clear answer, but it's greater than zero. Much later I came across an argument for something called "mindful disobedience" as a way to figure out when and how to resist. That sounds good to me. The trick is to know, as in poker, when to hold 'em and when to fold 'em. Figuring that out is another of life's mysteries.

I don't think my six years at Eaton Rapids High School were extraordinary. High school is largely about becoming independent and learning to deal with the opportunities, temptations and uncertainties the world throws at you—all while under assault by powerful emotions. You walk a tightrope. You experiment. You make decisions, see how they turn out, and learn. What's important is not so much to avoid mistakes (you learn from those) but to avoid disaster (it's hard to recover from disaster). I avoided disaster.

But maybe what Eaton Rapids added was a more comprehensive sense of life. Eaton Rapids was a microcosm. Underneath the small-town charm, it was like any other place: a seething mass of hope, fear, courage and passion. People loved, hated, dreamed, despaired, succeeded and failed. They struggled with their desires, their work and their neighbors. They were kind and they were cruel.

I got to see the whole picture in miniature. I was exposed to rich kids and poor kids going to the same school, having the same dreams and getting into the same trouble. It was all there in front of me. It was normal. That made it a good place to grow up.

Eaton Rapids high school broadened my horizons. I learned to get along with new and different people. I discovered that I was intelligent. I realized, particularly after reading *A Tale of Two Cities*, that there was a lot I didn't know about the world. I saw that I would go to college. I decided, despite liking math, science, and history, that I would not be an engineer, scientist, or historian. I had fun. But I didn't find a calling. I was like a bee going from flower to flower—and would continue doing that for many years.

And it was always clear that I would leave. Eaton Rapids was a great place to start, and I remember it with fondness. But it was not where I intended to end up.

OK, that's Eaton Rapids. It was hard to write. I'm not sure why. Mostly I was trying to figure out what to say. Despite all that happened and all I felt, I chose only to write about a few things. I had the most fun writing about the town of Eaton Rapids, and wonder why. But I mostly left out my high school friends (including those who were especially close—Vic Clark, Jamie Davidson, Mike Booth, John Banfield, John Taylor, Jim Huston, and Jon Eddy). I've stayed in touch with most, except Vic, who died tragically right after we graduated from college. And I barely mentioned my high school sweetheart, Terry Bristol, who was the love of my life back then. Why did I leave all that out?

I don't know. Something inside said to choose this and not that. It reminds me that memoirs are all about selection. Two of those I looked at (by Somerset Maugham and Carlos Fuentes) say almost nothing about their early years. But another (by Elias Canetti) starts at age two and goes on for three volumes and nearly 900 pages. It would be fun to ask those guys how they made those choices. They may not know either. I suspect they were simply moved in some mysterious way to include what what they included, and to leave out what they left out. (And two of them won Nobel prizes.)

For me so far it's grubby stuff. I'm reminded of my dog with his nose in a hole in the ground sniffing, hoping he'll find something wonderful. That's kind of what I'm doing.

What I do know is that you need to say things that are both true and in some way interesting. In her book on writing, Anne Lamott emphasizes the importance of finding your voice and writing about "the cold dark place within." She observes that "Truth seems to want expression" and therefore you should make every effort to "open the closet door and let what was inside out."

I think I'm fairly good at seeing what's true in my life. But not all of that belongs in a memoir. So the next step—deciding what's important, and interesting, to my audience—is crucial. For me that's where the mystery kicks in. I sit down, ask "What should I say?" and wait for my muse to answer. Often Mr. Muse is slow in getting back to me. And sometimes I'm tempted to go downstairs, grab him by the neck and wring it out of him. But sooner or later he offers up some tidbits, and I'm on my way. I see what I should write. And most of time it's fun.

On to another big change: college

V

MICHIGAN STATE UNIVERSITY

American Universities have seen radicals and revolutionaries come and go over the years, and all of them put together were not nearly so revolutionary as a land-grant university itself on an ordinary weekday. To give people with little money a chance to get the best education there is—that is true revolution.

—GARRISON KEILLOR,
TRUE DEMOCRAT

THERE WAS NEVER any doubt that I would go to college. It was going to happen, just as the sun was going to rise. That seems at least a little surprising, since it wasn't like we had a family tradition to uphold. No one in my family had ever graduated from college, and my father only managed to attend for a year. Maybe that fact caused my parents to make college a priority for their kids. I have no idea. But it was a sure thing. I don't even remember discussing it.

The only question was where. And even that wasn't really a question. I would go to Michigan State University. Why? Because it was nearby. And because I'd been going to football games there since I was a little boy (my father had season tickets; then once I joined the Boy Scouts, we served as unpaid ushers at the home games so got to see them for free). And because football was big at Michigan State and the team was good. End of conversation. I was fine with that.

A lot of kids made the same decision for the same reasons. In my circles, applying to college was not the high-stakes struggle then that it is now. We didn't agonize over where to apply and develop elaborate strategies for getting accepted. Only a few kids went, and just going was enough. Schools that were nearby and had good football teams were hard to resist. Even for kids who might have gotten into Harvard.

In my case, and at the urging of a teacher, I did consider one other school—Kalamazoo College—a private liberal arts college about 100 miles away, in western Michigan. But my heart wasn't in it, and I didn't apply. I was delighted to go to Michigan State.

Michigan State University was big, public, and lively. Established in 1855 as an agricultural college, it became the prototype for the nationwide land-grant college system established a few years later by the Morrill Act to "teach such branches of learning as are related to agriculture and the mechanic arts... in order to promote the liberal and practical education of the industrial classes in the several pursuits and professions of life."

By the time I got there, MSU had moved far beyond its roots in agricultural and mechanic arts to become a diverse, modern university. It offered everything (and more) in the sciences and humanities that a rural kid like me could want. It had first-rate professors and strong international programs. The students came from all over the United States plus many foreign countries. It was a great place to find out what higher education had to offer, and whether you could handle it. It also had a terrific marching band. And a pretty good football team.

MSU was growing rapidly, largely because baby boomers were turning 18 and opting for college. There was construction everywhere—new dorms, classrooms, arts and athletic facilities. There was hustle and bustle. You felt you were part of a dynamic institution. And there was what back then qualified as new thinking: MSU opened its first coed dorm the year I arrived, although coed just meant that women and men lived in separate buildings connected by common dining facilities. (University officials explained these new arrangements very carefully to uneasy parents.)

Going to college was the second most exciting thing I did in my life. (The first was joining the Ford Foundation, nearly a decade later.) It was in some goofy way like Tom Sawyer meeting Jay Gatsby. There were social events, fraternities, people from New York, rich kids, and courses in philosophy. I was, for the first time, completely independent. I had left my family and moved, delighted and excited, into a dorm (West Shaw Hall) filled with kids my own age who were just as eager as I to make friends and have fun. There was no curfew. I answered to no one. I didn't call my parents for three weeks. I was master of my fate.

Just about all freshmen had to live in the dorms, so the social life was plentiful, frenetic, and right in front of you. Everybody was new and looking for friends. You didn't have to break into any cliques, because there weren't any to break into. Mysterious "mixers" were announced that brought coeds from their dorms over for dinner at yours, and you could meet them in the line outside the dining room. All those women, your age, and probably lonely. Whoever invented that was a genius.

There were dances every weekend, along with concerts, plays, and movies. Each dorm floor elected a government and organized activities. You met new people, talked for hours, and stayed up all night playing poker. Fraternities offered parties for prospective members, meaning anyone could attend. Plus there were "grassers" that appeared out of nowhere, were fueled by word of mouth, and brought dozens of students together at night in a field somewhere to mill around and drink beer (which, for most of us, was illegal). It wasn't quite paradise, but it was a long way from Eaton Rapids.

Athletics were big. MSU had joined the Big Ten Conference many years earlier (replacing the University of Chicago, which left so as to focus on more serious pursuits), and had teams in just about any sport you'd ever heard of. Students got free tickets to all campus sporting events—football, basketball, ice hockey, fencing, wrestling, tennis, track, swimming, and more. There was an 18-hole golf course where you could play for free. There was a new and gigantic "intramural" building that housed all sorts of athletic facilities plus indoor and outdoor swimming pools. I spent a lot of time there swimming and playing paddle-ball. And, of course, the football team was pretty good.

All that activity brought you up against people whose backgrounds were very different from your own. I recall, in one of those dorm dinner lines, an attractive woman from Detroit leaning close and whispering in my ear "Is that guy ahead of us Jewish?" I had no idea, of course, and told her so. But I was flummoxed. I'd had almost no contact with Jews (except in the Bible, which doesn't really count) so I couldn't imagine why anyone would ask that question. What was this about Jews? My horizons were expanding in unexpected directions.

I also met Jim Corey, a kid from Grand Rapids who lived in my dorm and ended up changing my life. Jim was very different from me— ambitious, knowledgeable about politics and international affairs, and intent on becoming a diplomat. I was none of those—except maybe ambitious, but I had nothing to focus my ambition on. For some reason, Jim took an interest in me and began to instruct me in the ways of the world. He decided that I should get involved in campus politics. He told me about the leaders emerging in the freshman class (Bruce Osterink, also from Grand Rapids, was by far the star) and Jim was running against him for the Frosh-Soph Council presidency. He invited me to work in his campaign. That would give me some experience, he said, and might get me a student government position.

I did, we lost, and Jim was right. Despite my having worked against him, Osterink offered me a position (chair of the Newsletter committee) in his administration. I don't know why Bruce thought of me for the newsletter, or whether I was particularly interested in doing it. I probably would have taken anything he offered. But in fact I was beginning to feel a mysterious urge to write, so editing the newsletter wasn't a bad fit. Of course, I knew nothing about journalism, and even less about the mechanics of getting prose into print. And the previous class didn't even have a newsletter, so I had to start from scratch. I recruited a staff and wrote a few articles myself over the summer—aiming for a fall-term launch. Once we had articles written, I had to come up with a production process, and ended up laying out the newsletter myself, by hand, with technology that I discovered at an off-campus print shop. This was thirty years before desktop publishing made its debut. I still remember the look on Bruce's face—mostly of relief but mixed with some genuine delight—when I showed him the first issue. His Frosh-Soph Council had a face, and it looked pretty good.

In a more perfect world, or maybe in a good novel, editing the *Frosh-Soph Focus* (that's what we called it) would have been a major turning point in my life. I would have seen that what I really wanted to do was write. I would have gone on to write for the student newspaper (*The State News*). After graduation I would have managed to get a job as a reporter somewhere. Then I would have begun to submit articles to national magazines. Eventually, I would have gotten something published in the *The New Yorker*. Flush with success, I might even have begun work on a novel. I would have become a writer.

None of that happened, of course. I do remember signing up for a journalism course in feature writing, and suggesting that a good friend from Shaw Hall, Jim Sterba, try the course as well. He did and went on to write for the student newspaper. Then, after graduation, he wrote for the *Washington Evening Star*, got hired by Scotty Reston at the *New York Times*, became a Vietnam war reporter and spent the next three decades as a foreign correspondent in Asia for the *Times* and then the *Wall Street Journal*. He later wrote several books.

But I dropped the course after just one class. I don't know what I was thinking, but journalism wasn't singing to me. At that point in my life, I was probably more concerned with absorbing information than with sharing it. I remember feeling that I had a lot to learn, but don't remember feeling that I had much to say. I was still in discovery mode. The urge to write was way back in line.

Over the years, however, I've realized how important writing is and how much I like it. I've been moved to write op-eds now and again (with genuine pleasure), and of course I wrote a book after I left the Ford Foundation. But writing was largely a road not taken, and I'm a little sorry. I might well have become a real writer. Perhaps a career in writing was too big a jump for somebody with my rural background and limited horizons (but hey, Sterba did it). And maybe that's just as well. The road I did take was great. I had so much to learn back then that I can't imagine what I would have written about. Now I've learned a lot, and now I'm writing.

But what did happen was that I got into campus politics. For the rest of my four years at MSU I worked closely with campus politicians (including Jamie Blanchard, who later became governor of Michigan—and dropped "Jamie" for "Jim") in a variety of student government positions. Running for office was never my style, but I served in most administrations and participated in a committee that rethought the student government system. And I got invited to join the major honorary societies. I wasn't really a star, but I was a player.

That was important, not because I accomplished anything, but because it made me feel like I could operate successfully at that level. I had not previously even known that campus politics existed. Now I was in it and holding my own. That happened largely because Jim Corey pointed me in the right direction and gave me a push. I was an accidental campus politician at Michigan State, just as I had been an accidental senior class president at Eaton Rapids.

The other thing Jim did was steer me towards an international career. He hoped to join the Foreign Service and urged me to consider international work as well. That was new to me. I'd never met anyone who'd even traveled abroad, except for my father who served in Europe with the army during World War II and didn't talk about it. I don't know why I took Jim's suggestions seriously. I suppose it seemed like one way to make the world a better place, which appealed to my Lutheran upbringing. And there's no doubt that I was attracted by the prospect of traveling thousands of miles beyond rural Michigan. But it was Jim who crystallized in my mind the idea of an international career, and caused me to start down that path. After that it was more a question of what kind of international career, and how to make it happen.

After graduation Jim got into the Foreign Service and served a couple of tours in Africa. Then he left the State Department and worked on Shirley Chisholm's presidential campaign before dying of a brain tumor. I had lunch with him during a visit to Washington not long before his death. He didn't mention he was ill. As a mutual friend, Jack Armistead, observed, "he had a fine sense of irony and of the contradictions inherent in politics. He did laugh occasionally… but not the carefree belly laugh others seemed capable of. His was a thoughtful, amused laughter." Like so many people in my life, Jim knew much more about the world than I.

Also, at Michigan State I finally met Jews, virtually all of them, so far as I can recall, from New York. In retrospect that seems odd—this was the Midwest after all. What were New Yorkers doing there? But to me at the time, nothing at Michigan State seemed odd. It was supposed to be different and it was. I wasn't in Dimondale anymore. I assumed that everything I ran into was normal.

It turned out that Jewish kids from New York were attracted to Michigan State for several reasons: it was a long way from New York, so they really were "going away to college"; it was affordable, despite costing more than public universities in New York; the Greek system was open to them (Michigan State had three Jewish fraternities while many other universities had none); and (surprise) it had a good football team.

I liked the New York Jewish kids almost instinctively but found them different from my friends in Eaton Rapids—more direct, less inhibited and with a great sense of humor. And like my friend Jim Corey, they knew much more about the world than I did. They started me on a long and affectionate relationship with Jewish culture that would soon include a roommate, professional colleagues, numerous friends, the movies of Woody Allen, living in Manhattan, and marriage.

And there were classes. For me the classes at Michigan State were crucial. They were my entrée into a mysterious world I knew almost nothing about—the academy, knowledge, intellectuals—but for some reason found fascinating. It was like being presented with a long menu in a good restaurant and being told you could choose anything you wanted.

Well not anything. Some courses were mandatory. Michigan State assumed that students should get a basic grounding in the humanities and sciences, so freshmen had to take two courses that lasted all year— American Thought and Language and Natural Science. And men (we were men, now) had to take two years of Reserve Officer Training Corps (ROTC). Military service was still mandatory in the United States. Beyond that you could take pretty much what you wanted for the first two years. Then you had to declare a major and take whatever courses your major required. But you could declare what was called a "divisional" major (mine ended up being social sciences), which was the functional equivalent of a liberal arts degree. So there was lots of flexibility. (Later I realized that this scheme was remarkably like the "new College" that emerged in the late 1950s at the University of Chicago, featuring two years of general education plus two years of specialization.) For a kid like me who didn't have a clue about what to do with his life, and wanted only to sample as much as possible, it was perfect.

I especially liked American Thought and Language, which walked us through three centuries of U.S. history and culture and made us realize we had some of both. I'd been placed in an honors section, which meant we read original documents along with the work of distinguished historians. Our professor, Dr. Strandness, had us write up our impressions of what we read. Somehow that led me to poetry and I wrote a couple of poems criticizing the Puritans' apparent aversion to fun. One of those, a take on Sir John Suckling's poem "Song," I still remember it fondly. It began: "Why so pale and wan yon Puritan? Prithee why so pale?" Killjoys were an attractive target for clueless college freshmen.

I also wrote something quite different:

"'Tis a balmy afternoon
That glideth like a dove

On shimmery wings of easy breeze.
An afternoon to love

And cherish in its tranquil state
The beauty nature holds."

That fragment, which simply came to me and I can't explain, stuck. Several years later while on a blind date with a woman in North Carolina I spontaneously recited that poem, leading to the following exchange:

"Wordsworth?" she guessed.
"Puryear." I replied.

Poetry matters.

The course (it ran all year) turned what I'd seen in movies and read in novels into something real. The Salem witch trials really happened! What were those people thinking? And the slave trade, and the Mexican war, and…. It gave me the broad sweep of American history along with an intellectual framework for understanding it—the kind of horizon-expanding experience I needed.

Much as I liked ATL (as we called it) I decided to comp the remaining two quarters by just doing the readings during breaks and taking a comprehensive exam (therein "comp") for a grade and credit. Discovering I could do that and still get an "A" was liberating, although I suspect I would have been better off, i.e. more would have sunk in, had I actually taken the classes. But comping those courses made room for other courses in fields I knew less about, and my top priority was to sample broadly what the university had to offer.

Beyond the required courses I had no idea what I should take, so I simply experimented. During my first quarter I took elementary French (for some reason I'd always wanted to speak French) along with an introductory course in communications called "The Communication Process." I don't know why I chose that course and have always wondered whether it was in response to some deep urge to write. It turned out to be pretty good, and gave me at least one concept—"bias words"—that has stuck with me ever since, particularly when reading political journalism.

In that course I also found myself sitting next to Miss America 1961, Nancy Anne Fleming, who was also a freshman at Michigan State. I was, of course, too shy to introduce myself (we Lutherans didn't do that kind of thing) and that was probably just as well. Years later she said she'd felt like a freak at MSU, with so many people pointing and staring at her. But it was one more dash of excitement during my first week of classes, and another reminder that I wasn't in Dimondale any more.

Probably the most important thing that happened was getting invited, during my freshman year, to join the Honors College. Invitation was automatic if you got good grades, but I was surprised. I didn't even know the Honors College existed. Getting invited almost made me believe that I was intelligent and somehow special and maybe even a potential intellectual. It was a great morale-builder for someone with no academic background or sense of how he might fit into the bigger world. Maybe I could actually play on that field.

The Honors College was a great fit. Students were given special advisors and urged to experiment, so as to discover what really interested them. I was summoned to a meeting with the Honors College director, Stanley Idzerda, to discuss my coursework. He saw immediately that I had no idea what I wanted to study or do and decided to expand my horizons by suggesting I take courses in math and philosophy. I signed up for both. The math course (analytical geometry for math majors) was a disaster. The class met at 8 a.m. five days a week during winter quarter—early, dark and bitterly cold. I understood almost nothing about the material but somehow passed the course (the only D of my college career). But it was a good learning experience—I learned that math wasn't for me. The philosophy course was a delight, although I recall almost nothing except that we read Hannah Arendt's *The Human*

Condition, which I remember with fondness, but without substance or understanding. Mostly I think I was impressed that I was reading philosophy. It made me felt like an intellectual. I recently found the paper I wrote on Arendt, but have resisted rereading it. I decided that philosophy was not my cup of tea either, although it was certainly worth dipping into now and again.

There were also special classes offered only to Honors College students. I remember two. One was on contemporary theoretical physics, which we dubbed "Physics for Poets" and which did a pretty good job of providing a non-mathematical introduction to relativity and quantum theory. The professor, whose name I don't recall, had worked on the Manhattan Project at the University of Chicago, and wrote every word of his lectures on the blackboard to make sure we understood. I was fascinated by the otherworldly character of the material he presented, and even today perk up when I see a book on theoretical physics mentioned in the *New York Times Book Review*. By opening up non-scientists to science, the course was exactly what should happen in a liberal arts curriculum.

The other was a seminar on classics in sociological theory, taught by David Gottlieb, a recent PhD from the University of Chicago. We had to read one book each week and write a report. I especially remember Durkheim's *The Elementary Forms of Religious Life* (which I liked, but found repetitious), along with Weber's *The Protestant Ethic and the Spirit of Capitalism*. That seminar brought sociology to my attention. I was attracted to sociological theory as a way of understanding how people behaved. And, because of Professor Gottlieb, I became aware of the University of Chicago and its grand history in the social sciences. Both were to figure importantly in my decision, several years later, to study for a doctorate at the University of Chicago.

Another important thing that happened to me at Michigan State was what should happen to everyone who goes to college: I became unsettled, disoriented, and disturbed. Step one took shape during my sophomore year, the result mostly of new ideas chipping away at old ones. I wasn't sure how to handle that (who is?) and reacted with opinions that were overconfident, uninformed, and immature. I was, I think, trying to keep a steady hand on the tiller in the face of stiffening winds. I became sophomoric.

Fortunately I began to keep a journal that year and—I think you'll agree—my entries met college sophomore standards. Here are a few:

"One can misuse life only by ignoring it."

"A day cannot be ended by a TV commercial or a game of bridge: It ended long before."

"This aimless drifting over a far-flung continuum of ideas. This brush with knowledge. This hurried inquiry into how and why. This combination of rejection and absorption. This fretful and often indifferent nursing at the breast of some obscure goddess: This is my education."

There were more but I won't burden you. I find these charming, even today. College was doing its job.

Step two in the "unsettled, disoriented, and disturbed" process was an extension of step one. The further I got into new ideas, the more I began to change psychologically and the more I felt the strain of changing. That became clear when I started my junior year. I'd spent the previous summer hitch-hiking around Europe, partly with my high-school buddy Jamie Davidson, responding (of course) to my strong urge to get out and see the world. I had almost no money so slept in cheap youth hostels, and occasionally in parks or under bridges. Even so my parents had to wire me extra cash halfway through the summer (Thank God for those American Express offices scattered throughout European capitals). It was romantic, sort of.

Deep down I think I thought that spending a summer hitchhiking around Europe would solve my problems. It didn't, and finding that out was a revelation. Now what?

Psychologically, I was facing plenty of challenges. Going from farm boy to wannabe intellectual aiming for an international-career was a stretch, and I had to figure out how to deal with it. I was becoming a different person, but didn't yet know who. What did I stand for and what would I do? I remember feeling anxious, although not really depressed. And I don't remember ever being tempted to turn back. But I wasn't sure who I was.

That was upsetting, of course. On a good day, probably drawing on something I'd read in a psych course, I felt that I didn't have a self-image. On a bad one, I felt like something out of T.S. Eliot's "The Hollow Men": "quiet and meaningless as wind in dry grass or rats' feet over broken glass." That could be excruciating. But perhaps that was what college should do: make me, like Eliot's J. Alfred Prufrock, "spit out all the butt-ends of my days and ways" so I could become a different—or at least partly different—person. That's what boot camp does to army recruits, after all. Maybe it was something you had to go through.

I got through it. But the problem was that so far it was all journey and no destination. I was leaving my old self behind, but not making much progress in finding a new one.

That feeling stuck for a long time and didn't really change until I entered the Peace Corps in Colombia several years later. Getting my hands dirty working with poor peasants may have helped me reconcile my rural and Lutheran roots with my intellectual and international aspirations. For the first time I could see how I might put the two together.

My four years at Michigan State were mostly about discovery. I was experimenting—with courses, politics and people—in an effort to figure out who I was. I took classes in history, sociology, psychology, math, religion, French, political science, physics, economics, statistics, literature, business, and communications. Depth would have to come later. I wasn't remotely ready to choose a path forward. The only thing I saw clearly was that I wanted to be an intellectual. I used to carry around a copy of Sartre's *Being and Nothingness* (loved that title!), not because I'd read it—I hadn't, and never did—but because I wanted to tell the world I was an intellectual. It was a badge, like the decorations worn by military personnel (except I hadn't earned mine). I did read Camus, however, and in French, but remember only that I liked it.

I guess what I got added up to a liberal arts education. I certainly enjoyed it. I contrasted, in my only economics course, Max Weber's *Protestant Ethic* with R.H. Tawney's *Religion and the Rise of Capitalism* and saw for the first time how ideas interact with history. I discovered, by reading Bruce Catton, the glory and tragedy of the Civil war (years later I discovered that Catton had grown up in northern Michigan and had written a splendid history of the state). I took a course on Greek history (or was it Roman?). I studied Taoism (sort of). I read the Federalist Papers and got a glimpse of their brilliance. I discovered T.S. Eliot and still read him today, even though I barely passed the course. I took two courses in U.S. diplomatic history (I have no idea why) and began to understand, or at least pay attention to, how countries interact. I took one or more courses in psychology and can't remember what I learned. I took a course in contemporary Russian history and completely failed to appreciate the drama of the Russian Revolution—but was able to connect to that more easily years later when I finally started paying attention. I took several courses in sociology, and decided maybe I should become a sociologist. I may have taken a course in African history.

College for me was more about exposure and less about comprehension or appreciation: a making of lists; an introduction to texts; a learning what's out there so that later on when I needed—or could finally appreciate—it, I could remember it was there and where to find it. That was valuable, like meeting the wise men and knowing they were there even though you weren't yet ready to deal with what they were saying. You'd been introduced. A connection had been made. It set you up for later.

I suppose it's like joining a good club. You meet people, most of whom you won't get to know. But you've met them and, later on, if you need or want something, you know who to call. And they'll help you out.

This may be what happens when you grow up in a privileged circumstances: you develop connections—intellectual, emotional, social, professional, economic—that later you can come back to if you need, or simply get interested in, them. You become part of a rich and valuable network. It's an asset you can draw on.

If you grow up in non-privileged circumstances, as most of us do, education is a way of redressing—at least partially—the balance. You are shown what's important and you file it away until you're mature enough—or just find the time—to figure it out and appreciate it. Education fills in and compensates for what your family and community couldn't give you. That's why it's so important.

But you realize that education is a lifelong affair. You can't learn and appreciate everything when you're in school. You learn some and take notes on lots more to maybe follow up on later. Like a good detective you take names. Then, over time, you see what you can figure out.

I also began, gradually, to see myself as a social scientist. The social sciences seemed like the best platform for making the world a better place which, perhaps because of my Lutheran upbringing, was something I wanted to do. But that didn't add up to a profession. I didn't know what I should do with or in social science. I was still sampling.

Perhaps the most noteworthy aspect of my time at Michigan State is what didn't happen. I did nothing on Latin America, economics (except for the one course in economic history) or education. When I graduated, I could not possibly have predicted that those three would become central to my 40-year career. They didn't show up until later.

During my senior year I had to make some decisions about the future. Since I was a wannabe intellectual, and since all the intellectuals I'd met had graduate degrees, I decided to go to graduate school—more specifically, in sociology at Duke University. One of my professors had links there and recommended me for the PhD program. They offered me a full fellowship. I took it, mostly on momentum. I'd always liked sociology, and nothing else came to mind. I didn't have a job (although I turned down an offer from the CIA shortly before graduation). I didn't feel ready to go out into the world. In an interview for MSU's campus newspaper during my senior year I said (bravely) that I was going to get a PhD in sociology and then work in university administration. It was all I could come up with. And I thought graduate school would be more of the same. I was wrong.

I went off to Duke.

VI

DUKE UNIVERSITY

DUKE WAS A first-rate university that I was lucky to get admitted to. The campus was spectacular—a gothic masterpiece that looked exactly the way a university was supposed to look. Back then (this was 1965) Duke was in something of a time warp, still untouched by the '60s and maintaining the atmosphere of the genteel South—quiet, exclusive, and vaguely preppy. That would soon change, of course.

The professors were great, offering knowledge, guidance, and support. Ed Tiryakian (who had studied with Pitirim Sorokin at Harvard) introduced us to major social theorists like Emile Durkheim and Max Weber and helped us see how theory explained (and might predict) the way societies behaved. Joel Smith (who, it turned out, had begun his academic career at Michigan State!) introduced us to the canons of scientific methodology—something I had no interest in and signed up for only because the course was required. He helped me see the difference between good science and not-so-good science, and why research design was crucial in determining which was which. He also had us read a just-published book, Thomas Kuhn's *The Structure of Scientific Revolutions*, which challenged traditional views about how scientific progress happened, and has since become a key work in the history of science. (I'm impressed by how often I see that book mentioned even today.) The stuff

I got in Smith's class was clearly interesting, but I was skeptical about whether it would ever be useful. I was wrong.

Both areas—social theory and methodology—stuck with me for the rest of my career. They turned out to be key building blocks in understanding and interpreting the world I ran into, and especially useful in the work I did at Ford—strengthening the social sciences and supporting policy analysis. I could not have predicted that. A bunch of abstract principles and concepts turned out to have important real-world applications. The lesson I've since drawn is: Just learn them. Make them arrows in your quiver, so they'll be there when you need them. Sooner or later they'll pay off.

Duke is located in Durham, North Carolina, of course, so you were in the South, a place whose startling combination of religion, moralism, hospitality, warmth, and (for some, unfortunately) racism almost had to be experienced to be appreciated. I met many wonderful people there. And I got my first close-up encounter with evil when, with several classmates, I attended a Ku Klux Klan rally just outside of town. I got my second when someone I met by chance told me that the flesh of Blacks was inferior to the flesh of whites, something you could see if you cut into it. My God! Much more positively, I discovered the smell of curing tobacco, which permeated at least some of Durham's neighborhoods in the fall—one of the most delightful smells I've ever encountered. It was very different from the Midwest I'd grown up in.

Durham also provided an interesting link to the United States' storied history of prohibition. Alcohol was still highly regulated back then in North Carolina (and presumably in much of the South). Restaurants and bars could serve beer and wine by the glass, but not liquor. You had to bring your own (which you could only buy at government stores) and mix your drink at the table or bar using "set-ups" (glasses, ice, and mixers) that the establishment sold you. Most places offered lockers for rent, so you could store your liquor there rather than carrying it in and out. And, as in prohibition, there were illegal "speakeasies," usually in poor neighborhoods, where you could get a drink just like in a real bar. These places didn't have signs, and you had to have some kind of password to get in. This was good material for a sociologist (or a historian). We tried visiting one once, but they wouldn't let us in. No password.

All of this seemed anachronistic, and occasionally quaint, to a northerner, but it made you realize how serious and long-lived prohibition was. And how hard it is to restrain animal spirits. People like drinking alcohol. You can't stamp that out. All you can do is manage it. Much of life is like that.

I also had a couple of great roommates at Duke—Jack Armistead and Phil Kawesch. I had known both at Michigan State, but sharing with them the challenges of graduate school and of life in the South made us know each other better and become good friends. Both were different from me. Jack came from an academic family. His father had been a dean at Michigan State, and he had always expected to get a PhD and have a career in higher education. He was smart, decent, sensible, and conventional. He seemed to know where he was going. I always figured he would get there.

By contrast, Phil was a New York Jew whose father sold office furniture in the Bronx, and who bowled you over with his exuberance and warmth. He was emotional, irreverent, and liked to ask big questions. He'd been born with a genetic disease that seriously affected his physical abilities but didn't let that stop him. We played a lot of touch football. You had to like Phil. I had no idea what he might end up doing. A couple of years later when he was in between graduate school and his eventual career—and driving a taxi in New York—he gave me a late-night tour of the City, which included a famous delicatessen, a bar where a Black lady was belting out songs with a combo, and a burlesque show (they still existed). From Phil, I got my first glimpse of New York.

Jack became a professor, wrote a couple of books (at least) and went on to deanships at several universities. Phil founded a counseling and psychotherapy center in New York. Whenever I hear the Brahms Academic Festival overture, I think of Jack (*Gaudeamus igitur!*). With Phil, it's more like Zorba the Greek. We've stayed in touch for 50-plus years.

A future president of Chile, Ricardo Lagos, also defended his doctoral thesis (in economics) at Duke the year I was there. We didn't meet then. When we did, years later, it never came up.

Duke was a big step forward in realizing one of the three big urges I'd grown up with: to become an intellectual. The problem I ran into was that going to graduate school was serious. It was not about trying things out. You were expected to become a professional. You studied theory, methodology, and statistics. You tried your hand at research. You were on your way to becoming a card-carrying sociologist. I had nothing against sociology, and in fact enjoyed the classes in theory and methods. But I soon realized that I wasn't ready to make that kind of commitment. It was too abstract. I couldn't connect it to my urge to make the world a better place. I was going through the motions, but without the passion, or even much feeling. Pretty quickly I realized that I had to get out.

That posed a dilemma. The Vietnam War was in full swing, and young twenty-something males like me who dropped out of school would almost certainly get drafted. I didn't have particularly strong feelings about the Vietnam War at that point, but I didn't want to go there and fight it. That was clear. I briefly considered going to law school and even took the LSAT but couldn't get excited about studying law. So what should I do?

Then I had what later seemed like a stroke of genius: join the Peace Corps. Serving as a Peace Corps Volunteer would get my feet on the ground and my hands dirty, plus it would give me some genuine international experience—all of which I thought I needed. The Peace Corps was also trendy, since it was still the '60s, and the Kennedy aura hadn't faded much. And it would probably defer me from military service. Officially, Peace Corps Volunteers were not excused from their obligation to serve in the military, but in practice local draft boards had broad latitude regarding who they called and who they deferred. Rural boards like mine in Dimondale, where few youngsters went on to college, had no trouble filling their draft quotas and tended to defer Peace Corps Volunteers. (I heard later that I was the first Peace Corps Volunteer my draft board had ever had.)

These revelations came while I was writing my Master's thesis during a hot, humid Durham summer. They were strong, but I realized pretty quickly that I couldn't just decide—first I had to consult. So I wrote letters to my parents, and to my favorite Duke professor, Ed Tiryakian, laying out my concerns. What's interesting is how quickly everyone responded and how thoughtful their advice was.

My mom sent three pages typed single-spaced reflecting on how she'd dealt with big life decisions. It was kind of a tough-love document, emphasizing that you can't run away from problems and must face them, yet ended with unconditional love: "Jeff, should you decide to go into the Peace Corps, or whatever you will decide…you know we will always be proud of you in anything that you decide to do. You are that kind of person, one couldn't help be proud to the button-bruising point." It was clear and much-appreciated support.

My dad, in six small pages of graceful script, emphasized finding my inner feelings and using those to make my decision. I should not, he said, refrain because of his, or my mom's, comments. He mentioned one of his favorite sayings: "A man convinced against his will is of the same opinion still." And he signed off with his usual, slightly mysterious, exhortation: "Keep the faith." I felt supported.

And Dr. Tiryakian, writing from Dakar, advised "follow your heart's inclination—it knows best!" He also suggested, in comments that in retrospect look especially prescient, that I consider Latin America, which "is the place I would orient myself if I were in your shoes."

So I applied. And the Peace Corps responded right away, offering to send me to Niger.

What? I had never even heard of Niger. I said I would get back to them and went to the library. It turned out that Niger was a landlocked country in Africa, not far from Timbuktu and largely covered by the Sahara Desert. Its capital city had a population of around 70,000 and its main export was jute. At least that's what I remember. It didn't seem very appealing.

I got back to the Peace Corps and asked whether they had any other countries. A week or two later they got back to me, offering Nigeria, Honduras and Colombia. And Niger was still on the table, should I change my mind.

I said I'd get back to them and went to the library again. It didn't take long. I wasn't warming up to Africa in general, so I took Nigeria off the list. Honduras seemed awfully poor and something of a backwater. Colombia, on the other hand, looked interesting. It was relatively large, with several modern cities and a decent economy. It had mountains, beaches, jungle, and plains. It had a major international export—coffee (which Juan Valdéz regularly pitched on U.S. television). It sounded interesting. The only drawback was that it seemed awfully close to the United States. My goal was to get as far away as possible, preferably to Southeast Asia (Indonesia was my top choice, but Indonesia wasn't available, and you can't have everything.) Colombia didn't sound bad, even though it was only a couple of thousand miles away. I decided to take it.

Thus I made what would turn out to be one of the most fateful decisions of my life. I had not previously had any interest in the Peace Corps or in Latin America. I chose them only because something else (graduate school, for which I wasn't ready and wasn't the right fit even had I been) didn't work out. I needed to jump ship. There they were, like a life preserver. At a minimum, they met my urge to get out of rural Michigan and make the world a better place, so I'd still be on track. I made the decision almost casually. It profoundly changed my life.

⌘

So much for college and a year of grad school. Writing about Michigan State and Duke was fun, and a lot easier than writing about high school. They happened more recently and involved bigger changes, so were probably easier to remember. Leaving home and going to the university was a shock—like jumping into a cold lake. I loved the independence and challenge but had to figure out how to deal with it. And I realized that I didn't know who I was or what I would do with my life. That was good. The lesson, I think, is that all college students should resist the temptation to live at home if they possibly can. Get out. There's something startling about being on your own that concentrates the mind and forces you to grow up.

It may also be that I'm getting better at writing about my past. Now that I've written a bit, I think I see better how to do it. Mostly you plow straight ahead with whatever happened, saying what seems important (and true) and hoping that once you've laid it out you'll see how to separate the wheat from the chaff. Sometimes you take a small act, like dropping a journalism course or carrying around a book by Sartre, and mine it for meaning. You sniff, turn it over, write something, and see what happens. Always you keep your antennae up, hoping your muse will send something good your way—a feeling or insight that has real meaning. That happens more often than you'd think. Sometimes in the middle of the night.

But you can't simply expect the story to appear. You've got to recognize where there's potential, put your subconscious to work, and make things happen. And still, it's hard.

I'm also noticing that, starting with college, the stakes seemed to get higher. I began to take some things off the table, and leave other things on. I started down paths I would follow for the rest of my life. I was going to be an intellectual (whatever that meant) but I was not going to be a professor. I was going to have an international career. I was going to be a social scientist. I was going to work with elites. At the time, I didn't think much about the long-term consequences of my decisions. In fact, they were more like discoveries than decisions. And I didn't have a grand plan. Mostly I followed my nose.

VII

THE PEACE CORPS/COLOMBIA

Oh, do not ask, 'What is it?' Let us go and make our visit.

—T.S. Eliot,

The Love Song of J. Alfred Prufrock

On to the Peace Corps. Dropping out of graduate school ended stage one of my higher education. I had learned a lot, gotten a couple of degrees, and still not discovered what to do with my life. Michigan State and Duke were like the overture to an opera—all about introduction. The curtain had gone up, but the first act hadn't really begun. I was waiting for something to happen.

It happened quickly. The Peace Corps was the polar opposite of college. It was about fact rather than theory, people rather than books, the small picture rather than the big picture. It put you in the here and now. You were face-to-face with poverty, misfortune, incompetence, and evil. You were supposed to do something about them. Reading was over. It was time to act.

That made the Peace Corps serious. You left your culture behind and entered someone else's. It was like jumping into the ocean for the first time and having to stay there for two years. A shock. You wondered whether you were crazy. Maybe you were.

One of the most important aspects of the Peace Corps was that it took you outside the United States, and therefore outside your comfort zone. You lost a support system you hadn't realized you had. All the nice things you took for granted—friends, family, car, music, football, TV shows, cheeseburgers—were gone. The people you relied on for conversation, stimulus, identity, and approval were no longer there. Values were no longer shared. Words no longer meant what they used to. You had to speak Spanish. You couldn't go home for Christmas. The orderly, comfortable life you had enjoyed had disappeared, making you realize that it had been orderly and comfortable—and that you had enjoyed it. For 20-something Americans who had grown up middle-class, relatively pampered, and at least sympathetic to the rebellion and counterculture of the '60s, that was a shock. Our lifestyles had been taken away. We came face-to-face with a truth that Joni Mitchell would point out a couple of years later in *Big Yellow Taxi*: Some things you have to lose in order to realize you had them. For many it was a profoundly subversive experience. Maybe the U.S. wasn't so bad after all.

In fact it may be that the biggest impact the Peace Corps had on young Americans was to make them appreciate the United States. Many—perhaps most—of us assumed that the way we lived in the United States was normal. We learned that it was not, and that in fact we were extraordinarily privileged. That was a revelation and made many of us see life in the United States differently. We missed it.

I had no idea any of that was going to happen, of course. I had simply signed up for a rural community development program in Colombia's Antioquia province. I knew nothing about community development, Colombia, or Antioquia (which turned out to have steep mountains, beautiful valleys, fluffy white clouds, first-rate coffee and a long tradition of violence), but it seemed like a good thing to do if your goal was to make the world a better place, which one of mine was. And of course I didn't speak Spanish. I had a lot to learn. Again.

A couple of things were important about the Peace Corps I knew.

First, we weren't free-lancers. We had real jobs in a real program—*Acción Comunal*—as rural community development agents (*promotores de acción comunal*). *Acción Comunal* was a national government effort to promote grass-roots development. It sought to get communities (neighborhoods, really) to establish councils (*juntas*), elect leaders, and devise projects that would benefit the community, often using government funds set aside for that purpose. The goal was to reduce the passivity and paternalism that were so common at the local level in Colombia, and help communities take matters into their own hands—although always outside the formal control of political parties. The idea, at least on paper, was to empower local communities and thereby strengthen democracy. It was a kind of Rotary Club for the poor.

As *promotores*, our job was to expand and strengthen *Acción Comunal*. We were supposed to help existing *juntas* function better and create new *juntas* where they didn't exist. That meant visiting local communities and getting to know the leaders. It meant establishing credibility with people who were poor, isolated, had little education and no particular reason to think we could help them, and whose culture and values we were only beginning to understand. And it meant selling the idea of community development, and explaining how to conduct meetings, hold elections, establish priorities, organize projects, and manage money. And finally, it meant getting communities to take ownership of *Acción Comunal*. Our job was to facilitate but not to lead. Leaders were supposed to be local. Success depended on making sure the *junta* and its projects belonged to the community, not to us. Making all that happen was hard.

All of this had to be done in Spanish, of course, usually in isolated mountain communities (called *veredas*) that had no roads, no electricity and few people with more than a couple of years of education. You had to get there (on foot or horseback), get people together, get them to listen, and get them to act. Often we had help from the local priest, who would come and hold a mass in the *vereda* that would bring people out, and you would follow that up with a presentation on *Acción Comunal*. But it was a challenge. I often felt like a foreign missionary pushing, in imperfect Spanish, exotic ideas that I could only hope would work.

Having a real job in a real government program helped. We were official. We had a clear identity, clear goals, and clear methods. The local government, from the mayor on down, was supposed to work with us.

The parish priest shared our interest in helping the *campesino* community. We fit in. *Acción comunal* had a good reputation. And most of the *municipios* we worked in had lots of small landholders, giving *campesinos* a stake in community affairs. It added up. Had any of those pieces been missing, our work would have been much tougher.

But if there's a lesson here it's not that the Peace Corps should work with governments. Rather it's that the Peace Corps should tailor its strategy to local conditions. You need goals, methods, and partners that add up on the ground, where you're going to work. In our case, working with the government in *Acción Comunal* made sense. Elsewhere, a different approach might have been necessary.

The other important thing about the Peace Corps I knew was that it was a cultural immersion program. You were expected to learn the language and culture, and eventually to go native (although they didn't quite put it that way). Cultural immersion had always been part of the Peace Corps, of course, but our group was an experiment. We were going to be trained in-region and substantially by local authorities in an effort to take us faster and deeper into local culture. What none of us realized was how much stress "faster and deeper" would provoke.

We started with five weeks of language training at Camp Radley, high in the mountains of Puerto Rico. Then we got two months of training in Medellín, the capital of the Department of Antioquia, where we lived with middle-class families. Once training ended, each of us was assigned to live and work—alone—in a small village out in the mountains. You couldn't survive long by yourself in a small village without learning the language and the culture. You went native or you went home.

Camp Radley was boot camp for do-gooders. It was outside of Arecibo, up in Puerto Rico's green and rainy mountains and at the end of the road, secluded, and not served by public transportation. The only way out was a Peace Corps van. The atmosphere was mildly military. Johnny Delgado, a Black former Peace Corps Volunteer in Peru and Los Angeles native, was in charge and made that clear but we liked him— kind of a good-natured drill sergeant. Every morning at around 6 a.m.

the staff rousted us from our bunks with a bullhorn to do calisthenics and run. Then we took cold showers (only the staff got hot water). After that we gathered around the flagpole to raise the Colombian flag and sing the national anthem—in Spanish ("*O gloria inmarcesible…*"). Then it was breakfast (the food was pretty good—first time I ever had ice cream for breakfast) and off to Spanish class. We had something like six hours of Spanish each day, with instructors who as I recall were native Colombians. We were not allowed to speak English between breakfast and dinner. That made lunch conversation difficult. There's not much to say when you don't speak the language. (I remember a lame conversation with a professor from the Harvard Business School—James Austin, maybe—who had come down to give a talk and whose Spanish seemed no better than mine—but we were determined to follow the rules and not speak a word of English.) Having to speak Spanish for hours at a time was agony. By dinner we were dying to have a normal conversation. It was our first encounter with culture shock.

Our schedules were full. The Peace Corps brought in some pretty good speakers from the mainland to talk about politics and economic development, mostly in the evenings. And on weekends staff took us in vans to near-by towns, where we were encouraged to try our Spanish on the locals, often with comic results. We responded to the seclusion and pressure by developing a spirited social life based on beer, rum, and music. We drank. We danced. We poured our hearts out. We became fast friends, despite coming from all over the United States and having only just met. We fell in love. We published several editions of a newsletter commenting on the personalities, activities, and absurdities of camp life. We did our best to have fun.

After our five weeks in Camp Radley we got a couple of days of R&R in San Juan prior to flying down to Medellín for two more months of training. My brother and future sister-in-law surprised me by coming in from wherever they were to say good-bye. The night before getting on the plane we enjoyed a boisterous dinner with several other trainees at the *El Convento* hotel in Old San Juan. Just as at Camp Radley, we ate, drank, and laughed. But underneath at least a few of us were apprehensive. We were staring into the unknown, wondering what we had gotten ourselves into.

When we landed in Medellín, we gathered around the flagpole and sang the national anthem—in Spanish, of course (after five weeks of practice we were pretty good). Then the governor of Antioquia, Octavio Arizmendi Posada, welcomed us on the tarmac with a nice speech. The newspapers wrote it up. We were Colombia/51—the 51st group of Peace Corps volunteers to serve in Colombia. And Peace Corps/Colombia was one of the largest Peace Corps programs in the world. We were excited. We were going to help the people of Antioquia. We didn't know how, exactly, but that would become clear soon. We hoped. Our fingers were crossed.

Antioquia turned out to be impressive. It was 80% mountains interspersed with narrow, green valleys—a combination that generated gorgeous scenery, treacherous roads, and ideal conditions for growing coffee. Its capital, Medellín, was Colombia's second largest city and known, because it was located at nearly 5000 feet, as the "City of Eternal Spring." Most of Antioquia's *municipios* were perched on hillsides slightly above or below that altitude—with copious amounts of sunshine and rain. The region's mountainous terrain had made communication with other parts of the country difficult for many years, fueling a separate cultural identity.

Antioquia's people, known as *paisas*, were entrepreneurial and aggressive, and had produced some of the country's leading business and political leaders, including six presidents (most recently, Álvaro Uribe), Colombia's first Saint (Laura) and its most famous artist (Fernando Botero). Juan Valdez, the ubiquitous purveyor of Colombian coffee, is based on the *paisa* stereotype. Many argue that the *paisas* were descended substantially from Spaniards of Extremaduran, Basque, and Andalusian origin, along with a group of Sephardic Jews. That might help explain why the *paisas* had a strong sense of identity and weren't shy about letting you know how they felt. They also spoke a distinctive Spanish, peppered with exclamations (everyone's favorite being "*eh, Ave María!*"), diminutives (*momentico*) and delightful hyperbole ("...so tall he's got clouds in his eyes"; "…so ugly that, after making him, God sat down and laughed"; "…so thin you could x-ray him with a candle"). We took to the *paisa* style and quickly began to pick it up. They seemed like the Texans of Colombia (although they'd probably argue that Texans were the *paisas* of the United States).

Antioquia, and Colombia more generally, had a long tradition of local violence—"*la violencia*"—that was rooted originally in differences between the Liberal and Conservative parties, but had later taken on a life of its own, often unrelated to any specific grievances. During the 20 years between 1948 and 1968, some 100 to 200,000 people were killed. Violence was trending downward by the time we arrived, but was still common, particularly in rural areas. It had become a common way to settle scores, real or imagined. We would come across it regularly in the villages we lived and worked in.

In Medellín we had classes at the *Instituto Politécnico*—Spanish, of course, plus training in the theory and practice of rural community development plus some agriculture (I remember a class on breeding rabbits—which I'd always understood didn't require human intervention). But the bigger change was living with local families, which provided an immediate, and often vivid, look into Colombian culture. Most family members didn't speak English, and those that did had been asked not to, so as make sure we learned Spanish. For the first time we were inside the culture. We began to exchange impressions of "our" families and their often hard-to-understand attitudes and ways.

We were encouraged to participate in our families' social lives. That led to some memorable moments. I remember, on a Saturday outing with another trainee's family, discovering that the lady of the house (or maybe it was a cousin) was a *rejoneadora*, i.e. she fought bulls on horseback. We went to see her fight at the local *plaza de toros*. I took lots of pictures, and my Uncle Lloyd later turned one of them into a painting. A real contrast to the moms I'd known back in Michigan.

The head of the family I lived with was relatively young and studying law at the University of Medellín. We got along fine, although I don't remember much about our conversations. Every evening his wife served the two of us dinner—but didn't sit down. She wouldn't eat until we had finished and left the table. It was a low-key but clear introduction to the reality of *machismo*, which turned out to be pervasive, and taken entirely for granted.

Much of our training was about acculturation. The first message was that acting like *gringo* do-gooders wasn't going to cut it. Instead, we were introduced to the attitudes, values, and practices of Colombians, and urged to make them the starting-point for our work. That meant understanding the Colombian perspective, recognizing how things got done, knowing our job, becoming one of the boys, and earning respect. Their culture took priority over ours.

Doing that was easier said than done, of course. Most of us were young, inexperienced, and idealistic. Our first impulse was to please. Many of us were willing to bend over backwards to be loved. Some, myself included, had joined the Peace Corps because we weren't ready for the commitment and discipline of professional life. Now we were being told to get serious. Wagging our tails wouldn't be enough. We would have to get things done, and that meant figuring out how people thought, and making sure they saw us as professionals. It was a good lesson about dealing with the real world, but for many it was hard to swallow. We would have to suppress at least a few of the impulses that had led us to join the Peace Corps in the first place. We had signed up for peace, love, and adventure. We were being given jobs.

All of this was happening within the context of growing culture shock—a concept that was new to us and that we didn't see coming. Leaving our culture behind and learning to operate in a new one was a genuine shock. We were being asked to speak a new language, deal with people who were very different from us, behave in new ways and follow different rules. Doing that for short periods can seem romantic (psychologists call it the "honeymoon" phase of culture shock). But doing it all day, every day gets painful pretty quickly—at least until you adapt. It's hard to go cold turkey when it comes to language and culture. Culture is intimate. It's you. You miss it. We responded by clinging to what we were losing. We devoured the international edition of *Time* magazine as soon as it showed up at the newsstand each week. We sought restaurants that offered the food we had known back home—hamburgers, pizza, and even salami sandwiches. We engaged in long and animated conversations with each other, in part because doing so was the strongest link we had with the lives we'd left behind. We needed our shot of America every day. Once classes ended in the afternoon and we went home to our "families," the curtain would come down. We would have to shift into Spanish, and into our families' culture. It would be tough.

To give us a sense of what our lives were going to be like for the next two years, the Peace Corps sent each of us out to spend a several days alone in a small town up in the mountains. I was assigned to Santa Bárbara, which of course I knew nothing about, but turned out to be at the top of *tierra cafetera* (coffee country) about three hours away. I used my halting Spanish to locate, in the gritty part of downtown Medellín where long-distance buses came and went, the right bus line, check the schedule, buy a ticket, get there, and find a place to stay. Then I began contemplating what I might do for several days. I knew no one, of course, and don't remember having any specific instructions. I was on my own.

Santa Bárbara was a picture-post-card town. Billing itself as a "balcony with beautiful views" It sat at just under 6000 feet among rolling green mountains, deep valleys, bright blue skies, and fluffy white clouds that marched up the valleys every afternoon, dissolving occasionally into rain. It was gorgeous—about as good an advertisement for the beauty of Antioquia's coffee country as you could find.

It was also exotic, at least for a young *gringo*. Life in a small Antioqueño village was completely different from life in Medellín. Cars and jeeps were rare. People travelled on colorful open-sided buses, by horse or mule, or on foot. There was little direct contact with the broader world. Life was organized around the hills and valleys that surrounded the town, and powered its agricultural economy—which featured coffee, mangos, avocados, plantains and much more. *Campesinos* were everywhere, wearing wool *ruanas* to protect against the cold and rain, and with highly decorated leather *carrieles* (satchels) hanging on their shoulders, stocked with money, papers, and, more often than we realized, pistols.

I had gotten a (very) basic room overlooking the plaza in the town's only hotel and remember waking up my first morning to the sound of a horse galloping across the plaza. It felt like a cowboy movie. I could imagine the Lone Ranger, his spurs jingling, entering the café below to get some breakfast. I got up and looked out. He wasn't there. But I was a long way from the United States.

The only other thing I remember about my stay in Santa Bárbara was shock. Being there made me realize the enormity of what I had done. I was going to spend the next two years of my life in a town like this, alone. I was leaving behind all that was familiar to live in a place that was small, foreign, and poor. There would be no TV. Electricity would come and go. Telephone calls would require going to the phone company's booth on the plaza when it was open (and anyway, who would I call?). Leisure time would mean sitting in the café with the guys, downing shots of licorice-flavored *aguardiente* with mango chasers. I didn't even want to think about the food. No one would speak my language, share my culture, or understand my dreams. The things I was used to doing for fun would be gone. I would be alone. I was appalled. Did I really want to do this?

It turned out that I did. Although I no longer recall how I spent those few days in Santa Bárbara, the visit achieved its objective. I saw what I was getting into and resolved, with much trepidation, to stick with it. This was my opportunity to get the international experience I thought I needed for my career. I would get my feet on the ground and my hands dirty. I would have a shot at making the world a better place. Somehow I would find a way to deal with the boredom and isolation I feared were in store. Maybe it would get better as time went by. I would take a calculated risk, based more on faith than on conviction.

Most of us made the same decision. We saw that living in the village, and outside our culture, would be tough but went ahead anyway, largely because we had joined the Peace Corps to help others. Idealism carried the day. But we didn't realize what a hugely positive experience living outside our culture would turn out to be. By losing the familiar and the comfortable we found ourselves. We discovered that we were privileged. That we had been luckier than most people. That we had enjoyed advantages—education, security, prosperity, liberty, rule of law—that others had not enjoyed. That simple behaviors we took for granted, like punctuality and candor, were not simple, and should not be taken for granted. It was an unexpected education. Many—perhaps all—of us began to appreciate aspects of our lives we had never before appreciated. We began to feel thankful.

Just as important, we developed empathy for Colombians. We began to see how they saw the world. We came to understand, at least minimally, what they valued, why, and how it worked for them. We realized that their views were not only different from ours, but that they made sense and deserved respect. We began to take them seriously. We even began to share some of their feelings. Our world got bigger.

But the real surprise was that empathy pretty quickly led to imitation. We started behaving like Colombians. First came the accent. We began to mimic the pronunciation, exaggeration, and color that made the *paisas* so distinctive. We practiced in front of each other. Next we began experimenting with thinking and acting like Colombians. We tried on their values and perspectives like new clothes, adjusting them here and there, and seeing how they looked. We began resisting, for example, our impulse to arrive on time—learning to recognize when six o'clock meant six o'clock (which was seldom), and when it meant seven o'clock (which was often). We learned to express surprise—even dismay—when a market vendor told us how much something cost, and asked, with just the right facial expression, how the price could possibly be so high. We refrained from saying no when asked to do something we didn't want to do, and instead said we would make every effort to do it—which left people feeling respected even when we didn't do whatever it was we suggested we would. We tried to pass for *paisas*.

It was like acting in a play without a script. You had a part and some sense of the characters, but didn't have any lines, so you made them up—kind of an improvisational theatre. The important thing was to be part of their conversation rather than of ours. To operate on their terms. We started taking pride in that. We were becoming bicultural.

This was important. Becoming bicultural, it turns out, adds a dimension to your life. It's like getting a huge gift. Suddenly you can operate in two cultures instead of one. You're not just an American any more. You have a second identity—a Colombian, sort of. That's what "going native" is all about. When you're with normal Americans, you almost feel like a secret agent ("They don't realize who I really am..."). It's fun.

Just as important were the professional benefits. I discovered that it was much more productive, and satisfying, to work from inside a culture than from outside. You were on the team and in the game. You understood what was going on. You knew how to interpret what people said, and how to get things done. The difference was so great that I found it hard to imagine having an international career without being able to operate from inside the culture of the country where I was working. It seemed almost unprofessional. I decided I would try to work only in places where I spoke the language and understood the culture. Since it takes at least a year of total immersion to become bicultural, that meant effectively that I would spend my entire career in Latin America. I was not about to make the same investment in time, effort, and angst to become bicultural in some other part of the world. Once was enough. The die was cast. I would, without having intended it, be a Latin Americanist.

But putting acculturation so firmly at the center of our training program created problems. Our training was a little like military boot camp—demanding most of the time and painful some of the time. Having to adapt to a new culture was hard. The local officials who taught us weren't always impressive and didn't always communicate well. All of us were stressed, and many were angry. It was hard to see how the discomfort we were enduring would pay off. Several trainees complained that our training was a failure. An end-of-training evaluation commissioned by Peace Corps/Washington was, as I recall, highly critical.

I find it hard to assess all of this. Boot camp is by definition demanding. It isolates recruits and forces them to behave in new ways. No one enjoys it and many don't make it through. In our case nearly half of those who began training left before we started work. Maybe that was appropriate, given the difficulties of promoting community development in the mountains of Colombia. Moreover it's hard to evaluate a training program before its graduates begin working. And since we had no experience in the jobs we were being trained for, and were suffering from culture shock, our opinions about training may not have been reliable. How could we distinguish between good training and bad?

Personally I was willing to give the program the benefit of the doubt. Acculturation seemed like the right path. I was learning enough. And I was willing to put up with the stress. It was, after all, an experiment. My only serious gripe came at the end of training when my girlfriend got "deselected"—a wonderfully bureaucratic term for being sent home. That was too much. I started a petition drive to get her reinstated, and to my surprise we won. It was nice to get a victory in the midst of all that tribulation.

Some eighteen months later, after becoming the volunteer coordinator for Antioquia, I put together a survey of the training program's graduates. I was of course taking advantage of my graduate work in sociology (surveys being a core part of what sociologists did back then) but I was genuinely interested in seeing how our group was doing. We were an experiment. How'd we turn out?

The survey wasn't particularly sophisticated. But it did produce some interesting findings. The group had gotten a lot done, nearly tripling the number of functioning *juntas de acción comunal*, and getting them to undertake hundreds of projects ranging from construction (schools, aqueducts, latrines, roads, and bridges) to agriculture (ducks, chickens, yuca, beans, corn, vegetable gardens). Nearly all the volunteers said that *Acción Comunal* was functioning fairly well (or better) in their villages. Most felt they had significantly improved the attitudes of municipal officials toward community projects. And most felt their most valuable contribution was some form of attitudinal change. Examples included "fostering consciousness among campesinos of their problems and solutions" and "promoting responsibility and self-control." Only a few listed lack of money as a major impediment to their work; much more common were attitudinal problems such as apathy, fatalism, and a lack of social consciousness. A small minority felt that conditions in their towns (land distribution, for example) made it very difficult for *Acción Comunal* to work. But the picture was positive—certainly not what you would describe as failure. Those of us who made it through training seemed to be doing pretty good work.

Of course, assessing community development work is hard. The goal is to strengthen communities, so you can't just count projects. You have to change attitudes, develop leaders, and get people involved. How are you going to measure those? Some of the most important changes take place in people's minds, and may not show up for years. Once they do, they may change the world. But until they show up, nobody even knows whether they've happened.

So I'm inclined to see our training program as a noble experiment. It was on the right track in emphasizing acculturation and making the process tough. Maybe the execution was flawed. But maybe it was the best the Peace Corps could do at the time. It had the merit of taking culture and local authorities seriously—something that didn't come naturally to the U.S. government back then. I presume that the Peace Corps has since learned a lot about how best to settle volunteers into a new culture, and how to "deselect" those who don't appear to have the right stuff. But I'm glad I got the kind of training I did. It has had a large and positive impact on my life and career.

One more thing: The program was a smashing success on several measures of acculturation that no one anticipated. Six of the 15 volunteers who finished training and started work ended up marrying Colombians. A seventh (me) did his doctoral research in Colombia, lived in Latin America for a dozen years, spent his entire career working on Latin America, and married a Latin American (although not a Colombian) woman. Four of the volunteers (two men and two women) spent the rest of their lives in Colombia (or at least, were still there 50 years later). We acculturated.

Two other things happened during our training in Medellín that would connect to my career in interesting ways later on—although at the time I had no idea.

First, the Peace Corps invited an official from the Ford Foundation's office in Bogotá, Ralph Harbison, to come to Medellín and speak to us. I was impressed. Ralph was knowledgeable, articulate, and sounded (at least to my untutored ears) like a member of the east-coast establishment. He had studied at Princeton after all, and his father taught there. I remember nothing about what he said except that he sold me on the Ford Foundation. I came away convinced that the Ford Foundation was rich, powerful, sophisticated, visionary, well-connected, and hired the smartest people. It seemed far and away the most professional organization working on development in Latin America, and maybe in the world. It was where I belonged. That was clear. Listening to Ralph caused me to put something new on the table: I would—or at least, should—work for the Ford Foundation. The only question was whether they would hire me.

Second, the U.S. ambassador, Rey Carlson, came to speak to us. As I recall, Rey was not a career foreign service officer, but rather had been appointed ambassador after many years as a professor of economics at Vanderbilt University. So he was something of an outsider to the U.S. government. But to us he was simply an ambassador—the first we'd ever encountered. The one thing we'd heard was that he'd made an offhand but much-commented remark about instant coffee shortly after becoming ambassador to Colombia: "*Nescafé no es café*" ("Nescafé is not coffee") which we (and probably he) thought was funny but reportedly did not sit well with the Nestlé corporation. He had a folksy manner, and that was probably why I liked him. The surprise was that seven years later I had an office next to his at the Ford Foundation in Lima (They hired me!). He had taken a job with Ford after stepping down as ambassador. We became colleagues. When he retired, a year or so later, I took over the projects (all of them in economics) he had been managing. A total surprise, of course, but a good lesson in how hard it is to predict the future.

Training was over. Those of us who survived were going to be bona fide Peace Corps Volunteers (we called ourselves "PCVs") for the next two years. We were given our assignments and sent out to our villages to start work. I was sent to Pueblorrico, several hours southwest of Medellín, smack in the middle of coffee country. It was small, poor, and typical. I was excited. My international career was underway. I could finally start trying to make the world a better place.

I lasted just three months. My problem, apparently, was that I failed to impress the local *cacique* (political boss), who may also have been Pueblorrico's largest landholder. After looking me over (he invited me to ride out to his farm—on a high-spirited horse he provided—with his wife and kids for lunch), he asked the government in Medellín to send another *promotor*—a Colombian—to Pueblorrico. He never said anything to me (I only found out when the new guy showed up for work), but I assume he concluded either that I was incompetent or a threat (or probably both). And he had the clout to get the government to listen. Since it made no sense to have two *promotores* in the same village, I figured I would have to leave. I called my boss and he, after consulting with government authorities, agreed. I left. I'd failed.

The upside was that failure taught me a few things. I learned that local politics matter. That you need to understand where power resides, and what it can do. That when land is concentrated in just a few hands, rural community development is especially difficult. That making a good first impression is important—especially in a small town. I'm sure I understood all of these in some abstract and intellectual way before I started work. But now I understood them first-hand and emotionally. I'd seen what they could do. I felt them. They'd cost me a job. I wouldn't forget. I vowed that next time I would present myself differently—less casual, more serious, more professional, someone who expected and deserved respect. If I could sell that, maybe it would help. I would try.

I went back to Medellín and right away was assigned to Granada, a small village up in *tierra fría* (cold country) at just over 6,000 feet in what was known as Antioquia's "far east" or *oriente lejano*. It was cold only by *Antioqueño* standards (as a Michigander, I knew cold) but it rained a lot, and was gray a lot more. You could see why so many people—*campesinos* and town-dwellers—wore the thick wool *ruanas* that kept the rain out and the heat in. I bought one right away and became a believer. Looking out at shabby buildings, swollen gray clouds, rain-darkened hills, and wet cobble-stones, it was easy to find the atmosphere drab and dismal, which I did, although for some reason it never bothered me. When the sun did come out it lit up the place like a movie set. You wanted to cheer.

Granada was smaller and poorer than Pueblorrico. Nobody appeared to have much money, so there was no *cacique* to lord it over the others. Back then the real money in rural Antioquia seemed to be in coffee and cattle, and the altitude in most of Granada was too high for those. Most of the farms were small—an acre or less. I had the feeling that there wasn't much in Granada that would attract anyone looking to get rich. That seemed like a plus. The people were nice. I liked the place. It looked like something I could manage.

It's worth saying a bit about how important altitude was in Antioquia. Because the province was a labyrinth of steep mountains and deep valleys, altitudes varied substantially over short distances, causing major changes in temperature, weather and crops. Not surprisingly, places were often described by their temperature. *Tierra fría* was cold country—usually above 6000 feet, chilly enough to wear a *ruana*, and best for crops like potatoes. *Tierra caliente* was hot country, at 3000 feet or below, calling for a wide-brimmed hat to ward off the sun, and best for producing plantains, sugar cane, and cattle. In between was *tierra templada* (or *tierra cafetera*), where the climate was temperate, sun, clouds, and rain took turns all day long, and coffee flourished. You could experience all three in a single *municipio* and within a couple of hours by horse or mule, depending on how far up or down the mountain you went. Altitude also influenced atmosphere. *Tierra fría* tended to be reserved and maybe a little gloomy, while *tierra caliente* tended to be noisier and more upbeat. Granada was mostly *tierra fría*, although several *veredas* were down in coffee country where the temperature was higher and there was more sun. But overall Granada was up high, where things were chilly and serious. It seemed like a good fit.

One of the things I remember most about living in Granada was getting there. Transportation from Medellín to virtually all of Antioquia's villages back then was by rustic buses known as *escaleras*—each of which consisted of a colorfully painted wood body that had benches rather than seats, and open sides with low doors—all mounted on a metal chassis. Each bus was painted individually with whatever scenes and flourishes the artist or owner chose. No two were alike, of course, and each had the name of the village it served painted on the front, back and (maybe) the sides. So you knew where any bus was from just by looking at it. ("There's the bus from El Carmen"…or Abejorral,…or Sonsón"). People identified with them. They looked for their hometown bus. The buses' roofs were flat with a low metal railing all the way around to secure boxes, bags, baskets, live animals and, if the benches were full below, an occasional passenger. You sat shoulder-to-shoulder with villagers and *campesinos*, which got you into at least a few conversations.

Since the sides were open, you were exposed to wind, rain, and dust. Dust was the worst. There was a lot, and you couldn't keep it out by rolling up the windows because there weren't any. It clogged your nose and painted your face gray. You learned quickly to pull your hat down to your eyes and your *ruana* up over your nose. The backs of the benches were straight, hard, and vertical; there was no reclining. Like many passengers, I often fell asleep sitting straight up and then nodded forward, my head touching my chest or sometimes approaching (but never touching) my knees. I could sleep like that for maybe 20 minutes. It was a net positive, but hard to call refreshing.

The trip to and from Medellín was six hours if all went well, and a long time in an open bus. Granada wasn't all that far from Medellín, but it was more than a thousand feet higher and, once you got beyond the town of Rio Negro, the road was gravel, narrow, curved along steep cliffs and occasionally blocked by landslides. It felt like way out in the sticks. Most of the trip was up around 6000 feet and chilly. If you ran into a landslide, you had to stop and figure out what to do. Sometimes the bus could pick its way, slowly and carefully, through the debris. Sometimes it had to wait until a path could be cleared by workers with shovels. Or maybe heavy equipment would be needed, in which case you had a long wait. You learned to deal with acts of God like this. I never heard of a bus actually getting hit by a landslide, but I certainly thought about it.

The trips I remember most were the buses back to Medellín, which left Granada at around 5 a.m. For some reason I look back fondly on showing up at that ungodly hour, buying a *tinto* (black coffee) or a *té de manzanilla* (manzanilla tea) at the bus-station café, which was lively at that time of the morning, and finding a seat on the bus. I think it had to do with the thrill of escaping the village for the lights of the big city. You started out in the cold dark of pre-dawn Granada, with the stars spread out against the sky, wound your way along narrow gravel roads through neighboring villages—El Santuario, Marinilla, and Rio Negro—and finally, just at sunrise, reached the edge of the Aburrá Valley to find Medellín displayed a thousand feet below, its lights winking in welcome. Coming upon the city like that was a delight. So completely different from the drab streets and rocky trails of Granada. I began to realize that, despite my rural origins and love of the great outdoors, I was hooked on the big city.

Life in Granada was austere. You got the basics: enough to eat and a decent place to sleep. There was electricity most of the time. And running water. There was a hospital and a doctor. Also a dentist. You could sit in a bar and drink. But that was it. The streets were narrow and in disrepair. The buildings were old; many were crumbling. No one had a big house. Hardly anyone had a car. Or a telephone. I don't recall ever seeing a TV. There were no movies. No bookstores. There were practically no restaurants. You couldn't buy an ice cream cone. It was hard to find a newspaper. Life was often picturesque, and occasionally charming. But it was never luxe. You lived bare. There were no frills.

The exception was the church. It had gold, silver, linen, art, angels, saints, and stained glass. It dispensed not only religion, but also beauty and luxury—the only beauty and luxury in town. I remember stepping in one morning at around 6 a.m. while mass was being said and was struck by the relative grandeur of the place. Candles glowed under the vaulted ceiling and *campesinos*, wearing *ruanas* but often barefoot, listened respectfully. You were no longer on a mountain trail or in a drab village. You were connected to something greater. Part of it was spiritual, of course. You were listening to the word of God. But part of it was being in the presence of beauty and luxury. There was a richer, more beautiful world, and you could partake of it right here in town just by walking into the church. When life is mostly poor and ugly, that's a really big deal.

My apartment in Granada was spartan, consisting of a couple of bare rooms on the third floor of a nondescript building overlooking the plaza with no hot water and a shower up on the roof, partially open to cold breezes, so showering was something you didn't take lightly—or forget quickly. The floors were cement and tile. There was a bed, table, and some chairs. There was electricity, a sink, and a toilet. I could make coffee. I must have had a hotplate. The roof didn't leak. The view was pretty good. It was adequate—all I really needed. I never felt uncomfortable. I lived better than most.

Granada was where I became Colombian. No one spoke English or was from anywhere except Colombia, so the only option was to adapt. It was Spanish 24 hours a day, along with local people, customs, values, food, music, jokes, pastimes, gossip, priorities, and timetables. I did it their way. I became fluent—or at least, comfortable—in the colorful Spanish spoken by the *paisas*. I began to develop a rudimentary sense of how people thought, and why. I got pretty good at chatting up just about anyone, from the mayor and the priest to illiterate *campesinos*. Perhaps most importantly, I began to empathize with the villagers. Their concerns—or at least some of them—became my concerns. I really did care. After about six months I knew my way around the culture. I could walk into a cafe anywhere in Antioquia (and probably anywhere in Colombia), hold my own with the locals and feel comfortable doing it. I was at home. My fellow PCVs living alone in other villages did the same. We had been thrown into the deep end of the pool and learned to swim. We understood and identified. We acculturated.

This was, however, in contrast to at least some of the PCVs who lived in Medellín. They often roomed together, tended to speak English when they weren't at work and otherwise did not face the 24-hour-a-day pressure to assimilate that we faced out in the villages. They were good people, did good work, and got a lot out of living in Colombia. But it seemed to me that they were less happy. In a letter to a college friend a year into my Peace Corps service I noted that the city PCVs "are either thinking about what they left behind in the States or what they will do when they return." This was in contrast to the rural PCVs who seemed "a pretty well-adapted bunch." Rural Volunteers were different. I was biased, of course, But going native had its advantages.

It's hard to overemphasize how strong and important the fact of acculturation was for us. Our regional director and boss, Joe Mitchell, was a major reason for that. Joe was a Korean War veteran who had married a Cuban, bought a farm in Cuba and then lost everything to the Cuban Revolution of 1960. He also had an independent streak— the kind you'd expect from someone who grew up on a farm in North Carolina. Somehow he wound up working for the Peace Corps. Later someone suggested to me that during its early years the Peace Corps often attracted people like that—more adventurers than organizational types—unlike other parts of the U.S. government. I don't know. But Joe was certainly on the adventurer side of the scale.

Joe preached acculturation. It was what professionalism was all about. If we couldn't relate effectively to *campesinos* and municipal leaders, we might as well quit. He made that clear, and came off a little like a drill sergeant—criticizing and laying down the law. It was shape up or ship out. Not surprisingly, he rubbed some people the wrong way and eventually his contract was terminated six months early by our country director, Bill Dyal (who later became the founding director of the InterAmerican Foundation). I defended Joe when that happened and persuaded the U.S. Consul in Medellín to organize a going-away party for him. We couldn't just let him leave. Once the event had been announced and invitations sent, I called Bill in Bogotá and invited him personally. It was the diplomatic thing to do, of course. But I confess to enjoying the irony—inviting Bill to a reception we had organized to honor someone we appreciated, but that he had fought with and pushed out. Inside, I was smiling. He flew in for the reception and was of course the perfect gentleman. Bill and I would cross paths years later at the Ford Foundation, but that's another story.

I owe Joe a great debt. He got me (and many others) to take culture seriously, showing us how to fit in and get things done. No one else did that. It was valuable. Here are some examples:

As I was preparing to take up my second post, in Granada, Joe told me I had to change my name. "You can't tell people your name is Jeffrey" he said. "There's no equivalent in Spanish. They won't relate to it. They'll see you as a foreigner. You need a name people can say comfortably. Tell them your name is *Javier*. They can relate to *Javier*.'" I did. I became "Javier"—a name that rolled easily off the tongues of *campesinos* and municipal officials alike. My new name fit the culture. I was "*Don Javier*" for the rest of my stay in Colombia, and it worked perfectly.

Later, Joe helped me solve a drinking problem. Colombia's national alcoholic beverage is *aguardiente* (literally, "firewater"), an anise-flavored liquor made from sugar cane that Colombians usually drink straight, in shots, with a chaser. It was popular. As one observer put it: "You haven't lived until you've witnessed a seventy-year-old couple polish off a bottle between them on the bus from Bogotá to Medellín." Drinking *aguardiente* turned out to be an important part of the culture in the villages where we worked. Our professional peers (municipal officials, extension agents, and other mid-level functionaries) tended to gather in the café after dinner, to talk and drink *aguardiente*. There wasn't much else to do, after all. Since I needed to develop strong working relationships with these people, I joined them around the table and tried to make a good impression. That was how you became one of the guys.

The problem was that it was hard to avoid getting drunk. There was a ritual you had to follow. One of the guys (always guys, and usually three or more) would order a round and we would drink up. *Aguardiente* was not something you sipped. Sipping was bad form. You drank the entire shot in one gulp and followed it with a chaser, which might be diced mango, a slice of orange or maybe some soda water. And you did that in unison. Not keeping up with the group was also bad form. Then someone else would order a round, and you repeated the ritual. Since each round was paid for by the person who ordered it, you couldn't just drink one shot and leave. You had to stay and buy a round when your

turn came. After four rounds, I would be at the outer edge of my tolerance for alcohol. And the rounds would keep coming. Too often I drank
too much.

Like a typical *gringo*, I thought I could simply get up, say goodnight,
and go back to my room. I was wrong. When I tried, the guys responded
with alarm. "No, no *Don Javier*, you can't leave. We've got so much to
talk about—*eh, Ave Maria, hombre!* You have to stay." It turned out that
leaving early was also bad form. The pressure was strong. I couldn't say
no. So I stayed, drank too much, and didn't like it.

When I told Joe about the problem, he knew immediately what to
do. "You're behaving too much like a *gringo*—explaining how you feel
and what you're going to do. That challenges the group's camaraderie,
which is unacceptable and will never work. The way to deal with this is
simply to get up, say you're going to the bathroom, and then don't come
back. That way no one will have to acknowledge that you've left. They
won't feel uncomfortable or offended. They may not even notice you've
gone." I tried it, and it worked. No one said a word. I remained one of
the guys. And I stopped getting drunk. Joe taught me that.

Another example occurred a year into my tenure with the Peace
Corps, when I moved back into Medellín to become the volunteer coordinator for Antioquia. I rented a small apartment that needed some
repairs to the floor before I could occupy it. The work was supposed
to be done right away, but time went by and it didn't get done. After
many fruitless calls to the landlord, I asked Joe for advice. He suggested
that I tell my landlord that I had invited my boss over for dinner the
next week and was worried that the floor wouldn't be repaired in time.
"Latin culture is very hierarchical and people understand how important
it is to impress your boss." I called the landlord and told him my boss
was coming for dinner. The floor was fixed within a few days. It was
amazing—a thing of beauty, in fact. Joe had known which button to
press. Culture really did matter. I was thankful and impressed. I don't
recall whether in fact I ever invited Joe over for dinner.

I spent a year in Grenada, working as a *promotor de Acción Comunal*.
It was good work. I felt like I was helping people. I did what my fellow

PCVs in other villages did: traveled, by bus, horse, mule, and foot, up and down the mountains to reach the small communities (*veredas*) where the *campesinos* lived. Most of the time we were off the roads, and usually we depended on the *campesinos* to send us a mule or horse to ride—or we walked. We learned quickly to buy a good pair of boots, a wide-brimmed hat, and a *ruana*. I tried wearing spurs but found them unnecessary, and maybe even pretentious. I also tried a pair of leather chaps and discovered that they really did protect your legs from the rocks and trees you rubbed against going down a narrow mountain trail on horseback. But I decided I could get along without them. At times I felt like I was in a cowboy movie, although without having a six-shooter strapped to my leg.

Once in the *veredas*, we urged the *campesinos* to organize and work together to improve community life. We taught them the basics of *Acción Comunal*, including how to agree on priorities, hold elections, design and execute projects, and manage money. Most commonly, they wanted to improve the trails that led up and down the mountains (and were crucial for getting crops to market), build latrines, small bridges and rudimentary water distribution systems, and make repairs to the school. Sometimes we helped develop agricultural projects like community vegetable garden and raising rabbits or chickens. A few of us worked with cooperatives. The focus was always on making things better at the local level. And there was never any involvement in partisan politics.

But asking a community to tell you what they wanted could produce surprises. Sometimes, for example, their priority was to build a chapel. They took religion seriously and wanted it near and handy. If the *vereda* built a chapel, the priest could come and say mass. Wouldn't that be great? Most of us doubted that it would be great. Many of us were dismayed. Spirituality was not high on our list of community needs. These people were poor. Their priorities ought to be worldly—income, food, clean water, and education. Why waste time and money on chapels? Shouldn't we discourage them?

Answering that question turned out to be a learning experience. It introduced us to something we hadn't thought much about—the will of the people. It reminded us that the community belonged to them and not to us. It made us recognize that *Acción Comunal* was about helping people organize and make their own decisions. It forced us to consider the difference between kindness and paternalism. It suggested that democracy—and emergent order more generally—has its own, sometimes mysterious, logic.

Having to ponder those issues was great, particularly if you were a twenty-something kid from the United States. Fortunately I never had to take a stand on the chapel idea because none of the *juntas* I worked with seriously proposed building one. But some of them talked about it, and I had to consider how I might respond if they got serious. It was one of many ways in which those of us who were in the Peace Corps—the Volunteers—benefited from being there. Our work brought challenges that made us grow, quite apart from any benefits we managed to provide the people we were trying to help.

Since all of us were starting work at the same time, we faced together the challenge of establishing our credibility in the village. We'd been told that we needed especially to impress the mayor and the parish priest, because their opinions would sway the views of others. But getting that done was tough. Our Spanish was still shaky, and we were only beginning to understand the culture. So when we saw each other during occasional trips to Medellín, we talked at great length about how we were dealing with that challenge.

That led to some gallows humor. My favorite story (which I think was apocryphal) was about a recently arrived Volunteer who was sitting next to the village mayor at a community dance, and trying to impress him with his serious, professional demeanor. The mayor asked the Volunteer if he would like to dance with his daughter. The Volunteer was a terrible dancer and didn't want to dance with anyone. But neither did he want to offend the mayor. So he tried to find a graceful way out. Since he was wearing a pair of large boots, he said "I'm sorry, but I don't dance with boots." So far so good. But because his Spanish wasn't all that great and because he was nervous, he confused the English word "boots" with the Spanish equivalent, which is "botas," and said "bootas."

Unfortunately, in Spanish the word for "whores" is "putas." So when he said to the mayor "Lamento, pero no bailo con bootas" it sounded like he said "I'm sorry, but I don't dance with whores."

You can imagine how funny that sounded to a bunch of insecure Peace Corps Volunteers trying to figure out how to establish their credibility in a new and strange environment. We fell over laughing. We knew just how the poor guy felt. Screwing up like that was our own worst nightmare. The joke got retold a lot.

But in addition to channeling our anxieties, the story demonstrates how focused we were on the micro rather than on the macro. I don't recall ever discussing macro issues like history, politics or economic policy. Everything was micro—about the challenges of dealing with people face-to-face. We watched what people said and did and tried to understand why. Then we asked ourselves how we should respond. We saw close-up how poverty, ignorance, fatalism, greed, emotions, bad habits, bad ideas, and bad luck influenced daily behavior. Sometimes it was overwhelming. You wondered whether there was any hope. But you realized how important it was to change the way people thought. That's why, when I surveyed our group of Volunteers eighteen months later, they emphasized the importance of attitudinal changes like "fostering consciousness among *campesinos* of their problems and solutions" and "promoting responsibility and self-control." We'd all become anthropologists. It was the culture, stupid.

One of the things we learned early on was how common tragedy was in the lives of *campesinos*, and how they'd learned to accept it. People would ask, for example, how many brothers and sisters we had. When we told them (in my case it was two), their response was always: "Alive?" Since most of us were in our twenties, we wondered why they would ask that question. Of course, our brothers and sisters were alive. It was only when we asked them the same question that we began to see how different their lives had been. They always answered with several numbers, typically something like: "Eleven—eight alive and three dead." Not only were their families larger than ours, many of their brother and sisters had gotten sick and died. It was normal. We were taken aback by this reality. We'd never even imagined it. We soon got used to it.

A big payoff to focusing on the micro was that we got good at interpreting what people said, and at distinguishing what might work from what clearly would not. These were practical skills. They made us better managers and better decision-makers. But focusing on the micro also broke down cultural barriers between them and us. We came to understand what their lives were like. We saw them close up—the real reality. And that made us see how much we were alike. Moritz Thomsen, who was a volunteer in Ecuador and (in *Living Poor: a Peace Corps Chronicle*—the best book on the Peace Corps I've come across) captured this eloquently: "in the last analysis the Peace Corps is an intellectual exploration, the chance (if you are patient enough) to enter in some degree into the hearts and minds and feelings of alien peoples with exotic cultures. The final discovery, that we are all ultimately alike, is a hard-earned revelation. And it is well worth the trouble." That's what we did, and Thomsen was right.

What we experienced varied a lot from village to village, of course. I'd already had a taste of that in Pueblorrico, where I learned that a village strongman could get rid of me. More generally, villages where only a few *campesinos* owned land tended to be poor bets for rural community development. The *campesinos* just didn't have enough of a stake in the community to want to get involved. Politics also made a difference. Villages with lots of political conflict were tough to work in. Those without much political conflict were easier. Granada did fairly well on that score. It seemed to be dominated by the Conservative party—although parties and politics seldom got mentioned. I don't ever recall coming across anything that resembled a politician or an ideology while I was there, let alone a partisan battle. Maybe that made it easier for people to work together.

In other villages, however, politics was more important. One of the most idealistic PCVs in our group, John Lyle, was the target in his village of a whispering campaign accusing him of being an agent of the CIA. Since John was, as I recall, firmly left-of-center, those charges hurt. He responded by making clear his opposition to the U.S. government, and his commitment to helping the poor. The whispering campaign pivoted immediately and began accusing him of being a communist. I felt sorry for him but had to smile. Politics is certainly an unruly beast, but it can also be funny. Maybe there's a bigger lesson, but I never figured out what it was.

One of the nicest things about working alone in the villages was how seriously most of us took it. Whenever we got together, we would engage in long and passionate discussions about what we were doing and how it was going. We talked. We listened. We agreed. We disagreed. We laughed. It was like discussing football, or music, or maybe even politics. Our work seemed important.

Our conversations were often about impact, and whether we were having any. But because community development is largely about changing attitudes, it was hard to tell. My sense, from our discussions and from the survey I conducted at the 18-month mark, is that most of us thought we were having a positive impact. I certainly felt that way regarding my work in Granada. But beyond counting the number of active juntas and the projects they developed, we couldn't be sure. We had to be content with putting one psychic brick on top of another, and trust that we were building a wall. It was part of the mystery that was at the core of our work.

Most of these discussions, by the way, took place in the cheap and charming *Pensión Romania*, where we stayed when visiting Medellín. The *Pensión Romania* was cheap because it was a large, old, borderline shabby house in a neighborhood that had once been fashionable but was now overrun by an expanding downtown, and because you always shared a room with at least one other Volunteer, and often two or three, and so got into all sorts of conversations. It was charming for the same reasons. And the *Pensión Romania* served good breakfasts, my favorite being *huevos pericos* (eggs scrambled with chopped tomatoes and onions). We usually had breakfast with any Volunteers who happened to be in town and used that time to get caught up. It was the perfect place to gather and talk. I have no idea whether the owners were really from Rumania.

Al Woolston, one of the Volunteers who, after Peace Corps, spent the rest of his life in Colombia, told me later about feeling like he could have and should have done more in his village. He was very aware of what he failed to do. I don't know whether he was right or wrong. It's easy enough to look back and see where you could have done more. But that's hindsight. When you're on the scene and trying to figure out what to do, it's different. Looking ahead is a lot harder.

I've often felt the same way as Al, not just about the Peace Corps but about life in general. I've missed more opportunities than I can count. It's distressing. Much of the time I've been clueless. You'd think I had my eyes shut. One example: Many years later when I was developing an education policy program at the Inter-American Dialogue in Washington, two Colombian politicians asked me on separate occasions what I could tell them about education policy. In both cases I didn't have much to offer, and felt I'd let them down. My own thinking was still evolving, and I just wasn't ready to recommend much. But I never followed up with them. What made it worse was that each, Álvaro Uribe and Juan Manuel Santos, later became president of Colombia. Despite my desire to make the world a better place, I failed to seize a clear and direct opportunity to influence how two Colombian presidents thought about education policy. I could and should have done more. Fortunately (and not surprisingly) both presidents overcame my negligence and adopted first-rate education policies. But I keep thinking about it.

I think I see a couple of morals to this story.

First, most of us lack vision. It's hard to see the opportunities lurking in any given situation, and what might happen if we do x, y, or z—or if we don't. We can estimate, of course (and we all do), but there are lots of surprises out there. So instead of assuming you know what the opportunities are, assume you don't. Treat every situation as if it could be important and give it your best shot. Sniff around. Explore. Imagine. Try. And always take your "A" game. You may be surprised at how that turns out. This is not a new idea, of course. It's just another version of "Anything worth doing is worth doing well." But most of us overlook it. Don't.

Second, most of us need a nudge from someone else. It's hard to get it right on your own. You may lack vision. You may lack information. You may under- (or over-) estimate your ability. You may get caught up in things that don't really merit your time. You need someone who can look at what you're doing and tell you to stop—or start. That's what leaders do, of course. And what bosses are for. Good bosses are great assets and you should seek them out. But colleagues and other kinds of mentors can play similar roles. Even discussions at the *Pensión Romania*. The important thing is to engage with good people and listen to what they say. Sometimes what you need most is someone who can point out that an opportunity exists and tell you that you're the person who should make it happen. That can feel like a kick in the rear. But sometimes it's just what you need. Don't assume you can figure it out by yourself.

End of sermon.

Life in the village was routine punctuated by unexpected. In Pueblorrico, for example, I got a graphic introduction to Colombia's tradition of violence. Because no hotel room was available when I arrived, I had to spend a few nights in the hospital. On one of those evenings when I went back to my room late (after having a few *aguardientes* with the guys down in the plaza) I noticed that the hospital's lights were on. Since Pueblorrico had been without electricity for several days (this happened often), the lights should have been off. The hospital only used its generator for emergencies. As I entered, one of the doctors took me into the emergency room where two young *campesinos* were laid out on operating tables. They were bloody, having been hacked up pretty bad by machetes. The doctors (there were two) were sewing them up, but one had stomach wounds that were too serious for them to treat. He asked me to help carry the guy outside and put him in the bed of a pickup truck so they could take him to a hospital elsewhere that could treat him. I did. Then I went to my room. I was rattled by my close-up with the violent side of village life. A week or so later the doctor invited me in again to see how the first guy was doing. He had stitches all over but was smiling. I smiled too and wished him well. I don't recall ever getting an update on the guy I'd helped carry out to the truck.

I had another brush with violence when one of the *campesinos* I'd worked with in Granada, who had a small farm and a family and was doing well by local standards, shot and killed someone who tried to rob him on a mountain path. He apparently shot the robber with a pistol he kept hidden in his *carriel*. I found out about it when I ran into the mayor outside his office, clutching a holstered pistol and looking nervous and official in white pants. He told me what had happened and said he was going out to investigate and enforce the law. The surprise was that the *campesino* who shot the robber immediately took his family and disappeared. Had he stayed, the robber's family would have tried to even the score. That's how these things were settled.

Yet another experience with violence was less direct but also powerful. In Granada I worked with a young *campesino*—Don Nemecio—who, despite a humble background, seemed to be a natural leader. He was smart, respected, and had the maturity and people skills you look for in the community development business. I encouraged and tried to help him. A few years later, during a brief visit to Granada, I asked about him and was told the government had hired him to work as a *Promotor de Acción Comunal* in a nearby village. That struck me as a great decision. But shortly after starting work someone shot and killed him. I was shaken. A nice guy with a big smile, and now he was gone.

I never knew whether those attacks had been personal or political. But I concluded that violence was a lot more common than I had realized and was in some way an important part of the culture. It was deplorable, of course. But it happened. That experience colored my view for a long time. Six years later, when I arrived in Chile right after the military coup to start working for the Ford Foundation, I was surprised by how surprised my new colleagues in the office there were by the violence the military was using against supporters of the Allende regime. They hadn't expected all that violence. My reaction was: "Why are you surprised? This is Latin America. It's what people do." I may have come off as a little blunt, but my impression was that violence was to be expected. I'd seen it before. Our parallel surprises led to an interesting discussion about how Chile was different, how it had a strong civil society, how it had a long tradition of democracy, and how violence simply wasn't all that common. I was willing to buy their arguments. But I couldn't shake the feeling that violence wasn't as far below the surface in Chile as they thought. Pushing people hard is risky. And it looked to me like the Allende government (which the military had just overthrown) had pushed a lot of people hard.

Actually my scariest encounter with violence in Colombia occurred many years later during a business trip to Bogotá. While crossing a large and crowded plaza near the Hotel Tequendama, a young man in a dark suit walking towards me pulled out a pistol and told the guy next to me to raise his hands. Then he looked at me and said "You, too." He said he was a DAS agent—Colombia's equivalent of the FBI. The safest thing would have been to raise my hands. If I didn't he might shoot, after all. And what did I know? Maybe he was nervous. Maybe this was the first time he'd ever pulled a gun. I felt like I was on the edge of something. A cliff, maybe.

But raising my hands would make me part of the picture. While I was sure I could eventually convince him and the people he worked for that they'd made a mistake, how many hours in a DAS office would that take? Colombia is a very formal place and Colombian bureaucracy lived and breathed formality. Once you're in, it takes a long time to get out. I just couldn't do that. So I decided in an instant to opt out. I shook my head to indicate that I had nothing to do with this and moved off to the right, trying to look nonchalant. I figured he wouldn't want to take his gun off the guy he'd already identified, and risk having him run away. So if I put space between us he'd have to make a decision. I was right. He decided to stick with the first guy and forget about me. I continued on to wherever I was going. It was just one more day in Colombia.

Mostly though, the unexpected we ran into in our villages was less serious, and often comic. For example, a couple of months after I helped one of the *juntas* start a community vegetable garden with seeds the Peace Corps gave me, a *campesino* sat down beside me, pulled something out from under his *ruana*, and asked "What's this?" It was a radish. I told him about radishes—that you ate them in salads. He smiled and said it was pretty good in soup, too. I've always remembered the puzzled look on his face when he asked his question. It's the first and only time I ever ran into someone who didn't know what a radish was.

On another occasion I was out on the mountain and some *campesinos* offered to loan me a horse. The horse was beautiful—young and strong, completely different from the loaners I was normally offered. It would get me up and down the mountain in style. I was delighted. The *campesinos* held the horse while I mounted. Then they let it go. The horse took off like (as my mother would have said) a bat out of hell. It plunged, bucking, down the trail and then began running in haphazard circles. I was startled. This wasn't what I'd expected. Fortunately my experience riding horses with my father as a little boy kicked in, and I managed to stay (more or less) on top of the horse. I tried to keep it away from large rocks. Hitting one would hurt. The *campesinos*, on the other hand, were shouting and laughing. They were having great fun watching the *gringo* try to ride a horse that (I now realized) was only partially broken. It was a prank. I had become entertainment. Pretty quickly they headed the horse off, stopped it and, still laughing and grinning, helped me dismount. They said the horse was "*brioso*," which meant "spirited." I'd never head that word before. I've never forgotten it.

My work in Granada was ordinary but had a couple of highlights. First, in addition to strengthening *juntas* in the *veredas*, we managed to establish a village-wide federation of *juntas* called the *Asociación Central de Acción Comunal*. It was, as much as anything, a statement that *Acción Comunal* was alive and well in Granada and looking to do bigger things. We never did bigger things, so far as I can recall. But it felt like a real achievement. I think that's because, if community development is chiefly about changing attitudes, setting up a village-wide federation of *Juntas de Acción Comunal* served notice that attitudes were changing. People were finding common ground. They were interested in working together. The social fabric was getting stronger. And maybe establishing a federation would get even more people to collaborate, making it both a cause and an effect.

This was progress. But it would all come crashing down in the early

1980s when Granada became the center of a bloody conflict between groups that moved in from outside. First, the National Liberation Army (ELN), one of Colombia's two major Marxist-Leninist guerrilla organizations, decided that Granada's location was strategic and took over the town. A few years later the other major guerrilla organization, the Armed Revolutionary Forces of Colombia (FARC) showed up and dislodged the ELN in a battle that destroyed over 200 homes and shops, plus the hospital. Occupation for more than a decade by the ELN and the FARC gave Granada a reputation as a "guerrilla haven." That got the attention of a right-wing paramilitary organization (the ACCU), which moved in to expel the FARC. And that finally brought in the Fourth Brigade of the Colombian Army.

Granada was a battleground for more than two decades, and its people became pawns. A 2016 report by the National Center of Historical Memory described a "total war" that included car and canister bombs, killings, disappearances, and citizen displacements. Some 460 "selective assassinations" were reported, along with another 59 killings in 10 "massacres," 2992 disappearances, 98 kidnappings and 50 reports of sexual violence. This in a village of, at most, 18,000 inhabitants—rural and urban—when the violence began.

The conflict was brutal and personal. It included "house bombs" that detonated when someone opened the door, and fatal injections of cyanide or gasoline. Mothers were shot in the presence of their children. The dead were sometimes exhibited as trophies. People were forced to become "human mules," carrying the remains of family members or neighbors to other locales for burial. Many who survived suffered psychological trauma. It's hard to read the report.

I had heard about this in general terms but had not gotten any details. Once while on a Ford Foundation business trip to Medellín, friends told me I must not visit Granada. It would be too dangerous. So I didn't. After that I didn't get back to Medellín for a long time. Only years later when I read the report did I realize how bad it had been.

But there were rays of hope. The National Center of Historical Memory's report praised the way civil society and victims responded to the violence, along with Granada's "strong social fabric." It also praised the work of the *Comité Interinstitucional*, a federation of non-governmental organizations (including *Juntas de Acción Comunal*, cooperatives, producer associations, and the Catholic Church) that had been established several years earlier to address common development problems like clean water and agricultural production. Once the violence began, the *Comité* shifted its efforts, calling for armed conflict to be suspended, and warning armed groups to respect the political neutrality of local institutions and the vulnerability of the civil population. It declared the village a "territory of peace," organized workshops on coping with fear, and requested support from national and international organizations. It established a campaign—"Everyone United for Granada"—to collect funds and promote reconstruction. It played a key role in helping the village respond, resist, and rebuild. Granada's response, according to the report, was "unprecedented." It became "a veritable laboratory of peace" and a lesson for communities elsewhere.

I'd like to think that Granada's resilience in the face of brutality was due at least partly to the work we did more than a decade earlier. The *Comité Interinstitucional* sounds a lot like the village-wide federation—the *Asociación Central de Acción Comunal*—that we set up well before political violence erupted. That initiative blazed a path, raising the profile of collaboration among civil society groups, getting people involved, and giving them some experience. Later, when things got bad, Granada did not have to start from zero. It had something to build on, and that helped.

You never know, of course. But community development work is like that. You target attitudes even though they're hard to influence and harder to measure. You realize you won't know for sure whether you've had an impact. But you have to try. And what you do might pay off big-time, even if you can't prove it was you who made it happen. It's probably a lot like raising kids.

The other highlight of my year in Granada had nothing to do with changing attitudes and everything to do with making money. I helped set a guy up in the poultry business. It was I think mostly about instant gratification. I wanted to do something more concrete than community development. Something with immediate, visible results. (Please, can we achieve something now?) I'd heard that a Volunteer in a nearby village—Guarne—had developed a successful poultry project and went out to see it. He'd set a guy up with a few hundred laying hens. The guy sold the eggs in Medellín, made a nice profit and had since expanded. I was impressed. It didn't look all that hard. I decided to try it in Granada.

I knew a guy—Don Antonio—who had a little store in town and seemed to understand business. So I outlined the idea and said I'd provide the technical advice if he'd put up the money. He decided to do it. I explained the kind of facility he'd have to build to house the chickens. And I boned up on chicken health and nutrition. We were on our way.

A few months later I purchased (with Don Antonio's money) several hundred just-hatched chicks and had them shipped out to Granada on the bus. I don't remember the breed, but they were certified egg-layers—big-time chickens. For the first couple of weeks. I raised them in my apartment in a pen I'd rigged with a couple of heat lamps (keeping newly hatched chicks warm is crucial to keeping them alive). They chirped a lot. It was exciting. I felt responsible for all those little lives. I worried more about the chicks than I did about Don Antonio's money.

Once the chicks had grown enough feathers to keep themselves warm, and I'd vaccinated them (against what I don't remember but it involved putting a drop of liquid in each chick's eye), we transferred them to the coop that Don Antonio had built (for some reason I've always referred to it as the "chicken ranch"). I told him everything I knew about raising chickens, which wasn't much, and came from reading books. Then I turned the project over to him, and left town. Goodbye Don Antonio. And good luck.

I didn't plan it that way, of course. I'd gotten an unexpected promotion. I was going to become Volunteer Coordinator for Antioquia and would now live in Medellín. Although I would try to visit now and again, Don Antonio would have to figure out the rest by himself. He did, raising the chickens and selling the eggs, and was still managing that first flock a year later when I left Colombia and returned to the United States.

That's all I knew for three years until I went back to Colombia to do dissertation research in Bogotá and took advantage of a trip to Medellín to visit Granada early one Sunday morning. After three cups of coffee and one *aguardiente* with some *campesinos* I ran into in the plaza (Sunday was market day, after all), I made my way up the hill to Don Antonio's house—and the chicken ranch. I was nervous. I'd gotten Don Antonio into the chicken business. Was he still in it? Or had it turned out to be a bust? As I approached the house I heard clucks. Lots of them. Don Antonio was still in the chicken business! He invited me in and showed me around. He now had 2000 purebred laying hens and was getting a 40 percent return on his investment over 18 months. That was good money. He was happy. I was happy too, but more than that relieved. My project hadn't been a fiasco.

Looking back, I'm amazed at how flimsy our business plan was. It wasn't really a plan but more of a precedent. Someone in another village had been successful raising purebred laying hens. So maybe it would work in Granada. The only thing I did research on was how to raise chickens—which seemed pretty straightforward. Plus I did a few back-of-the-envelope calculations about costs and revenue. But I had no real idea about expenses, prices, markets, supply, or demand. I didn't know where to sell the eggs, or how to get them there. I just figured it would work. A business school would have given me a failing grade had I proposed the project in class. A bank would have turned me down for a loan.

But somehow Don Antonio trusted me and somehow I trusted myself. Maybe that's what small-scale entrepreneurs in poor countries do much of the time. They see something that looks promising, try it, work hard, and figure things out as they go along. Sometimes it pays off, sometimes it doesn't. It's an inexact science. Still, in retrospect, I'm aghast. I wasn't playing with my own money. My approach was somewhere between cavalier and stupid. Fortunately it worked out.

I spent one good year in Granada. The people were great. I liked the work. But I never liked living there. Mostly that was because, aside from work, there wasn't much to do. No movies, no TV, no restaurants, no bookstores (or even newsstands), no concerts, no theater, and no sports (except for the occasional pickup soccer match on a field that occupied one of the few level surfaces in town, or maybe a little basketball with students at the liceo's outdoor court if it wasn't raining—and it rained a lot). Most of the time when you came in off the mountain in the afternoon, you either went to your room and read, or went down to the plaza and drank *aguardiente* with the guys. That's pretty much all there was. I'm an introvert, but even I needed more.

Part of the problem was that there weren't many people like me to talk to. I was OK with being the only foreigner in town. But I was practically the only college graduate as well. I remember just two others, a lawyer and a dentist. Both were young government officials doing their mandatory couple of years of service in the *campo* before being allowed to take government jobs in Medellín. Later I heard they got married (the lawyer was a woman), which may suggest that having only a few romantic options stimulates romance. Or maybe it confirms Say's law—that supply creates its own demand. Probably both. But whatever the explanation, there wasn't much for a college grad to do in Granada except work. And catch up on your sleep.

There were, of course, other people I could talk to, and I did. I made friends with the nuns who ran the *Hogar Juvenil*, a home for girls on the edge of town, and occasionally taught classes there (perhaps on raising vegetables, but I don't recall). That got me lunch now and then (best food in town, alas). And I did spend some time talking (and drinking *aguardiente*) with the guys down in the plaza, among them the extension agent from the National Federation of Coffee Growers and the mayor. There were also a couple of nurses who I think had eyes for me, although unfortunately I didn't have eyes for them. But it just wasn't enough. I was an aspiring intellectual sitting in a small, poor mountain village, and lacking the commitment and perspective of an anthropologist—or of a Buddhist monk—either of which would have been helpful. I wanted more.

Another part of the problem was that I missed the broader world. There was, of course, no internet back then—nor up in Granada even

TV. The radio provided national news at most. I don't remember seeing a newspaper—although I'm fairly sure a few Medellín papers arrived every afternoon on the daily bus. Forget about anything like *Time* magazine, or even its Colombian equivalent. You were cut off. Pretty much everything was local. I yearned for news, movies and being able to go to an Italian restaurant at night and eat lasagna. It was about lifestyle. I was a do-gooder realizing there was more to life than doing good. I missed the buzz of the big city.

The best response most of us could muster was short-wave radio. I had a decent portable that picked up the Voice of America, the Armed Forces Radio and Television Service (AFRTS), and the BBC World Service. Tuning in was a kind of enchantment—a precious link to the Land of Oz. It connected you to news, music, politics, and sophistication—to a world that had once been yours and you were sure still existed but had largely been cut off from. Listening to the BBC discuss world events in posh English while sitting in poor, remote Granada was magic. It provided reassurance and contact. The world was still out there and you could still partake—at least a little.

AFRTS had the additional merit of carrying sports events live from the U.S.—a particular passion of mine. I could get college football (any game anywhere was a delight), and even the Indianapolis 500. I remember spending one Memorial Day listening to the Indy 500 on the roof of my apartment while looking down on the hustle and bustle of Granada's Sunday market and feeling distinctly blessed. Thank you AFRTS. My government was doing something right.

The other thing I did was read a lot. In a stroke of genius, the Peace Corps gave each Volunteer a box of paperbacks—maybe a hundred, mostly fiction and thoughtfully selected. I vaguely remember books by Steinbeck and Twain, but there were many others. They were water in the desert, exactly what a young, educated American living alone in a small foreign village needed. The books offered us the world, and we had plenty of time to take them up on it. Plus we were needy. I read nearly all of them.

My other problem with Granada was the food. I didn't like it. It wasn't bad, exactly, but it certainly wasn't good. Bland is probably the nicest thing I could say. I ate my main meals at the hotel, which by my reckoning had the only real restaurant in town. There was no menu; you ate what they offered. Generally that was some combination of rice, potatoes or plantains, with some meat and maybe a little carrot. Or the same ingredients in soup. There was almost no seasoning. Sometimes you got boiled beef with cold rice. Or fatback fried and served at room temperature. Or blood sausage, which I couldn't imagine eating. You might also get lettuce or sliced tomatoes, but you couldn't eat them because, as the Peace Corps doctor warned us, they would give you intestinal parasites. (He was right. We had diarrhea much of the time, even when we didn't eat lettuce or tomatoes.) Dessert was an afterthought, maybe some guava jelly or fruit compote. You seldom got avocados or fresh fruit. Or bread, cookies, or cake. In fact, I never remember seeing a bakery in Granada.

A local staple was the *arepa*—a substitute for bread, but unleavened and made of corn kernels that had been soaked in water and then ground into flour, moistened, shaped into a round patty and cooked over a fire or burner. Theoretically, the *arepa* was Colombia's version of the *tortilla*, but in fact, at least in Granada, it was something else—rounded rather than flat and therefore slightly hard on the outside and almost gummy on the inside. *Arepas* were usually served cold, with no accompaniment, at every meal. They were completely unappetizing and I stopped eating them, except when I was out in the *campo* and a *campesino* family served them, in which case I tried gamely to eat at least half. Another local favorite was *mazamorra*, a soup consisting of crushed corn grains (sometimes soaked in soda lye) that were cooked until soft and then served, often at room temperature, with milk and an unrefined sugar called *panela*. I never understood its charms, and regularly avoided it.

Sometimes while out on the mountain a *campesino* family or a teacher at a rural school would do their best to prepare a nice lunch and I would do my best to eat it. But I always found it a challenge. Two meals have stayed in my memory. Once a school teacher served me what she said were sliced onions but turned out to be sliced garlic. Not bad, actually. Certainly not bland. Another time a parish priest in a small hamlet several hours down the mountain served me dinner, complete with a small piece of cake for dessert. Unfortunately there was a beetle underneath the cake. A live beetle. I can still see it today. It's hard to keep eating when that happens.

It wasn't that Antioquia didn't have good food. It was famous for its beans, which could be delicious. A bowl of red beans served hot and topped with crisp fried fatback and avocado slices was a favorite of mine (and of my parents as well, when they visited). And there was excellent beef, pork, chicken, avocados, mangos, and much more. Even plantains tasted good if you prepared them like french fries or potato chips—which wasn't hard. The problem was that you seldom got those things in Granada. It was small and rural. People were poor. Their priority was keeping themselves and their families fed. Taste was a distant luxury. So far as I could tell, no one cared about cooking. I seemed to be the only fussy eater in town.

And of course part of the problem was that I really was a fussy eater. I had been for years, starting when I was a little boy and stopped drinking white milk. Couldn't stand it. It was chocolate milk or nothing. Things that most people would just swallow and accept, I simply couldn't eat. I might even gag. That limited my options in a place like Granada. There wasn't much I wanted to eat.

My response was to eat cookies. I bought large tins of cookies at a local store and ate them in my apartment to compensate for the food I wasn't getting at the restaurant. The cookies were delicious—by far the tastiest food in town—and since I wasn't eating much else, I ate a lot of them. Munching on cookies and reading paperbacks became my favorite form of leisure. When I finished a tin (each was more than a foot tall and six inches in diameter) I would place it on the floor along one wall of my apartment and buy another. The tins began to pile up, and the wall began to look interesting. But I began to wonder whether my behavior was becoming what in polite company might be called "strange." Very few people ate that many cookies. Or lined their wall with cookie tins. Fortunately just as my cookie mania reached full strength I moved to

Medellín, where good food was easy to find, and I could go back to normal eating. But the experience made me realize that extreme circumstances (and I considered the food situation in Granada to be extreme) often elicit extreme responses. I was living proof. It was a good lesson.

I have contradictory feelings about the year I spent in Granada. On the one hand, I felt isolated and stuck. But on the other, it was one of the best things I've ever done. Living there full-time forced me not only to acculturate, but to acculturate with a group of people—*campesinos*, village officials, shopkeepers, parish priests—that I would seldom encounter again for the rest of my life. It was a once-in-a-lifetime experience that justified any psychic distress I had to endure. Comfort isn't everything. Sometimes, maybe often, being uncomfortable is worth it.

But what I also should have done was what Moritz Thomsen did when he was a Peace Corps Volunteer in rural Ecuador: write. Most days Thomsen would come in from work, sit down and take notes on what he'd seen and done, turn that into articles and send them to the *San Francisco Chronicle*, which published some, maybe most. Then he turned the articles into a book, *Living Poor: A Peace Corps Chronicle*, which (I think) is still in print nearly 50 years later. I did none of that—no notes, no articles, and only a few letters back to parents and friends, most of which have disappeared. Now, half a century later, I have to rack my brain to bring up something worth saying about life in Granada. Writing would have been a great way to spend my free time (and I could still have eaten all those cookies). It's frustrating that I didn't do it. Once again I lacked vision. The lesson, I guess, is that even when things are tough there's usually something worth doing. The trick is to find it and do it.

I spent the second of my two years in the Peace Corps living in Medellín and serving as the Volunteer coordinator for Antioquia. That meant I was the liaison between the regional office and the Volunteers out in the field. I travelled a lot, mostly driving a Peace Corps jeep. It was a great combination. I'd already gotten the benefits of acculturation, and so was perfectly happy living in Colombia. I'd spent a year out in the campo working in *Acción Comunal*, which made me a veteran who might possibly know what he was talking about. And I got to live in

Medellín, which kept me off cookies, in Italian restaurants, and at the movies. I was happy.

My second year was rewarding but not life-changing. I had probably already gotten the most important things the Peace Corps had to offer during that first year in Granada. After that it was downhill. In Medellín I became a manager, which was more inside my comfort zone. I planned, organized, and offered advice. I dealt with Volunteers, Peace Corps staff, and occasionally with village officials. The work was hard and the hours long, but I liked it. I shared a small apartment above a café in a slightly seedy part of town (near the *Pension Romania*, in fact) with another Volunteer (Chris Bunn) and we scrabbled together enough furniture to make the place comfortable. It was home.

One of the biggest differences was that now I had plenty of people to talk to. I got to know the Volunteers living in Medellín, and crossed paths with many who lived in other parts of Colombia, usually because they were traveling on business or I was. One of the most interesting was Dave Coolidge, who was part of a Peace Corps program that brought recently graduated MBAs to Colombia to help local businesses raise their game. Dave was a child of privilege and so was quite different from me. He was related to former President Calvin Coolidge (great-grandson, I think). He'd grown up on the north side of Chicago, and had a scar on his face that he said came from diving into a half-full swimming pool while at a party—which seemed Gatsby-like. He had a BA from Williams College and an MBA from Harvard, and later became vice-chair of an investment banking and asset management firm in Chicago, and a trustee of the University of Chicago and of Williams College. Almost what you'd expect from somebody with that kind of background.

(I should, by the way, probably stop using the phrase "child of privilege" since in fact I had plenty of privilege myself—great family, teachers and friends being chief among them. Those count a lot, so maybe I should just say that Dave's privileges were different from mine. On the other hand, judging by what I saw of him, he must, like me, have had a great family.)

Dave was also (like most Peace Corps Volunteers) a nice guy. He stayed at my apartment for a few weeks while laying the groundwork for the arrival in Medellín of several new MBA Volunteers. He was wonderful about taking care of me after I'd drunk too much *aquardiente* one evening—bringing me coffee and toast for breakfast and assuring me that I'd feel better soon. We talked about all sorts of things, including (I can't imagine why) about calculus, which he said wasn't all that difficult as long as you remembered that it's about rates of change. A year or two later when I took my first and only calculus course at the University of Chicago I remembered his observation and it helped.

Dave was also my introduction to the world of management and MBAs—which turned out to be fundamentally different from the world of intellectuals I aspired to join. He was instinctively pragmatic, while I was instinctively introspective. He wanted to get things done; I wanted to figure them out. A few years later while working on my PhD in education at the University of Chicago I took some courses in the Business School and got a clearer sense of that difference. I met lots of business school students, most of whom were smart and motivated, and most of whom I liked. But they were different from me. In class my first impulse was to try to understand the material, while theirs was to find the most efficient way to get (at least) a passing grade. They weren't against understanding the material, but their first priority was getting what they needed for their careers with the least amount of effort. They were businesslike. I'd never seen that before and appreciated it even though it wasn't me. I got a lot out of my courses (mostly in economics and statistics) at the Chicago Business School. I even completed half of an MBA. But I always felt like an outsider dabbling in a new and exotic culture.

One of the things I still missed out on during that second year in Medellín, was politics—specifically, U.S. politics. This was 1968, when so much happened in the United States. Opposition to the Vietnam War was beginning to spill over into the streets. The Civil Rights movement was generating demonstrations (riots, even), along with historic legislation. Lyndon Johnson decided not to run for re-election. Martin Luther King, Jr. and Robert Kennedy were assassinated. It was, as David

Halberstam pointed out in *The Best and the Brightest*, "..one of those landmark years in which everything came to a head—or as in this case, seemed to come apart...."

But we (my fellow Volunteers and I) weren't there to feel and witness our country falling apart. We were in Colombia, largely cut off from the drama and emotion our friends were experiencing stateside. We got the highlights from the local papers, of course. And we tried, via short-wave radio and *Time* magazine, to connect more directly and deeply. When new volunteers arrived from the States, we would all gather around, eager to hear their stories. But the turmoil seemed distant and our experience vicarious. It was like not showing up at a major family event. We missed it, and we felt at least a little guilty.

What was nice, however, was how Colombians responded. There were live radio broadcasts from Los Angeles and Memphis, and long articles in the newspaper. During visits to Granada people came up and put an arm around my shoulder to convey their sympathy. The *Junta Coordinadora* passed a resolution expressing its condolences to me regarding the death of Bobby Kennedy. I was amazed and pleased. I'd always liked the people in Granada, but now they felt like family. One of the core goals of the Peace Corps was to promote brotherhood. It was, almost to my surprise, doing just that.

One of the unexpected pleasures of being a Peace Corps Volunteer in Colombia was travel. We weren't allowed to go home during vacations, but were encouraged to get to know the country, and given a moderate but reasonable vacation stipend to do it. So we traveled a lot. There were plenty of places worth visiting—beaches, jungles, snow-covered mountains, colonial towns—in addition to modern cities. And air travel was relatively inexpensive, as long as you were willing to fly on second- (or third-) tier airlines, and stay in one-night cheap hotels, which of course we were. That's how we lived and was all we could afford.

That meant we flew exclusively on propellor aircraft—mostly DC-3s, DC-4s and C-47 Skytrains—and never on jets. Flying on a prop plane was very different from flying on a jet. Not only were they slower, they flew at lower altitudes, down where there was weather and turbulence.

And because the terrain was mostly mountainous, there was always weather and turbulence. So your plane rose like a condor and dropped like a rock. Out the window you got close-ups of rugged mountain peaks, ominous clouds and spectacular lightning—always beautiful and sometimes scary. You crossed your fingers a lot (or maybe you prayed). You understood and appreciated seatbelts and airsickness bags. On some flights the turbulence was so great you might not get served lunch, or even coffee. But it was never boring, the way flying jets was. It made you tough.

Travel to smaller venues was on single- and twin-engine Cessna-type aircraft that often landed on grassy airstrips (or at least they looked grassy—and resembled airstrips). You could get to a lot of places that way. Back then little airlines were flying little airplanes everywhere in Colombia—a kind of Wild West of air travel. Even the twin-engine planes were small, so you might get to sit in the co-pilot's seat (there were seldom copilots) and chat with the pilot. I did that once. The pilot, it turned out, also owned the airline. He pointed to a mountaintop below where a few years earlier one of his planes had gone down, killing a couple of Peace Corps Volunteers—the first Volunteers to die in service anywhere in the world, he said (with maybe the slightest hint of pride, which I resolved to ignore). I never checked his story out. All I remember is looking down at the spot (I can see it today) and having nothing to say.

A good example of how serendipitous those trips could be was when a few of us decided, at the last minute, to spend Easter Week in the Department (province) of Chocó—a remote jungle area that runs south from Panamá along the Pacific Ocean, is inhabited largely by Afro-Colombians, and is known, because it gets nearly 400 inches of rain a year, as the wettest place on earth.

We flew to Quibdó (Chocó's capital) with neither plans nor hotel reservations, and by sheer luck ran into the provincial Governor in the airport, who it turned out had chartered a plane to spend Easter in Bahía Solano, a remote resort due west on the Pacific coast that was reachable only by air (although you could get there by foot and canoe if you didn't mind spending a week in the jungle). He had some empty seats and invited us to go along. We did. (Full disclosure: one of the people we were traveling with was from a very influential Medellín family and was dating one of our fellow Volunteers—a vivacious blonde from Minnesota—whom he would later marry. The governor knew who he was. That's why we got invited. Peace Corps charm did not get us on that chartered plane.)

This was my first trip to the jungle, and it did not disappoint. We spent several days swimming, paddling around in dugout canoes, and exploring Bahía Solano's extraordinary ecosystem—a combination of leafy rainforest and pristine Pacific beach. Most of the people were descendants of African slaves brought by the Spanish many years ago and thus very different from the Spanish-descended campesinos I'd gotten to know in Antioquia. On Good Friday there was an all-night funeral for Jesus, complete with casket, candles, flowers, armed guards, and wailing. No Easter Bunnies and egg hunts here. Easter was serious. Walking across the village at 3:30 in the morning and listening to the mourners (who were still at it) felt more like being in Africa than in Latin America.

On Easter Sunday we flew back to Quibdó (population 39,000 at the time) and spent a day there, buying baskets and handmade gold jewelry. Quibdó was like something out of Conrad's *Heart of Darkness*—primal, mysterious, and forbidding. There seemed to be a battle going on between nature and civilization. I described my feelings in letters to my good friends and former Duke roommates, Jack Armistead and Phil Kawesch. Here are excerpts:

"The town lies on the Rio Atrato and appears to be rotting away into the jungle. You get the distinct impression that a gigantic struggle is going on between the forces of the jungle and the forces of civilization and that the latter are losing…We stayed in the best hotel in town ($2.50/night), which is well-enough built but in such a state of disrepair that one feels that the owners have given up hope and left it to the primitive forces of the jungle. The steamy heat and decay throughout the town give an air of pervasive evil. The church looked as if it had been bombed out several years ago and left to rot….Throughout there was an air of malaise and corruption which suggested that anyone living here was subject to dark forces much greater than himself…I felt that at any minute a leafy tendril would come creeping into my room and drag me into the wilderness."

It was a strong reaction, of course. And no self-respecting Tourist Board would have anything to do with it (or with me). But that's how I felt. Quibdó was different. Nature wasn't any bigger there than in Bahía Solano, but somehow it seemed more of a threat. I've never understood why.

The two years I spent in Colombia with the Peace Corps were probably the most important two years of my life. They opened a door to a new world—Latin America—where I would spend my entire career. But not only did they open a door, they dragged me inside, forced me to speak Spanish, demanded I put my culture aside and adopt theirs, and made me enjoy it. It was like getting kidnapped and held by the good guys. I came out a different person—a kind of aspirational Latin American.

How much I'd changed hit home when I returned to the United States at the end of my tour. I cleared customs at Chicago O'Hare, stepped into the terminal and was surrounded by Americans. They seemed orderly, well-dressed, satisfied, and prosperous—none of which I was. I didn't know what to do. I didn't belong and couldn't relate. Either I was an alien from outer space or they were. My response was to hope they wouldn't notice me—and how different I was. I feigned nonchalance and tried to pass as American. That was hard because I kept running into truly amazing things—like vending machines, which I hadn't seen in two years and had forgotten existed. But I dared not stop and stare. That might blow my cover. So I looked at them out of the corners of my eyes. Struggling to keep your cool in the presence of a machine dispensing candy bars is something you remember for a long time.

I got over feeling strange. It was great to be back in the States, reconnect with family and friends, and prepare to begin graduate school at the University of Chicago. Finally I'd seen enough and done enough to feel comfortable going ahead and getting a PhD

I'd gotten a start on two of my three goals: getting out of Dimondale and making the world a better place. Now I'd tackle the third and try to become an intellectual. But I was a different person. Peace Corps/Colombia had connected me first-hand to poverty, greed, misfortune, and ignorance. And it had given me a second culture. Now I understood and identified with Colombians, not just Americans. I had an extra dimension.

My experience wasn't typical. No Peace Corps experience is. What the Peace Corps does is set you up to do good in a poor country. After that it's up to you. There's no product to sell, quota to meet, T-shirt to wear, or flag to wave. Once you're up and running, the Peace Corps fades into the background, largely forgotten. You're one more professional struggling to do your job. Moritz Thomsen captured this beautifully in *Living Poor: a Peace Corps Chronicle*: "The Peace Corps exists as a vehicle for acting out your fantasies of brotherhood and, if you are strong enough, turning the dream into a reality." Each Volunteer makes of it what he or she can and will.

But quite apart from doing good, all Volunteers confront the drama of poverty, connecting in some important and unforgettable way with the people around them. For me, the Peace Corps wasn't so much about helping others as it was about connecting to others. It established a relationship with Latin America and Latin Americans that has endured for over 50 years. Much of what I've done since—work and play—started with Peace Corps/Colombia. It put me on the road.

A couple of new (or maybe not new) thoughts:

Writing about the Peace Corps was long and hard. I didn't realize how strongly I felt or how much I had to say—although I probably should have. Now that I've written it, the story seems obvious. But when I started all I knew was that I'd done a lot of different things in the Peace Corps and some of them were important. The details I had to figure out. I couldn't have outlined in advance what I was going to say (just as I couldn't have outlined any of the chapters I've written so far). It was only when I worked my way through the memories that I began to see what was there, what was important and what needed saying. Before that I just didn't know.

I think I see a process. First I target some part of my life—one that seems important, like high school or the Peace Corps. Then I ask myself what I want to write about. It may be something I did, something I saw, or just something I felt. But the urge has to be there. I'm writing a memoir, so I don't have to say everything. The urge points me towards what I need to write about.

Then comes the hard part: What do I say? Feeling the urge isn't enough. I still have to find the substance and meaning lurking behind it. Often I just sit at my desk and stare. I know something's in there. I don't know how to get it out. I wait. Maybe my muse will show up. What's interesting is that if I wait long enough the ideas almost always appear, one at a time, and I start writing them up. And they're usually more interesting than I expected. It's a kind of magic. I'm concluding that most of us have a lot more to say than we realize. In fact I'm tempted to think I could find substance and meaning behind practically anything if I worked at it hard enough. Like a rock, for example. (After all, if John McPhee can do it....) But so far I haven't felt the urge to write about a rock, so I don't know. What's hard is believing you have something to say, sitting down and trying, and then waiting until the good stuff appears. Fortunately, it's also kind of fun—at least for me. Like working on a puzzle. I just wish it didn't take so long.

My other thought is in fact a conviction: I'm convinced—against my better judgment—that I'm a pretty good writer. At least good enough to get published and read. I know I'm not supposed to think this way. Most writers do and they end up disappointed. You write because you have something to say and not because you expect to be read. But it's really hard not to think you're good enough to be read. Maybe not best-seller material, but good enough to get a book contract, sell some books, stay in print for a few years. And who knows? Word of mouth, social networks—a lot could happen. Right?

Probably not. But I'm like the parents (most parents, maybe) who believe that all their children are above average. I can't help thinking that way.

And that may be a positive. I worry a lot about my readers. I ask myself whether what I'm saying is worth reading. Will they enjoy it? Will it be useful? I take Elmore Leonard seriously ("Leave out the parts that readers tend to skip") and try to eliminate the fluff and the wordy. I try to say only what deserves saying, and to say it well. I read good writers to see what makes them good, and then try it myself. I'm looking out for you, dear readers. Don't worry. And thanks for helping me raise my game.

Finally, it continues to feel good. I know I've said this before. I'm not just trying to write. I'm trying to write well. There's something luscious about writing well. It's the act of creating beauty. When I think I've managed to do it, I'm delighted. It's a major reason why I write.

VIII

THE UNIVERSITY OF CHICAGO

SITTING AT THE FEET...

It must be remembered that the purpose of education is not to fill the minds of students with facts...it is to teach them to think.

—ROBERT MAYNARD HUTCHINS,
WHAT IS A UNIVERSITY?

So I WENT to the University of Chicago, a major research university with an unwavering emphasis on academics and little interest in anything else. It was, of course, the opposite of the Peace Corps. And unlike the universities I'd previously attended—Michigan State and Duke—there was no marching band, and no football team. There was no rah-rah, period. There was folk dancing. And there were distinguished professors. And world-class libraries. And students who had all been high school valedictorians (or at least that's how it seemed). It was serious.

In fact, one of my most enduring memories is of how rarified the intellectual atmosphere was at the University of Chicago. Where at a normal university casual conversation might be about movies or sports, at Chicago it would be about the *Iliad*, general-equilibrium theory, or the Russian famine of 1921. Nobody talked about sports. Everybody talked about books, classes, and ideas. Those of us who enjoyed more conventional chitchat tended to choose our words carefully while on campus. Anything frivolous felt odd. Like telling jokes in church. Later some wag would refer to the University of Chicago as the place where fun goes to die. That was close. It became a popular T-shirt.

Actually, Chicago once did have a football team (the Maroons), and a good one thanks to Alonzo Stagg, who was recruited to coach football in 1892 by Chicago's first president, William Rainey Harper, and stayed for 41 years. Stagg was a major figure in college football, introducing innovations like the huddle, lateral pass, numbered jerseys and the tackling dummy. No less than Knute Rockne, Notre Dame's renowned coach, observed that "All football comes from Stagg." The University's 50,000 capacity football stadium was named Stagg Field, and the University of Michigan's fight song "The Victors" was written after Michigan defeated Chicago 12-11 at Stagg Field in 1898. The Chicago Maroons were national champions in 1905 (defeating Michigan 2-0 in "the game of the century"), and again in 1913. In 1935 they produced the first Heisman Trophy winner, Jay Berwanger. Chicago had an illustrious football history.

But it didn't last. Chicago's young and idealistic president, Robert Maynard Hutchins, dropped football in 1939—considering it incompatible with the academic and intellectual purposes of a modern university. "Football, fraternities, and fun" he famously opined "have no place in the university. They were introduced only to entertain those who shouldn't be in the university." In 1946 Chicago pulled out of the Big Ten Conference (which it had co-founded). Stagg Field was initially abandoned, and then in 1942 became, with the kind of irony that seems exactly what you would expect from the University of Chicago, the site of the Manhattan Project—the first man-made self-sustaining nuclear reaction—under the direction of Enrico Fermi. Shortly thereafter Stagg Field was demolished and replaced by Regenstein Library. The ivory tower supplanted the gridiron. Chicago opted to become the lofty community of great scholars that I would encounter a few decades later.

(By the way, Berwanger was the only Heisman trophy winner ever tackled by a future president of the United States—Gerald Ford—during a 1934 game between the University of Chicago and the University of Michigan. This may have portended Chicago's fall from college football greatness, and Michigan's rise.)

Also (and perhaps of interest only to me), after the University of Chicago left the Big Ten in 1946 it was replaced by my first alma mater—Michigan State University. And after Hutchins left the University of Chicago in 1951, he became an associate director at my first employer—the Ford Foundation. And after F. Champion Ward resigned as Dean of the College at Chicago in the late 1950s, he worked in education at Ford—and was one of my bosses. And after McGeorge Bundy turned down an offer to become president of the University of Chicago (my third alma mater) in 1966, he opted instead to become president of the Ford Foundation (my first employer—did I mention that?), where he put together the extraordinary collection of talent I was so privileged to work with when I finally got hired there several years later.

I was fine with Chicago's devotion to the ivory tower. I'd had enough of the real world, at least for a while, and was ready to go back to books. Chicago was a giant in the social sciences. I was a fledgling social scientist. The sheer talent of the place was captivating. Chicago's world-class intellectuals were calling out to me like those neon signs on the Las Vegas Strip: "Come. Try your luck." I was only too happy to accept. I'd see what it was all about and whether I could handle it. And I'd probably learn a lot.

Curiously, I was enrolling in the department of education—a field in which I had no experience and no particular interest. That was an accident. I'd intended to study international development and had applied to some of the country's best-known programs (Harvard, Princeton, Johns Hopkins/SAIS), all of which turned me down. And I'd gotten accepted in a couple of less-celebrated programs, but with little or no financial aid. However while in the Peace Corps I'd met Richard Pelczar, who was doing his doctoral research in a program on comparative education at the University of Chicago. He said it was a great program that focused almost entirely on developing countries, and that I should apply. I did, without giving it much thought. To my surprise, Chicago offered me a full fellowship—by far the best offer I received. I decided to take it. Education was crucial to helping the poor, after all. And it was the University of Chicago. I'd get my foot in the door of one of the best universities in the world. The rest I'd figure out.

The program at Chicago—the Comparative Education Center—turned out to be first-rate. Its staff were internationally known, and at the center of global debates on education and development. C. Arnold Anderson, the director, was highly regarded for his work on the sociology of education and had co-founded the International Study of Educational Achievement (IEA), which carried out the first cross-national student achievement tests. Mary Jean Bowman had pioneered work in the economics of education and its international implications. Both had worked at Iowa State College with Theodore Schultz (later a Nobel laureate in economics), who recruited them to teach at Chicago. Philip Foster was internationally known for his critique of vocational and technical education in developing countries (which would influence World Bank policy and inspire my doctoral research). And Robert Myers was an expert on the brain drain in Latin America, and would soon move to the Ford Foundation, where several years later he would smooth the way for me to apply for a job. These people were insiders.

Also, I liked the program's emphasis on social science disciplines. Students were encouraged to choose a discipline, like sociology or economics, and make that their intellectual base for focusing on education. That added rigor and meant we could go beyond the department of education to take courses taught by the many distinguished professors in other departments—which most of us did and was a major reason I'd wanted to come to Chicago in the first place. And the program was one of three (the others were at Harvard and Stanford) partially funded by the Ford Foundation in an effort to strengthen work on international education. There was a skeptical, empirical, and brainy feel to the place that I liked. I was lucky to be there.

It was, however, a tough place to settle into. I knew no one, of course. The campus was located in Hyde Park on Chicago's gritty South Side, cheek-to-cheek with poverty, violence, and police. You were smack in front of an urban ghetto you couldn't ignore. You worried about getting mugged, or even picked up by the cops. (They stopped me once for no reason I could see and scared the hell out of me.) And it was the fall of 1969, when anti-war and civil rights protests were spilling into the streets. Students were digging foxholes on campus to defend against presumed attack by fascist security forces. Black Panther leaders were denouncing racial injustice in the University of Chicago's library. The trial of the Chicago Seven for criminal conspiracy and incitement to riot during the 1968 Democratic National Convention was getting underway downtown, with more drama than jurisprudence (e.g. defendant and Black Panther Chairman Bobby Seale was bound and gagged after calling the judge a "fascist dog"). I got some great pictures of Chicago police brandishing billy clubs on top of boxcars. Rebellion was in the air. I was a long way from Colombia.

I never really came to terms with all of that. I'd been out of the country for a couple of years and hadn't experienced directly the incidents and debates that fueled the rage of so many. I had to catch up. And I was never much of a radical. I wanted to make things better, but step-by-step rather than all at once. At a gut level I distrusted radicalism and the chaos it could unleash. I didn't think all-at-once would work. (Reading de Tocqueville on the French Revolution in a political science course at the University of Chicago only reinforced my view.) I preferred to operate from inside, analyzing, figuring out what to do, and getting it done. Protest just wasn't my métier.

It's worth asking, though, what leads some people to take to the streets while others take jobs. Some of it has to do with psychological makeup, I'm sure. And some depends on the nature and gravity of the threat. You probably couldn't have gotten very far combatting Hitler's Germany from the inside (or Stalin's Russia, or Mao's China). And de Tocqueville himself took to the streets to protest Louis-Napoléon's 1851 coup. But I had the good fortune, later at the Ford Foundation, to support people who opposed dictatorships in Chile, Argentina, and Uruguay. All of them operated from inside the system, some with real success. So it can be done. Of course, that's hindsight. It's never simple and seldom predictable.

I also never bought into the University of Chicago's single-minded devotion to the life of the mind. From the start I told my professors I had no intention of becoming a professor. That was fine for some people, but not for me. The academy, in my view, was a resource to be employed. Something I would take and use elsewhere—in the real world. The ivory tower was a great place to visit, but I didn't want to live there.

Partly that was my temperament. While I saw myself as an intellectual, I also saw myself as a doer. How else to make the world a better place? I wanted to get back out there and do good. And partly it was because I didn't see how academics could influence the real world. The business of academics was truth, after all. Their job (drawing a bit on Herman Hesse) was to preserve the purity of all sources of knowledge. That's why they resided in ivory towers. Impact was for others, and happened elsewhere.

Later I came to see how wrong I was, and how important and influential the academy could be in the real world (as long as you were comfortable with impact that was slow, unpredictable, and indirect). But understanding that took a lot of living and learning. I lacked vision, judgment and confidence, and needed to get them. That probably wouldn't have happened in the ivory tower. Had I stayed, I suspect I'd have become a competent academic, but not much more. I was better off getting my PhD and getting out.

Fortunately, the Comparative Education Center was a good place to land. It was small—maybe twenty-five students—and the professors gave students lots of personal attention. The standard introductory courses were good, and we were encouraged to explore outside the department of education (which had me reading de Tocqueville in Lloyd Rudolph's marvelous political science course). As usual, I was in discovery mode. I'd studied sociology at Duke. Now at Chicago I was studying comparative education— something I knew nothing about.

Pretty quickly I realized that education isn't a discipline. It's an activity you can study from many different disciplines. So if you try to include them all you risk spreading yourself far too thinly across psychology, sociology, economics, philosophy, management, pedagogy, and politics (I've probably left out a couple). Not a good idea, particularly in a PhD program. You're better off concentrating on one discipline and applying its tools to education. I decided to do that, but immediately ran into a problem. I'd come to Chicago thinking I was a sociologist but now was having second thoughts.

Indeed. Probably the most important thing that happened to me at the University of Chicago was that I discovered economics. Before, I'd taken just one course, on economic history, at Michigan State University. We'd compared Max Weber's *The Protestant Ethic and the Spirit of Capitalism* with R.H. Tawney's *Religion and the Rise of Capitalism*—which introduced me to the complex relationship between thought and action. I loved the course but somehow it didn't move me to take more economics. (Instead, I took more history.) At Chicago, however, my advisor (Bob Myers) told me I should take Mary Jean Bowman's course on the economics of education. I did, and it turned out to be a totally different experience. Since most of the students had no background in economics, she began by sketching out the basic elements of microeconomic theory: supply, demand, price, quantity, utility, and how they interact. That was new to me. I was surprised. It was as if a light had come on. I was seeing a powerful explanation of human behavior—how people made decisions and how their decisions affected the decisions of others. And curiously, it was an explanation that was at some distance from politics. That may have made it more appealing. I'd always been uncomfortable with politics. I distrusted the certainty and the emotion that politics seemed to be built on. I was a skeptic by nature; grand schemes generally left me cold. And I'd always kept my emotions close to my chest. I wasn't going to jump up and down and wave the flag for much of anything. (Well, maybe for Michigan State football.) So finding a system like microeconomic theory, that explained so much in non-political, non-emotional, and empirically testable terms, was exciting. I wanted more.

I know. You'll tell me that economics is just as susceptible to politics and emotion as any other discipline. And I'll agree with you. But there was something basic about microeconomic theory—something that applied and was going to operate no matter what your politics or ideology. People were going to maximize utility (however they defined it) whether they were communists or libertarians. That's how people were. That's how they thought. There was, it seemed to me, a powerful and universal principle lurking at the base of microeconomic theory. It provided a theory of action that sociology (the discipline I originally identified with) didn't seem to have. In fact Gary Becker was at that moment applying the principle to sociological phenomena in Chicago's department of economics, and would later win the Nobel for doing it. His lucid, groundbreaking book, *Human Capital*, on how economics applies to education had recently been published. I read it. It was a great time to be at the University of Chicago.

But at the same time, I was worried about getting a good job in international development, and figured I needed some non-academic skills, perhaps in management, to strengthen my chances. That meant the business school. Chicago back then had no equivalent of, say, the Woodrow Wilson School of Public and International Affairs at Princeton (where I had applied, and been turned down) or the Kennedy School at Harvard (which I hadn't even heard of). Management resided in the business school. It was the refuge of doers in Chicago's exclusive community of thinkers. So I worked out a deal with my advisors and the business school to get a joint MBA/PhD, and began taking a few courses in the business school—most of them in economics.

The business school was different. Not surprisingly, the professors were first-rate. But the business school acted at least partly like a business. It saw its students as clients, whose interests needed to be served. That meant teaching was important. To improve teaching, students were asked at the end of each course to evaluate their professors along several measures of performance. Their responses were tallied and distributed right away, before students chose their courses for the next quarter. I have no idea whether those evaluations eventually had any influence on tenure decisions. But they certainly got professors' attention. They had to worry, at least a little, about how students reacted to their course and their teaching. They had to ask themselves whether they were presenting the best material, and making sure their students understood it. That's probably why the teaching was so good in all the courses I took. The business school (as an economist might put it) got the incentives right.

Business school students were also different. For one thing, lots of them were rich. I remember a kid from Oklahoma who seemed to be on the phone every day with his broker, trading commodities. I barely knew what commodities were, although I figured it out pretty quickly. He was also losing a lot of money, which I thought was interesting. Another kid told me he'd just bought gold, on the theory that the U.S. would soon go off the gold standard and the price of gold would skyrocket. Which it more or less did a few months later, causing the dollar to plunge and him presumably to make a bundle. And there was a Chinese-American (or maybe just Chinese) student who talked about establishing a national chain of fast-food Chinese restaurants, à la McDonald's. This was all new to me. These kids had money. They thought big. And they expected to be in charge. I'd never met kids like that. I was wide-eyed. I felt like I'd stumbled onto an exclusive club—one that was fascinating but that I clearly wasn't a member of. I didn't have a single extra dollar I could use to buy gold or trade commodities. And I couldn't imagine starting even one restaurant, let alone a chain. But I was paying attention and taking notes. It was certainly interesting.

I never finished the MBA. Finishing would have required an additional year of courses, plus funds I didn't have. I began to believe I was employable even without the MBA. And I got tired of being a graduate student. So I did just half, and stopped.

But I had a great time. I took courses in economics (micro, macro, and labor), along with some math (the kind you need for economics—differential calculus and linear regression, plus a peek into linear programming). The microeconomics course was special, turning the introduction I'd gotten earlier from Mary Jean Bowman into a broad theoretical base that made me think that maybe I could really become an economist. My professor, John Gould, was first-rate and later became dean of the business school. I set the curve on his final exam—probably the only time I ever did something like that—largely because he inspired me.

I took a course in marketing research that made me realize how unreliable statistics are in predicting human behavior, and a course in Bayesian statistics that changed my approach—or more accurately, gave me an approach—to probability. My statistics professor, Harry Roberts, was extraordinary—a pioneer in applying Bayesian statistics to business decisions, and in developing interactive computing. One of his doctoral students, Eugene Fama, later won the Nobel in economics. (Unfortunately I never took Fama's Introduction to Finance course, which many business school students did back then.) Harry agreed to serve on my dissertation committee and was a great help. Not only did he make sure my analysis was solid, he arranged for me to analyze my data on an experimental interactive computer he was developing for some company. That made work a lot faster. I was able to order up analyses from a keyboard, and get results in just a few minutes, and without going back and forth to the computer center, years before doing that became commonplace. And I've always remembered his advice—perhaps unexpected coming from a statistician—about analyzing data: "Start by just looking at the data, running your hands through it and getting a feel for what it's like. That will help you avoid misusing statistics."

The big challenge in my business school courses was calculus. I've already mentioned the disaster my one math course was at Michigan State. Calculus at Chicago started out the same way. It was gibberish—like trying to decipher Egyptian hieroglyphics. Halfway through I was flailing and failing.

Then two things happened. First, I realized I was approaching calculus (and math more generally) the wrong way. My approach was the same as for the social sciences. When asked a question, I either knew the answer or I didn't. If I knew something I wrote something. And if I knew nothing I wrote nothing—I was out of luck. But math turns out to be different. Just because you don't recognize it doesn't mean you won't recognize it. Throwing up your hands when you don't know the answer is the wrong approach. The right approach, apparently, is to play with the question. Restate it in various ways and see if it becomes familiar.

Often it will turn into something you recognize and can solve. Math's like that. For a long time, I didn't know that little secret.

Second, I got lucky. After class one day I noticed a small group of students huddled around a table. One of them claimed to have three or four rules that would let you solve any calculus problem (or at least, the kind our course covered). It was, according to him, a piece of cake. All you had to do was apply the rules. It sounded suspicious, of course—like a get-rich-quick scheme. Maybe he was studying to make money fleecing consumers. (Business school does attract those kinds of people, after all.) And since there were so many well-heeled students who knew so little about math, it was probably a spectacular business opportunity. But he was passing out the rules for free. And when I tried them, they worked. Suddenly I could analyze functions with ease. So easily, in fact, that I started doing it for fun (and to show off), covering page after page with long, exotic-looking equations. Once I woke up in the middle of the night realizing that I'd been taking derivatives in my sleep. I was proud. I'd cracked gibberish. I'd become a math whiz.

The rules (which I wrote on the inside cover of my textbook) were so miraculous that I showed them to our professor, who said he'd never seen them before but that they ought to work. They did, for the rest of the course at least, after which I promptly forgot them. I have no idea why the rules worked, or what they had to do with calculus. What mattered was that they got me through the course just fine. Which was probably how most students in the class felt. It was one more example of the find-what-works-do-it-and-move-on attitude that was so common among business school students, and so uncommon among wannabe intellectuals like me, whose first impulse was to stop and wonder why things worked. We were from different subcultures. I was learning about theirs.

Business school didn't turn out as I'd planned. I went there looking for management credentials, but came away with economics, statistics, and an appreciation for the down-to-earth. I got enough economics to understand, think like, and identify with the economics profession, even though I never became a card-carrying economist. I got enough statistics to do my own research and interpret the research of others—which came in handy later on at the Ford Foundation. And I got exposed to the world of business, and its pragmatic ethos, which balanced my tendency to keep my head in the clouds. But I got no management credentials. And I completely ignored whole areas of the business curriculum, like finance, accounting and (surprisingly) management. That was fine with me. I discovered that my priority was economics. I didn't get the MBA, but what I got was remarkably useful. It was one more example of how hard it is to predict how things will turn out. Mostly, all you can do is aim in what looks like a good direction, move forward and figure it out.

Still, there is an obvious question here unanswered: Why didn't I take courses in Chicago's vaunted department of economics? It was world-class. It was right there in front of me. I was shifting toward economics. My education professors knew many of the economics professors. All I had to do was register. I didn't. A golden opportunity, missed. How come?

The answer is mostly that it never occurred to me. We were, of course all aware that Chicago had a great economics department. My courses had me reading work by Friedman, Schultz, and Becker, each of whom sooner or later won the Nobel. And Friedman's warning. "There's no free lunch," floated over the campus like skywriting. But I was more concerned about getting some management credentials, and that led me to the business school. I needed to take courses there for the MBA I thought I needed and was going to get. The business school taught economics too, and well. Many of the professors had joint appointments in economics. I was happy with the economics I was getting. And certainly no one nudged me towards the economics department. Even though my advisor (by then Mary Jean Bowman) had a joint appointment in economics, she never suggested I take courses there. She'd negotiated the joint MBA/PhD agreement with the business school, so probably thought it should take precedence. The topic just didn't come up.

I have no complaints. I got a good education at the business school. It served me well. And I liked the students, in part I suspect because they were so different from me—a respite from the unremitting seriousness of graduate student life at Chicago. Adding coursework in the department of economics probably would have been too much. Sometimes a nudge is what you don't need.

That meant, however, that I didn't get to know the Latin American students studying in Chicago's department of economics—who, over the next couple of decades and under the soubriquet of the "Chicago Boys," would revolutionize the region's economic policy. Our paths just didn't cross. The one exception was Miguel Kast, a German-Chilean who was finishing his MA in economics just as I was finishing my PhD in education. By then I'd accepted a position with the Ford Foundation in Chile, and Jean Bowman summoned the two of us to her office shortly before graduation to make sure we'd met. Miguel went back to become the director of Chile's national planning agency, where I thought he did a good job of creatively applying economic theory to the challenge of reducing poverty. But I only saw him a couple of times. He'd become part of General Augusto Pinochet's repressive military government, from which the Ford Foundation was distancing itself as it shifted toward preserving independent, critical thought in Chile. That didn't leave much common ground. A few years later, he died of bone cancer.

I did, however, regularly run into "Chicago Boys" around Latin America over the next several decades, as part of my work with the Ford Foundation. We had no shared experience to draw on, of course, but I always understood where they were coming from. I'd studied enough economics at Chicago to know what it was about and why people bought into it. We spoke the same language, even if we didn't always have the same politics.

The courses and professors at Chicago were for the most part great, but I still had to write a doctoral thesis. The thesis is a big deal—the capstone. Without it you don't become a PhD. It's required because the doctorate is a research degree. You're being trained not only to master a field but to contribute to it. Research is how you contribute, so you have to show you can do it. It's your ticket to the dance.

This sounds simple, but in fact it's a major hurdle that some students never overcome. That's partly because doing research is the opposite of taking courses. It's production rather than consumption. Students are used to consuming knowledge but now they have to produce it. Most have never done that. It's a big adjustment.

And partly it's because students tend to overestimate the requirements for a doctoral thesis, turning what ought to be a simple research exercise into a magnum opus. You can understand why. The research they read in their courses is nothing like the typical doctoral thesis. It's first-rate. That's why they've been assigned to read it. They seldom read doctoral theses, which tend to be narrow, peripheral, and forgettable. And all of us dream that our doctoral theses will be wonderful. We're human. So we aim too high. We try to build a wall when all we need is to make is a brick.

I worried a lot about that. I'd seen too many fifth- and sixth-year doctoral students hanging around campus trying to finish their theses. They were good students but seemed stuck—like deer in headlights. A few probably just didn't have it. And some lacked the funding to work full-time on their theses. But I always thought that for many the problem was more emotional than intellectual: they were intimidated by doing thesis research. They assumed standards that were higher than most graduate students could meet.

I resolved not to get derailed by high standards. I decided that the most important characteristic of my doctoral thesis would be that it got done. I didn't care about making a name for myself or getting published. I just wanted to get a PhD. My thesis would be as simple and easy as I could make it. I would ask, and answer, a single question. I would analyze the data and write it up. The thesis would be approved. I'd be finished. That's all I would do.

So I kept my thesis proposal simple. I started with Phil Foster's much-commented article challenging the practicality of vocational training in developing countries. Then I proposed to evaluate an industrial apprenticeship program, known as SENA, in Colombia. Was it a success or not? Was it attracting the kind of students it sought? Did its graduates get jobs? Did they make good money? Were they doing the kind of work they'd been trained for? That was it. Nothing fancy. It was so simple I feared my committee might turn it down. But they didn't. They approved it.

Personally I was worried. My proposal didn't seem very academic. I could imagine answering each question with a simple yes or no. That might lead to a short thesis. "Skimpy" was the word that came to mind. But on the other hand, it certainly looked doable—and that was my priority. Gather the data, answer the questions, write it up and I'd be done. I could see how to get there. And my committee had told me to go ahead. So I didn't tell anyone that I was unimpressed.

Finding support to do doctoral research is always a challenge, of course. I was fortunate to get a grant from the Social Science Research Council to spend a year in Colombia gathering data. SENA gave me an office in Bogotá and access to their files—along with the moral support of their staff. And I had a small research budget that let me hire a couple of interviewers and track down the graduates, including the few who'd migrated to other parts of Colombia (1 interviewed one beside his ship on a naval base in Cartagena). And when I came back, the University offered me a one-year lectureship that required I teach a graduate seminar and help with recruiting but gave me time to analyze the data and write. So I had the necessary funds—which also meant I had no excuses.

The surprise was that I was wrong. What I thought was simple wasn't. To be sure, the questions I'd posed were easy enough to answer. And the answers were mostly yes. The SENA program attracted good students. Its graduates got jobs, made good money, and largely worked in the fields they'd been trained for. The program was clearly a success. So my doctoral thesis was done. Right? And maybe Phil Foster was a little too pessimistic about vocational training, at least in the case of SENA. That probably would have been an acceptable thesis, although maybe borderline skimpy.

But not so fast. It turned out that analyzing the data brought up all sorts of issues I hadn't thought of. I realized, for example, that I couldn't just report positive findings. I had to say something about why they were positive. The standard explanation was that the training made students more productive, enabling them to get good jobs and make good money. It added value. I called that the SENA effect.

But there were other possibilities. I discovered that the SENA graduates weren't average; they were a select group. Just to get into SENA they had to have good grades, good records, and pass a personal interview. Then they had survive three rigorous years of classes and apprenticeship (many dropped out). They were winners, the kind of kids employers love. They were going to do pretty well even without SENA's training. So some part of SENA's success was due to qualities (intelligence, motivation, discipline) that the kids brought to their training, and not just to the training itself. I thought about that as the Harvard Business School effect and called it the selection effect.

And I realized that each student was sponsored by, and did their apprenticeship in, a modern, capital-intensive firm. That connected them to the high-wage sector of the economy. They learned how to knock on the right doors, and they developed a network of contacts that could help them navigate the labor market. This I called the information effect.

So all of a sudden I went from saying that SENA was a success, to having a theoretical explanation for why. There was a value-added effect, a selection effect, and an information effect. I didn't foresee any of this in my proposal. To my surprise, it was beginning to look like I might have not only a thesis but a publishable article.

There was more. I noticed that, even though the SENA program was supposed to be terminal, after graduation most kids continued to study (usually in night schools), and their studies were academic rather than vocational. These kids weren't satisfied with becoming factory workers. They wanted to move on and up. Many aimed to go to college. SENA, quite unexpectedly, was acting as a capital market: It gave ambitious and talented blue-collar kids a free vocational education that enabled them to get good jobs and to use their wages to finance an academic education—which was what they wanted all along. This was a surprise (although Foster had suggested something like that might happen).

And finally, once I was on the ground I realized that I could easily gather enough data on costs and benefits to estimate private and social rates of return, which turned out to be high, suggesting that SENA's apprenticeship program was an economically efficient allocation of resources. This wasn't in the original proposal either. It was a target of opportunity.

So what started as a straightforward program evaluation turned into a surprisingly respectable academic exercise. But that only happened after the research process got underway. Doing it changed it. I learned a lesson: It's hard to see where your analysis will take you, particularly if you're a novice researcher. You have to let the story go where it wants. Your best bet is to start with a few good questions and some decent data. Have a plan. Be humble. Dig in and produce. Be alert. You should get an acceptable thesis at least, which is all you need. And maybe you'll get more.

I got more. Over the next couple of years my thesis produced three academic articles, and was translated into Spanish and published by the United Nations International Labor Organization. That was a surprise. I was thankful. But it was icing on the cake. I'd have been happy even had none of that happened. My thesis would have been done. I could, after four years in the ivory tower, go back out into the real world. I was Dr. Puryear and I was free. That's what I wanted most.

My thesis had one other totally unexpected consequence that was so valuable—and stressful—that I've always remembered it. Several years later SENA organized an international conference to celebrate its 20th anniversary and invited me to present my thesis findings. By this time I was working for the Ford Foundation, living in Peru and busy, so I told them that I would be delighted to attend, but couldn't speak because I wouldn't have time to prepare. They said fine. I didn't think much about it.

When I arrived at the event in Bogotá I discovered I was on the agenda that afternoon as a speaker. Not only that, I was part of a panel that included Gary Becker (future Nobel laureate from the University of Chicago) and Dudley Seers (head of the Institute of Development Studies at the University of Sussex and one of the first people I'd read on development economics). These were intellectual heroes of mine. And now I was supposed to speak on a panel with them, surprised and unprepared. I was aghast. I'd been invited to perform onstage with the stars and was about to screw it up.

But I realized I had to do it. In fact, I never should have turned down the offer to speak in the first place, since I had done what back then was the only empirical study on how SENA graduates had fared in the labor market. That kind of privilege comes with an obligation. I owed it to SENA. I also had a reputation to uphold. I was a Chicago PhD and worked for the Ford Foundation. I had to act the part.

So I did it. There was really only one option: pull the thesis up out of my memory. I sat down and remembered what I could. I took a few notes. Then I spoke unscripted for about 15 minutes. I don't know how good I sounded, and I certainly struggled, but I felt good. I knew my thesis pretty well and could recall the key findings and what they meant for policy. And, unlike Becker and Seers, I could talk about what had really happened on the ground in Colombia (and in Spanish). I think I did better than I expected. The lesson is that when you have to do it, you do it.

I was, finally, done with the University of Chicago, and I left. Leaving was vivid. I remember, after successfully defending my thesis, walking out of Judd Hall feeling free (at last). I left most of my books and papers behind in my office and never looked back. I'd finished with the ivory tower and was returning to the real world to work for the Ford Foundation in Chile, and so would no longer need them. It was a symbolic act; a declaration of independence.

Today, of course, I wish I had at least some of those books and papers. And I never got as far away from the ivory tower as I thought I would. But that's hindsight. At the time the only thing on my mind was exhilaration.

But I still dream about the University of Chicago—mostly a recurring nightmare. In the dream I've signed up for a class and then failed to attend or do any of the readings and tomorrow a paper is due and I have no idea how I'm going to write it. I can't believe I've been so irresponsible. I'm screwing up. The gods of knowledge are unhappy. All the pressure and apprehension I endured in Hyde Park are back.

This dream shows up at least a couple of times every year, reminding me of where I've been. It's always painful. Then, almost miraculously, I wake up and I'm OK. I even smile, as if encountering an old friend.

And the expectations my professors set have not ebbed much. When I put together an analysis or an argument I find myself asking—at least occasionally—whether it would pass muster. Would Phil or Jean or Arnold approve—or would they roll their eyes? Does it meet standards? It's a high bar that I'm delighted to find still in front of me.

So how was it studying at the University of Chicago?

The standard definition of a great university is one that is dedicated to producing world-class research. A wholehearted commitment to producing knowledge—and not just to transmitting it—is what sets great universities apart. There aren't many, and the University of Chicago would be on anybody's short list. That's why I wanted to go there. It's worth asking what I got out of it

It's hard to say it was fun. For me at least, studying at Chicago was a little like taking your medicine. Strong medicine. You didn't look forward to it. You didn't enjoy it. You were glad when it was over. But it was going to make you better. Really. So you did it. It was a virtuous investment.

It was also relentless. You'd been tapped to enter an intellectual community. The solemnity, the demands, and (even) the rituals verged on life in holy orders. You were urged, mostly by example, to make the academy the center of your life. You were bombarded with theories, concepts, information, and reasoning that you were supposed to understand, assimilate, master, and use. You took courses from professors you'd read, or read about, as an undergraduate. You spent most of your time in class or in Regenstein library—your body in a carrell and your head in a book. I remember speculating, mostly as a joke, that on any given day more students entered Regenstein than came out, but that the University wouldn't admit it because those who didn't come out were being sacrificed—quietly, of course—to appease the gods of knowledge.

Maybe that's what happened to those poor kids who couldn't finish their doctoral theses. Maybe it was part of what it cost to be a great university. I never knew for sure. And I couldn't prove anything.

But it was hard to escape the ivy tendrils. The campus had a serious feel to it—like church. There was no natural social center. You were there to learn, and that's how the place was set up. In fact (and unfortunately) the best place on campus to meet girls was probably Regenstein Library. You can imagine what that was like. It just wasn't a social place.

The big exception was Jimmie's—a venerable bar just off campus whose chief attractions were alcohol, pandemonium, and shallowness, making it a magnet for desperate graduate students. There you could drink beer and talk football (mostly about "dah Bears"). You could say stupid things. You could shout. You could even meet girls. Nobody talked about the *Iliad* at Jimmie's. I recall running into the dean of students of the Business School there once, and thinking how nice it was that he came by to show his students he cared. I also recall meeting a medical student—a real live girl—who, like me, seemed shell-shocked by the demands of coursework and just needed someone to to talk to. Jimmie's was an oasis. It was human.

Jimmie's had its limits, however. As I recall, most of the kids I ran into there were studying in the professional schools—like business, law or medicine—and planning to go back out into the real world once they got their degrees. Kids studying for PhDs, and therefore planning on life in the ivory tower, seemed less likely to show up at Jimmie's. Perhaps they were worried about remaining pure. The gravitational pull of the academy was strong. You weren't supposed to escape. But at least Jimmie's was there when you needed it.

The other exception, at least for me, was Chicago's Near North Side, where the Business School had its downtown campus, and where one evening a week one quarter I took a course in marketing research. The Near North Side was probably the city's trendiest neighborhood. It was about commerce and entertainment rather than academics. One of my Business School buddies who was taking the same course had a membership in the Playboy Club—the original Playboy Club—which was conveniently located just a couple of blocks away. So after class we would go there for drinks. You can imagine how it felt for a University of Chicago graduate student who'd been hanging out in the library and overdosing on the staples of academic life—theories, concepts, analysis, statistics—to suddenly be surrounded by scantily clad Playboy Bunnies offering cocktails. "Oh my God! Are you kidding me? Wow!" It was magical, and about as far off-campus as you could get.

Still, studying at Chicago was one-hundred percent worth it. Chicago put me into a different world. It was like being in the Peace Corps all over again. I had to learn a new culture. I experienced academia from the inside and from the top. I sat at the feet of giants (so to speak), got exposed to their brilliance (if that's what it was), and learned from them. I was able to see what extraordinary academics were like: how they thought, how they taught, their values, and even their foibles. I got a more realistic sense of how the academy operated. And I began to see how I stacked up.

I got three big things from the University of Chicago—all of which you should get from a great university, and some of which you might get from any university.

First, I got a good education. My professors were often leaders in their field. They knew what they were talking about and wanted me to know too. Like ancient mariners bearing wisdom, they imparted not only knowledge, but values, standards, attitudes, and expectations. Perhaps most importantly, they showed me the way. They sorted through all manner of theories, perspectives, studies, and people, and told me which I should spend time on—and which not. That was important. There's so much out there, and you know so little, that you can't sort it out yourself. You need someone to show you around—a guide. Mapping the terrain and telling you what to read may be the two most important things professors do.

So I listened, read, discussed, and wrote. And I learned—about the traditions and literature of comparative education, economic theory, statistical analysis, and a lot more. I was taught and challenged. I was pushed to make connections and spot patterns. I remember particularly a paper that Phil Foster had me write on the history of vocational/technical education in the UK during the late 19th century—which turned out to have a lot in common with the pattern I found later when I did my thesis research in Colombia.

I discovered that studying with first-rate professors goes beyond transmitting knowledge. You have the opportunity to meet, take classes from, and otherwise interact with some of the world's most extraordinary minds. You see them closeup and in real time. You get a sense of how they think, how they talk, and how they decide. They teach you to think and to express yourself. They inspire. Their standards are high and they make you up your game. Anything less seems like bad form. The "sit at the feet of giants" trope turns out to be real. If you're lucky, you'll get close enough to a couple so as to be really influenced by them. I got that from three or four. The potential for mind-changing growth is enormous. There is a Chicago effect. You get smart by being around other smart people.

Of course, it's always chancy putting yourself in the hands of someone you don't really know and hoping they'll steer you in the right direction. You could get indoctrinated. Professors, like the rest of us, have agendas.

But much of life is like that. You have to take what comes and sort the good from the bad. My professors had their views, and didn't disguise them. Still, this was a great university and they didn't get hired by accident. And they were careful to show the various sides of issues that had various sides. I felt that I got a proper introduction to whatever it was they were teaching—that I was getting as good an education as you could get, or needed. They opened doors. They set examples. They said what they had to say. The rest was up to me.

The second thing I got at Chicago (and this is probably just another part of getting a good education) was skepticism. My professors routinely challenged conventional wisdom. Their message was that some part of what we blithely consider to be true doesn't pass muster when subjected to careful, empirical analysis. Conventional wisdom, they argued, should be taken with a grain of salt. Doubt is a professional responsibility.

Skepticism, of course, has long been dear to the University of Chicago's heart. A faculty committee published the *Kalven Committee Report* in 1967, shortly before I began studying there, reiterating the university's duty to question the established order: "A university faithful to its mission will provide enduring challenges to social values, policies, practices, and institutions. By design and by effect, it is the institution which creates discontent with the existing social arrangements and proposes new ones. In brief, a good university, like Socrates, will be upsetting."

Interestingly, though, the report concluded that it was not the university that should take positions, but rather the individual professors and students. "The instrument of dissent and criticism is the individual faculty member or the individual student. The university is the home and sponsor of critics; it is not itself the critic." This was, of course, at odds with calls for the university to take stands on issues of the day, like South Africa, the Vietnam War or race relations in the United States. The committee's position was that the university could only protect the full academic freedom of its individual members if it remained ideologically neutral. It was not a club, trade association or lobby; its first and special obligation was to sustain "the widest diversity of views within its own community."

For me the message was clear. I should be skeptical. I should consider unpopular views. I should resist what we now call political correctness.

That was an important tonic for a kid from rural Michigan who grew up unconnected to elites and tended to be dazzled by the personalities and conventions of established thinking. My instinct, in the presence of experts, was to trust them. But my professors' instinct was to question them, applying facts and logic. They alerted me to the politics, emotion, ignorance, and just plain inertia that often lurk behind established thinking. And to my surprise, they conveyed the impression that, since I was now aware of these problems, I had some responsibility for sniffing out and exposing them. I could no longer just observe. I was supposed to act.

The third thing I got at Chicago wasn't intellectual at all, but more like a blessing. Graduating from a great university admits you to an exclusive club. You become a graduate of the University of Chicago—or Stanford, or wherever. That's important quite apart from anything you studied or learned. Something magnificent and mysterious has been bestowed upon you. You've been certified. You become part of a community.

For me, the blessing had at least three parts.

The first, and probably the most important, was emotional. I could stop worrying—or at least, now I could start worrying about other things. A great university had given me two thumbs up. I'd made it. I was finally an intellectual. I wasn't a star, of course. But I could play on the same field as the stars. That was a relief.

Thinking you belong at least near the top makes a difference. You get over something. Your confidence grows. You begin to feel responsible for what goes on in your field. You go from being a spectator to being a player. You're part-owner of the academic enterprise and expect to have influence. That can be powerful.

The second part of the blessing was more about how others reacted to me. I'd acquired a label that made people take notice. I wasn't just Jeff Puryear any more. I'd gotten a prestigious seal of approval—a Chicago PhD. It was a little like the selection effect I'd found when I did my doctoral research on SENA graduates in Colombia. Chicago, like SENA, was shorthand for "this kid has something on the ball." It got attention and opened doors. It was the first time in my life that I'd carried an elite label.

Nearly a decade later, when I began recruiting for the Ford Foundation's program in Latin America, I came to realize just how powerful those labels can be. My first question when I reviewed an applicant's CV was usually "Where did this person go to school?" Anyone who'd managed to get into, and graduate from, an elite university was a good bet to have something—brains, motivation, character, a good education, connections—and deserved a second look. Particularly if they were a *magna* or a *summa*. It was a convenient way to identify talent.

I know that's unfair. And I tried to resist it. But it wasn't easy. Our work at Ford required extraordinary people (or so we thought). They were going to have to deal, on a more-or-less equal basis, with high-level academic, policy and political leaders from across Latin America. They needed to be smart, sensitive, well-educated, confident achievers who could push through adversity and get things done. There weren't many out there. And if you needed to find them, elite universities were a good place to start.

Moreover, because we sought extraordinary people we tended to ask extraordinary academics for suggestions. They were usually at elite universities and tended to recommend their best students. It was an informal recruiting network that in fact worked quite well. But if you hadn't studied at an elite university, it was hard to break in. Which, once again, was unfair.

Still, we were a small organization that couldn't try out a lot of staff to see who might make it and who not. If we hired the wrong person, an important part of our work might get held up for the couple of years it took to find that out. We needed to get it right the first time.

This wasn't new. Recruiting from elite universities was the norm at the Ford Foundation back then. When I took up my first job at Ford's office in Santiago, Chile, all my colleagues had graduate degrees from elite universities—Yale, Princeton, Stanford, Columbia, and MIT. Nowhere else. Interestingly, only a few came from privileged backgrounds. But all of them were smart and strong. The Ford Foundation I joined was like something out of *The Best and the Brightest*. It made every effort to hire top talent. Frankly, that was one of the main reasons I wanted to work there.

The third part of the blessing was about contacts. A great university puts you into a great network. It starts with your professors, who are known and respected by leaders (academic and otherwise) elsewhere, and therefore can provide you with entrée.

My first advisor at Chicago, Bob Myers, left within a year to take a position at the Ford Foundation. A few years later when I was ready to look for a job, he asked whether I was interested in working at Ford ("Of course!"), put my CV into their recruitment system, and (I'm pretty sure) put in a good word. I got the job.

Another professor, C. Arnold Anderson, was editor of the leading academic journal in my field, the *Comparative Education Review*. When I finished my dissertation and was ready to submit my first article for publication, he already knew me and my research. I didn't have to get his attention. I got published.

More generally, our professors heard about things in advance—faculty positions, research opportunities, or just interesting ideas and people, and could let us know. And people asked them for advice. Their information was good and their endorsements mattered. You wanted to be in their network. Now, it's true that every university has well-connected professors. But great universities have more, and that raises your odds.

I'm not suggesting that our professors compromised high professional standards to promote their students. That could happen, of course. But their credibility depended on providing good advice. If they didn't, people would stop listening to them. So they were careful about who they recommended for what. And they could only recommend people they knew. If you were outside their network, too bad. They couldn't even consider you.

Student contacts were just as important—and usually more fun. I stayed in touch with several of my Chicago classmates—mostly those who, like me, took non-academic jobs in international development. We helped each other by trading impressions about issues and people. Sometimes we let each other know about jobs, or provided some kind of entrée. But occasionally the network led to something more elaborate.

My favorite—and most impactful—example involved my former classmate Steve Heyneman, who spent more than two decades working for the World Bank and then became a tenured professor of international education at Vanderbilt University.

Steve had been appointed to a prestigious body (the Board on International Comparative Statistics in Education—BICSE) set up by the U.S. government to address growing concern about the world's capacity to monitor and assess the performance of its education systems, and specifically UNESCO's management of the international education statistics database in Paris. The group decided it needed to document the problem. Steve, after consulting with colleagues at the World Bank and UNICEF, asked me to go to Paris and write a report.

I was astonished and told him so. While I knew something about the statistics used in survey research, I had no background in statistical databases and knew nothing about whatever it was UNESCO was doing. I doubted I could come up with the kind of report they wanted. But Steve told me not to worry. He was sure I could handle it. That's where, I think, the network effect really kicked in. Steve and I had enough experience together for him to have a good sense of what I could do. He saw no need to sort through a bunch of applicants.

That may get at what's most important about networks: they help get you past the hard work of figuring out who's capable of doing what. Network members already know something about each other. They reduce the guesswork. Steve knew enough about me to think I was right for the job. And I knew enough about Steve to trust his judgment—even though I couldn't see how I was going to do it. So I went ahead and took the assignment.

Then it was my turn to draw on our network. I contacted John Smyth, who'd studied with us at Chicago and was now at UNESCO/ Paris directing its *World Education Report*. John, it turned out, shared the concerns of the BICSE folks and offered to set up my appointments. As an insider, he knew who I should see and could get them to see me. I put myself in John's hands. He made everything easier.

The upshot was a report that sketched a disturbing picture of the world's capacity to monitor and evaluate its education systems and found serious problems with UNESCO's international statistical database on education. It concluded that "the world has only limited information with which to evaluate one of its major investments" and "No major global organization has taken up the issue of educational statistics, assessment and research, and sought to make them part of what constitutes good governance in a modern state." Those were strong statements, but I was pretty sure I'd gotten it right.

And the report wasn't as hard to write as I had feared. The people I interviewed were experts. They knew the story. All I had to do was listen and pull it together.

The report was shared with a group of senior international education professionals and published in a European academic journal. It set in motion a process that led, some six years later, to a complete restructuring—and relocation from Paris to Montreal—of UNESCO's education statistics operation, and then to an expansion. For me it was maybe three months' work. The bang for the buck was enormous. Steve had been right. I was up to it. Partly it was about being in the right place at the right time. But more importantly it was about being in a network that, when opportunity knocked, knew me and realized I was a good fit. And then helped me set up those appointments in Paris.

Networks, of course, can be good or bad. They can protect unwarranted privilege, resist new ideas, restrict competition, and deny access to new and deserving groups (the "old boys' network" often gets those accusations). But networks can also be the most efficient way to steer the right people to the right spots. And they can act as a quality enforcer. You're more likely to do your best for someone in your network—and they for you—because your relationship is at stake. You don't want to let an ally down.

What's important is not to be on the outside looking in. Networks are a fact of life—starting with the original network: the family. People use them every day, and they're probably becoming more important with the spread of social media. That's why it is so important that universities—and especially elite universities—have admissions policies that prioritize talent rather than privilege. Any young professional looking to break into a field is well-advised to find a network (or several) and to get inside. And If you want a great network, study at a great university.

෴

It became clear once again as I wrote about the University of Chicago how hard it is to go from feeling you have something to say to knowing what it is. Feeling is different from saying. It's the smoke that signals fire. I knew there was a lot there. But I couldn't see it until I sat down, pulled up the memories, and let them settle and take shape. Writing forced me to make sense of what I knew and felt—to put it into words. That was hard, sometimes painful, and usually took forever.

Frequently I drew a blank. I sat there and waited, hoping something would emerge from the mist. It did, most of the time, but often it was something I hadn't expected to say or hadn't thought much about. Remembering is at least part discovery. Maybe it's like giving birth. You know something important is on its way but you don't know the details. And even when it arrives you may need some time to figure out just what exactly you've got. You can't hurry it, and you don't have much control. It's a process you can only recognize and respect.

Then, once I figured out what was there I had to decide whether it was worth saying. That's a separate decision. A lot of what you come up with isn't. You have to step back from what you've discovered you know, and ask whether it's something you ought to say. Is it important, beautiful, dramatic, useful, funny? Does it offer a lesson? Would anyone besides you find it interesting? Answering that is seldom obvious, and often personal and mysterious. But you have to do it. It's your story.

And finally, once I'd decided what was in and what was out I had to figure out how to say it. That meant finding a style. I didn't want to continue with the academic and policy writing style I'd used for years. It seemed dry and impersonal. I wanted something different but didn't know what. So I started checking out writers (some of whom I'd read before) to see how they wrote. I looked at books by John McPhee, Carlos Fuentes, Bruce Catton, Stephen King, George Orwell, Anne Lamott, Elmore Leonard, Richard Cohen, Robert Gottlieb, Ernest Hemingway, James Michener, Somerset Maugham, and (much later) Winston Churchill. Those were the ones who stuck. There were others.

That was fun. Some of them wrote memoirs, often about writing, and offered advice. Others just wrote. But it didn't make much difference. The style was the thing. What was interesting was that all their styles worked even though each was different. I realized I had options. I experimented a bit, trying out the style of one or another. But mostly it was inspiration. When I got stuck, I would dive into one of them, hoping it would jolt me out of my dismay, like a cold lake on a hot day. Sometimes it did.

The problem was the downside, which was often huge. They wrote beautifully and I didn't. Reading them made that crystal clear. I'd never be able to write like that. I was an interloper, eyeing mountains I couldn't climb. Or worse, I was a pathetic, wide-eyed fool with the preposterous idea that somehow I could write well if only I worked at it. It wasn't going to happen. I might as well quit.

That took some getting over. My solution was to quash any impulse to write the way they did. No. Trying to do that would be madness. I had my own contribution to make, and was just mining them for ideas. I would let my real voice develop and be heard. Doing that would lead me sooner or later to the promised land, where I would mingle with the writing gods and bask in perpetually elegant prose.

Most of the time that worked. I felt better. But it was hard not to worry.

The two I kept coming back to were McPhee (pretty much everything) and Orwell (the *Essays*). I'd read a lot of both over the years but hadn't thought much about their styles. Now I'd become style-conscious and could appreciate the choices they made and the effortless quality their writing seemed to have. Both write in a style that is personal—you feel you know them—but somehow their egos don't get in the way.

And their styles were different. For Orwell, good prose is "like a windowpane." It takes you right to the essence without your noticing it's there. Also, his writing is natural and conversational. You feel like he's talking to you. He wasn't afraid to use the passive voice now and then (even though he warned against it); nor did he pare his prose down to Hemingway standards. That was contrary to the edicts of Strunk and White, which I had followed for years. Reading Orwell helped me relax my style a bit, giving me permission to experiment.

In *Draft 4: On the Writing Process*, McPhee argues that a "relaxed, unself-conscious style is not something that one person is born with and another not" but instead has to be developed. It takes work. That sounded right to me. I had no natural style I was happy with, so my only option was to develop one. That was hard, but maybe there was hope.

From McPhee I also learned to value detail—to see its beauty, and its capacity to enlighten. McPhee had a marvelous ability to capture, organize and present the multiple features of a topic in a way that was interesting rather than tedious or overwhelming. His books on geology—lively writing about rocks—are a good example. By contrast, I had always been detail-averse. Pithy was what I liked. Detail seemed dangerously close to clutter and made me nervous. But reading McPhee made me see that detail could not only be your friend, it could be done with grace and style. His mantra (paraphrasing, to my surprise, Cary Grant) was "a thousand details add up to one impression." I could see how that might work. It was a matter of selection. That was amazing. I vowed to give it a chance.

I don't, however, think you can consistently imitate the style of any writer. Style is too personal—an extension of personality. I got more from both by simply reading their writing and letting it push me in one or another direction. I also realized that I was looking for something specific. The words simplicity and elegance kept appearing in my mind. That's what I wanted. I didn't know how to get it, but I'd know if I did. My style was a work in progress. These guys gave me a jumping-off place. You learn to write by reading great writers. At least that's what I hoped.

IX

THE FORD FOUNDATION

SOME HISTORY

To give away money…is an easy matter. But to decide to whom to give it, and how large a sum, and when, and for what purpose is neither in every man's power nor an easy matter. Hence it is that such excellence is rare and praiseworthy and noble.

—Aristotle, *The Nicomachean Ethics*

The Ford Foundation…is a large body of money completely surrounded by people who want some.

—Dwight Macdonald, *The Ford Foundation: The Men and the Millions*

It's a nice job. You meet so many interested people.

—Robert Maynard Hutchins, quoted in Dwight McDonald

I WENT ON to the Ford Foundation. Getting that job was one of the most important things that ever happened to me. And perhaps the most unlikely. It put me into a segment of the Establishment—a far-off place I'd barely heard of and couldn't imagine I'd ever inhabit. And I was getting a chance to make the world a better place big-time.

My path to Ford was straightforward but far from certain. While I was working on my doctoral thesis, I knew I should also be looking for a job but did almost nothing. Partly that was because I wanted to make sure I got my thesis done. Time spent looking for a job was time not spent working on my thesis, which was by far my top priority. I was still spooked by all those graduate students I saw hanging around campus trying to finish their doctoral theses. And partly it was because the only place I really wanted to work was the Ford Foundation, and Bob Myers had already put my CV into the hopper there. So why apply anywhere else? No other employer struck me as interesting; hardly any even came to mind. The logic was appealing, although hardly prudent. I tried not to think about it and concentrated on getting my thesis done.

Fortunately, I heard back from the Ford Foundation. They asked me to come to New York to interview for a couple of positions in Latin America, one in Mexico City, having something to do with rural development, and the other in Santiago, Chile, in education. Either would have been fine with me. In fact, anything, anywhere would have been fine with me, so long as it was with the Ford Foundation.

The Mexico City job didn't look a great fit, but the job in Santiago did. My interviews with Bill Carmichael, the director of the Latin American program, and Peter Bell, the head of the Santiago office, went well. I liked them both. But it was going to take a while to decide. A few months later they invited me to go down to Santiago for interviews, and I did, and that also seemed to go well. Then they offered me the job.

I couldn't believe it. Opening that letter was like winning the lottery. Six years earlier I'd set my sights on Ford. Now I'd made it. They'd lifted the velvet rope and were motioning me inside. I'd gotten to where I'd worked so hard to get. I was ecstatic.

Here it's worthwhile stepping back a bit and understanding what the Ford Foundation was and represented at that point in time. Ford wasn't just any foundation. It was the largest private foundation in the world. It had been established in 1936 as a Michigan foundation that largely assisted Michigan philanthropies. But in 1950 the Ford family endowed it with 90 percent of the Ford Motor Company's stock, making it almost overnight a titan in American philanthropy.

During its early years, the sheer size of the Ford Foundation was astounding. In 1951, for example, it spent five times more than the University of Notre Dame and seven times more than UNESCO. Its budget in 1954 was four times that of the Rockefeller Foundation and ten times that of the Carnegie Corporation. Its endowment in 1960 was over half the endowments of all U.S. institutions of higher education combined, and it spent more than did the entire United Nations and its specialized agencies. Ford was "a towering giant," and its main challenge in the 1950s was finding good ways to spend its money.

But the Ford Foundation wasn't just big. It thought big and it acted big. In 1948 the Foundation's trustees, anticipating the monumental size that the gift of Ford Motor Company stock would bring, established the Gaither Study Committee to chart a path for the future. As Dwight Macdonald notes in *The Ford Foundation: The Men and the Millions*, the Committee concluded that a modern foundation should no longer seek "to merely treat symptoms…but rather to eradicate the causes of suffering." The Gaither Report recommended turning Ford into an international philanthropic organization that targeted world peace, freedom, democracy, economic well-being, education and knowledge.

This was revolutionary, of course, but the trustees bought it and promptly turned Ford into a national and international foundation. They hired Paul Hoffman (formerly head of the Marshall Plan and a key advisor to Dwight Eisenhower) as president, and he brought in Robert Maynard Hutchins, former chancellor of the University of Chicago, as one of his associate directors. Neither was a stranger to big thoughts, and a bold new foundation began to take shape. Instead of funding hospitals and other traditional charities, it was trying to save the world. And it was led by people who thought big. And it was the largest foundation in the world. That was interesting.

Ford dramatically increased spending in 1951, established its first office abroad in 1952 (in New Delhi), and moved its offices to New York in 1953. Between 1951 and 1954 almost half its expenditures went for education and a third for international programs. Just under a fifth went for work on civil liberties, the behavioral sciences, and economic development. Michigan philanthropies ended up in Ford's rear-view mirror, getting just five percent of the budget.

What stands out in those early years is how visionary and experimental Ford was willing to be. It put up real money to advance civil liberties (as defined in the U.S. Constitution's Bill of Rights), broaden humanistic (i.e. non-vocational) education in the United States, and develop "mature, wise, and responsible citizens who can participate intelligently in a free society." It supported aid to refugees in Europe, research, and exchanges to make Americans more knowledgeable about other countries, and "overseas development" (which included activities as diverse as helping peasants adopt modern agricultural practices in India, setting up an Institute of Business Administration in Istanbul and establishing an International Institute for Advanced Buddhistic studies in Rangoon). As Dwight MacDonald notes in *The Ford Foundation: The Men and the Millions*, it funded a "plan for world peace," a "restatement of the principles American society," a "study of the fundamentals, workings, and problems of democratic society," "research on a European Constitution," and what J. Mortimer Adler's Institute for Philosophic Research describes as a "dialectical examination of Western humanistic thought, with a view to providing assistance in the clarification of basic philosophical and educational issues in the modern world." There was more. Some of it was probably foolish. But much was bold, high-minded, and pioneering. Ford's president, Paul Hoffman, was, in the words of McDonald, "the glittering ringmaster of a philanthropic circus."

Not surprisingly, Ford's combination of size, erudition, globalism, and independence got it into a fair amount of trouble. This was the early 1950s, and McCarthyism was revving up. Significant voices in politics and the press felt that the American way of life was under attack, and that the social sciences and internationalism were suspect. Ford was a good target, Macdonald points out, and got accused of "un-Americanism, subversion, eggheadism, and general Left deviationism." Westbrook Pegler's 1952 column illustrated one extreme: "Ford Foundation is Front for Dangerous Communists." Tennessee Representative B. Carroll Reece charged that the Ford Foundation was using the Ford fortune to "undermine and subvert our institutions." The accusations prompted two congressional investigations—but no legislation. Closer to the mark, however, might have been journalist George Sokolsky's lament: "Why cannot some of the money the Ford Foundation is piddling away on trivia be used constructively for the saving of opera?"

None of these accusations had much substance or led to any consequences. But they made Ford's trustees, and particularly Henry Ford II, uncomfortable. And they were coming to believe that Hoffman was too independent, too casual a manager, too indifferent to public relations. So in 1953 they fired Hoffman, eased out most of his associate directors, and brought in as president Henry Gaither, whose Study Committee had produced Ford's Magna Carta just a few years earlier. That created a new regime—cooler, more low-profile, and less likely to make waves. The "Gaitherized" Ford Foundation pulled back from its adventurism and played it safer. Gaither spent Ford's prodigious wealth, but largely avoided controversy. As one scholar put it a few years later: "They don't make the mistakes they used to, but they don't take the chances, either."

But a precedent had been set and an image established. Whatever the merits of Ford's initiatives during those early years, they were big and they were idealistic. As Ford trustee John J. McCloy put it: "It's hard to be daring in a big foundation…But some of the things Paul Hoffman did rang round the world." The Ford Foundation got a reputation for being bold and visionary—even though few people knew what exactly it did.

Now, fast-forward to 1966, when McGeorge Bundy left government to become president of the Ford Foundation. Ford was still the world's largest private foundation, and still highly regarded, but had become cautious in its grantmaking, and its trustees were looking for new ideas. As Kai Bird notes in *The Color of Truth: McGeorge Bundy and William Bundy, Brothers in Arms*, they told Bundy he could be his own boss and would have the freedom to make mistakes. He took them seriously.

Bundy was an exemplar of the American establishment—a gifted, self-confident Boston Brahmin, a graduate of Yale (where he became a member of the secret society Skull & Bones), a former military intelligence officer, an internationalist and "vital center" liberal, dean of Harvard's Faculty of Arts and Sciences at age 34—despite never having completed a PhD—and then national security advisor to presidents Kennedy and Johnson. Some thought he was a future secretary of state. But he'd stumbled badly in Vietnam. Many charged him with giving too much priority to political expediency, with lacking a firm moral compass and with failing to reflect deeply enough on the issues he faced. His reputation had taken a hit, and it never really recovered. At the Ford Foundation, though, he'd have the opportunity to turn the page and to use his brilliance, breadth, and energy to do real good.

What Bundy did, I think, was to take Ford up a notch, making it smarter, more visionary, and more willing to disturb the status quo. He made racial justice a top priority, spent hundreds of millions to establish a public broadcasting system, and undertook major initiatives in public interest law, environmental protection, arms control, and community development. He got into a huge fight over decentralizing New York City's public school system. He strengthened Ford's international and developing country programs. And he attracted a talented and strong-minded staff. Bundy was determined to bring the best minds to bear on contemporary problems and then do what seemed right, even if it meant taking risks and ruffling feathers. "Our job" he told the *New York Times*, "is to make our decisions, defend and explain them, and then go on to the next one with serenity. Otherwise, we might as well just throw the money up and see where it blows down."

That's the Ford Foundation—Bundy's—that caught my eye while I was in the Peace Corps, and then became the place I wanted to work. It called out to me—a philanthropic version of the shining "city upon a hill" that Jesus mentioned in his Sermon on the Mount, and then John Winthrop quoted in his "Model of Christian Charity" sermon in Southampton in 1630 to the pilgrims who were setting out for the New World to establish the Massachusetts Bay Colony, and politicians like John F. Kennedy, Ronald Reagan, Barack Obama, and others have used to great advantage in speeches ever since.

That's sophomoric, I know, but it's roughly what I felt. Ford, under

Bundy, had gotten its edge back and added some sparkle. It was smart, muscular, and demanding. Its liberal values fit my desire to make the world a better place. It was led by a president whom many thought was brilliant and who wasn't afraid of controversy. It had a reputation for quality and attracted top talent. It had money. And it was strong in Latin America. To a young outsider looking to do good big-time, it was a dream come true.

Please forgive this lengthy discussion of Ford's past. I think it important to make clear why Ford attracted me back then, and what made it special. It appeared, and turned out to be, an extraordinary group of people who imagined, attempted, and sometimes accomplished extraordinary things. You don't find many institutions like that. And they seldom perform at high levels for very long. It's important to recognize and understand them.

X

FORD/CHILE

WHAT IT WAS LIKE

So, Ford was what I wanted, and what I got. Then what? The next step was pretty tough, actually—and a long way from what I might have expected had I'd given it any thought, which I hadn't. I stepped off the plane in Santiago, Chile on a beautiful Southern Hemisphere spring day in December, 1973 into a world that was not only new and exciting, but absolutely bewildering.

Think about it. A kid from the rural Midwest with no connections and little background manages—because he's smart, works hard, was a Peace Corps Volunteer, went to a good school and LUCKY—to get hired into one of the country's premier international foundations, and a pillar of the US establishment. Now he has to show a bunch of sophisticated, over-achieving, Ivy League-trained professionals that he can cut it.

And he's starting out in Chile—a country that had just suffered a brutal military coup, and where people are being arrested, tortured, or worse, and he doesn't have a clue about what's going on, why or what should be done. This country he's signed up to work in has fallen apart. He doesn't understand the politics, and the programs he's been hired to oversee might close. Grad school didn't cover this. Welcome to your career.

That was disorienting. It was a while before I could even begin putting together the pieces.

Let's start with how it felt. I'd landed in post-coup Chile. The military had taken over and weren't taking chances. They believed that too much politics and an unscrupulous left had pushed Chile to the brink of social disaster. They responded by forbidding politics and vowing to "eradicate the Marxist cancer from our homeland". They declared a state of siege, suspended most civil rights, dissolved Congress and began a massive campaign to find, arrest, and sometimes execute persons thought to have leftist sympathies. Criticism of the military regime was prohibited. All political parties were banned. There were armed soldiers everywhere. People were being arrested for their roles in, or just having expressed support for, the now-deposed Allende regime. Some were sent into exile abroad. Some simply disappeared. There were reports of torture. A curfew had been established from 11 in the evening until 6 in the morning. Outside my little house in *El Golf*, an upper-middle class neighborhood in Santiago, there was automatic weapon fire in the street almost every night after curfew. But when I peered over the garden wall, I could never see anything. Maybe they were just trying to intimidate us.

At the office, people connected with Ford's programs were coming in with tales of woe. They were worried—even scared—and didn't know what to do. Some feared for their jobs; a few feared for their lives. Some came on behalf of family members who had been fired or arrested or had disappeared. Most needed someone to talk to, and some perspective on what was going on. There was an air of threat and emergency that we hardly understood and had no preparation for but had to deal with. We did what we could.

Every day brought emotion, uncertainty and surprise. What had been abstract—arrests, disappearances, and torture—became real. Not for us, of course, but for people we talked to or for people they knew. It wasn't clear what might happen next. And it went on and on. Sometimes you felt like you were in a movie, or maybe had a front-row seat at the opera. Except it was real. I still tense up when I talk about it. And prefer not to.

Understanding post-coup Chile was even tougher for me because I knew so little about Chile before the coup, during the government of Salvador Allende. What little information I had was second-hand and anecdotal. I was struck by how disorderly Chile appeared to have been back then. The country seemed to be grinding to a halt. You couldn't find toilet paper, cooking oil, or rice. (The Ford Foundation's office in Chile, taking advantage of its semi-diplomatic privileges, regularly brought staples in by truck from Argentina for its staff. But they were a privileged exception.) There were demonstrations and rumors.

I had visited once, but just for a few days in early 1973, to interview for the job I eventually took. And that visit left just one clear memory, which in retrospect was probably telling. Upon arriving in Santiago I'd gone to a restaurant to have lunch, and asked for a menu. The waiter informed me that there was no menu, but that the cook had just come back from the market where he'd managed to find oil, fish, and rice, so therefore I could have fried fish with rice—which is what I had. That got my attention. What kind of a market only had a couple of things for sale? Why? How did people cope with that? And how did they feel about it? This was new to me, and extraordinary. But I was busy and didn't think much more about it. A decade or so later, when I was regularly visiting Cuba for the Ford Foundation and eating in Havana restaurants where there were few choices and the waiters almost always told me what I was going to eat, I remembered the little restaurant in Santiago with no menu. That, I concluded, was how socialism operated.

The other poignant insight I got into pre-coup Chile came in late-1974 when, upon arriving in Santiago (by then I was living in Lima but traveling at least half the time), I cleared immigration and customs only to be directed to stand in a long line under the sign "International Police." I was annoyed by the delay and said so to no one in particular but out loud. A gentleman ahead of me, who looked decidedly middle-class, turned and said: "We must return order to Chile. We've had far too much turmoil. It's time to establish order." He spoke from the heart, obviously fed up with the conflict and disarray that Chile had experienced under Allende, and willing to put up with a military government if it restored order. I've always remembered him. I suspect he was expressing what a lot of Chileans felt. He made me realize how important order is to most of us, and what we'll give up to get it.

Interestingly, the person behind me in line was wearing a clerical collar and smiled warmly when I expressed my discomfort. We introduced ourselves and he turned out to be Father Ted Hesburgh, president of the University of Notre Dame. That was a surprise. I asked him what he was doing in Chile and he said he was traveling incognito in an effort to get the military government to return the *Colegio Saint George*, the only private high school it had taken over, to its original owner (and his order), the Congregation of Holy Cross. We chatted until the line started to move. I didn't see him again. And he didn't have much luck. It was more than ten years (1986) before Saint George was returned to the Congregation of Holy Cross—although the *junta* did transfer control of the school provisionally to the Archbishopric of Santiago in 1977. Later I discovered that during the Allende years the *Colegio Saint George* had, under the leadership of its director (and fellow Michigander) Father Gerry Whelan, become famous for its efforts to translate the principles of Liberation Theology into practice at the primary and secondary school level. No surprise, I guess, that the military government took it over.

I hate standing in lines. But this one turned out to be the best I've ever stood in, all because I talked to myself out loud and in public. That's probably not a good idea most of the time. Too many people who do it are schizophrenic or in some other state of impaired contact with reality. If you talk to yourself out loud you're probably going to get lumped in with them, rather than recognized as the distinguished representative of the world's largest private foundation that you are. But if you can do it without sounding crazy, it can pay off big. I got valuable insight into why people supported the military coup, and I got to talk with the president of the University of Notre Dame—who by then had become a major figure in U.S. public affairs. And in no time I was at the head of the line. It was great. So I'm not suggesting you rule out talking to yourself out loud and in public. Just be careful.

My new colleagues in Ford's office were appalled by what was happening after the coup. Chile wasn't like this, they said. It had been democratic for most of the past 140 years. It was civil. It was tolerant. It wasn't violent. But now it had been taken over in a hail of bullets by a military *junta* that showed no interest in democracy or civility. The place had been turned upside down. How could this have happened? They were surprised and indignant—and even a little shell-shocked.

I, on the other hand, was neither surprised nor indignant. I was bewildered. I knew nothing about Chile, so had no expectations to shatter. My starting point was that the world was complicated and tough, and that Latin America had a long tradition of dictatorship and violence. I'd spent three years in Colombia, after all. What I'd walked into in Chile seemed one more example of that tradition—deplorable but hardly surprising. My immediate problem was that I didn't understand what the military *junta* was doing nor where it might be going. Or what it might mean for us, the Ford Foundation. That much I probably had in common with my new colleagues. We would come up with several answers over the next several years.

And none of us, I think, was ever able to express to folks back home how it felt. When I tried, my family and friends would listen politely, nod, and not really get it. And how could they? It was all so strange, immediate and personal. You had to be a Tolstoy to convey the color and feeling. The only thing I ever found that managed to communicate the emotion of being in Chile right after the coup was the 1982 Costa-Gavras movie, *Missing*. I tell people to watch it if they want to know how it felt. You can quibble with some of what the movie says are facts—and I do—but it gets the job done.

Most of the people we were talking to right after the coup were high-level academics or policy specialists. Ford's work in Chile back then still followed the Magna Carta created by the Gaither Study Commission 25 years earlier—that it should seek not "to merely treat symptoms... but rather to eradicate the causes of suffering." That meant establishing the skills that were crucial for social and economic development, by strengthening universities, improving training in economics, sociology and political science, and beefing up the management and planning capacity of government agencies. Doing that, the theory went, would lead to better policy, better decisions, more economic growth and stronger democracy.

And it was a perfectly good theory. But you had to realize that development is messy. There are no guarantees, or even straight lines, in the development business. Things might well get better, but at their own pace and in their own way—and often with major surprises. Clearly, the military coup was one of those surprises.

Anyway, none of the people coming into our office worried or scared right after the coup were coming in to see me. I was new and knew no one, so could only stand by and watch while my colleagues engaged in heroics. My most common reaction was something like "What the hell's going on?" (I always remember one of my new colleagues, Nita Manitzas—New Yorker, Jewish, and a graduate of Columbia University—rolling her eyes at my observations and saying, "Is that what you think, buby?") None of that was surprising, of course. I knew nothing. My job was to watch, listen and learn.

Especially about politics. I realized immediately that politics was big in Chile and central to the work we were doing and that I didn't understand it. I had arrived in Chile a political innocent. My politics were, so far as I could tell, buried somewhere inside me, unseen and unconsidered. The closest I'd gotten to politics was wanting to make the world a better place—which of course was political small potatoes. I was an ingénue.

But now I had to deal with pros. Chile may have been the most politically sophisticated country in Latin America. Politics was everywhere and conducted at an extraordinary high level. Political parties were strong and numerous. They influenced, and sometimes controlled, all sorts of institutions, like student groups, university departments, professional associations, labor unions, and community organizations. Many people looked to their party for inspiration and guidance.

Equally important, in Chile politics was not just a game of interests but also a game of ideas. Interest groups didn't just slug it out the way they did in the United States. They felt compelled to justify themselves in grand ideological terms. That led to a rich brew of political philosophies, models, and arguments. People—particularly the high-level academic and policy types that Ford worked with—took political ideology seriously. It was an important part of their identity. They talked politics the way people back where I came from talked sports. If you didn't understand that, you'd have a hard time dealing successfully with them. And your job was to deal successfully with them.

Politics was also polarized. Catchphrases like "big," "grand," and "revolutionary" floated in the air. Party leaders had, over several decades, become more committed to their ideologies than to the democratic process. They favored change from the top down rather than from the bottom up. Each had, in the words of José Joaquín Brunner, one of Chile's leading intellectuals, "a great project for totally rebuilding society." They proposed comprehensive, nonnegotiable solutions to social and economic problems. They disdained the give and take that made democracy work. And they refused to compromise. Compromise was for sissies. Ideological purity was what mattered.

This wasn't new, exactly. The shift toward rigid politics began with the emergence of an authoritarian, Leninist left in the 1950s. Then in the 1960s an uncompromising center emerged, followed by an antidemocratic right in the 1970s. Trust and understanding across political groups dwindled. Whichever party was in power—left, right, or center—would go as far as it could without making any deals. Democratic politics stopped working. Politics became an all-or-nothing game. That led to the breakdown I parachuted into in 1973.

There was also a strikingly human side to Chile's polarized politics. People with different political views didn't talk to each other much. They seldom even met. Some had been classmates at the university, so at least knew each other. A few came from the same families, which made for tense conversations at family gatherings. But most moved in separate and mutually exclusive social circles. They didn't attend the same cocktail or dinner parties. They didn't intermarry. The left and right referred to each other with contempt, as either a *momio* (mindless right-winger) or a *rojo* (mindless left-winger). Whichever you were, the other was beyond the pale. (Curiously, there was no comparable label for people in the center, which probably demonstrated the center's declining relevance as people increasingly moved left or right.) Chile's political culture was rich and sophisticated, but it had split into two isolated communities that had little contact with and often despised each other.

This kind of political tribalism was new to me. I'd always worked and socialized with people without paying much attention to their politics. It never occurred to me that politics might be important. But I couldn't do that in Chile, especially in the circles Ford moved in. Politics was the elephant in the room. You couldn't ignore it. You had to understand who you were dealing with. Their politics determined how they were seen, and what they might—and could—do. Moreover, Ford's money and prestige mattered. Who you talked to and who you supported sent a political message—like it or not. People were watching.

These divisions extended even to my social life. I couldn't just socialize with whomever I wished. There were consequences to consider. If I hung out with the right, people would assume I shared their politics. Ditto if I hung out with the left. And if I hung out with both, people would wonder whether there was something wrong with me. Maybe I was shallow. Or naive. Or untrustworthy. It might complicate my work. So socially I pretty much had to choose sides.

Which I did by going in the same direction the Ford Foundation was going: away from the right and toward the center and the left. My colleagues and I were aghast at the violations of human rights by the military *junta*, at its authoritarian character, at its restrictions on freedom of speech, and at the witch hunts it was unleashing in the universities. We couldn't sign on to repression. And back then the right generally kept quiet about what the military *junta* was doing, preferring (I think) repression from the right to the repression from the left it was certain Allende would have precipitated had he remained in power. So social chitchat with the right was awkward, at the very least. But chitchat with the center (well, most of it) and the left was easier because they shared our dismay. We could relax with them.

Early on I dated a woman who, although she wasn't very political, identified more or less with the right (and was, she said, related to General Augusto Pinochet, the leader of Chile's military junta). She took me to an Independence Day celebration at the Argentine Embassy (where she worked) and, to my surprise, I found the four members of Chile's military *junta* standing resplendent in their uniforms like gods, paying their respects. In the reception line I shook hands with Pinochet. It seemed perfectly natural at the time, and kind of a kick. I'd met my first head of state.

But I immediately had second thoughts. What was I doing shaking hands with this guy—hands that were, well, bloody? Did I want to be in that position? I realized I didn't and from then on avoided social situations where I might have to engage in symbolic acts that made me uncomfortable. And I realized that socializing with the right was more likely to put me into those situations than socializing with the center or the left—at least then and there. So I avoided socializing with the right.

Still, I have to recognize that I never fell in love with a woman who was on the right. Suppose I had? I mean, I wasn't against the right per se, just against how they'd cozied up to Pinochet. (After all, had I been working in Cuba, it's quite possible I'd have been hanging out with the *damas blancas*). So had I fallen in love with a woman on the right, maybe things would have turned out differently. And maybe today I'd be writing a novel instead of a memoir. Who knows? But I didn't. It was another road not taken.

Two more thoughts on the complicated etiquette of dictatorship: A year or two later when I finally met McGeorge Bundy at our offices in New York I asked him when he was going to visit Chile. He said he had no intention of visiting Chile because if he did he'd have to meet with people he didn't want to meet with. That sounded just right. It was a variation of the "avoid awkward situations" rule I'd stumbled on. He never did visit, and had already sent his vice-president, Dave Bell, whom my boss, Dick Dye and I had shepherded around for a couple of days. We talked mostly with dissidents and, I think, a few high-level, relatively low-profile government people. That was enough. I don't remember any awkward moments.

Tougher is the blood-on-the-hands issue. I've known several people over the years who visited Cuba and for a variety of reasons were introduced to Fidel and shook his hand. Most got their picture taken (which some might later have hung in their office). A few were even invited to sit down and talk politics and policy with him. Most saw this as something of a privilege; a few perhaps even an honor. They didn't have a problem with it. I know of no one who turned down the opportunity.

But I'm pretty sure that many, perhaps most, of those same people, had they visited Chile under similar circumstances, would have resisted being introduced to Pinochet, and shaking his hand, and getting their picture taken—let alone sitting down and trading ideas. For them, Pinochet was different. You only shook his hand if you had to. And you didn't hang his picture in your office.

How do we explain that difference? Both were dictators. Both opposed democratic institutions, civil rights, and academic freedom. Both had a lot of blood on their hands—arguably the same amount, but certainly well over any threshold of decency that I can imagine. One area where they differed was in where they took their countries: Pinochet's Chile managed impressive economic growth and, after 17 years, returned to democracy while Fidel's Cuba has stagnated economically and remains, after more than 60 years, an authoritarian police state.

So why is it OK to shake hands with Fidel and not Pinochet?

I can hear at least a few people sharpening their knives. You're not supposed to bring this up. It makes people uncomfortable. Fidel was a folk hero and Pinochet was a monster. That's all you need to know.

But obviously you need to know more. The other glaring difference is that Pinochet governed from the right while Fidel governed from the left. There is a long tradition, in Latin America and among people who study Latin America, of teaching that the right is bad and the left is good. And certainly there are cases where that's been true—where the right has behaved badly and the left has behaved, well, at least better. But the terms "right' and "left" have taken on a kind of mythic character that's hard to get past, and often keeps us from looking at the details— which of course is where the devil usually resides.

That opens the door to indiscriminate political correctness. We're not supposed to criticize the left, so we don't. But we're supposed to criticize the right, so we do. We cut Fidel plenty of slack because he's a leftist and therefore a champion of the people. And we demand much more of Pinochet because he's a rightist and therefore cares only about the rich.

If that's your position, fine. But you should take responsibility for it. And recognize what it might imply: that repression from the left may be acceptable, while repression from the right is not. And if you disagree with that position, also fine. But you should disagree out loud—even if doing so is considered politically incorrect. Otherwise you risk committing the sin of omission. People get hurt when governments repress. We should not avert our eyes. It's important see clearly and to speak out. I like Martin Luther King, Jr. on this: "In the end we will remember not the words of our enemies but the silence of our friends."

Personally, I wouldn't want to meet with either Fidel or Pinochet. Both were brutal dictators who committed acts and promoted values that I find reprehensible. They belong in the same category, and it's a category I don't like. Had I needed to meet with either—as part of my job, for example—I'd certainly have done it. But I'd have rather not.

In the case of Fidel, this could have come up. For roughly five years in the early 1980s I managed the Ford Foundation's Cuba program, visiting Havana once or twice a year and meeting with government officials and academics. Our objective was to build informal, non-governmental relationships between academic and cultural leaders from the two countries. Given Ford's prominence, and Cuba's contentious relationship with the United States, you could imagine someone thinking maybe I should meet with *El Presidente*, at least as a formality. Had I been invited, I'd have accepted, and shaken his hand. And probably gotten my picture taken. It would have been part of my job. But no one, so far as I know, ever thought I was important enough to meet with Fidel. It didn't happen. I was neither surprised nor disappointed.

I probably got a little carried away on this topic. When I sat down to write I had no intention of comparing Fidel with Pinochet. In fact, I'd never even thought about it. It simply appeared in my mind, and I had to write it down. Which suggests that I cared more than I realized. I suppose that kind of gut reaction is appropriate in a memoir, as long as you don't overdo it. I hope I haven't. I think I'm responding to watching, over the years, so many intellectuals pull their punches regarding transgressions by left-wing governments while screaming bloody murder at anything questionable that right-wing governments do. I got tired of ignoring it.

But back to life in Chile. I don't want to give the impression that Chile's political conflict made living there nonstop misery. That would be an exaggeration. The repression was deplorable and distressing. But Chile still had its charms, particularly if you were a foreigner who was largely out of the line of fire. And for a youngster like me who wanted a career in Latin America, already spoke Spanish and had just gotten his first job, it had a lot to offer. I didn't know that, of course, until I got there. It was just one more piece of luck.

Let me count the ways.

Geography comes first because as soon as you get off the plane you see the towering mass of the Andes—high, jagged, and snow-covered— shimmering in the sun and hinting at mysterious pleasures and secrets. The Andes are young (for mountains), high (topping out at well over 22,000 feet just south of Santiago) and long, marking Chile's entire eastern border from north to south, until finally dropping to nothing where Patagonia ends at Tierra del Fuego. In addition to being beautiful and accessible, they block rainfall (and people) from the east for much of the country's length and give it the feeling of being walled off from the rest of South America. That made Chile feel special, almost cozy. It was a place where people felt obliged to deal with each other.

And Chile is extraordinarily long and skinny. Sandwiched between the majestic Andes and the equally majestic Pacific, it runs for more than 2500 miles from Peru and Bolivia in the north to the Antarctic in the south, making it one of the longest countries in the world, and also one of the narrowest—just 217 miles at its widest point, twelve times as long as it is wide. (That much I already knew and had noted in my junior high school paper "Chile-The String Bean Country.") On a good road, you could easily drive from east to west in a few hours. But driving from north to south would take days, and down south you'd eventually have to detour over the mountains into Argentina to reach the world's southernmost city, Puerto Williams, on the Beagle Channel in Chile because no road runs all the way through the deep and spectacular fjords that dominate the southern fifth of the country.

Way up north was the starkly beautiful Atacama desert, the world's oldest and near-driest, where some weather stations have never recorded rain, and NASA has tested instruments for future missions to Mars. Most of the desert is high—nearly 8,000 feet—and empty, but punctuated dramatically in a few places by vicuñas, flamingos, geysers, and salt flats. The high altitude, cloudless skies and absence of towns producing urban light pollution have attracted a multinational group of astronomical observatories. Desert and stars made Chile's north special.

Way down south—in Patagonia (which locals routinely call the "end of the world")—was some of the world's most dramatic and bleak terrain, including fierce winds that blow rain sideways half of the year— "stripping men to the raw" as Bruce Chatwin put it—along with a dazzling collection of animals, birds, glaciers, icebergs, mountains and fjords. (Patagonia also had a long record of attracting colorful eccentrics, dreamers, nomads, and oddballs, many of them British, which Chatwin does a great job of capturing in his *In Patagonia*.)

In between the drama of north and south, Chile had the Mediterranean-like Central Valley, where the capital, Santiago, was located and where most people lived. There the climate was hot, dry, and sunny half the year—just plain delightful—and cool and rainy the other half. The land was fertile, irrigated during the rainless summers by meltwater coming down off the Andes, and great for nectarines, cherries, kiwis, raspberries, avocados, tomatoes, lettuce, walnuts, and more. And for grapes, which meant wine. Good wine and lots of it. Chile's Central Valley was the Southern Hemisphere's version of Northern California.

Santiago, nestled in the Central Valley where the foothills begin, gave you quick access to the Andes. It was easy to go up and back in a day, which meant you could leave home on a Saturday morning, hike all day in Andean splendor (or ski all day in powder), and still make a concert or dinner party that evening back down in Santiago. And only a little further away, to the west, was the Pacific coast, a near carbon-copy of California's Big Sur—big waves crashing on big rocks—and a great weekend escape. In between was wine country, rolling, green, and peaceful. All of it so close, beautiful and easy—as if the gods were conspiring to make you happy. It was hard to complain.

There's more. A little further south, maybe eight hours by car (did I mention that Chile is long?), was the Lake District, a collection of deep blue lakes, snow-capped volcanoes, temperate rainforests (among the world's few, and harboring 3000 year-old alerce trees) that separates Chile's Central Valley from Patagonia. This is one of Chile's most beautiful areas and feels a little like Switzerland (except for the active volcanoes). The Lake District was extraordinarily wet in the winter ("where the rain was born," according to Chile's Nobel Prize-winning poet, Pablo Neruda, who grew up there). But in the summer it was sun and fluffy clouds, and where you spent your vacation, hiking and camping—if you hadn't gone to the beach.

The European feeling was enhanced by German settlers who began arriving in the late 1800s and became, by the early 20th century, Chile's fifth-largest immigrant group, behind Bolivians, Peruvians, Spaniards, and Italians. Most settled down south, and in some towns a majority still spoke German. (Years later my wife and I visited a Lutheran church in a small town on Lake Llanquihue, and discovered that the bible on the altar was in German). But the Germans didn't have the place to themselves. Alongside, and outnumbering, them was Chile's largest indigenous community, the Mapuches. They were much poorer, however, and had never been properly represented in national life. They made the Lake District feel thoroughly Chilean.

I'm leaving out, by the way, not only Easter Island, but also Robinson Crusoe Island (yes, the very same). Both of which are extinct volcanos, by the way…

One summer while on vacation in the Lake District, my good friend (and journalist *extraordinaire*) John Dinges and I climbed the snow-covered *Villarrica* Volcano, one of Chile's most active, that topped out at just over 9000 feet and towered splendidly over the lake and town of the same name, some 460 miles south of Santiago. *Villarrica* had experienced a major eruption a couple of years earlier, but now was just smoking. And the top glowed a bit at night. We'd camped at the base (probably in the national park) and drove well up the mountain to a ski resort just below the snow line on a beautiful sunny day (which, in the Lake District in summer, most days were). We understood you could reach the crater without much difficulty from there but didn't know what the terrain was like or how long it might take.

The first part of the ascent was over gravel and rock—basically a trudge. Then the trail arched upwards and the snowfield began. Both of us carried ice axes—elegant constructions of steel and wood you could lean on in snow and ice and use to brake yourself if you fell and began sliding down a steep snowy slope. (In Chile everyone called them by their French name—*piolets*.) And John, more serious a mountaineer than I, carried crampons. But I didn't and quickly realized I had a problem since my hiking boots, although fine for dirt and rocks, could barely grip the steep snowy surface. It was two steps forward and one step back, and I began thinking I wouldn't make it. Fortunately, a party of Chilean hikers making their way back down stopped to tell us what was ahead and, seeing I had no crampons, offered to loan me a pair. They said I wouldn't reach the summit without them and were probably right. It was a spontaneous act of kindness—something you often ran into up in the mountains. People who've reached the top know how hard it is, and how you always run into something you didn't expect. That makes them want to help. We agreed I'd return the crampons to them that evening at their hotel at the base of the mountain once we got back down.

The crampons made all the difference. I marched slowly but steadily up the snow, now at 45-degrees and steepening a bit as we neared the top. It was hard but somehow not a problem. Being out there in the bright sun, crisp air, blue sky, and vast expanse of dazzling white snow was what mattered. The view was spectacular—crystal-clear Lake *Villarica* immediately below and mountains all around, several of them snow-covered volcanoes, and with Mapuche names like *Quetrupillán, Lanín, Llaima,* and *Lonquimay,* pushing up through green forests. You felt like you could see a hundred miles. And in front loomed the fat, white snow-covered crater that we'd been climbing patiently for hours, inviting us finally to stick our heads over the rim and see what was inside.

Which we did once we reached the summit—and were aghast. It was like looking into the belly of hell. Mysterious forms glowed below and threatened to erupt. Sulfurous fumes scoured your nose with a wire brush. It was fire and brimstone, the devil, Dante. You imagined falling in and dying. Or worse, being dragged in by some preternatural tendril. The contrast with the beauty we'd climbed up in couldn't have been greater. Smoking craters were fine from a distance, but not something to hang around and savor close-up. You just wanted out. Both of us pulled back, turned around and started down. We'd reached our limit. Which, I think, is largely what climbing is all about.

The trip down was delightful. Maybe a vertical quarter-mile, mostly on snow. We draped the crampons around our necks and *glissaded* down the cone on the heels of our boots, shifting our weight left or right like skiers across the soft white snow in bright sunshine. Gliding down the mountain after working so hard to climb up, and after encountering what amounted to evil at the crater's rim, was a great way to end the day. Exertion followed by elation. We stopped at the hotel to return the crampons, and maybe we had a beer. Then we went back to our tent to clean up and figure out dinner. It was the kind of perfect summer day that Chile's Lake District made available.

So, geographically at least, there was a lot to like. But more than anything it was the people that made Chile a great place to live. Cosmopolitan, open and friendly, with an addiction to politics, a taste for art, and a penchant for living well, Chileans were charming, at least to most Americans. Part of it is that they were very middle-class, in ways that Americans could identify with. I remember attending a wedding reception shortly after arriving and thinking it could have been my brother's wedding in suburban Chicago. You felt like you knew the Chileans you met; it was almost like being home.

They were also sociable. You got invited to dinner at the drop of a hat. I'd get off a plane from Lima on a Friday afternoon and within a few hours have a dinner invitation, sometimes for that evening. People loved to talk. Dinner was where you did it. So come to dinner. A charming custom.

Of course, the Chileans we worked and socialized with were a highly educated minority, different from the country's poorer, less-educated majority. But I've gotten to know similar groups in other Latin American countries, and Chileans were clearly different. There was something—a kind of openness, heterogeneity, irreverence, and egalitarianism—that set them apart. Society in Chile seemed more diverse and less rigid than in the more thoroughly Spanish countries of Latin America.

Perhaps it was their multiple national backgrounds that made Chileans feel different. Chile was less Spanish and more broadly European than much of Latin America. In addition to Germany and Italy, its people had roots in a dozen or so other European countries including Croatia (Chile has more Croatian descendants than any other country except Croatia), and the British Isles, particularly in the port city of Valparaiso (much of Chile's middle class drinks tea in the afternoon). Plus France, Greece, Hungary, and the Netherlands. There were even migrants from Russia, Lebanon, Palestine, and Syria. And quite a few Jews, mostly Ashkenazi but a few Sephardi (one of whose descendants I would marry). Some of these, particularly the German- and Anglo-Chileans, retained their original language and some of their customs, despite integrating fully into Chilean society. The result was a charming hodgepodge of national and ethnic identities that opened the country up and encouraged people to recognize their different backgrounds. I was bemused sometimes by the non-Spanish and almost exotic last names of people I met or read about in the paper (e.g. Garafulic, Münchmeyer, Bitar, Frühling, Subercaseaux, Matthei, Mackenna, Brunner, Sunkel, Chadwick, Benmayor, Foxley, Knapp, Zalaquett, Kast, O'Higgins, Radic, and Boeninger). It was a little like the national origin mélange of the United States. Just two of the country's most recent seven presidents have had Spanish surnames (Lagos and Piñera). The others were British (Aylwin), Swiss/German (Frei), French (Pinochet and Bachelet) and Croatian (Boric). My secretary when I joined Ford's Santiago office was Patricia Nagel; our other senior secretary was Anita Meyer; our office manager was Andrew Wallace. The place just didn't feel like the stereotype of Latin America. It drew from and reflected a broader world.

There was also a tendency to look outward and find and appropriate the best of what the world had to offer. Chileans didn't spend a lot of time looking inward. Their impulse was more to look abroad for good ideas and consider bringing them back to Chile—whether it was jogging (known as "footing" back then), music (the day after Elvis Presley died, my housekeeper offered her condolences), or economic policy (Chile's "Chicago Boys" revolutionized economic policy with ideas they'd picked up studying there). What was foreign commanded attention because it was different, and might be useful, or at least fun. Worth a try.

And there was a subtle, almost British sense of politeness, formality, discretion, and tact that could leave you bewildered if you didn't understand it. Even though the culture seemed informal, you needed to observe "good form" or "*buena educación*." And some things you expressed only indirectly and never directly. That was a code you had to figure out. I once had a long conversation with a grantee over how the project we'd been supporting was going. Afterwards, a colleague asked "Did you realize that he asked you for more money?" Nope. He was so polite and indirect that I completely missed it. I've since thought that comparing Chilean and Japanese culture would be interesting. Both are wide open to outside ideas but somehow retain their distinct national identity. And neither is casual. Forms and standards are important.

There was more—food, wine, literature, art, the beach, skiing. But I don't want to bore you, dear reader. Take it from me. I liked it and you would too. Chile, despite its serious problems back then, was an attractive place to live for a foreigner like me.

But let's get back to the Ford Foundation, and to Chile's high-powered political culture and how Ford dealt with it.

During its first dozen years in Chile, Ford steered relatively clear of partisan politics. To be sure, its instinct was to favor the political center, and that tilted it towards people who sympathized with the centrist Christian Democratic Party. But in 1970, when Peter Bell took over as head of the Chile office, it made a deliberate effort to broaden its programs to include academics identified with the right and the left. The goal was to diversity its work, and better reflect what was going on in Chile, without taking a partisan political stand. Ford's work, moreover, was almost entirely academic, supporting teaching and research at universities, and aiming to provide Chilean students with the technical know-how to promote economic growth and social justice. The centerpiece was a commitment of $10 million over ten years to strengthen the University of Chile through a program of exchanges with the University of California's university system. (Back then, $10 million was a lot of money.) Ford funded other universities as well, and some of its support went to agriculture, veterinary medicine and basic science—fields that were a long way from politics. But some went to economics, including helping (along with the Rockefeller Foundation and USAID) fund the department of economics at the Catholic University of Chile—which gave birth to the now-famous Chicago Boys, who would later revolutionize economic policy in Chile (under Pinochet) and more broadly across the region. That turned out to have political implications, although I doubt that Ford could see that far ahead when it decided to put up the money. Ford also invested millions of dollars to send Chilean students abroad for graduate training so they might acquire the technical know-how to promote economic growth and social justice. (I wrote about Ford Foundation activity in Chile at this time in my book, *Thinking Politics: Intellectuals and Democracy in Chile, 1973-1988*, published in 1994.)

After a few years Ford also began supporting work in sociology and political science in several universities. In a report to the Ford Foundation Board in 1983, I described the initiative as part of a region-wide—and innocent-sounding—effort to "increase the ability of Latin Americans to make rational choices among important policy options facing their societies." That took it closer to politics, and made it consider the political implications of its work. But still, politics wasn't high on its agenda. It saw no reason to tilt one way or another and remained largely above the political battles playing out in Chile.

That changed after the 1973 coup. In part because the people and institutions that Ford worked with—particularly the universities—were fundamentally disrupted by the military government. The Chilean coup was not only anti-communist, but also anti-politics, and the changes it made were dramatic. The *junta* appointed a rear admiral as minister of education and installed military rectors in every university. It set in motion a "cleansing" process aimed at eliminating all elements it judged were dangerous to the functions of higher education. And that quickly became a political witch-hunt. Known leftists were dismissed. Programs identified with leftist viewpoints were either closed or re-organized. Academic freedom and due process were eliminated, and intimidation became commonplace. Even those in the political center were suspect. If you weren't a whole-hearted supporter of the military regime, you could easily find yourself in trouble. Clearly, the military was going to do whatever it thought was necessary to get the country back on track

For Ford, that was a lot to swallow. Most of its work was in universities, and the military *junta* was redefining what being a university meant. Gone was academic freedom and the notion that social issues could be freely debated and that government actions could be analyzed and criticized. The components of intellectual creativity—curiosity, discussion, diversity, criticism, security, merit, and tolerance—had been severely weakened. And more broadly, democratic institutions and procedures had been suspended, and human rights were being violated and political violence was far too common. All these changes were motivated by politics, of course, and Ford now had to decide whether, for its work, politics mattered.

Ford had already responded, quickly and provisionally, to the new conditions, rolling out several emergency measures to help academics (mostly social scientists) adversely affected—and those who thought they would be adversely affected—by the new government's policies. These included programs to evacuate, relocate, and find jobs for those who'd been forced out of university positions, provide promising young scholars with funding to pursue graduate studies abroad, and try to help intellectuals who had been imprisoned without charges. (I described these programs in my article, "Higher Education, Development Assistance and Repressive Regimes," which appeared in 1982 and was reprinted by the Ford Foundation the next year.) These programs helped. But they were temporary measures, designed to deal with immediate problems. The bigger question was what stance Ford would take over the longer term.

It didn't start by knowing what to do. The terrain it faced was largely uncharted, and it had to figure things out. But Ford was still Ford. The values and standards and extraordinary staff that I'd signed up for were intact, and if anything on full display in the face of the challenges posed by the sudden and (largely) unexpected military coup. Watching Ford respond was a dramatic tutorial for a newbie like me. I was delighted, and privileged, to be part of it.

Ford went into full-deliberation mode. Bill Carmichael, Ford's director for Latin America and the Caribbean, came down and, along with Peter Bell, the head of the Santiago office, met with Ford's grantees, government officials, political leaders, and other notables to try and get a clearer fix on what was happening, and what might happen next. And to canvas the opinions of people on the ground regarding how Ford should respond. Their starting point was that Ford should make clear its disagreement with the measures taken by the military government, probably by closing its office.

I sat in on some of these meetings and remember particularly a heated discussion with Charles "Chuck" Young, the chancellor of the University of California, Los Angeles—UCLA, over whether Ford should continue business as usual (which he more or less favored) or change course in response to the military government's measures (which we were considering). Young was breathing fire. This was, he argued, no time to disengage because the University of California might now be one of the University of Chile's few connections to the principles of free speech and democracy. That was a reasonable argument. But since we were funding—generously—that program, the stakes for the California system were high as well.

I confess that my own reaction was not always noble, in part because I was so new to all of this. In a letter home to my parents I observed that "It was good to get in a few licks against the school which beat MSU in the Rose Bowl." But it wasn't just because I was new. I suspect that even today if I met with the chancellor of UCLA, the same mischievous imp would be sitting on my shoulder, leering at him or her. You don't get over college football.

But quite apart from the University of California, the stakes were high more generally. It wasn't just Ford's money that was important, but also its prestige, and the international legitimacy its prestige conferred. Whatever it did would have a symbolic, as well as a financial, impact. That gave it a special responsibility to come up with a proper response.

And the proper response wasn't immediately clear. One argument, coming from at least a few people in Ford/New York, but also from quite a few in Chile, was that Chile was better off now that Allende had been deposed. The Allende government, elected with just 36% of the vote, was never popular but insisted on governing as if it had a broad mandate to institute massive—even revolutionary—economic and political change. It was, in the words of political scientist Arturo Valenzuela (who later became assistant secretary of state for Latin America in the Obama administration) "a minority coalition dominated by Marxist parties dedicated to a fundamental transformation of that country's economic, social and political structures." The Allende government regularly bypassed parliamentary debate and adopted bold social and economic policies by *fiat*. And it led the country into hyperinflation, shortages, strikes, rationing, economic failure, and growing political conflict. Allende (went the argument) had taken Chile to the edge of chaos, and that provoked the military intervention. For everyone who deplored the coup there was someone who applauded it. Chile was now on a better path and would eventually regain its democratic ways. It was important to help the country recover and move forward.

The counter-argument was twofold. First, the military regime's decision to abolish democratic procedures, violate human rights, engage in torture and suppress independent viewpoints ran counter to the core values of the Ford Foundation, and Ford needed to make that clear. Otherwise it risked providing the new regime with tacit approval and legitimacy. Ford was large, prominent, and respected. It couldn't fly under the radar. Doing nothing was doing something. It had to decide where it stood.

A similar argument, it's worth noting, can be found in a 1971 paper on how Ford should behave in "distasteful regimes," prepared by Kalman Silvert, its distinguished advisor for the social sciences in Latin America: "Closing our eyes to evil elements on the grounds that we are helping governments only to do their focused good is a very dangerous practice...If we cannot make a very strong case for distinguishing our activities from the support of politically repressive behavior in the host country, then we should withdraw." Silvert was writing about Brazil, but had anticipated at least some of the issues Ford ran into later in Chile.

The second part of the counter-argument was more practical: Chile's new military government had created conditions that made it hard—perhaps impossible—for Ford to achieve its objectives. The intellectual absolutism sweeping the universities seriously threatened the pluralistic and free process of academic debate that was essential to good scholarship. That placed Ford's efforts to develop first-rate universities and establish a modern social science in peril. Universities were no longer allowed to operate like universities. So it no longer made sense for Ford to work with them.

What I find interesting about that argument—today, at least—is how much it shared the view laid out in the University of Chicago's 1967 Kalven Committee Report (which I mentioned earlier) that universities should harbor critics: "A university faithful to its mission will provide enduring challenges to social values, policies, practices, and institutions. By design and by effect, it is the institution which creates discontent with the existing social arrangements and proposes new ones. In brief, a good university, like Socrates, will be upsetting." I have no reason to believe that anyone at Ford back then had read the Kalven Report. I hadn't read it myself. In fact, I didn't even know it existed. But many Ford staffers were applying more or less the same logic: a university that ceased to be "the home and sponsor of critics" ceased to play one of its essential roles. It wasn't doing what a university ought to do.

The bottom line was that Ford couldn't just ignore politics in post-coup Chile. It needed to decide where it stood. That was pretty clear. What wasn't clear was what it would decide. That's what the debate was about.

Bill and Peter concluded that Ford should take a strong stand—sharply reducing activities in Chile, closing the Santiago office, and relocating international staff (like me) to other field offices in Latin America. The message was that Ford disapproved of the new conditions and would wind down its activities—perhaps even to zero within a few years. It was a condemnation of the Pinochet regime.

I agreed, although I was so new there was no reason to have much faith in my opinions about what Ford ought to be doing. For me this was more than anything a golden opportunity to watch several world-class minds sort out a complex problem of institutional strategy and politics. I'd learn a lot. But I didn't have much to offer. My position was more like "If that's what you guys think we should do, then it probably is."

But this was not a decision that Bill and Peter could make. It was too big and too entwined with politics. Dave Bell, the vice-president of Ford's International Division, had to be consulted. But ultimately the decision had to be made at the top, by Ford's president, McGeorge Bundy.

So Peter went to New York a few weeks later to discuss the course of action he and Bill were recommending. They met first with Dave Bell and Dave's deputy, Frank Sutton, prior to meeting with Mac. (I wasn't there, of course. My account of the meetings in New York is based entirely on an interview with Peter Hakim, assistant director of Ford's Santiago office at the time who, because he happened to be in town, was invited by Peter Bell to sit in.) Dave and Frank were not happy. They questioned whether Ford should close its office. They argued that

Ford was not a political institution and did not shift gears in response to political winds. Its job was to solve problems and in Chile problems continued to exist, so it should continue trying to solve them. (Frank reportedly said something like "Doesn't Chile still have an inflation problem?") Politics wasn't what Ford did.

But before they could get very far, a message came from Bundy's office that he was ready to see them, and only had a few minutes. So they went in. As he often did, Mac started out playful and conversational, asking about family and travels. Then he asked Bill why he and Peter were there. Bill beautifully laid out the facts and recommendations. And Peter just as beautifully backed him up. Mac was clearly taken with their argument. But he seized on the distinction between politics and academic activity. "I understand exactly what you're saying" he said. The gist of his argument was that, although the Ford Foundation was officially apolitical, it was intellectually, and ethically, opposed to what was going on in Chile, and particularly in its universities. Given those changes, Ford could no longer achieve its objectives, and so must withdraw. Its decision was, at least officially, practical and professional.

It was over. Mac said that unfortunately he had to run. Dave never had a chance to present his views. Ford would wind down its work in Chile. Just like that.

Two things are interesting here. The first was Mac's apparent decision to base Ford's decision, at least formally, on academic rather than on political grounds. He understood perfectly, of course, the politics of changing course in Chile. But he was saying that Ford had no business taking a formal political stand. It wasn't set up to do that. And, as a non-profit (and tax-exempt) institution, it wasn't really supposed to. So it wouldn't. Ford would remain officially apolitical, even though its decision would, de facto, send a strong political message. Formally, it was reducing activities in Chile because conditions no longer allowed it to achieve its objectives. QED.

Some might find his argument too clever by half. But it's worth noting that it enabled Mac to do several things at once: address the concerns of his staff in Santiago, minimize the Foundation's political exposure, maintain at least some common ground with his vice president—who might have reached a different conclusion—and do the right thing.

The second is the role of luck in big decisions like this. Preparation matters, of course. Bill and Peter were prepared. When they got their chance they made their case. But suppose they hadn't gotten to talk to the boss? Or suppose the personal chemistry had been different? Or suppose there'd been more time and Dave Bell had decided to make the counterargument? Their case was strong, but you never know. Ford, after all, did not take the same position in other parts of the world. It all happened fast. Luck played a role. It probably always does.

So the decision was made. Ford would wind down its work in Chile. Grants already approved would be allowed to run their course if their original objectives could be met. The agreement with the University of California would be reduced and limited to sending Chilean students abroad for graduate study. There would be no new grants to government agencies or universities. Grants to other institutions would be considered only if they could operate independently of the military regime and promote academic freedom. Ford wouldn't quite close its office but would no longer designate it as a field office. And it would dismiss most of its local staff and transfer international staff who were staying on, like me, to offices elsewhere in Latin America. Ford's presence in Chile would steadily decline. It was a sharp, conspicuous change.

I would be shipped off to Ford's field office in Peru. I was fine with that. I still had a job, liked Ford, and was up for just about anything. Lima sounded interesting. And I'd be going back to Chile every month to tend to business there. Plus they were giving me more and more responsibility. I'd been hired to work on education, but they'd already given me the economics portfolio in Chile (and Argentina). Now they were giving me the education program in Peru as well (Bob Drysdale, who'd held that job, was leaving to head Ford's Office in Mexico City). In part this was the inevitable consequence of downsizing. Programs were winding down in Chile. People were leaving. Somebody had to pick up the slack. So it wasn't a clear vote of confidence. But at least it wasn't a vote of no confidence. I was getting a shot. It would be up to me to show my stuff.

Here I want to stop and say something more general about what it was like to work at the Ford Foundation—at least back then and there. And especially for a youngster (I'd just turned 30) starting out in his first real job. I was, formally at least, a kind of junior philanthropist, but knew nothing about the implications of giving away money, or how to do it. I was setting foot in new terrain—wide-eyed and inexperienced.

The first and most important aspect of the job was the simple fact that you had money to give away. Lots of money. Enough to make a difference. That got people's attention. Ford was still the largest foundation in the world. It was serious about Latin America. The dollar was strong. You could do things. This was the big league. You were expected to perform like a big-leaguer

Second, the Ford Foundation had prestige. It didn't just bring money to the table. It brought visibility and status. Ford was recognized and respected worldwide. It was, presumably, a high-quality operation. Anyone Ford was funding must be pretty good. That got attention too.

And third, Ford didn't target the grass roots; it targeted the best and the brightest. It worked almost entirely at the top. Its clientele of choice were academic and policy elites—the highly educated and the well-connected. Ford believed that if you strengthened academic, intellectual, and government leaders, and connected them to the work of experts worldwide, the result would be better policy, faster economic growth, and more social progress. So it concentrated on improving graduate training, research, and policy analysis in fields related to social and economic development. It saw elites as being key to helping the poor. They, it calculated, would get you the most bang for your buck. Your job was to help elites do better work.

That was quite a combination, and it thrust you into an exclusive world. You dealt routinely with first-rate academics, policy experts, opinion leaders, intellectuals, and department deans, and the occasional university president, minister, or politician. It was your job to establish good working relationships with people like that. And because you might have a say in whether some of them got funding, you became, overnight, someone to be reckoned with. That's uncommon for a young professional just starting out. Most toil long and hard before they go shoulder-to-shoulder with top people and get anything resembling real power. We got both of those right away. It made working for Ford special.

Giving away money is great, of course. It makes you feel important. People want to meet you. They return your calls. They invite you. They ask your opinion. You feel almost like royalty. You've been anointed with an extraordinary quality—the capacity to dish out money. That gives you an attractive, golden glow. You're somebody. Part of the orientation Ford colleagues traditionally gave new staff was: "Welcome to the Ford Foundation. You've just had your last sincere compliment and your last bad lunch." They meant it only partly in jest.

I don't mean that negatively or cynically. It's just a fact. The people we dealt with were, by and large, good, serious, and professional. They were responding to a stark reality: You had something they needed and they were trying to figure out how to get it. You and I might respond the same way. We probably have. The important thing was to recognize what was going on and not have any illusions about your somehow being special. You'd been invited to participate in a serious and complicated dance. You needed to choose your partners and learn the steps.

What were they? Figuring that out took a couple of years and came mostly from my new colleagues in Santiago and Lima. What's clear is that it isn't hard to give away money. What's hard is to do it well. And to figure out what "well" means. Neither is obvious or easy. As a beginner, you can only hope that you've landed in an institution that takes these questions seriously, has come up with some thoughtful answers, and recruits people who will criticize and improve on whatever is considered best practice. And be good mentors. Fortunately, I landed in that kind of institution.

Formally, Ford didn't do much to orient new recruits (except for the standard stuff in New York—there were forms to fill out and people to meet). After that they tossed you into the water and expected you to swim. If you didn't, well, maybe you weren't cut out for this. Ford, after all, wasn't for sissies. A lot, therefore, depended on your new colleagues in the field office. They were the ones who would show you the ropes. Or try. The process was largely informal, but remarkably intense. I got my first and only lesson in how to write grant evaluations from Peter Hakim over beer in a bar in Buenos Aires. And it helped. Other colleagues told me what they thought when I asked, or when the spirit moved them. The most important message it seemed to me was that our work was serious and our standards high, and that I needed to meet them. I'd better not screw up.

That was fine with me. None of the casualness about learning how to do the job seemed like a problem. If anything I preferred it. I had great colleagues who would help if asked, and I was used to figuring things out. What I wanted was a chance to try, and to find out whether I was good enough.

We started, of course, with the Foundation's program guidelines, which were usually pretty good. They set goals and established boundaries. You could see what to aim for; what was in and what was out. And you could look at grants that others had made, and see what they were like. I was amazed to discover that a copy of the RGA (Request for Grant Action—a brief, highly summarized document describing grants submitted to the president for approval) for every single grant that Ford made anywhere in the world—automatically came to my inbox (as it did for every other program staff member in every other office). I could see what my colleagues had proposed, the arguments they'd made, the objectives they'd set, and the activities they'd funded. I got, in just a few pages, a snapshot of what Ford was doing worldwide, along with a sense of its modus operandi, values and standards. That was helpful.

After that it was talk to colleagues, take some steps and see how you did. My new boss in Santiago, Peter Bell, kindly started me out with purely routine assignments—responding to simple inquiries, evaluating existing grants, and reporting on changes in the universities—just right for a newbie trying to get his sea legs. I met grantees and began learning how to deal with them. I saw how grants had been structured, and how they'd turned out. I had to determine whether objectives had been met and figure out why. And I began to explore the environment we worked in by documenting how Chile's military dictatorship was trying to reshape higher education. It was low-risk/high-reward, at least for me. Step one in learning the ropes.

Here I want to stop and say a bit about my first boss, Peter Bell. Peter was a great example of the extraordinary people working at the Ford Foundation when I joined. He was what, in my most idealistic moments, I expected from the elite: smart, well-educated, principled, and serious. He was also the product of a world very different from mine—a Massachusetts yankee with Jewish roots (his father, the son of a Jewish immigrant from Poland, had gone to Yale and then started an outerwear manufacturing business with his brother—and married a WASP from western Massachusetts). Peter had degrees from Yale and Princeton. He'd done volunteer work in the Ivory Coast, and had been an intern in the U.S. Department of Defense. He'd gotten his start at Ford's office in Brazil and was now director ("representative" was the title we used) of Ford's office in Chile. He spoke well and wrote well. He was a rising star.

And I was not. I was just starting out. I wanted desperately to understand the mysterious world of international development I'd gotten myself into but knew little about, and he seemed so sure of himself in. That and the East Coast Ivy League establishment something or other—I couldn't even describe it—that he seemed to represent. Peter had the keys to that stuff. I didn't. And he was willing—determined might have been the more appropriate word—to pass on at least some of it. So I watched and listened. It was a good match. The fact that someone like him was my boss was an amazing stroke of luck. This was what I'd signed up for.

Peter Bell was also straitlaced. He may have been the most responsible, careful, ethical, and professional person I've ever met. And he was that way pretty much all the time. He seemed to embody the Puritan tradition I'd read about in college—maybe that was it. Or maybe it was just his family. I don't know. But the message he sent was that we were placed on this earth to do important work and needed to keep that fact front and center, always. Frivolity wasn't anywhere on his list. (Peter's wife, Karen, organized a 50th birthday party for him and invited each of the guests to speak to his "frivolous side"—a nice spoof.) He was serious. You couldn't imagine Peter Bell telling a joke.

Most striking was that I always felt I had to be at my best whenever I was in Peter's presence. There was something mesmerizing about him. He seemed to be watching. I worried about what he might see. So whenever we were together, and that included social occasions, I automatically shifted gears, thinking twice before speaking so as to make sure that whatever I said was responsible and well-considered. I didn't want him to find me wanting.

That didn't bother me. I was serious too, although nowhere near his level. It was probably the Boy Scout meeting the Puritan. I knew about hard work and high standards. I wanted to become a first-rate professional. This was what the Ford Foundation was like. It came with the territory. And Peter was not only splendidly professional, but also positive, decent, and scrupulous. He just didn't fool around much. So it was OK. At least for me.

Peter and I worked together for less than a year but established a relationship that lasted until his death, four decades later. He may have been my most important mentor. Certainly he was my first. And I kept learning even after we stopped working together. He cast some kind of a spell that I liked. We stayed in touch.

I particularly remember an incident several years later when Peter was president of the Inter-American Foundation in Washington and I'd just started working at Ford/New York. He'd been appointed during the Carter administration, but Ronald Reagan had just become president. I was meeting with someone at the White House who suddenly asked whether I knew anything about the Inter-American Foundation because he'd been sounded out about becoming president. That was news. I went straight from that meeting to the nearest OEOB pay phone (no cell phones back then) to tell Peter the knives were out. They sacked him not long after.

That left Peter at loose ends (at the Carnegie Endowment for International Peace in Washington—not a bad place to land) and I was able to hire him to do some consulting for us (Ford) in Chile. The most memorable part of that visit was having drinks with Ambassador Harry Barnes on the patio behind his house ("residence" in diplomat-speak) and discussing whether Chile might return to democracy any time soon. Harry would later play a small but important role in that return.

I also remember our breakfasts at the Yale Club later on when Peter was president of the Clark Foundation in New York. We seldom had an agenda. Mostly it was about catching up. Peter often reacted differently to ideas than I did, so I got a lot out of hearing his perspective. Plus it was fun. And he was the only person who ever invited me to breakfast at the Yale Club.

I always thought that Peter Bell should have become president of the Ford Foundation.

Shortly before Peter died, I sent him an email reflecting on our friendship, which his wife, Karen, read to him in his hospital bed. I mentioned some of our encounters, and thanked him. By expecting so much, he got me to raise my game year after year (or at least to try). Later Karen told me that he sometimes affected her the same way.

That's my discourse—appreciative and affectionate—on Peter Bell. Now let's get back to what it was like working for the Ford Foundation back then and there.

A couple of things became immediately clear. One of the most striking—and surprising—had to do with writing. Writing was a big deal. Just about everyone in our office, and in the Latin American program more generally, wrote well. Not just well, but exquisitely. There was, back then, a self-assured, eloquent, knowledgeable smoothness about the Ford writing style that communicated not just a command of the facts, but also grace and aplomb. It assured you that these were people who knew what they were talking about, and wanted nothing more than to help you understand it. Often, your gut reaction when you read their memos was to thank them for setting you straight. It was gorgeous.

I loved it. I'd always cared about writing and now was confronted with some of the best I'd ever seen. And I was expected to write like that. I decided that everything I wrote, even the shortest, most routine memo, would meet the standards of my new colleagues. So I read what they wrote with great care and tried systematically to imitate their style. My chief model early on was Peter Bell, in part because he was my boss but also because he wrote so well, and his style epitomized what I thought Ford was all about. During those first few months I often began writing tasks by asking myself how Peter might write about a similar topic. I'd reread a paragraph or two of his to get me going—like priming a pump. It wasn't about emulating his positions on things; I had no problem with taking positions that were different from Peter's. It was about channeling his reasoning, standards, and style. Reading Peter's prose reminded me that I had to write well, and what writing well looked like. It got my attention and pointed me in the right direction. That was, I think, when I first realized that you learn to write by reading great writers.

Peter wasn't my only model, of course. The writing of my other colleagues in Santiago, particularly Nita Manitzas and Peter Hakim, also inspired me. And the people we dealt with routinely in New York—Bill Carmichael, the director for Latin America, and Kal Silvert, the social science advisor—wrote beautifully. When you read their memos and then looked at yours, you knew you had to do better. Otherwise you'd lose face. Good writing was essential at Ford—a form of jousting. If you couldn't do it, you probably didn't have the right stuff.

That started what for me has become a lifelong passion. Writing well is like learning to play the violin, or play chess, or ski. You take lessons. You practice. You polish. It's slow. It never really ends. And often it takes on a life of its own. But it's worth every minute, quite apart from any impact it might have on the rest of the world. I'm reminded of Steve Jobs' insistence on making things as beautiful as possible even if they were inside the box where no one would see them. Writing well is a form of grace. Its value is inherent. That's why you do it.

Another thing that became clear right away was that you had to figure out how to relate to elites. At Ford we didn't start at the bottom. We were supposed to identify the top people and help them make good things happen. Our starting point was always the director, or the dean, or the rector, or the minister, or the country's leading expert, or the head of this or that. Most were intellectual or academic elites, but some were political (in Chile the line between academics and politicians was particularly blurry) and a few were religious. They were our counterparts—the people we had to engage, understand, learn from, impress, and sometimes negotiate with. Dealing with them successfully was fundamental to the job. We had to learn how to do it.

This, of course, was new to me, and didn't come naturally. Growing up in Dimondale and Eaton Rapids, I'd had no contact with elites. That changed a bit at Michigan State, Duke, and the University of Chicago, where I began sitting at the feet of giants, and mixing with people who expected to run things. But still, when it came to knowing how behave with elites, I was essentially in diapers.

One of the first things I realized was that I had to get over a psychological hump. Dealing with elites wasn't just about knowing the moves; you had to feel you belonged. That may be almost automatic for kids who grow up in privilege. They come from elite families, go to elite schools, hang out with elite friends, and expect to operate at elite levels. It's normal. Of course they belong.

But for kids who grow up in less exalted circumstances, which is most of us, dealing with elites can be intimidating. You look around and realize you're in unfamiliar territory. No one told you this was coming. You have no experience with university presidents, government ministers, or the Cardinal Archbishop of Santiago. All the stuff that was second nature to Winston Churchill because he grew up with it is new to you. You've never been there. You suspect there are unwritten rules no one's told you about. You worry they'll notice you're nothing special. That maybe you're trespassing. You're not sure this land is your land. It's an adjustment.

Here, the prestige, authority, and staff of the Ford Foundation were a great help. Ford was indisputably an elite institution and had given me its seal of approval. I was on the team. And Ford didn't hire just anybody, so I must be pretty good. My colleagues in the field office were first-rate, and assumed I was too. I watched them in action; they took me by the hand and showed me what to do. It was a tutorial.

And—let's be honest—Ford's money helped. It got you in the door and gave you something to talk about. You had something everybody wanted. You might be a complete unknown but you'd still get a chance—at least for a while—because of the dollar sign that was blinking cheerfully on your forehead. At some level, you were the kid with the ball. Having money to give away is a great equalizer.

Of course, adjusting successfully to the world of elites depends in part on your motivation. There I was in pretty good shape because—for reasons I've mentioned but can't really explain—I'd long felt I should work with top people. But that's seldom enough. What Ford did was set me up for success with elites. It got me into the country club, gave me some golf clubs, arranged for lessons, and teed up the ball. All I had to do was hit it in the fairway. I was happy to try.

Two aspects of working with elites—at least back there and then with the Ford Foundation—stand out.

First, working with elites tends to rub off on you. You become something of an elite yourself. This is close to automatic. Elites are your clients—the people you talk to most. They and you have roughly the same levels of education, sometimes at the same elite schools, so you're at least a candidate for membership in the same elite circles. You meet. You talk. You get on a first-name basis. You see them at seminars, receptions, and dinner parties. You get to know them. They get to know you. Some you end up funding. Others you simply stay in touch with, making clear you value their knowledge and opinions. But you're on the inside. First and foremost, you're a potential source of money. And because you represent the Ford Foundation, you may also provide prestige, a stamp of approval, and valuable international contacts. The bottom line is you've got something elites want.

Plus, all that exposure gives you the opportunity at least to become more than a funder.

You may impress a few with your knowledge and judgment and develop deeper professional relationships that last for decades. Some may even become friends. This happens more often than you might expect. And it sets you more firmly into the elite network.

What's notable is that you start to get comfortable. You begin to understand the world of elites—their values, concerns, strengths, and weaknesses. You learn to speak their language and to navigate their terrain. You are in fact part of their terrain. It's where you do business. You get socialized. You begin to identify. You belong.

This is at least a little seductive. Working for a large foundation connects you to power and gives you entrée into exclusive circles. You begin to take for granted that the dean or the rector or the minister or the ambassador will return your call, give you an appointment, and maybe even invite you to lunch. It seems normal. You guys (it was mostly guys back then) were playing on the same field. So of course you needed to talk. One example: I regularly accompanied my boss for lunch with Cardinal Archbishop Raúl Silva Henríquez at his residence in Santiago. The conversation was frank and occasionally funny. He mixed the pisco sours himself—and always offered seconds. Followed by good food and wine. It was useful, but it was also fun. Years later I hosted a lunch for him at Ford's headquarters in New York and made sure to have several bottles of good Chilean wine on hand. It's pretty easy to get hooked on that kind of thing. Rubbing shoulders with the stars is attractive; you'd just as soon keep doing it.

This is big. Very few of us get into any kind of elite network. Because of Ford, you've done it. You're on a first-name basis with people who are, or will become, distinguished scholars, deans, ministers, senators, and ambassadors. Some may run for president; a few might even win. You may enjoy being in their company or not. You may wish to remain in those circles, or not. But working at Ford—back then at least—set you up. You got your foot in the door and had a shot at making something of it should you wish to do so. That's a major privilege.

And if you're one of those people who didn't grow up in elite circumstances, the most important benefit may be psychological. No longer is the elite world some distant, alien community you've had no contact with. Now you're there. It's a mountain you've climbed. You know the place. It's yours. That's no small achievement. It's also a privilege.

The second aspect of working with elites that stands out—at least while working for Ford back there and then—is very different. It has to do with Ford's money. It turns out that money is a double-edged sword. It gets you into elite networks and enables you to have an impact—which is great. But it can become a crutch—which is not. Recognizing and adjusting for these contrasting aspects of giving away money is key, not only for doing good work but also for your personal development.

Money is a crutch primarily because it's so attractive to so many people that it's enough to justify your existence. You don't need to bring much more to the table. Keep in mind that people don't knock on Ford's door looking for you (notwithstanding your unquestionable talent and charm). They're looking for money. You are a means to an end. It's an important end, and that makes you an important means. But you're still a means. The people you fund won't demand that you have exceptional intelligence, knowledge, charisma, or judgment. They'd like that, of course, but they're not going to demand it. All you really have to do is come up with the money. That's your ticket.

Initially, that's fine. You're happy to be there. The people are great, often inspiring. You're learning a lot. And you're making an important contribution.

But the problem is that it's too easy. If money is all it takes, what happens to excellence? Who's going to maintain standards? There aren't, after all, many external incentives in philanthropy. You don't have to make a profit. There's little or no competition, and not much oversight. Your clients generally have no one else to turn to. The world is not checking to see whether you're doing good work. No one, in fact, pays much attention to foundations. So most of the time you don't have to please anyone except your boss and your board of directors. In philanthropy, excellence is always desired and often assumed, but ultimately voluntary. You're relatively free to do as you see fit.

So how do you go beyond practicing mere philanthropy to practicing smart, principled, and effective philanthropy? There's no fail-safe recipe, but this is where institutions and colleagues matter. They set and enforce standards—hopefully high standards—in an arena where money and good intentions rule, and standards are vague and often discretionary. The most reliable path to becoming a good philanthropist is to work in a place that demands excellence, sets high standards, and hires people dedicated to both. And encourages them to argue about what all that means. That still doesn't guarantee you'll produce great work, but it increases your chances.

Fortunately, I got into that kind of institution. Ford's then-president, McGeorge Bundy, was determined to let "large and constructive forces" loose in society. He insisted on excellence, and hired people he thought shared his commitment and met his standards. The result was a potent mixture of talent, aspiration, debate, and experiment, leavened with real money. Smart people were tackling tough problems. I'd been recruited to help.

What I found most striking was that the bar was high. From the time I arrived I was surrounded by people who were smarter than I was and knew far more than I about what was going on. The New York staff we dealt with most—Vice President Dave Bell, Latin America Directors Bill Carmichael and Jim Himes, and Social Science Advisor Kal Silvert— were glittering stars in the Ford firmament, offering (well, most of the time) authority, wisdom, eloquence. and inspiration. I couldn't imagine producing at their level, but that was fine. Just being in their orbit was enough, and a privilege. (The only downside was that I didn't want them to see me screw up, so I was real careful what I said when they were around.)

My colleagues, first in Ford's Santiago office, and the following year in Lima, were formidable as well, but the dynamics were different. You got to know them better, learned more and had more fun. They were smart and strong, so you had to be at your best. You debated principles, strategy and what it all meant. You agreed and disagreed. Occasionally you fought. But you formed friendships that lasted decades. Dealing with that talented and contentious group of colleagues early in my career established standards and expectations I still have today. It put me on a good path. I wouldn't have missed it for anything.

But the process was slow. Excellence was out of reach for me at the beginning. The best I could hope for was to hold my own. Then learn, which took time and depended heavily on being blessed with good teachers—and which, thankfully, I was. I made my share of rookie mistakes. Early on, for example, after being given responsibility for the economics portfolio in Chile, I met with the dean of the department of economics at the Catholic University and assured him that we would renew our funding for their work. (It was in our budget projections, after all). We wouldn't, of course. And soon I had to tell him that, which made me feel foolish and untrustworthy. Obviously I didn't know what I was doing. Later Nita Manitzas and I put together a brand-new grant—the first I'd watched developed from start to finish. But she did almost all the work, including drafting the RGA (Request for Grant Action), which set out, in lucid prose, what we proposed doing and why it absolutely had to be done. When finally, much later, I worked up a new grant all by myself, it was like flying solo for the first time. Mostly, though, I watched and learned. During my first two years at the Ford Foundation I never really felt like I knew what I was doing. I relied, appropriately but more than I like to admit, on the knowledge and judgment of others. It was an apprenticeship.

The bottom line, then, is that Ford's money can get you into elite networks but isn't enough to guarantee elite performance. It may even get in the way. To be excellent you need standards and pressure to meet them. Neither comes attached to money. You're most likely to get them from colleagues, especially if you're just starting out. There's no substitute for having to contend with people who know more and reach higher than you do. If you can get into an institution that offers that combination, do it, even if you have to take a lower salary. It's an investment. You'll learn and you'll grow. Smart, demanding colleagues are the ultimate fringe benefit.

The other important aspect of Ford's money, of course, was that it paid your salary. My starting salary was $15,000 a year, which was nothing special, but way above the meager graduate student stipend I'd lived on for so long—and nearly double the instructor's salary I'd had during my final year at Chicago. Plus because I was posted abroad I got a free place to live (they told me how much rent they'd pay; I got to choose the house), free use of a car (I paid for gas), and was, by living outside the United States, exempt from most income taxes (thanks to U.S. government policy). Oh, and I had an expense account. I could take people out to lunch. So suddenly I was rich, or at least I felt rich. I no longer spent every penny I made. It added to my sense of having hit some kind of jackpot when I got hired by Ford. I remember thinking that if someone offered to pay me this much, adjusted for inflation, for the rest of my working life, I'd take it.

It's worth saying something more generally about the economic side of working for the Ford Foundation. Did we make out like bandits or not? The answer, I suppose, is that it depends on your expectations. If you'd gotten an MBA and were seeking a career in the world of business, you'd probably turn up your nose at what Ford offered. Business offered more. But if, like me, you'd gotten a PhD and your alternative was an academic or a government job, and you wanted a clear shot at making the world a better place, the salary was pretty good. It was comparable, perhaps, to the salary of a university professor (except we didn't get summers off). And living abroad was a big plus because of all those freebies. You could save a lot of what you earned. It was comfortable. But it was not lavish.

We did not, for example, have a guaranteed pension. Ford offered a "defined-contribution" retirement plan. You put money each month into a 401(k) account that you owned and, within limits, decided how to invest. Ford matched part of what you put in. When you retired, you'd draw on whatever was there.

Nor did we have job security. It wasn't like working for the government or a university or maybe the World Bank, where once you were in you could probably stay until you retired. At Ford, the assumption was always that you were going to move on. No one at what was called the program level got tenure—at least not that I ever heard of. Maybe they'd extend your contract a few years, and then later maybe a few years more, but there was always an end date. I'd been hired on a two-year contract, extendible for a third year by mutual consent. That was standard. Soon they offered to extend my contract to six years total, the last of which would be a sabbatical at a university of my choice. That was unexpect-edly generous, and driven I think almost entirely by the unexpected risk, uncertainty, and travel associated with my job. They'd have had a hard time finding, at least in the short term, an acceptable replacement. So they figured they'd better nail me down for a few years. Whatever they thought of my performance, I was clearly in the right place at the right time. As it turned out, I managed to stay for seventeen years. But that first three-plus-three contract was the longest I ever had. That was fine with me.

⋟

Here I need to step back (again) and reflect on what I'm writing. What's striking is how much I have to say about the Ford Foundation. It was, of course, the most important part of my career so maybe I shouldn't be surprised that there's a lot—and that there's more to come. I'll try not to bore you.

But let's remember that a big part of what I'm trying to do is write well. Or at least better—much better—than I've written in the past. I want my writing to be beautiful, to have zing, or at least to make people want to keep reading. That's what got me started. So every once in a while, I need to stop and look at my writing rather than at my life. How's that going?

Hmmm. Slow as hell, I have to admit.

I simply haven't learned to write fast. The experts all tell you to write fast and fix later. Just push through and say what comes to mind. You'll get warm, vital stuff out there wriggling on the table where you can see it and decide whether it's a keeper. Then you fix what needs fixing. Writing is bad until it's good.

I realize that's sound advice. Moving forward uncritically helps tap your subconscious (another name, I assume, for your muse), which is where the good stuff lies sleeping. You need to wake it up and drag it out.

But doing that is hard. When I signed up for the religion of writing I somehow got assigned to the Church of the Precious Word—which is led by a jealous God who demands that members write only what's perfect. And beautiful. And, somehow, writerly. It's a narrow path that only a few can follow (Matthew 7:13-14 provides a sense of this: "small is the gate and narrow the road"). It requires full devotion.

So I'm acutely aware of what's wrong with what I write. I go over my stuff five times, trying out four verbs and six adjectives. Then I change it again. I've spent half a day writing one paragraph. And still it's not right. This is the cross I bear. It's hard. I worry, in fact, that the problem isn't just my prose, but me.

Fortunately, having been raised Lutheran I can deal with this stuff.

And—hallelujah—the fact is that once I finally pronounce something written, I like it. I'm happy—almost delighted with the final product. My muse has weighed in. The bells have rung. The pain and loathing have faded. This is what I was after. It's pretty good.

The sad truth is that I almost like the slow, painstaking approach I seem stuck with. The payoff—getting it right—feels great and I'm willing to work hard to make that happen. I'm getting what I signed up for, even though I had no idea it would be like this. Writing well is worth it.

And I'm getting better. Now I write faster (although I still can't just let it rip). I also get stuck less. I see more quickly whether the problem is that I've chosen the wrong topic, don't know enough about it, haven't figured out what's worth saying, or have muddled my train of thought.

I've also learned to keep it simple, concentrate on verbs, distrust adjectives, and avoid adverbs (mostly). And I'm developing an ear for good prose—something that seems more aesthetic than rational. I listen to what I've written. Does it sound good? Have some rhythm? Sing? Leap off the page, even? I'm looking for grace in words.

And, thanks to William Safire, I avoid clichés like the plague.

So it's not like I'm not making progress. It just takes forever. I can only hope that, as Aesop promised, the turtle ultimately beats the hare. But if I had to earn a living writing I'd probably be broke.

XI

FORD/CHILE

WHAT WE DID

Now LET'S MOVE on to what we actually did during my first five years with the Ford Foundation—which, I promise, was surprising and interesting.

Chile first. Once Ford decided, in early 1974, to downsize and downgrade the Santiago field office, things changed fast. Several program staffers had already left. We quickly laid off much of the local staff and moved to smaller quarters—a house we'd converted into an office. The director, Peter Bell, and deputy director, Peter Hakim, both left mid-year and went to New York. Dick Dye, a senior official in Ford's New York office, was appointed to run the program from there. Nita Manitzas moved, like me, to Lima and continued to direct the social science portfolio. Gary Horlick, a recent Yale Law School graduate who'd arrived in Santiago just before I had, was appointed deputy director of the Santiago office, but operating out of Ford's office in Bogotá, Colombia. I was based in Lima but had responsibility for both the education and the economics portfolios in the Chile office. So we became a staff of four, two of whom had been with the Foundation for less than a year, living in three different countries, none of them Chile, and expected to fly in and out. And it wasn't clear where, if anywhere, the program was going.

Moreover, the Santiago office also oversaw a small office and program in Buenos Aires, the remnant of a full-scale operation that had been downsized several years earlier when Ford decided that Argentina was rich enough to get along without it. That office still had a program and a small local staff that needed tending, adding a layer of time, travel and thought to our responsibilities.

Plus I had, as I mentioned, been given the education portfolio in Peru, which had previously been managed by a full-time professional—Bob Drysdale. So now I had three programs to manage in two offices, with two bosses, two sets of colleagues and responsibilities in three countries. I lived officially in an apartment in Lima but stayed just as often in a guest house we'd established in Santiago. And regularly in the Gran Hotel Dorá in Buenos Aires. I was on airplanes much of the time and occasionally woke up in the middle of the night not sure what country I was in. All this after slightly more than six months on the job.

A dream come true, right? I'd wanted an international career and now I had one. In spades. But I never expected anything so sprawling, strange, and unpredictable. The job in Peru was fairly straightforward, but in Chile it wasn't clear what we should do. Or what might come next. Or whether I could handle it. It was a little like being asked to ski down difficult mountain terrain for the first time and in a snowstorm. Uncertain for sure; maybe a little dangerous.

The dangerous part had to do with the fact that we were supporting social scientists who didn't like the government, in a country whose government didn't like social scientists. That exposes you, in a repressive military dictatorship, to some level of risk. Bad things were happening. People were disappearing. There was torture. You had to wonder what would happen if the government decided it didn't like you. We assumed, for example, that the Chilean intelligence services had tapped our phones and were monitoring our calls. And we suspected that they'd searched our office. My colleague, Nita Manitzas, reported one morning that some Tampax she kept in a desk drawer had been removed from its packaging, slit open and left lying there. That seemed to us like a pretty clear message. We worried.

We were especially nervous about discussing what we were doing on the phone with colleagues in New York. They'd never had their phones tapped, of course, so had a hard time realizing that ours might be, and how touchy we might be about it. They sometimes asked questions we didn't want to answer, at least not on the phone from Chile. More than once, I had to cut off higher-ups in New York, saying I'd be glad to answer their questions and discuss their concerns once I was back in Lima, but not there and then, sorry. We operated in an atmosphere of menace that we couldn't ignore.

We also watched, often with alarm, what was happening to people we knew, and to people they knew. Early on, for example, I visited one of our grantees in jail. He was a Jesuit priest (Patricio "Pato" Cariola), a decent, intelligent, mild-mannered fellow with a master's degree from Harvard, a big smile and, I soon realized, a backbone of steel. Everybody loved Pato. He ran an education research center that we funded (the Center for Educational Research and Development—CIDE). He was not, so far as any of us could see, politically active, or even politically committed. He was simply a Jesuit working, like so many, in education. But a year or two after the coup the head of a clandestine extreme left party (the Revolutionary Left Movement—MIR), Andrés Pascal Allende, who was on the verge of being captured by the military, asked several priests to help get him and his wife into an embassy where they'd be safe. Since the alternative was probably death (a year earlier the military had killed his predecessor in his home), Pato and his fellow priests felt they couldn't say no. They agreed to meet him and his wife on the street, took his automatic rifle and ammunition, and somehow got both of them into the Costa Rican Embassy. I never knew how they managed to do that. Then they turned the weapons over, and themselves in, to the government and were jailed.

So I went to visit him. He was being held in the "white collar" section of the Santiago jail—which meant better accommodations and better treatment. He was a little sheepish about what had happened. "What could I do?" he said. His jailers had been almost deferential, since he was a Jesuit and wore a clerical collar. The Church, of course, expressed its concern and asked that he be released. He was, fairly soon, and that was the end of it. But he'd made a remarkable moral decision, the kind people had to face all too often back then. Not many of us has ever had an experience like that, or would have responded so courageously. For me it was one more bizarre episode in what had become an uncommon job. I was not surprised. And it was the only time I ever visited anyone in jail.

I wasn't particularly bothered by these strange working conditions—except for the travel, which left me feeling disoriented. I realized right away that I needed a place of my own to come home to, where I could relax, recharge, and have a personal life. That was my ballast. My relative nonchalance about the rest was due mostly to being young, single, and naive. I'd never seen any of this stuff before and had no framework to fit it into. Life, I figured, was like that. You dealt with what came your way, even if it wasn't what you'd expected. I was, after all, getting my chance. I liked the people. It was interesting. And I was dealing with some of Latin America's leading social scientists, which was a privilege. So yes, it was still a dream come true. I'd hang in there. But I couldn't imagine how it would turn out.

Pato Cariola and I, by the way, became good friends. A year or two later we hiked well up the 14,000 foot *Tinguiririca* Volcano, where he may have saved my life. This was a multi-day trip organized by his brother and some buddies (two of whom were German-Chileans) complete with *arrieros* (mule-drivers) who packed food and drink in wooden boxes on the backs of their mules, and brought along a couple of saddled mules that we took turns riding when the trails weren't steep. The Tinguiririca Volcano, of course, had been made famous by Piers Paul Read's book, *Alive*, which documented the 1972 crash, on its western side during the winter, of a plane carrying a Uruguayan rugby team, and their struggle in the Andean snow over the next couple of months, where they'd survived by eating the flesh of their dead comrades. Eventually two of them found a way out, and summoned help for the rest. I'd heard the story and read the book. It turned out we were going up the same trail they'd come down. There was nothing to see, because the government had obliterated the crash site with explosives so it wouldn't become a macabre tourist attraction. But one of the *arrieros* told me his father had been the first to make contact with the two survivors who'd hiked out, and helped get the rest back to civilization, making me feel I had a direct link to that unspeakable and unimaginable drama.

We worked our way up beautiful mountain terrain over several days. Since we'd started well up the mountain, where the Rio Azufre enters the Rio Tinguiririca, the only trees we saw were ancient gnarled *maiténes*, known for their extremely slow growth. The rest was all meadows, streams, rocks and gravel, bending upward toward the majestic, snow-covered volcano waiting in front of us. Initially we couldn't see the volcano at all because it was hidden behind a couple of 11,000-plus foot peaks, San Hilario and El Brujo—also majestic and snow-covered. But as we worked our way higher, Tinguiririca began, little by little, to reveal her charms.

I confess to obsessing about mountains. I fall in love with anything over 5000 feet tall, and Tinguiririca was no exception. That breathtaking volcano was a sensuous woman inviting me to come closer and sample her delights. So much so that a week or so after the climb I began writing an article for a magazine on Andean exploits that was published in Lima, and whose editor I knew. I never finished it but still have the draft, and it's full of imagery that, while borderline sophomoric and possibly sexist, was certainly inspired. Some examples: "She was appropriately wide at the bottom and curved up to a rounded, snow-covered cone." "She had rounded, boulder-strewn flanks nestled firmly among the surrounding peaks, and snowy shoulders suggesting hidden treats for those able to find the key." "…expansive, earthy and hinting at unimaginable experiences"…"a Fellini fat lady basking in the summer sun." You get the drift. I was into it. Any psychotherapist worth his or her salt would have a great time analyzing the titillating article about big sexy women that I started writing but never finished.

Anyway, it was as pleasant an Andean hike as you could ask for. The terrain was relatively easy, and the sun was bright. Occasionally we rode one of the mules, but mostly we walked. There were hot springs which, stripped down to shorts, we jumped into a couple of times. And there were huge condors riding the swirling currents of wind above us.

A striking feature at that altitude were the large flocks of a noisy Andean parrot called the *loro tricahue* that lived high in cliffside nests. Each morning groups of six or eight— dark blue, about 14 inches in length—streaked down the valley, their cries echoing off the mountain-sides. Late in the afternoon they came racing back (exhausted by a long day of squawking, I presume). We hiked for nearly an hour up to their nesting site at sunset on our first day. As we worked our way along a sandy ledge just below their nests, hundreds rose in a feathery cloud that swirled and squawked above us in the darkening sky. The effect, with a fat, full moon rising in the background, was worthy of Hitchcock.

Each evening we stopped to camp and eat the food the *arrieros* prepared over a campfire, and of course drink the wine and pisco. One of my memories of those meals was the goat meat they'd brought, rubbed with salt and grilled over the fire. Hot, crisp, juicy, and consumed with plenty of red wine, it tasted great. Another memory was of getting up early the first morning, ready for breakfast, to find one of the *arrieros* tending a large soot-blackened kettle over the fire. "What's that?" I said. "Goat's head soup" he answered. I could think of nothing more to say and moved on. Breakfast would wait.

On the second day I struck out ahead of the group, took a wrong turn and managed almost to get lost. I did this on pure enthusiasm. I get excited when I'm in the mountains, especially on warm sunny days, and can't resist following my nose. This time I missed a crucial turnoff and headed straight up the valley into a horseshoe-shaped dead-end, when instead I should have traversed a steep side trail that led out of that valley and into the valley above.

The upside was my closest encounter with condors ever. Because condors live high in cliffside nests and spend most of their time floating lazily on updrafts, climbers seldom get close to them. One exception, it turns out, is to work your way up a rapidly ascending valley that has condors living at the top. As the valley rises, the distance between its floor and the clifftops decreases, bringing you closer and closer to the condors' front door. That put me maybe a few hundred feet below half a dozen condors soaring gracefully overhead, followed by a youngster about half their size practicing his moves. It was a stately mountain spectacle normally witnessed only by other condors, eagles and the occasional mountain goat. I was a privileged intruder, and watched until they glided off.

Then, noticing that my colleagues hadn't shown up behind me, I decided to wait. There was a waterfall nearby—more a drip than a fall, really. Water was emerging far above over broad, uneven stretches of rock and breaking into droplets as it went over the edges rather than hanging together in a stream. I stripped off my pack, boots, and shorts, and stepped naked into the falling mist. It was cold, soft, and good. Especially in the hot sun. While drying off on the green grass nearby I heard a shout and saw two of my comrades well down the valley, on muleback, pointing to the cliffside where the rest of the group was snaking its way up the trail I had completely missed. I dressed, retraced my steps and got back on track. I'd be the last one into camp. But that was fine. I was delighted. Following my nose had paid off.

I don't think we ever really got to the top. 14,000 feet is high. You'd probably feel the altitude, and I didn't. Since Tinguirrica has seven cones, it's more likely we climbed one of the lower ones. I have no idea how high that would have been, but it was high enough. By day three, the trail got steeper. There was snow. *Fumaroles* appeared. The air seemed alive with smoke and steam, as it probably should atop an active (or near-active) volcano. I marched steadily upwards, feeling very much the seasoned mountaineer. I was proud I could handle this stuff. Then a little kid appeared at my side bounding along in flip-flops cut from the treads of old truck tires. Maybe twelve years old, he was probably the son of one of the *arrieros*, on a summertime lark and having a great time. I felt a little sheepish, with my French climbing boots, crampons, and *piolet*. Perhaps the terrain wasn't as tough as I thought. But still, it was a beautiful day, and I was enjoying myself. So more power to him. He may even have taught me something, although I'd have to think a bit to figure out exactly what it was. Meanwhile I'd stick with my fancy gear.

We got to the top of the cone, celebrated, and looked inside. The volcano had been quiet for nearly sixty years, so the crater was solid and snowy. There was even a field of *penitentes*—thin blades of ice pointing dramatically toward the sun. It was beautiful, of course. After much surveying of the scene and hailing of the views, we hiked back down to our camp. We'd done what climbers are supposed to do and were happy.

But back to getting my life saved. That happened on the way up, a day or two before we reached the summit, and after we'd stopped to make camp one afternoon in a green and pleasant valley. I started to mount one of the mules just for fun—probably inspired by the horseback rides I used to take with my father as a youngster. I was wearing my hiking boots, of course, which lacked the distinct heel that riding boots have to keep your foot from sliding through the stirrup. My mule took off unexpectedly, causing my foot to slide through and me to fall backwards to the ground, my left foot caught in the stirrup. Suddenly I was being dragged across the boulder-strewn terrain like a bag of rags by a mule determined to rejoin the rest of the herd grazing fifty yards or so off. I was helpless and knew it. Fortunately I was wearing a small backpack with a parka inside that cushioned my back. But nothing protected my head. It was going to strike a rock.

My great luck was that Pato was standing between me and the other mules, saw what was happening, quickly stepped forward, grabbed the mule's bridle, and stopped it dead. It was brief and it was over. I was OK. Disaster had been averted. I was shaken and thankful and told him so. I get goosebumps thinking about it.

For years afterwards each time he told the story, Pato always said that before grabbing the mule's bridle he shouted "Now Jeff, how about that Ford Foundation grant to CIDE? You'll recommend it, won't you? We need the money." (Jesuits were famous for their ability to raise money, and he was no exception.) It was droll to hear him tell it and we always laughed. But we both knew I could've been killed. He may well have saved my life.

CIDE got its grant. And it was one more step in a beautiful friendship. We got together regularly over the next couple of decades, talking politics, education, and people. Pato had a remarkable ability to combine being nice with being tough. At a minimum he made me realize the value of trying to do both. When I finally got married, Pato blessed our wedding (Myriam being Jewish and I Lutheran, he couldn't officially marry us). Not long after, he was awarded the prestigious National Prize for Education; then he died of cancer. I remember him fondly.

The other guy whose life he'd probably saved, Andrés Pascal Allende, was, the last I knew, living in Cuba and working for the government tourist agency.

Let us resume our discussion of work. How did we go about spending Ford's money in the dark and confusing conditions that characterized post-coup Chile?

Initially the only clear option we had was to go out of business. The Foundation had decided to wind down its work in Chile in the most responsible fashion, and our job was to get it done. I don't think any of us really liked that, but we saw few alternatives. Early on we thought maybe the military government would ease off on its repression, enabling us to go back to our old nation-building ways. But it didn't, so we couldn't. Repression looked to be the norm for the foreseeable future.

To be sure, in the short term we could clearly play an ameliorative role, supporting the few independent social scientists still hanging on in the universities, sending their junior colleagues abroad for graduate study, and helping others find work outside the country. There were a number of such opportunities, and we were happy to seize them. And I, optimistic by nature, thought that maybe we'd touched bottom a year or so after the coup, and that space for criticism and free expression in the universities might start growing rather than keep shrinking. I was wrong, of course. It showed my lack of experience. What I failed to understand was that the left and the right had both gone too far. The wounds were serious. Things weren't going to get better for a long time. Attractive program opportunities for Ford probably wouldn't drop to zero, but they would keep declining. Winding down the program continued to be our main option. Call it palliative care. We couldn't see a clear alternative.

That had some interesting upsides. By terminating our support for universities, we eliminated a powerful vested interest from our work. Deans and department heads stopped coming by to talk up their programs. We no longer had to respond to their pressure or set aside significant sums for their projects. Our biggest and strongest clients faded away, leaving us free. And by abandoning much of the conventional wisdom that had guided our work—because it wasn't appropriate in a repressive regime—we became willing, able, and even anxious to consider new strategies, even though we had no new strategies to consider. For better or worse, we were clearing the stage.

What was clear was that we would not support—substantively or symbolically—the military regime. And that we cared about maintaining critical, independent thought in a country whose government had become repressive and authoritarian. Beyond, it was largely fog.

One of the first new strategies to appear was human rights. We had no experience in that area. (My initial reaction was that it was an important issue but not one we knew anything about—therefore we should not work on it.) But human rights violations were dramatic and growing, and our colleagues in New York (particularly Bill Carmichael) supported seeing what we might do. We did—providing support for the Church's Vicariate of Solidarity and the Chilean Commission of Human Rights. A year or two later, after the military coup in Argentina, we began supporting human rights groups there. Human rights would become a major program area.

More generally, we looked and listened. We couldn't see a way forward, so we talked to people who might—mostly talented academics and former university officials, plus the occasional politician. These included Alejandro Foxley, who headed a highly regarded economic research center at the Catholic University, the Center for National Planning Studies (CEPLAN), that was being threatened by the new authorities, and Eduardo Boeninger, former rector of the University of Chile, and José Joaquín Brunner, who headed FLACSO/Chile. (All three would become ministers in the new democracy that emerged fifteen years hence.) And of course the Catholic Church via Cardinal Silva. Most were frustrated and pessimistic—which was appropriate. Academics not fully on board with the military regime had either been pushed out or pushed aside.

The universities were beset by a kind of creeping conformism that admitted neither criticism nor diversity. It was, according to Genaro Arriagada, one of Chile's brightest political analysts, like a neutron bomb that "saved the buildings but killed the spirit, at least in the social science area." The picture was dark.

CEPLAN was a good example. Despite producing solid research, it was under a cloud because its leaders and staff were centrist and identified with the Christian Democratic party rather than being clear supporters of the military dictatorship. CEPLAN's smart and politically astute director, Alejandro Foxley, could see which way the wind was blowing and didn't like it. He took two giant steps.

First, he enlisted the help of Rodrigo Botero, former minister of finance of Colombia and a member of the Ford Foundation's board, in setting up, in Colombia, a legal base for CEPLAN, should the group find it necessary to leave Chile. They'd have a place to land.

Second, he worked with some first-rate lawyers to establish a legal status in Chile for an independent, non-profit research organization—called the Corporation for Latin American Economic Research (CIEPLAN). This was done well under the radar of the government, which might have tried to block it had they realized what was going on. Once complete it produced a *fait accompli*: CEPLAN announced it was leaving the Catholic University, renaming itself as CIEPLAN and setting up shop as a private research center in Chile. And the Ford Foundation, which had supported CEPLAN since its establishment, and had given me responsibility for that support, approved a two-year grant enabling the repotted and rebranded CIEPLAN to get work underway.

But more generally the prospects for Ford Foundation work were not encouraging. The military dictatorship ruled with an iron fist. There was no sign of a thaw. On the other hand, the people we were talking to were highly motivated, knew the terrain and looking to test the waters. If anyone could find effective responses to the regime's severe restrictions on academic freedom, it was them. Maybe they'd figure something out. We, by contrast, knew little. Our strategy, if you can call it that, was to listen to their ideas and see whether we could help.

Slowly, things began to happen. The social scientists who'd been purged from the universities wanted to keep working but couldn't go back. Professionally they were operating in the academic wilderness, surviving on consultancies, producing what amounted to *samizdat* (i.e. underground publications by dissident groups in the communist block of Eastern and Central Europe) and hoping something would turn up. They had to find new institutions. Or else new professions. Maybe even new countries.

What to do wasn't obvious. Research in Chile had traditionally been limited to universities. There were only three private, non-university social science research centers at the time of the coup, and two of those were run by the Catholic Church. So the dissident social scientists didn't have many alternatives. But there was one positive fact: although the military government had flatly prohibited politics, it generally permitted research. That meant that displaced social scientists could remain intellectually active as long as they found a friendly institution. And funding. And kept their heads down.

That turned out to be exactly what they did. Chile's dissident social scientists began establishing private institutions in which they could continue doing academic work. And Ford, along with other foreign donors and the Catholic Church, stepped up to help. I don't think anyone saw that coming. It simply happened. And it happened in a way that seemed natural and appropriate. A network of private think tanks began to emerge, completely unconnected to the universities or the government. They had high-quality staffs and strong international contacts. They became a robust, independent, and parallel intellectual community. Fifteen years later there were nearly fifty of them, employing well over six hundred professionals, many of whom had done graduate work in Europe or the United States. They were publishing more than twenty periodical journals and had produced hundreds of books. By contrast, only some two hundred social scientists were carrying out research in

Chilean universities. Government repression had induced a sea change. Much of Chile's social science mainstream took refuge in private think tanks.

The change was brusque. Social scientists went from the relatively comfortable confines of universities to the realities of raising money from international donors. They were subjected, in the words of José Joaquin Brunner, one of Chile's leading public intellectuals, to "three Anglo-Saxon formulas: 'publish or perish,' 'no nonsense,' and 'accountability.'" Arriagada described the shift more vividly as going from the traditional university "where you spent four years producing a book, or one year producing a twenty-five-page paper," to "the most cruel free market of competition for projects...You had to have an implacable rigor to produce, because you had to fulfill obligations to the Konrad Adenauer [Foundation], to the Ford Foundation, to ECLA, to the University of whatever...." Chile's dissident social scientists found a way to survive but took on a whole new set of demands.

These new, private think tanks became the core of a new Ford Foundation strategy: to maintain critical, independent thought within a repressive regime and keep high-level social science talent in the country so it could eventually guide national policy once democracy returned. We left our old strategy—establishing strong universities and a modern social science—behind for something that better fit the realities of dictatorship. During the next fifteen years of military government, we provided startup assistance to many of the new centers, helped others make the transition away from university and government affiliations, and supported several with core or project funding. Finally we'd found a way to deploy Ford's money and continue working in the academic social sciences, without sacrificing our values.

But what was more interesting, and surprising, was that the new think tanks began to influence opposition politics. This was partly because they had talented staffs who were politically inclined. But it was also because the military government had, by outlawing politics, created a political vacuum that the think tanks could expand into. Politicians and political parties had been made illegal in one of the most politicized and politically sophisticated countries in Latin America. That generated pressure for spaces in which political topics—ideology, dialogue, strategy, and policy—could be discussed. The think tanks provided those spaces, but on their own, distinctly academic, terms. They convened and they set agendas. Politicians showed up and listened; often they talked. They had almost nowhere else to gather and discuss these issues.

What happened then, during the remainder of the military government, was that the new think tanks, staffed by these well-trained, dissident social scientists and funded by foreign donors, played a key role in Chile's politics, and in its return to democracy. The story is long, complicated and fascinating. I wrote a whole book about it (*Thinking Politics*), but here I'll just offer a summary—which you can skip over if you wish.

The new think tanks:

- provided a sanctuary for critical, independent thought during a time of official political repression;
- led a forceful critique of opposition thinking that eventually produced a democratic left and a more tolerant and flexible center;
- criticized the regime when politicians could not do so;
- provided information and analysis that were crucial to developing a realistic approach to democratic transition;
- helped opposition factions overcome their bitter divisions;
- advocated fundamental changes in transition strategy;
- imported a new campaign technology and sold it to political leaders;
- designed the successful 1988 plebiscite campaign that ensured that democracy returned sooner rather than later; and
- took up, once democracy returned in 1990, key political and policy positions in the new government.

It was a tour de force, and largely unexpected. And it was funded almost entirely by foreign donors, many of them private like Ford, and others public—largely Canadian and European government aid agencies.

The key point, though, if you're a philanthropist is that the new think tanks had a clear positive impact. And positive impact is the holy grail of philanthropy. All philanthropists seek it. Most claim it. But few can be sure they got it. Here they did. Philanthropic dollars were well spent. It took fifteen years and lots of persistence, but philanthropy made a huge positive difference in Chilean politics.

I want to make two other points. First, the Catholic Church, under the leadership of Cardinal Archbishop Raúl Silva Henríquez, played a crucial and historic role in enabling the new private think tanks to set up shop. That was noteworthy because the Church had no spiritual reason to do that. None of the new think tanks were religious in character, and almost none engaged in the good works that the Church traditionally favored. But the Cardinal was appalled by the government's repression and violations of human rights. He decided to take a stand.

The Church had a crucial comparative advantage: It could establish private institutions, hold public meetings, and publish without getting government permission. Others could not, and found it hard, if not impossible, to jump through the legal and political hoops the government had established to keep private institutions under control. So the Church decided in 1975 to establish the Academy of Christian Humanism as an institutional umbrella for academic groups cut adrift from the universities. The Academy's mission was not religious but rather to support "intellectual work, intended to promote research, development and communication of the social and humanistic sciences." It provided the legal framework that dissident social scientists needed.

We—the Ford Foundation—helped get the Academy up and running by providing seed money for an initial three-project, six-researcher program. (Cardinal Silva, in a charming example of how religious leaders seek help from on high, announced when we started grant negotiations that he'd already spoken to Ford's president, McGeorge Bundy, and had a promise of "prompt and substantial" funding.)

Over the next fifteen years of military government, the Academy became a major center of dissident debate and discussion on social issues. It grew to eight programs employing more than three hundred persons.

Ford helped fund some of these, but other foreign donors did as well. There were risks, of course, and therefore limits on what groups affiliated with the Academy could do. Political activism was out of bounds, along with attacks on Church orthodoxy. Either might endanger the Academy's survival. The operating principle for the intellectuals working under the Academy's umbrella, according to its director, Duncan Livingston, was "not so far away that you freeze; not so close that you burn." That produced an unspoken agreement in which the Church respected intellectual freedom, and the intellectuals respected Church values. It worked just fine. The Church, under the leadership of Cardinal Silva, took a risk and it paid off. It was an inspired and heroic achievement.

My other point is that, at least in the world of philanthropy, strategies sometimes come from the bottom up rather than the top down. We—Ford—didn't know, at the outset, what to do going forward in Chile. We only knew what *not* to do—collaborate in any way with a repressive regime. And we knew that we cared dearly about academic freedom, democracy and human rights. That led us to stop doing what we'd been doing—a decision that was arguably bold and made at the top (although in response to a recommendation from the bottom). But beyond that our stance was largely "Let's see if we can help." That kept us busy for a while, but it wasn't a long-term strategy. We had values, but no program.

It's worth pointing out, though, that our first glimmer of a new strategy came from noticing that Ford had, five years earlier in Brazil, helped a group of academics expelled from universities by the military dictatorship to establish an independent social science think tank (CEBRAP) that managed, despite serious repression, to become a respected center for independent research and critical thought. That was interesting. We wondered whether there were any lessons for Chile. (A key figure in CEBRAP's founding was a brilliant social scientist named Fernando Henrique Cardoso who several decades later would be elected president of Brazil, but of course we didn't know that yet.)

The strategy we eventually adopted came together over nearly two years, and was based primarily on watching, waiting and talking to talented people. They told us what they thought might work. And began trying. We came to see how and why their plans made sense. And began helping. That turned into a strategy. It was a kind of emergent order—more spontaneous than calculated. There was no clarion call from on high; no blue-ribbon committee devising a strategy that we then implemented. Mostly it was us reacting to talented people on the ground, putting two and two together and taking one step at a time.

To be sure, our colleagues in New York played an important role. They were beacons that helped us find our way. They established the values, standards, and program areas within which we worked. They inspired, stimulated, informed, and challenged. We had to pass muster. But they also trusted us more than I would have expected. Their starting point seemed to be that, because we were reasonably competent and on the ground, we might find the best way forward—within, of course, the parameters they'd set—and so ought to be taken seriously.

This was a pretty common dynamic in the Ford Foundation back then. I was amazed by how much responsibility I was given early on—more, I suspect, than I would have been willing to give myself. Bundy's Ford Foundation, or at least the Latin American portion, was like that—demanding but decentralized. The assumption was that staff in the field, even junior staff like me, had been carefully selected and therefore had something important to offer. You got listened to. You had power. I always appreciated that.

My final thought on what Ford did after the military coup in Chile is a meditation on the realities of power and responsibility. Donors have power, and Ford was no exception. It had several forms—money, visibility, and prestige—mostly within Chile's academic and intellectual community, and possibly, but to a much lesser extent, within the political community. That was simply a fact. The question was how we would use that power. In answering that question it's important to recognize that power is always accompanied by responsibility. If you have power, you are responsible for how that power is used—or not used. So when conditions change, and especially when conflict rears its ugly head, you, as a donor, have a decision to make: business as usual or not? You may choose one or the other, but you need to understand that either will have consequences and encumber you with responsibilities. There's no getting around that.

The temptation Ford faced after the coup was to keep its head down, refuse to take a position and continue business as usual. That would have involved a lot less conflict, soul-searching, debate, and disruption. But you rarely get away with that. If a donor has any power, it is responsible for how that power is used. We would, had we continued business as usual, have been responsible for signaling that conditions weren't bad enough to make us change course, and for failing to challenge the new authorities' assault on academic freedom. People would have noticed that we did nothing. The lesson, I think, is that not to exercise power in a repressive situation is, paradoxically, to exercise it, in that not doing something sends a message, and makes it easier for something else to happen. Power brings responsibility. Even when you don't use it.

XII

FORD/ARGENTINA

I MENTIONED THAT the Ford Foundation also had a significant program in Argentina, part of which I was responsible for, making it necessary for me to visit Buenos Aires regularly. That was a cross I did my best to bear. Buenos Aires was a delight, starting with the endless blue sky dotted with fluffy clouds and extending across the endless *pampa* that you encountered when you stepped out of the Ezeiza airport. It was big. It was grand. And you were only at the airport. You hadn't yet entered "the city."

When you did, it felt like Europe. Buenos Aires was (and is) the least Latin American of Latin American cities. It exudes European style and culture—in art, music, dress, theater, and books. The architecture is more *belle époque* than colonial. The downtown is dominated by broad avenues (Avenida 9 de Julio) is twice as wide as the Champs Elysees) and marked by an imposing obelisk. The people are not only Spanish in origin, but Italian, German, and British. It has the largest Jewish population in Latin America. The food—grilled meats, pasta, fresh vegetables and fruits, pastry, and wine—is not just good but lavish. The atmosphere is warm, cosmopolitan, and elegant. Buenos Aires was often called "the Paris of Latin America." Most other Latin American capitals seem provincial by comparison—or, at least, part of another world.

I always loved visiting, and soon established a dinner ritual. On my first night I'd go to my favorite *parrilla* (whose name I don't recall) and order a *chorizo* (grilled pork sausage), *bife de chorizo* (basically, a New York strip steak), French fries, watercress salad, and a half-bottle of red wine. Dessert was always a hot-fudge sundae—called, I think, a *charlotte*. This meal, which I preferred to eat alone, was a kind of personal celebration—like visiting a shrine. It got me settled and ready to work.

Ford staff stayed mostly at the Gran Hotel Dorá in Buenos Aires, a comfortable but not luxurious hotel on Calle Maipú, just off the Plaza San Martin. The location and staff were great. The hustle and bustle was just a block away, the breakfast was good (especially the croissants) and the guys at the front desk greeted us by name, and exchanged our dollars for Argentine *pesos* at a decent rate—which, given Argentina's chaotic economy was important. They'd also loan us cash against a credit card if we forgot to bring dollars, which I once did. It was very much a full-service hotel. But what was really great about the Dorá was Borges—Jorge Luis Borges—Argentina's world-class writer of short stories, essays and poetry who never got the Nobel Prize for literature but probably should have. Borges lived across the street and regularly dined at the *Dorá* with his personal assistant, Maria Kodama, whom he married a few months before he died. It was great fun to sit at the bar sipping local scotch with my friend and Anglo-Argentine Jesuit, Michael Petty, and watch Borges shuffle in (he was blind by then) behind Kodama. It felt historic—like spotting Hemingway a few tables away. You were in the presence of greatness; it was a privilege. Today the hotel offers a penthouse "Borges Suite" and informs guests that Borges usually ate boiled white rice with butter and grated cheese, mineral water, and *dulce de leche*. That, coming from one of the giants of Argentine culture, was disappointing—where's the beef? It was like discovering that James Bond drank Pepsi Cola rather than dry martinis. But I only heard about Borges's gastronomic preferences later. Just down the street there was a little bookshop that offered signed copies of Borges' *Complete Works* in Spanish. When I finally went in to buy one, they said they'd run out and that he was currently taking a nap but if I'd come back later they'd have one for me, which I did and they did. I found that charming.

My first visit took place just before Christmas, right after I started work in Chile, when my boss, Peter Bell, sent me over to Buenos Aires to meet grantees and get a grant evaluation underway. The timing was exquisite. I'd left my girlfriend, Angie Kappner, behind in Chicago and she was, it turned out, visiting her family in Buenos Aires over the Christmas holidays (her father was president of Bayer Chemical in Argentina). The fact that I'd left her behind said something about my priorities back then: career was more important than love—at least any love I'd experienced to date. The job with Ford was my big chance, and it was going to take an awful lot for me to turn it down. Also, my then-girlfriend was a professional with a good job in Chicago. Asking her to give that up and follow me to Chile (and who knows where else) was asking a lot. So our prospects weren't great. And I think that, deep down, both of us realized that we weren't really made for each other. But those things are never easy; spending Christmas with her and her family in Buenos Aires was a nice way to avoid reality, at least for a while.

I think, though, that there's a lesson here about navigating life in the face of rapid and major change. It's hard enough to figure out whether you're in love, whether love is enough, and whether you should get married. It's harder when you're pretty sure, as I was, that your future will be significantly different from your past. I'd embarked on major change but knew no one who'd done anything similar. The people I'd grown up with in rural Michigan—family and friends—for the most part had futures that were fairly similar to their pasts. So for them deciding on marriage was more straightforward. You bet on what felt like love and hoped you'd gotten it right. They didn't have to worry about moving to Chile, and then to Peru, and then to San Francisco, and then to New York, and then back to Peru, then to New York again, and then to Washington, as I would. I didn't think their approach would work for me. I'd already lived for two years in Colombia, acquiring a second language and a second culture. I expected to continue doing things like that and wanted to. But it complicated choosing a mate. I couldn't see what kind of person would be comfortable going along on my journey, or how to find her. It's probably the price that comes with opting for major change. In hindsight I can see that one good strategy is to find someone who's no stranger to the journey you're on and see whether you fall in love. That's eventually what I did. But I didn't know about that strategy when I started out. Anyone starting on a similar journey might want to keep this in mind.

I faced similar decisions over the next several decades and decided in each case against marriage, and in each case, looking back, think I made the right decision. I was like a guy on a train who, while stopped at a station, meets someone he finds attractive but then has to say goodbye because the train is about to leave and he's on his way to somewhere else. I said goodbye a lot. And I didn't get married. Had I taken that step in any of those cases, I suspect I would have ended up getting divorced. It was only several decades later that the skies finally cleared and I could see what to do. And it turned out to be great.

But back to Christmas in Buenos Aires. The family lived in the upscale suburb of Martinez, and I drove out there on Friday afternoon in a Ford Falcon the office had given me. What was interesting about that drive, aside from the splendor of the *Avenida del Libertador*, was the person I heard on the car radio chatting and telling jokes. Normally I wouldn't listen to that kind of thing, but the guy had a folksy quality that drew me in. I soon realized I was listening to Argentina's thrice-elected president, Juan Domingo Perón, who had returned from exile earlier that year and would die the following year. He had exercised his populist spell on the country for nearly three decades, and clearly he was a charmer who might talk you into anything. And he came to symbolize, as I learned more, Argentina's great mystery: how a leader who took his country from the fifth or sixth richest in the world (richer than France or Germany) down to the fifth or sixth richest in Latin America (richer, arguably, than Mexico), and who routinely resorted to organized violence, dictatorial rule, and torture, undermined freedom of speech, praised Italian and German fascism, and welcomed and protected Nazi war criminals after World War II—could nonetheless be the symbolic head of a political party that continues to be broadly popular and to win presidential elections half a century later. I've never understood it. But listening to that radio broadcast gave me a sense, at least in part, of how he managed to get away with so much for so long.

The family was interesting—Germans who'd left Germany decades earlier (in opposition, as I recall, to the Nazi regime) for China (where my girlfriend was born) and then moved around Latin America while he climbed the ladder at Bayer. Now they had a nice house in an upscale suburb with a pool, a Mercedes, and a couple of German Shepherds. It was all very German—real candles on the Christmas tree, Christmas Eve services at a Lutheran church, lunch at the German Club downtown. Since I had a German background (my maternal great-grandparents migrated from there), I related and appreciated. And it underscored how diverse and cosmopolitan Argentina was. Right after Christmas we drove down to Mar del Plata, a traditional seaside resort, for a few days. All I remember about that trip were the huge Patagonian sea lions lolling on a waterfront dock, and her father's insistence on driving there in a Ford Falcon he borrowed from his office rather than in the family Mercedes because, he said, American cars were more reliable. We got along fine. He even told his daughter that he approved of me as a future son-in-law, which I found surprising. When my parents visited me the following year, we spent a few days in Buenos Aires and the family invited us over for a pleasant lunch. Family-wise, it may have been a good fit, or at least good enough.

But it was not to be. And that was probably for the best. Angie and I were different people moving on different tracks. Not long after we got together again, also at her parent's home in Buenos Aires, and she observed (rather cooly, I thought) "Our time is past." She could say it. I couldn't. She was right.

I mentioned earlier that the Ford Foundation had already downsized sharply in Argentina, leaving just a skeletal office (which we soon closed) and a program that was perhaps one-third the size of our work in Chile. It was a mix of old grants that were winding down (e.g. a troubled endowment at the Instituto Torcuato di Tella), and newer grants for work similar to what Ford was supporting elsewhere in Latin America. It was pretty normal stuff. That changed, however, in March, 1976, when the military took over and began purging leftist and critical academics from the universities. Suddenly Argentina began to look like Chile (except that in Argentina academic repression was not new, and historically had come from both the left and the right). So we reacted by replicating, approximately and on a much smaller scale, in Argentina the strategy we'd developed in Chile: preserving critical, independent thought, and nurturing policy expertise for a future democracy. It seemed like the right thing to do. We'd learned how to do it. So we did it. And in both countries we added work on human rights—a topic we knew nothing about but decided, given the alarming scale of violations, we should take on.

Within just a few years, then, our programs in both countries had shifted from fairly standard development work, emphasizing economic growth and government policymaking, to work that addressed the unique challenges and perils of repressive regimes. (In fact, we did something similar but even smaller in Uruguay, which had experienced a military coup in mid-1973, but I don't want to overwhelm you with detail. This is a memoir, not a history.)

Argentine was different, however, in that human rights violations there were more dramatic and cold-blooded. Leftist guerrillas had, prior to the 1976 coup, killed over 600 people, most of them military or police. Their violence helped spark the coup, and caused the military *junta* to believe it was confronting an attack on Western and Christian values. They were in a war. The *junta's* head, General Jorge Rafael Videla, articulated their attitude: "A terrorist is not just someone with a gun or a bomb but also someone who spreads ideas that are contrary to Western and Christian civilization." So the *junta* targeted not just members of guerrilla organizations, but also students, intellectuals, and community activists. And it sought not just to silence and control, but to eliminate. The result was darker and more murderous than in Chile. Some 10,000 (maybe more) people disappeared. Nearly all were kidnapped, tortured, and killed, their bodies dumped into the ocean or buried in secret graves. If the Argentine security forces picked you up, you were probably going to die. It was brutal.

That extra dimension of brutality, which too often descended intro depravity and sadism, may explain why it is to Argentina, and not to Chile, that I owe my closest and most memorable brushes with state terrorism. Shortly after the 1976 military coup I got a phone call in my office in Santiago from Michael Petty, the Jesuit friend I mentioned earlier, who headed an educational research center in Buenos Aires that we funded—and for whose funding I was responsible. Michael was an Anglo-Argentine, from one of the British families that played such an important role in the country's history beginning in the early 19th century when they came to "the Argentine" to exploit its abundant beef and wool, and stayed to establish the railroads, utilities, and all sorts of businesses. Michael had been born into privilege, gone to an elite boarding school in England (Winchester, perhaps; I don't quite remember), and joined the Jesuits. He was also a friend because we'd studied together at the University of Chicago.

It was Michael, by the way, who introduced me while we were at Chicago to the concept of the hair shirt—something you wore over your skin as a penance—which I knew nothing about but apparently had been part of his Jesuit training. He was moved to bring it up, I'm sure, by the quasi-monastic lives we led as graduate students, complete with vows of poverty, chastity, and obedience (well, that's how it felt), our need to atone for our ignorance, and our hope that one day the Gods of Knowledge would admit us—at least provisionally—to the Ivory Tower. The hair shirt fit nicely into that narrative.

Anyway, what surprised me about the call was that it happened at all. I don't think he'd ever called before. There hadn't been any need. And the conversation was curious. "Michael, how are you?" I said. "Fine" he responded. "How are you?" "Fine." I said. "What's up?" "I just called to say hello" he responded. "Is everything OK?" I asked. "Yes" he replied. "Maria del Carmen has been sick, but we're hoping she'll get better soon." "I hope so, too." I said. "Well," he said "Great talking with you. Good-bye." "Good-bye, Michael." I said, and hung up. I sat there thinking for maybe thirty seconds and then called my secretary: "Get me on the next plane to Buenos Aires." Obviously something was wrong.

I showed up early the next morning at their offices and, sure enough, Maria del Carmen had disappeared. She'd gone out to run some errands prior to visiting her parents' home for lunch and never returned. A few hours later security agents appeared at her parents' home saying she'd been detained but would be released soon and asked for her typewriter. That was the last anyone heard of her.

Not surprisingly, Michael and the staff were devastated. They had no reason to believe she was involved in anything that would make her the target of security forces. So how could this happen? What surprised me was that they felt guilty—that they were somehow to blame. They thought they'd done something wrong, and that's why the security forces took Maria del Carmen. I sat with them for several hours trying to be a counselor (not my strong suit), and especially trying to convince them that they weren't guilty of anything. I argued that they and Maria del Carmen were victims, and that the real guilt belonged to whomever had taken her. It was an uphill battle. I hoped I'd made some progress. I wasn't sure.

Then I took Michael to lunch with Rudolph Rausch, *Time's* correspondent for South America, whom I'd gotten to know through my good friend John Dinges, then *Time's* stringer in Santiago. After a morning steeped in tragedy, it was a relief to have a more upbeat conversation, and a gin and tonic, at a nice restaurant—like climbing out of a dark hole. Ru offered to make some inquiries of his own, which I thought was kind of him. After lunch I went to the U.S. Embassy and met with a couple of political officers to report Maria del Carmen's disappearance. That had become our standard practice after the military coups in Chile and Argentina. If someone from an institution we supported were arrested or disappeared, we immediately notified the Embassy and asked them to make inquiries. We figured that if the U.S. government asked about someone, the military would have to think twice before treating them badly. Maybe we were right, although I don't recall ever seeing any evidence to that effect. But it was certainly worth a try. You did what you could. Most of the time you felt helpless.

What stuck in my mind, though, was the sense of guilt that Michael's staff had. They kept asking what they might have done to cause this. It seemed that there was something about being absolutely powerless in the face of anonymous terror that produced guilt rather than outrage. There must be a psychological principle there; I couldn't imagine what it was. It just seemed strange. Faceless government brutality had, somehow, made the victim feel guilty of the crime. It was a striking, and for me wholly unexpected, consequence of repression.

Maria del Carmen was never heard from again.

My other brush with the impact of state terrorism came, also just after the Argentine coup, when my boss, Dick Dye, called from New York (I was in Santiago) to inform me that a prominent Argentine social scientist had gone into hiding after being labeled a subversive in the press, and that I was to go over to Buenos Aires, find him, and get him out of the country. Dick had no more information, nor advice, so it was a short conversation.

My first reaction was that our conversation sounded like that old TV show, *Mission Impossible*, which was later transformed into at least one Tom Cruise movie. Some of the lines were unforgettable: "Your mission, should you decide to accept it, is…" and "Should you be caught or killed, the Secretary will disavow any knowledge of your actions…" and "This tape will self-destruct in five seconds. Good luck." Dick didn't say any of this, but it came to mind. I felt like I was in the movies.

My second reaction was that I'd better go home and shave off my beard. Like many in the counterculture (which we graduate students liked to think we were part of), I had a full beard when I joined Ford, and had kept it. But suddenly I had doubts. I wasn't in graduate school any more. If I were going to help some Argentine intellectual elude the secret police and flee the country, it wouldn't do to arrive in Buenos Aires looking like Che Guevara.

Then I started thinking about the reality of doing what I'd been asked to do. I had no experience smuggling people out of countries. And I'd never even met the guy I was supposed to extract. But I figured that someone in Argentina's social science community would put me in touch with him. Then I'd offer to get him to an airport and on a plane. How hard was that? The Foundation had given me an airline credit card (an IATA card, I think it was called) with a "q"' on it that meant I had unlimited credit on just about any airline in the world, so that I could get a lot of people on airplanes in a hurry if I had to. This would be the first time I'd used it. I more or less had a plan. I made a reservation on the first flight to Buenos Aires the next morning. Then I went home and shaved off my beard.

I mentioned that we maintained a guest house in Santiago where Ford staff stayed when they were visiting Chile. That's where I was staying, and where that evening my colleague, Nita Manitzas, appeared, arriving from Lima, to report she'd just seen, in the Santiago airport, the fellow I was supposed to find. He'd gotten out on his own and was on his way to Los Angeles where he had an offer to teach at a university. So my mission was no longer necessary.

I was relieved, but disappointed. There'd be no derring-do for me. It was the only time I was ever asked to find someone who'd gone into hiding and get him (or her) out of the country. And that was probably just as well. I'd been on the brink of doing something that sounded romantic, but was outside my job description, outside my competence, and almost certainly dangerous. Now my feet were firmly back on the ground. It probably wouldn't happen again. It didn't.

But I never did let my beard grow back.

One more observation—this one about the Catholic Church. I've already mentioned how in Chile the Church, under the leadership of Cardinal Silva, played a key role in challenging government repression. Based on that experience, we thought the Church would do something similar in Argentina, and that the Ford Foundation might even provide some support. So I asked my Argentine Jesuit friend (and Ford grantee) Michael Petty how we might gauge the Church's thinking. He organized a meeting with several bishops, and we—my boss, Dick Dye, and I— went over to Buenos Aires to talk.

The bishops weren't interested. They acknowledged that there were violations and lamented them. Then the conversation lapsed into generalities. They didn't want to discuss action. Clearly they had no intention of doing anything on human rights. Nor, it seemed, on any issue that might put them at odds with the military government. In the face of state terrorism, the Catholic Church of Argentina would remain silent. We returned to Santiago, surprised and disappointed.

Later I came to realize how different Argentina was from Chile. I've already mentioned that in Argentina leftist guerrillas had killed more than 600 people prior to the coup. This was armed struggle—an extended campaign that included kidnappings, assassinations and bombings, and was led by the *Montoneros*, Latin America's most powerful urban guerrilla movement. That traumatized plenty of people and fed the narrative of a subversive threat from the left. It helped bring on the coup. And it prompted the Church to defend, and even collaborate with, the new military government, despite its widespread violations of human rights. All of that is clear. For me it was a graphic example of how even an institution as hierarchical and doctrinally homogeneous as the Catholic Church could take radically different positions in different counties. I'd thought the Church was monolithic. I was wrong.

But much more importantly, it demonstrated how precarious our notions of right and wrong can be. The Argentine Catholic Church, part of an ancient, global institution long identified with morality, virtue, and compassion, decided to support, through omission and commission, massive violations of human rights by the government, including the killing of defenseless civilians. It did so, apparently, because it felt its values and interests were under serious threat.

If that can happen, what shields us from the logic and values of the Crusades? How certain can we be that the moral principles we share and take for granted, and that enable us to live in harmony despite our differences, can endure? Not very, I think. What happened in Argentina was a warning. The small amounts of peace, unity and fellowship we've managed to establish are fragile. Push too hard and they crumble. And what's beyond is awful. I'm reminded of a comment by José Zalaquett, Chilean human rights leader, Amnesty International deputy director, and MacArthur Foundation "genius" awardee (and good friend): "Inside every one of us there is the potential for the beast." We don't like to face that, but it's true. We are neither perfect nor perfectible.

Argentina was always a small part of the work I did with the Ford Foundation, but it remained a part throughout my seventeen-year tenure. That meant regular visits, a look into Argentine affairs, and a connection to the country's distinguished community of social scientists. I was exposed to one of the most interesting countries in the world, but one I've never felt I understood. For all its bonhomie and laughter, there was something elusive about the place. Something dark and inward-looking, like the tango. I never figured it out.

Borges, with his emphasis on dreams, allegory, and fantasy, may have been on the right track: "We accept reality so readily - perhaps because we sense that nothing is real."

I don't know the real Argentina.

I may have gotten well into the weeds here. Those first few years with the Ford Foundation were so charged with surprise, unfamiliarity, challenge, and emotion that I've had to dig deep to clarify and communicate what I saw and learned. This was, as well, when I finally began to work and produce at a professional level. And where I think I was on a team that did some extraordinary things. So I felt that I had to make sense of it. I've struggled with capturing and communicating that. I think, given the privileged position I occupied, I had an obligation to try. Few have seen and dealt with this kind of thing. I have a responsibility to make sense and communicate. I can only hope you find it interesting.

XIII

ON PSYCHOTHERAPY AND ART
(BOTH OF WHICH ARE GOOD FOR YOU)

PSYCHOTHERAPY

A FEW YEARS into my job with Ford, I decided that I needed to do some psychotherapy. It wasn't a sudden decision, but rather one that had been building for a while in ways that, although undramatic, mounted steadily like pebbles piling up on a sandy beach and making it hard to walk. Something had been bothering me—for years so far as I could tell. It was never urgent, but always there. Eventually I began to pay attention. It may be that, having gotten my PhD and a good job, I could finally lift up my head and see what else I ought to be dealing with. The vague collection of worries, anxieties, and unease I'd been carrying around rose to the top of the list.

I didn't grow up knowing much about mental health. Health was physical, not mental. My one brush with mental health had come when I was maybe seven years old and my father had some emotional problems. I knew that only because my mother told me. I don't remember any symptoms. He seemed normal. But she said he was doing some sort of group therapy, so clearly there was a problem. Then my parents announced that we would take a month-long road trip to visit his brother in California. Apparently, the trip was part of his treatment; he needed a break. And since we were departing in the middle of the school year rather than waiting for summer vacation, whatever he was feeling must have been serious.

So we piled into our four-door Hudson and took off cross-country. For me and my brother Gary, the trip was great: Carlsbad Caverns, our first-ever Mexican restaurant (in Albuquerque), the Grand Canyon, Griffith Park in Los Angeles, the casinos of Las Vegas (which we saw only from our motel room while our parents were inside playing the slots), and the Zion and Bryce Canyon national parks (where, it seemed, all the cowboy movies we'd ever seen must have been filmed). We met my uncle Merrill, from whom I'd gotten my middle name and who'd gone into real estate in southern California. We saw the Hoover Dam, the Black Hills, and Mount Rushmore. It was a little like discovering America.

Then we were back, in early spring, and somehow managed to make up the time we'd lost at school. My father changed jobs (which may have been part of his therapy). His new job, managing a large gas station on Lansing's south side, went well. (Pumping gas there would become my first part-time job when I turned 16 and could work legally.) We seemed to have enough money. Then he was promoted to an executive position, where he remained for a decade or more. So far as I could tell, he'd put behind him whatever emotional troubles he'd had. I don't remember the topic coming up again, except once my mother mentioning how it felt to "have your back against the wall." It didn't seem terribly serious to me. I wish I'd asked my father about it later on. I never did.

I say all this simply as preface to discussing my own emotional ups and downs. It's standard procedure to assume that what you're feeling today is based in part (and maybe a lot) on what your parents did, or didn't do, yesterday. Perhaps my father's problems had an impact on me. I just don't know. These things are more typically mysterious than obvious. So maybe.

I have, however, already mentioned the vague feelings of anxiety I had while at Michigan State. They were real. But I'd chalked them up to the new world of people and ideas that college was exposing me to. Change was hard. I'd get over it.

Still, there was another feeling that was different, and that I've always remembered. It had to do with getting married. I'd had an on-again, off-again relationship with my high school sweetheart—Terry Bristol, my first real love—and was wrestling with what to do. The passion was strong, and in a more traditional world we might well have gotten married and lived happily ever after. But I couldn't commit. Something was holding me back, and I didn't know what. At the rational level, it bothered me that she had gone to nursing school rather than to college. I was aiming to become an intellectual; she had become a nurse. I felt we'd chosen different paths, and that those differences didn't bode well for marriage. I even wrote a letter to my parents making that point. (They would have been delighted had I married her.) I was targeting a different world.

There was something else, though—a problem of my own—something vague about feeling uncomfortable in social situations, which I couldn't really put my finger on but needed addressing. I didn't know what to do. All that was clear was that, given the way I felt, I was not ready to get married. So I wouldn't. And I didn't. We broke up for good—eventually, finally, and painfully. That night I got in my car and drove too fast for too long down a dark country road, feeling hurt and frustrated. I let rage take over. That was a bad decision. I could have gotten killed.

I continue to think I was right not to get married. But I have to recognize that I also continued to dream about Terry for years (decades, in fact) afterwards, usually with strong feelings—love, of course but also, curiously, a feeling of being rejected. That may say something about whatever darker emotional problems I needed to deal with. Now, half a century later, those dreams have pretty much gone away. But recently I had a dream in which Terry, my high school sweetheart, and Mary Jean Bowman, my doctoral thesis adviser, two of the most important women in my life back then, were talking with each other—about me. So maybe they're still out there, tapping on my window after midnight. Some things you just don't get over.

That feeling of being "uncomfortable in social situations" stuck with me. But it wasn't until my last year at the University of Chicago that I was finally moved to take it seriously and made an appointment to see a psychologist. Something must have prompted that. I don't remember what. What I do remember was seeing, as I was entering the student health service (which was in the University of Chicago Hospital), someone jump out of a window several floors up, obviously to their death. I still remember the thud. I'd witnessed a suicide. I was shaken. It wasn't a great way to start off your first visit to a mental health professional. I told the psychologist what I'd just seen, and her gut reaction was to hope it wasn't one of her patients. I thought that was nice. That's all I remember. I didn't go back.

The other step I took towards mental health during my final year at the University of Chicago was to sign up for a weekly "encounter group" that met downtown and brought young professionals like me together to discuss their feelings and become more self-aware. I liked it immediately. There was a trained facilitator who got us to talk, and to see the feelings lurking behind our talk, and who didn't let us get away with much. She opened a door. I began to see that I was filled with strong feelings that wriggled and flopped like salmon spawning in an Alaskan river, and affected how I felt and what I did but that I didn't even realize were there, let alone understand. I was amazed. This was important. I needed to know more.

I attended those group sessions right up until I left for Chile to work for the Ford Foundation. It was a good first step. I'd learned something useful and filed it away for future reference. It was something I should probably follow up. But it wasn't high on my to-do list.

Later I realized that the encounter group was my first contact with something much bigger that was bubbling up and didn't yet have a name but eventually came to be called the human potential movement—the idea that individuals are unique and can flourish if that uniqueness is recognized and cultivated. Or something like that. It was coming out of humanistic psychology, an upstart that had emerged alongside the more traditional branches of psychology: psychoanalytic theory and behaviorism. It began coming together at the Esalen Institute in California's Big Sur in the mid-1960s. It emphasized self-knowledge, feelings, expression, and confrontation. It eventually embraced all sorts of forms (like yoga, est, meditation, and rolfing) in addition to group therapy, and it attracted all sorts of people (including even the Beatles). It was a disorderly but well-founded effort to make people, and the world, better. And it had legs. I didn't know any of that then, but the human potential movement would provide the framework for the psychotherapy I would eventually do.

Now, fast-forward two or three years. I was a junior program officer with Ford, residing legally in Lima but spending only about a week a month there. Most of my time I spent in Santiago, with regular trips to Buenos Aires, and occasionally Montevideo. I'd finally gotten comfortable in my new job. I'd made good friends in Peru and Chile, and had established a social life in both. And I began to think that I needed to do some kind of psychotherapy. I don't recall any single driver; it was just a feeling, or more likely an accumulation of feelings. The stress of my job and lifestyle may have played a role. But I think I'd have done it regardless. I decided to act. It was time.

A real plus was that many of the people I'd made friends with in Chile actually knew something about psychotherapy. Some had done it; others knew people who had, or even who were therapists themselves. They moved in those kinds of circles; I didn't. I took advantage of what they knew. One of the people they recommended was Arturo Mardones, a psychiatrist who'd spent several years in the Bay Area sampling the fresh winds blowing through traditional psychotherapy. While in California he had done work with Claudio Naranjo, a Berkeley-based Chilean therapist who became a key figure in the human potential movement. Arturo had incorporated many of the new ideas he found there into his practice.

I made an appointment, liked him, and saw him once a week for the next year or so. It was largely an exercise in getting me in touch with my feelings. Which is a big deal, and turns out to be harder and take longer than you'd expect. Just seeing what you're doing, and what emotions might be driving what you're doing, are huge steps forward. Like realizing that the earth is round and circles the sun. He got me to talk, and he probed. One thing I realized is that wanting to get in touch with your feelings isn't enough. Even if you want to, deep down you don't want to. A powerful part of you has got that door locked and is sitting on the key. That's why you need professional help.

Perhaps because of the time he'd spent in the Bay Area, Arturo was willing to try uncommon approaches. Once he had me smoke marijuana and then talk about my feelings, with moody classical music playing in the background. That was dramatic and seemed to work. To this day I can't listen to Schubert's Unfinished Symphony without thinking about my mother. But mostly it was straightforward: him getting me to talk, especially about things I didn't realize were there and wasn't keen on talking about. And me rummaging uncomfortably among my feelings and talking.

My bottom line was that this was good stuff. It got me to explore how my childhood, and particularly my relations with my parents, had affected my feelings and my choices in life. It shined light into dark spaces. I saw things I'd not seen before. They seemed real. The veil was coming off. And that was helpful because, when we started out, I didn't even realize there was a veil.

After a year or so, he suggested a change. He was organizing a group to do something called the Fischer-Hoffman Process. It was a two-month intensive program that would take you through a mini version of a full psychoanalytic process, identifying negative thought and behavior patterns, replacing them with positives, and making you a happier and better person. That's a brutal approximation, but you can see the concept. This was something he'd encountered in Berkeley (Naranjo had been key in developing it), had done himself and was convinced worked. He had organized and led the Process several times in Chile. I spoke with one person who'd done it, and he was happy. So I signed up. (A year or so later, while on sabbatical at Stanford, I would visit Bob Hoffman, who'd started all this, at his place in San Francisco, chat a bit, and buy his book—*No One Is To Blame*. He'd been a tailor before getting into psychotherapy. Naranjo was convinced he was a modern-day shaman. But I'm getting ahead of myself.)

There were five or six of us. We met once a week as a group so Arturo could explain concepts, show us techniques, and give us assignments. Then we worked at home. And we met with him individually, as needed. It was intensive. There was a lot of homework. The process pretty much took over your life—at least after work and on weekends. We were not allowed to communicate in any way with our parents. A central feature was visualization (AKA "mind trips"). We sat quietly with our eyes closed and visualized whatever it was we were working on. Step one was to establish a kind of sanctuary in your mind that you could always go to and feel safe—and where you would do most of your work. I chose a spot up in the mountains, with blue sky, snow-covered peaks, a babbling brook, and a sweet little *araucaria* tree. Then we imagined a guide who was always in that sanctuary and would help us through the process. And then we visualized the villain—our negative emotional child, who embodied the pain and trauma we had inside us, and whom we needed to understand and engage. He was what we needed to fix. Then we began to visualize our parents, and all the bad things they'd done that had created the negative emotional child. We were introduced to a key concept: "Everyone is guilty, but no one is to blame." Finally, we discharged all that pent up anger and resentment by crying, screaming, beating on pillows, or whatever. Some of this we did alone, but I recall doing one of those discharge sessions with Arturo in a remote canyon up in the mountains.

The overall goal was to see your trauma, understand where it came from, get it out of your system, and forgive. Then you'd be at peace. Exciting, no? I certainly thought so. It was one of the most exciting things I've ever done.

In addition to examining our relations with our parents, we could work on issues that were less clearly parent-specific. The one I remember most was smoking. I'd been trying to stop smoking for years without success. Arturo put together a visualization exercise in which, in my sanctuary, my guide and I confronted my negative emotional child about his attachment to smoking. I stopped soon after, and never smoked again. Nor even felt tempted. Another, which I think I did by myself later on, took on my deep and long-standing fear of public speaking. I visualized speaking in front of a group while my guide hovered above them and reassured me that I was doing fine. That got me over my fear. I've since become a good enough—and relaxed enough—public speaker.

I came out of the Fischer-Hoffman Process satisfied. I'd seen, I'd understood and I'd come to terms. It was a great feeling. Like getting out from under something. It wasn't that I no longer had any problems. It was more like I'd made real progress on some, could see most of the rest and was confident I could deal with them. The lights had been turned on, and they would stay on. I felt at peace. I look back on the experience with great fondness.

And I thought the Process added up intellectually. Recognizing your emotional baggage, identifying how you'd gotten it, discharging the inevitable rage, and then forgiving those involved made sense to me. There was a logic and completeness to it that I liked.

I know this sounds pie in the sky, so let me try and extract some lessons.

First, I think that virtually everyone should do some kind of psycho-therapy. We routinely see a doctor for knee pain or a sore throat. Why not see a psychotherapist for anger, anxiety, or a broken heart? There's so much about each of us that we don't realize and that gets in our way. Some will benefit more than others, of course, but all will benefit some. And my suspicion is that most will benefit a lot. I had no idea that this was the case when I started out. I wish I'd started sooner.

Second, how much and what kind is not clear. One size doesn't fit all. Psychotherapy is the sort of thing you have to wade into and figure out. Each of us has different problems, and those problems come in different sizes and shapes. What worked for me won't necessarily work for you (although it might). Nor is it clear when you're done (or whether you're ever done). It's a process and an adventure. To be sure, there's a substantial body of work about psychotherapy out there, and you should learn something about it before jumping in. Read. Ask people you trust. Listen to your gut. That will establish options. Then try something and see how it goes. Just don't think there's a sure thing. Ultimately, the therapy that works is the therapy that works for you.

Third, people matter. It's not just the kind of therapy you do. A lot depends on the talent, commitment, and integrity of the therapist you work with. And the chemistry you have with him or her. I worked with someone who was recommended by people whom I thought knew what they were talking about, and whose talent and integrity I came, over time, to trust. But psychotherapy draws its share of amateurs, and even char-latans (a small share, so far as I can tell). You just have to figure that out.

And fourth, psychotherapy isn't everything. Other parts of life are important—love, work, education, friends, community, spirituality, a healthy body. One danger of psychotherapy is that it's potentially self-ish. It's mostly about us and has to be. But we need to recognize and manage that. The Fischer-Hoffman Process promoted "quadrinity," the idea that humans operate in four domains, the physical, rational, emo-tional, and spiritual, and need take care of each. In the Process we were dealing mostly with the emotional, and that was fine. But we needed to pay attention to the others as well. I'd never seen that scheme before but it made all sorts of sense. What we were doing was one step in a bigger undertaking.

I concluded that the idea of figuring yourself out has practical limits. Ultimately, we're all mysteries. Like quantum mechanics. Why should we ever expect to fully understand ourselves?

I finished the Process (and was pronounced, ceremonially, "finished" by Arturo). Several months later I left for a year's sabbatical at Stanford University. I never felt that I needed to do more psychotherapy. I'm sure I would have benefited from more. But the urge was gone. I was happy enough. And finally I felt I was ready to get married. That was a big step forward. What's more, and to my surprise, at Stanford I'd meet my future wife. But, and maybe not so surprising, it would take me almost a decade to realize that. What a dope. That's another story I need to tell.

ART

One more noteworthy aspect of my years working and living in Chile was that I discovered art. This was, I suspect, another case of something I'd long had inside me but couldn't get to until I'd gotten my PhD and a job (and maybe a little money). My mother and uncle had both painted, but those were just hobbies to which I'd never paid much attention. And I'd taken a course in art history at Michigan State, which I enjoyed but never followed up on. In Chile, though, something happened. Shortly after I arrived a well-known artist, Alister Santos Chavez, came by the office with some prints to sell and I perked up. I liked them and bought a couple (they weren't expensive), but more importantly I felt an attraction to art. It was visceral. I liked how it looked and felt. I wanted more. That was new.

It was the beginning of a long-term love of art—contemporary art generally, and painting, specifically though not exclusively—something that flowered inside me quite unexpectedly. I started paying attention. I discovered that Chile had a lively modern art scene—one of the liveliest in Latin America. Over the next year or two I met a few artists, all of them young and relatively unknown, and began getting a sense of how they viewed their work. I began dating an artist—Francisca Cerda—who sculpted and was part of that world. I discovered that artists were all different from each other and hard to categorize. That probably says something about what art (and creativity more generally) is and requires. I started visiting galleries. I bought a few pieces, always by unknown artists whose prices were low enough for me to afford. That started me on the long process of developing at least a rudimentary sense of taste. I even signed up for a few drawing lessons. I'd taken my first steps into the world of art and liked it.

Most of the artists I met were young, of course, but one of those I remember most, Delia del Carril, was not young at all but old, probably in her 80s when I met her. And she was Argentine rather than Chilean, the second wife of Pablo Neruda, one Chile's two Nobel Prize-winning poets. Delia was from a wealthy family in Buenos Aires; Pablo had been born into humble circumstances in southern Chile. She was 20 years older than he. Some say she introduced him to society. They'd met in Spain and married (the year I was born) in Mexico. Eventually they divorced. Then she took up painting and had some success. I saw her work in a gallery in Santiago, liked it, and bought some. The gallery owner, Carmen Waugh, told me that Delia was bedridden but enjoyed receiving visitors, so why didn't I go and introduce myself. I did and went back several times. We talked about her art. She'd started out drawing horses, and they'd kept getting larger than the canvas she was drawing on so she had to get a larger canvas. "They just kept getting bigger" she said. I found that charming. Apparently she saw her work more as description than as invention. She let things happen, and that probably took her in directions she couldn't predict or control. It seemed like a good way to practice art. Much later I would realize that writing is like that, too.

One of the most interesting things I learned was that artists, or at least the ones I met, weren't comfortable talking about the meaning of their work. A good example was Sergio Soza, a young artist I'd gotten to know and liked during those early years in Chile. I asked him specifically what he'd had in mind in a painting that showed the bust of a man in a jacket and tie balanced precariously on a narrow pedestal, facing the bust of a voluptuous woman sitting firmly on a wide pedestal that was on rollers, wearing a diaphanous gown that revealed her breasts, and blowing steam in the guy's face from a hot cup of tea. "What were you thinking?" I asked. "What do you see?" he responded. I told him I saw a conventional guy who was very uncomfortable in the presence of a sexy, contemptuous woman. "Interesting." he said. That's about as far as we got. He just wasn't willing to commit to having intended anything. Meaning was something that was ambiguous, even mysterious. That attitude was pretty common among the artists I met, and I soon stopped asking them what they'd had mind when they created whatever they'd created. It almost seemed beside the point.

The idea that meaning in art was subjective—in the eye of the beholder as much as the artist—was driven home to me many years later in Washington when my wife and I organized a reception at our house to welcome a couple of old friends from Chile and Colombia (Carlos Portales and Fernando Cepeda) who'd just been appointed ambassadors of their respective countries to the Organization of American States. I'd become a fan of a well-known Chilean painter, Ricardo Yrrarázabal, and had (finally) had enough money to purchase a few of his paintings. They tended to portray men who looked simultaneously respectable and deeply uncomfortable, their faces blurred and perturbed. We'd hung two of his paintings in the living room, one above the other. At some point

I noticed that Jesus Silva Herzog, Mexico's ambassador to the United States (and former finance minister), was standing in front of the paintings and staring at them intently. "Chucho," I said, "What are you doing?" (His nickname was Chucho.) He turned, looked me straight in the eye and said "That's me." I was taken aback. If art has any use beyond pure decoration, this was probably it. Those paintings spoke to him in a personal way. He saw himself. I felt that I understood art a little better, having seen how someone outside the world of art could be touched by it. What was important was what you saw and how you reacted. That gave art its impact.

I began rooting around in art more or less like a pig, happy but unsophisticated. I looked for art, artists, galleries, and museums in the countries I visited—in Chile of course, but also in Peru, Argentina, and Colombia. And several years later, after I'd moved to New York to manage Ford's Caribbean program, in Cuba, Jamaica, and Haiti. That was fun. I discovered that you could find good art at good prices if you looked around enough, talked to knowledgeable people, developed a sense of what you liked and were patient. That happened—I picked up a couple of splendid pieces by Afro-Cuban artist Manuel Mendive for peanuts courtesy of the Center for Cuban Studies in New York. Today they're among my favorites. The hard part was not finding but seeing. You could find a lot of art; seeing what was good was harder, and always mysterious.

Moving to New York was a big step up art-wise—like striking it rich. There was more treasure there than I could ever consume. I discovered the Museum of Modern Art and quickly became a regular. Walking up and down those stairs and through those galleries and finding all that beauty at my fingertips was delightful. The artists—Matisse, Gauguin, Van Gogh, Monet, Picasso, Rousseau, Toulouse-Lautrec, Hopper, Klee; the furniture—Alvear Aalto, Charles and Ray Eames; the architecture— Mies van der Rohe, Frank Lloyd Wright; the idea that industrial design was art (that red Porsche! the Bell helicopter!) It was everywhere, gorgeous, and a feast.

I was particularly taken with Picasso's *Guernica*, which back then was still in its own room on MOMA's third floor surrounded by the sketches that had preceded it and photographs of the work in progress. I used to stop by every month or so just for a quick look. It reassured me in a way I can't explain. It was like touching base with an old friend— except "old" was hardly what was going on; I'd only recently seen the painting for the first time. In 1981 they shipped it back to Spain and I soon missed it. Years later I visited the *Guernica* at its new location in the Reina Sofia Museum in Madrid. It didn't feel the way it felt at MOMA. Something had changed. I didn't know what. Probably me.

Art would wind in and out of my life for the next several decades. It got a big boost from José "Pepe" Zalaquett, the Chilean human rights leader (and MacArthur "genius" awardee) I mentioned earlier whom I met in Washington in the early 1980s, where he was in exile and a fellow at the Carnegie Endowment for International Peace. Pepe referred to art as his "predominant passion." He'd started in 1967 when he managed to scrape together $800 to purchase a print by Paul Klee from a Chilean collector and then became a lifelong Klee fanatic. He argued, in an interview with journalists Patricia Hidalgo and Constancia Toro, that Klee offered a uniquely human quality that couldn't be explained. You either saw it or you didn't. "He gives you the powder, you add it to the water of your experience and knowledge, and you've got a soup." I never saw that in Klee, nor even tried much. But I was drawn to Pepe's passion.

Pepe and I became art buddies. Once he was allowed to return to Chile in 1986, and I was visiting Santiago at least once a month from my post in Lima as head of Ford's regional office there, he began taking me to galleries and introducing me to artists, sometimes at their studios. It was very much a teacher-student relationship. Pepe knew what he was talking about; I was feeling my way. He would ask, diplomatically, my opinion about art and artists. Then he'd tell me what he saw, which was always several levels beyond me. It was a great way to learn about art. And a privilege.

Pepe had gotten to know a group of young, emerging artists who later became known as the artists of the 1980s, or the "80s Prom," and introduced me to several. Samy Benmayor, Bororo, and Pablo Dominguez were the ones I remember most and got to know best, but there were others. All were young and struggling, so we could afford to buy their work. That led to some unexpected adventures. They'd ask us for money to go somewhere and paint, offering to pay us back in paintings. The first request came from Pablo Dominguez and José León for money to spend a couple of months painting in Peru—just below Cuzco in the Sacred Valley of the Incas. Pepe argued that this was an offer we couldn't refuse: "Think of Van Gogh and Gauguin painting together in Southern France, or of Braque and Picasso." How could I say no? We came up with the money. They came back with a bunch of lovely of paintings. We chose a few.

The most memorable of these adventures happened, surprisingly, several years later once I'd moved back to New York and was still working for Ford. I got a call from Samy Benmayor saying he and Bororo were passing through New York on their way to Vermont where someone had invited them to spend a month painting. They needed money to buy materials. Could I help? These guys were good, so of course I was interested. By sheer coincidence, Pepe was in New York that week so I suggested that the four of us get together for coffee, which we did, and then we wrote them a couple of checks. A few months later Pepe and I went by their respective studios in Santiago to choose our paintings. These have become favorites of mine, including a Bororo showing a pair of disembodied hands playing a piano with Vermont mountains in the background (the guy who'd invited them was a pianist) and a couple of Benmayors that seem to depict Lewis Carroll's Red King and Queen (which of course had nothing to do with Vermont but looked great, particularly when hung together). I refrained from asking either what he'd had in mind when he painted what he'd painted.

What was interesting about our agreements to provide travel expenses in return for art was that they were always informal. No one specified in advance how many paintings we would get. It was always "You give us some money and we'll give you some paintings." Later we'd show up at their studios to see what the deal was. I like to think that we were trying to find a number that both sides felt was fair, but that you could only discover once you were face-to-face. Typically what happened was that we said: "OK, how many can we select?" And they told us. I don't remember ever feeling dissatisfied. Several things were in play. They were calculating not only how much those paintings were worth if they managed to sell them to someone else, but also how much it was worth to keep us happy. After all, they might want us to finance another trip in the future. And they hoped we'd recommend their work to other people who bought art. So they had reasons to be careful. But so did we. We wanted to treat them fairly and remain friends. Plus we wanted to maintain good relations with Chile's artistic community more generally, which was a small world back then. Those considerations, almost magically, yielded a number. That's probably how markets ought to work.

Pepe and I remained active art buddies for nearly a decade. Occasionally we overlapped in New York and went out exploring galleries together in Soho and on the Upper East Side. That was always fun, but sometimes left me scratching my head. I remember in particular him taking me to see an elaborate installation by, I think, a German artist that occupied an entire room in a gallery. Pepe thought it was marvelous; I thought it was awful. I couldn't see what he saw. This happened occasionally, but often enough to be unsettling. There was art out there that he thought was good, and that galleries were asking high prices for, but that I wouldn't buy even if I could afford it, or hang in my home, or even spend time looking at in a gallery. It just didn't speak to me. Pepe had apparently crossed over to a place I couldn't get to and didn't much want to. What to make of that? Was I missing something? Was I insensitive to the deeper and more sophisticated levels of art? Was I (gasp!) a lowbrow?

Those turned out to be a good questions, although not ones I answered any time soon. They echoed the times at the MOMA I'd stood in front of paintings by artists like Pollock, de Kooning, Rauschenberg, and Rothko (along with a growing number of mysterious "installations" by artists I'd never heard of) wondering why I wasn't excited. I thought art was supposed to look good. This stuff didn't. It lacked that ineffable quality that I called beauty but was beyond beauty—some combination of the visual and the emotional that had drawn me to art in the first place. What was going on?

I never really answered that question. I'm sure that part of the answer was that I simply didn't know enough. Had I known what the art cognoscenti knew, I'd probably have appreciated some of that art more. Fair enough. I was swimming in unfamiliar waters. But still, I couldn't resist considering a more skeptical view: maybe some of this stuff just wasn't all that good. Could that be?

I wasn't sure, and eventually came to terms with simply not liking some, perhaps a lot, of what I was seeing in galleries on the Upper East Side and in Soho, and occasionally in the MOMA. That was my taste and I'd live with it. But much later when I read Tom Wolfe's *The Painted Word* my skepticism revived. Wolfe didn't like a lot of that stuff either and argued essentially that the emperor had no clothes. What was going on with Abstract Expressionism, Minimalism, Conceptual Art, Op Art. and much more, he said, was a combination of elitism (the culturati looking to set itself apart from the crass and the middle class) and a sort of intellectualism (high-brow art critics arguing that you couldn't really see a painting unless you had a theory to go with it). This latter he summarized wonderfully in his book: "Not 'seeing is believing,' you ninny, but 'believing is seeing." I loved that. It captured the idea that you couldn't appreciate the art if you didn't understand the theory behind it—a position I didn't like at all. The immediate pleasure that art was supposed to deliver had apparently gotten hijacked by intellectuals and theorists. The rest of us either had to trust them and fall into line or turn our backs.

(Wolfe also reported a wonderful pun he'd spotted in the mainstream press, referring to Jackson Pollock as "Jack the Dripper." I'll bet he wished he'd come up with that.)

I don't know how much truth there was (and is) to Wolfe's theories. My own not-at-all-original position is that art is a series of experiments—creative experiments—that can take you to beauty, or to dead ends. We should hope for the former but not be surprised by the latter. And we can't trust, at least in the short run, art critics, or the art-buying public to tell us which is which. Time, and our gut, will make that determination.

None of this, however, got in the way of my friendship with Pepe—or my respect for his art cred. We agreed on much more than we disagreed. He got me not only to be more serious about art but showed me what serious meant. And in 1991 he took me to an art auction at Sotheby's in New York, in preparation for him selling his Klee print there a few days later for $85,000 to a couple of Japanese collectors and using the money to help buy an apartment in Santiago. Letting go of that Klee print was a milestone for him. I was privileged to share it.

We had a great time discussing other topics as well, including astrology, which he took seriously, and Chilean wine, which both of us did.

Pepe's claim to fame, of course, was human rights, where he was a major international figure. I remember a long conversation about what Max Weber might teach us about human rights. When *Death and the Maiden* (which featured a Latin American woman confronting a former agent of the military dictatorship she thought tortured and raped her decades before) debuted on Broadway in 1992, with Gene Hackman, Glenn Close, and Richard Dreyfus, he took me to see it with tickets he'd gotten from Ariel Dorfman, who'd written the play based in part on a conversation he'd had with Pepe.

My favorite anecdote about Pepe's work in human rights comes from one of his students at the University of Chile's law school who reflected on a classroom discussion:

"I'll never forget that class:

Professor Zalaquett: 'Today no one can say he doesn't know someone who was the victim of human rights violations during the dictatorship.'

Student: 'I don't know anyone,'

Professor Zalaquett, walking over and extending his hand: 'Pleased to meet you, I'm José Zalaquett.' "

That's the Pepe I knew.

When I finally got married, Pepe was best man. We remained friends right up until his death decades later of what he described in an email as a particularly "nasty" strain of Parkinson's disease, and which took him downhill fast. I visited him nearly a year before his death and by then he could no longer move, swallow, or talk. So it was me telling him what I was up to, and how much I appreciated our friendship over the years. His eyes were alert, but he could only respond by raising or lowering a finger his wife held in her hand—up was yes and down was no. He was receiving oxygen via a tube in his nose, and food via a tube in his arm. Parkinson's doesn't affect your mind, but steadily erodes your motor functions.

He was special. I miss him.

Tom Wolfe, by the way, has long been a favorite of mine. His first book, which I remember reading back when I was in graduate school at Duke, was *The Kandy-Kolored Tangerine-Flake Streamline Baby*, which vividly documented the new culture bubbling up in the United States after World War II—including Las Vegas (which he called "the Versailles of America"), stock car racing, rock and roll, and Cassius Clay. I still have my much-underlined paperback copy. The quote that rings truest today is "Suddenly classes of people whose styles of life had been practically invisible had the money to build monuments to their own styles." Precisely. I'd seen it while growing up, particularly in the customized ("chopped and channeled") cars that appeared on Eaton Rapids' Main Street, the ducktail haircuts (my own brief foray included), and the demolition derbies I watched on TV (which Wolfe called "a form of gladiatorial combat for our times"). He held a mirror up to society in a way that was dramatic, exuberant, entertaining and mostly accurate. It was also useful. We need him today to decode Donald Trump.

XIV

PERU PLUS

SO FAR, DEAR reader, I've said nothing about Peru. It's the Latin American country I've lived in longest: seven or eight years over two tours with the Ford Foundation, depending on how you count. It's also the most exotic, populated appreciably by people of indigenous descent, inspired by Indian cultures that stretch back a thousand years (the Chavín, Huari, and Inca being most important), and dominated politically and economically over the past several centuries by descendants of the Spanish conquerers. Peru's politics have been exotic as well, including the revolutionary and left-leaning military dictatorship of General Juan Velasco Alvarado, the bloodthirsty terrorism of Abimael Guzmán's *Shining Path*, the glittering populism of Alvaro García, and the *Fujishock* and *Fujigolpe* of Alberto Fujimori—all of which I experienced over two decades. Peru has the best cuisine in Latin America (sorry, Mexico), punctuated by wonderful Chinese restaurants (AKA "*chifas*"). And it has some of the warmest, friendliest people I've ever encountered. So for me it's always been a special place.

I first visited Peru in 1970 while still a graduate student, to attend a workshop on the economics of education organized by a professor of mine at Chicago, Bob Myers. That visit was memorable for two reasons: 1) One of the participants was Alejandro Toledo, who decades later would become Peru's president; and 2) I had a one-on-one with Dick

Dye, the head of Ford's office in Lima, that left me petrified. Dick was one of the most tight-lipped people I'd ever met. He said hello and then waited for me to talk. I'd assumed he was going to talk, but he didn't. I couldn't think of anything to say. There was silence. It was excruciating. Here I was meeting for the first time with a Ford Foundation bigwig and failing to impress. Half a decade later Dick became my boss, and pretty quickly a good friend. But it sure didn't feel that way when we started out. There's probably a lesson there: even if you fumble the first impression, you may get another chance. Learn. Keep at it.

By the way, something similar happened to me several years later in New York when, now a junior staff member at Ford, I met for the first time with the Foundation's vice president for international programs, Dave Bell (who'd been JFK's budget director and head of USAID). It was also a one-on-one, and I had no idea why it was even taking place. Dave was a smart, no-nonsense guy. He asked me several questions about Peru and Chile. I gave him flabby answers. He let me know that. The meeting was over. I was dazed. Once again I'd failed to impress. Would I ever learn? But both these incidents illustrate, I think, why I was attracted to the Ford Foundation in the first place. You were forced to deal with tough, first-rate minds. That could be painful but was what I'd always wanted to do. I could take it. I would learn. It was good for me.

I began actually living in Peru in July of 1974 when, six-plus months after joining the Ford Foundation to work in Chile, I was transferred to Lima—where I resided legally for the next four years and worked for five. That was unexpected. I'd spent half a year getting settled in Santiago, not only learning to navigate the turmoil and repression of military dictatorship, but getting to know our grantees, making friends, meeting a couple of women, getting a taste of Santiago's (very middle-class) social life, sampling the food and wine (decidedly first-rate), experiencing the city's delightfully sunny, hot and dry summer, and checking out the nearby majestic snow-covered mountains and Big Sur-type coast. It wasn't a bad start, and I was feeling good. Now I had to give that up and start over in a new country, Peru, and a new city, Lima. But I was too young to be fussy, and this was, after all, the Ford Foundation, where I'd always wanted to work. So I'd do it and not complain. Still, it was a challenge.

In Lima, July is the cruelest month. You're below the equator so it's winter. You're on the Pacific coast so the Humboldt Current is bringing frigid water up from Antarctica that the weak winter sunlight can't fully warm up and instead turns into mist—thick clouds of grey mist—that hug the city for a couple of months, turning everything chilly and damp. It doesn't rain, although you get a bit of morning drizzle (*la garúa*). The temperature is in the 50s or 60s. Most July days you don't see the sun at all. For much of the rest of the year, clouds are still the norm. Annually, Lima gets less sunshine than London. It's not a place that makes a good first impression.

(Later I learned that for foreigners like me July was a month to avoid in Lima. Either you drove up into the mountains to the village of Chosica on weekends, above the clouds and in the sun, or you tried to schedule travel abroad, on business or vacation. You did what you could to get out of that unremitting cold cloud.)

Driving in from the Jorge Chávez airport provided a good introduction to Lima. First came the shanty towns (*pueblos jovenes*)—vast, mysterious and impoverished—that surrounded the city like supplicants. They were composed largely of migrants from Peru's interior seeking work or (later) fleeing terrorism. Their streets were ugly, dark, and deep. Their buildings—of adobe, brick, boards, corrugated metal, and sometimes cardboard or straw—seemed unplanned and unfinished. Their inhabitants were barely shadows moving in the dim light. You couldn't imagine their problems and would rather not. It was Dickensian, perhaps beyond. I never wanted to turn off the main road and actually enter those slums. They frightened me. But neither could I ignore them. Sometimes I felt I saw more poverty driving into Lima from the airport than I saw during my entire two years as a Peace Corps volunteer in Colombia. Lima bared its soul to anyone who came near.

Then you entered more developed neighborhoods. These were working class, and in some sense modern. They had paved streets, traffic lights, running water, and sewers. The architecture was nondescript but was architecture. The houses were modest but designed by some-one—and finished. There were apartment buildings, restaurants, bars, shops, *discotecas*—even bingo parlors (who would have expected that?). There was neon, often garish. They felt a little like a strip mall in the United States—cheap, but lively. You could get a pizza or a hamburger or Chinese takeout or a whiskey. There was a lot of bad taste, but a lot going on. People had money. They were spending it. There was a kind of vitality. These neighborhoods were a big step up.

If you were heading to a hotel in the center of town, around the Plaza de Armas, where visitors had traditionally stayed, you were treated to the splendid colonial architecture at the city's core. The buildings were often hundreds of years old, featuring hand-carved wooden balconies that felt like Madrid, or maybe Seville. They reminded you that Lima had once been the capital of the Viceroyalty of Peru and thus the center of the Spanish Empire in South America—big, strong, and wealthy. They provided a huge sense of history.

More and more, though, people like me stayed at hotels in the modern neighborhoods of Miraflores and San Isidro, which were out-side the city's core and on the sea. These were clearly upscale. They had fewer people and more money. The houses were larger. The brick walls protected lawns, gardens, and garages. It was quieter. This was the Lima of the modern, educated elites—the people we dealt with and consid-ered ourselves part of. Entering these neighborhoods was, in an almost subliminal way, comforting. You identified. You knew what to say and how to behave. You felt at home.

That's where I landed in the fog of July, and quickly rented a one-bedroom furnished apartment (in *Lince*, as I recall, on the border with *San Isidro*) from an elderly couple—missionaries who'd settled in Peru long ago. He was British and she was American. They connected me to the world of idealistic foreigners who'd come to Peru many years before to make things better and stayed. (He always referred to Argentina as "the Argentine," a phrase I'd never heard before and assumed was some-thing that British of a certain age said.) The office assigned me a Toyota. I began to settle in.

I've said before that one of the great things about working for the Ford Foundation back then was the high quality of its staff. Lima was no exception. Nobody was average. All were first-rate professionals, good people, and even fun. Jim Trowbridge, my new boss, was a Chicagoan who'd studied at Princeton's Woodrow Wilson School and had worked in Ford's Caribbean program before coming to Peru. We hit it off; I'd be fine with him. Rey Carlson, who I mentioned earlier had been U.S. ambassador in Colombia when I was in the Peace Corps there, managed the economics program and turned out to be a great guy. He and his wife Patsy invited me for Thanksgiving dinner—much appreciated by a newcomer missing a family ritual. (A year or so later, when they were spending post-retirement time in Buenos Aires, Rey and Patsy invited me and my visiting parents to dinner at a fabulous steakhouse. I still remember his animated discussion with the waiter about which sausage, cuts of beef, wine, and dessert we should order. Jovial was an understatement.) Nita Manitzas had also been transferred to Lima from the office in Santiago, so I already knew her and her husband Frank, who worked for CBS News. There were others—Peter Cleaves, a Berkeley-trained political scientist who managed the social science program, Peter Knight, a Stanford economist in charge of agricultural economics, and Antonio Muñoz-Najar, our Peruvian office manager who also oversaw our work in population. All were all special, in terms of talent, motivation, education. You expected them to do special things. The local support staff were just as impressive, including senior secretary Diana Davis, an Anglo-Peruvian who helped us remember that the British had an important presence in recent Peruvian history, Angelica Hirata, a Japanese-Peruvian who helped us remember the same about the Japanese, and our driver, Federico ("Freddy") Herrera, who had grown up in a remote mountain village where there were no roads at all, and got his start driving a tank in the Peruvian army. There were others, all of whom I liked. It was a good group to talk to, work with, and learn from. I'd be fine.

The process of inserting yourself into a new country and culture is probably more art than science. You start with your office colleagues simply because you see them every day and they know the ropes. They share, inviting you to dinner, telling you what's out there and introducing you to friends. You follow up. You begin to map the terrain and see what you like. You establish relationships. At some point you begin to navigate on your own. You're in.

In my case I asked Peter Hakim, my former colleague in the Santiago office who had, a few years earlier, worked briefly in Peru, whether he had any suggestions and he gave me a name—Mayu (short for María Jesus) Hume—who turned out to be intelligent, strong, and charming. Mayu was the first woman to get an engineering degree at the Catholic University of Peru, and followed that up with an MA in Economics. She worked at the Catholic University, under its distinguished rector Father Felipe Mac Gregor. We hit it off. She introduced me to her boyfriend, Julio Vargas, a civil engineer who specialized in anti-seismic construction (crucial in earthquake-prone Peru). We became friends. So much so that within a year or two, when I began spending less time in Peru and more in Chile and Argentina, they suggested I stay at their apartment while in Lima rather than at my own, and promptly christened theirs the "*Pensión Vargas*," which we laughed about. Since I was no longer using my apartment, I loaned it to a couple of U.S. graduate students (and their dog), who appreciated the boost to their limited finances. Mayu and Julio introduced me to their friends; I began to have a social life with Peruvians, and not just with foreigners. It was a good start.

So pretty quickly I got a solid introduction to Peru. I met Ford grantees, got to know a few of the country's social scientists, read the newspapers (along with *Caretas*, the country's premier newsmagazine), and sampled the politics. I began to appreciate the richness and weight of Peru's indigenous culture—something I'd not seen in Colombia, Chile, or Argentina. I got exposed to the government's "revolutionary" agenda (which, frankly, I never thought had much promise). I made friends. I began reading Mario Vargas Llosa (starting, I think, with *Pantaleón y las Visitadoras*, which explores, with subtle wit, what happens when a conscientious and recently promoted captain in the Peruvian army gets a secret order to establish a prostitution service aimed at keeping troops happy in the jungle region of Iquitos). I made my first of several visits to Cuzco and Machu Picchu. And to Huancayo, via the world's second-highest railway. And to Pucallpa, where I experienced the green screech of the tropical rain forest. I discovered *ceviche, causa, rocoto*, and Peru's version of pisco sours (drier, sweeter, and tastier in my opinion than the Chilean version). I began feeling like I knew the place.

Working in Ford's office in Peru at that point in time seemed almost normal. Peru was, like Chile, governed by a military dictatorship. But that dictatorship was less repressive. So there was less political violence, more freedom of speech, and more space for political opposition. In Peru we didn't have to worry about people who'd been arrested or had disappeared, and whether our phones had been tapped or our office searched. The universities functioned almost normally. And in Peru we didn't feel uncomfortable working with the government (although that generally wasn't our style).

I want to emphasize also that Ford's core strategy back then was to strengthen the capacity of Latin American people and institutions to understand and address their social and economic problems. We believed that well-trained, internationally connected academics and analysts, most of them social scientists operating from modern universities and think tanks, could and would play positive roles in their countries. That was a macro- rather than a micro-strategy. It was long-term rather than short-term. And it put us behind the front lines rather than on them. We were like bankers, making long-term investments and hoping for long-term payoffs. My job in Lima, and that of my colleagues in most of Latin America, was largely to help strengthen institutions and capacity, both of which took time. If we were successful, the benefits would flow for decades. I found that approach attractive. And, having been raised a Lutheran, I was used to deferring gratification. Long-term was fine.

But wasn't it boring? A little dull, maybe? Like laying bricks on a foundation or nailing siding to a wall? I never felt that way. For me it was fascinating. We had a shot at making a major contribution to a country's welfare by strengthening the quality of the people who made decisions on social and economic policy, and the institutions that produced and housed them. That was big. It spoke to my abiding desire to make the world a better place, something I'd grown up with and was now getting a chance to try. Doing that well was a responsibility and a privilege. It was God's work. How could it be boring?

But I didn't really know what to do. I had plenty of education but little knowledge about building institutions or strengthening capacity. And of course I wasn't going to build anything myself. The people we funded would do the building. Our role was to put up money—to decide who to fund and under what conditions. I needed to understand the nuts and bolts of doing that.

It turned out that the methodology was right in front of me—in the minds of my colleagues and in our grant documents. Ford had tried a lot and learned a lot. You tapped into it by talking and reading, which I did lots of. Pretty quickly the outlines of a methodology emerged. But just the outlines. The details I had to fill in myself because every case was different. Here are some basics.

First, the work we supported needed to be housed in an appropriate institution, which for us was usually a university, occasionally a private think tank or international organization, and almost never a government agency. That framework had to be relatively sturdy, committed to high standards, and insulated against political pressure. Otherwise its work might be ignored. Or be of such low quality that it ought to be ignored. So we paid a lot of attention to the institutional framework that surrounded any project we might fund.

Second, we needed to fund the right people. That meant the best. Our job was to find and develop top-quality professionals and help them get in positions to address their social and economic problems. We did that in various ways. Step one was getting to know the relevant professional community. That meant tapping into networks. We identified key people. We had lunch. We listened to what they were saying about research, policy, politics, and each other. We looked at where they'd studied and what they'd written. We asked their opinion about what we should do. We developed our own opinion (hopefully accurate) about their motivation, intelligence, training, judgment, credibility, leadership, and integrity. We sized them up.

We paid special attention to leaders. A good leader was likely to do good things. He or she had high standards, sound judgment, the ability to inspire staff and respect in the broader professional community. These were the people who might influence university training and national policy over decades. We tried to find and nurture them. They were the horses we wanted to bet on.

But most importantly we tapped into international networks to get their take on the people and work we were dealing with. We hired distinguished social scientists from Europe, the United States, and elsewhere in Latin America as consultants to discuss our plans, meet the people we were talking to and inform our decisions. It was, I think, a good formula. They brought international perspectives and standards to bear on national activities and provided local scholars and analysts with authoritative feedback on their work. They gave us a good sense of who had the right stuff. And the consultants we brought in often established professional and personal relationships with local scholars that kept paying off long after they returned to their universities.

Third, we had to grapple with the how. What was it going to take to get the job done? What combination of inputs should we fund, at what level and for how long? Were we willing to be the only funder, or should we require complementary support? What made sense and might work?

There were no magic answers to these questions. It depended on their (and our) objectives and the realities they faced. If, for example, the goal was to establish a modern discipline of sociology in a university, we'd have to fund generously and broadly—staff salaries, research, international travel, publications, visiting foreign professors, graduate training abroad, overhead—for a decade or more. Building institutions and capacity is a big job and takes time.

If, on the other hand, the objective was simply to do research on a specific topic and the capacity to do that research were already in place, our funding would be smaller, narrower and shorter. It all depended.

I need to say more about objectives. Choosing objectives may be the single most important thing a donor does. That choice allocates money and effort to one area rather than to another. It stimulates activity, builds expertise, and (hopefully) generates progress. It determines the kind of staff a donor needs, and the kinds of people it consults and supports. It sends a message about what's important. It can have a significant ripple effect, causing others to reallocate their own resources in response to the objectives a donor—especially a credible donor—has chosen. It has consequences.

It also promotes, or at least permits, creativity. One of the marvelous things about philanthropy is that it enables donors, at least in principle, to put their money where their hearts and minds lead them—which often is very different from what a government might do. They can take risks, think outside the box, challenge conventional wisdom, explore wild ideas and champion the politically incorrect. They can criticize the status quo, or defend it. They can do that not just with ideas but also with money. Philanthropy combines freedom with power.

That freedom brings with it responsibility. You need to choose objectives clearly and deliberately. You need to know what you're trying to make happen, and what not. You need to know why it's worth doing, whether it can be done and what it will take to do it. You need to know these things regardless of whether the gleam in your eye is about feeding the poor or strengthening capacity to do research in macroeconomics. They are the guidelines that help you see the big picture and decide whether your plans pass muster.

So the magic (and I think there really was some) in working for the Ford Foundation at that point in time was in figuring out what ought to be done, whether it could be done, who could do it, and what it would take. And then, once those questions had been answered, overseeing the efforts by grantees to do what they'd proposed to do, and what we'd agreed to fund. Some combination of that is what I did for seventeen years. It always seemed important and never seemed boring.

I've probably gotten a little carried away here. And I don't want to suggest that Ford's approach was the only or best way to do philanthropy. Plenty of other institutions are out there doing good work. And

I still have a couple more thoughts on the donor profession that I think are important but that you may or may not want to sit through. If not, feel free to jump ahead a few paragraphs. Quite a few paragraphs, actually.

One of the biggest challenges donors face is saying no. You're a philanthropist. Your job is to give away money. You've invested a lot of time and effort in figuring out how you might do that. You've met some great people. They need help. You care. How can you say no?

There's no clear answer to that question, except to focus on the guidelines I've suggested above. If the institutions, people and plans don't measure up to your objectives, strategies, and resources, what's the argument for giving them money? Maybe there's one that you've simply failed to see. You should consider that. But often there isn't. And you should say no.

But it's hard. The downside of having money to give away is that everyone expects you to give them some. And is disappointed when you don't. People screen out any suggestion that you won't provide funding. They won't hear you say that funding is unlikely, and may not even hear you say no. They will continue to hope, even with no encouragement and perhaps without realizing they're doing it. That's normal. I'd probably do the same.

So you need to start by assuming that, for most people, you are a glittering pot of gold, and tailor your behavior to that reality. Be nice. Be modest. Don't waste people's time. Concentrate on objectives, requirements, and facts, and not on the great lunch they've just given you. In fact, buy lunch. Cultivate a poker face. Utter a discouraging word. Utter two. Tell them you love them, but that money just isn't in the cards. Blame it on your boss in New York. Don't suggest there's any possibility of funding unless you're willing to fork it over. It's easier to start an avalanche than to stop one. Be responsible. Those practices are fundamental for the professional philanthropist.

The temptation, of course, is to dabble. You've decided you're not going to provide real money to an institution you've been talking to, but hate to say no completely and so offer to fund at least something, like a conference or some travel. It's kind of a consolation prize. You feel better. Maybe they do. Spread it around a little.

Dabbling is OK in small quantities. It's a way to let someone down easy, establish your credibility or recognize their achievement. It may, occasionally, address a strategic need. And sometimes planting many seeds in many places is how you bring new ideas into the mainstream. It can also help you test the waters: fund something small at an institution you think has potential and see how they do. Then use that to decide whether they merit a larger investment later on.

But dabbling can be habit-forming. Doing a bunch of little things can feel bigger than doing one big thing. Your list of activities is longer, and your sense of accomplishment greater. You've got more people smiling and saying thank you. You have more to talk about with your boss and more to report to your board of directors. It always feels good.

The problem is that action is not the same as impact. Doing many little things may get in the way of doing the one big thing that makes a difference. And dabbling is labor-intensive. It can fritter away your time and your institution's money, making it harder to see and do what really matters. You need to set a high bar. Avoid making small grants just to make yourself feel better—as, let's be honest, I've done myself more than once. And when you dabble, be clear about why. Recognize that you are facing huge temptation.

Your default response, though, should be no. It's not fun, but it's responsible.

I said no a lot. One of the toughest cases came several years later while I was managing the Foundation's work in the Caribbean. The program was small, and focused on Jamaica and the Dominican Republic, with a smidgen in Barbados and Puerto Rico. I was wondering whether we should start work in Haiti, the Caribbean's poorest country, where we'd done almost nothing. I made several visits on my own, and then a couple with Bill Carmichael, my boss, and with Harriet Rabb, a member of our Board.

There was no lack of things to do. The people were great, the culture fascinating and the needs enormous. Poverty was broader and deeper than anywhere in Latin America. The government seemed barely to exist, let alone function. Much, perhaps most, of the population could neither read nor write. Most kids didn't even go to school. Only about ten percent of the few who did went to public schools. The other ninety percent had parents who could afford private schools. But most were uneducated. The politics were nearly incomprehensible and soaked through with corruption. It looked like a kleptocracy and felt like a disaster. I'd never seen anything like it. I remember especially visiting a health clinic for desperately ill children that was funded entirely by foreign donors like us. Standing at the bedside of those sick kids was heart-breaking.

My recommendation, though, was that we do nothing. The logic was simple: Haiti was so different, and its problems so deep and widespread that, at least in the fields in which we worked, only a substantial, prolonged, and intensive effort had any chance for success. The dominant language was Creole. The official language was French. The culture was a mix of Africa and France. We spoke neither and understood neither. We'd have to hire someone who did, and I doubted that we would. We hadn't discussed objectives, but all those that seemed worthwhile and leveraged our comparative advantage would require significant time, effort and money. I saw little appetite within the Foundation for that kind of commitment. The most I could see us doing was dabbling. Why do that? The case was weak. Making ourselves feel good wasn't enough. So no.

I was surprised that I reached that conclusion. All I did was survey the scene, look at obstacles as well as needs, and try to be realistic about what it might take to make a difference and whether we could provide it. You can still get it wrong doing that, of course, but there's probably no better way to get it right.

Here, since we're talking about Haiti, I want also to pass on a random experience there that captures some of the country's uncommon feel and color—and, to my surprise, some fundamental aspects of the Ford Foundation I worked in.

It was a conversation I had with some Evangelical Christians (my label—I don't recall exactly how they identified themselves) I ran into by chance. Haiti attracts all kinds of foreigners wanting to do good. They were one of many. We chatted.

"What are you doing in Haiti?" I said.

"The Lord brought us. He told us to come here. We didn't even know where it was."

I found that interesting because it was way beyond anything I'd ever done. I'd always known where I was going, or at least thought so. These people didn't, and didn't worry about it. They'd been called, and they answered.

But clearly they'd gotten some preparation: "We were told before we came that we'd better know our Jesus because the people here really know their voodoo."

I found that charming. And a sound principle. Back in the Peace Corps I'd discovered how important it was to understand what it was you were trying to do and why it should be done. If you didn't, it was going to be hard to get people to move beyond the status quo. And that same principle was maybe even more important at the Ford Foundation where the objectives, like establishing a modern discipline of economics or promoting human rights, were broader and more abstract. Change didn't happen just because you thought it should. You (or at least someone) had to make the case. People knew their voodoo; you needed to know your Jesus.

Just as interesting, the Evangelicals felt they'd gotten results. They told me "There was a little girl at one of these services. She was deaf and dumb, and we prayed for her, and she began to speak. The words came slow, you know? 'b-b-bonjour'…just a few words you know, not a whole dissertation. And then we whispered 'Jesus' in her ear and she understood."

That affirmed their faith. They explained "I guess that if he makes you feel that way, he must be the Lord. If he weren't the Lord, he couldn't make us feel that way."

I was a little envious. At the Ford Foundation we didn't get results— at least not immediate, short-term results. We'd rejected that siren song.

It wasn't part of our catechism. Ours was the noble, long-term game. The money we were investing in training people and building institutions wouldn't pay off right away but would eventually change the world—or at least our part of the world. Once the youngsters we'd sent off to study at Stanford, Harvard, and Chicago came back and took charge, it was gonna be great. Short-term was for sissies. We had the vision, judgement, and patience to play the long game. We'd thought it through. We believed.

So we were different from the Evangelicals when it came to results. We neither got nor expected them any time soon. They did. But I'm not sure this particular difference was all that important. What seemed more important was what we had in common: faith. Theirs was based on religion, ours was based on reason. Both were powerful. Both fueled commitment. Both transcended short-term results. Both were probably key to any effectiveness we had. Both made each of us feel we'd found the way. The Ford Foundation would never call itself a faith-based organization, but in some important ways it was just that.

I'm reminded of a conversation I once had with Rodrigo Botero, a former finance minister of Colombia and a particularly thoughtful member of Ford's board of directors, in which he said that the Ford Foundation reminded him of the Jesuits. I'd not thought of that, but it made sense. Like the Jesuits we had a strong sense of mission, took the long view, tried to recruit the best and the brightest, placed a high value on education, and thought money was important. Not a bad comparison.

I'm also reminded of the argument that James March, a Stanford professor whom I'll tell you more about shortly, made about Don Quixote and what he can teach us about leadership. Quixote, March contended, shows that "Great acts of leadership in history have often involved the ability to see things others could not see." They are, first of all, matters of vision and faith. In his film, *Passion and Discipline: Don Quixote's Lessons for Leadership*, he observed "Quixote does not accept reality. He imposes his imagination, his commitment and his joy on it. He produces a world of beauty and of meaning."

The Ford Foundation did that, at least back then in Latin America. It had a robust and attractive vision and was committed to turning that vision into reality. And there was something joyful about the place. I think that's part of why I wanted to work there.

The Evangelicals did something similar, even though their vision was very different from ours. Both of us were playing a game in which the rules were unclear and the opponents strong. But both of us were convinced we were right, and that gave us not just strength, but comfort. We were more like each other—and like Don Quixote—than either of us might have cared to admit.

Go to Haiti. You'll be amazed.

Once again I've gotten carried away. Haiti will do that to you. Let me try to get back on track by emphasizing that for philanthropists results are in fact important. But they're tricky. Philanthropy is all about doing good. But sometimes, maybe often, you can only hope and believe that good really will flow from what you do. It's easy enough, of course, if your goal is something relatively straightforward like feeding the poor. You can watch people eat. And even take pictures.

But good luck if the good you're trying to do is more abstract and longer-term. It may take years for any impact to occur and even longer to see it. In fact, you may not see it even if it happens. And forget about taking pictures. Or even getting credit. You can only do what you think is right and hope.

That was Ford's predicament in Latin America in the 1970s and 1980s. We wanted economies to grow and societies to become more equal, tolerant, and democratic. Initially we figured that strengthening competence in areas like the natural sciences, engineering, agriculture, and management would make that happen. Soon we also began to emphasize "increasing the ability of Latin Americans to make rational choices among important policy options facing their societies." That led us to focus more on strengthening the social sciences and building local capacities to carry out basic and applied research that might improve economic and social policy.

We were happy with those strategies, and confident they would eventually pay off. But there was no point in expecting any near-term impact. And even when impact began to happen, it would probably be hard to document. We could only do our best to upgrade talent in the social sciences. The rest would have to work itself out.

Two examples, both from Chile, illustrate how hard impact is to predict. Between 1961 and 1971 Ford, along with the Rockefeller Foundation and USAID, sought to strengthen the country's two leading university-based economics programs. The goal was to establish a modern discipline of economics, and thereby promote economic growth. Yet, after a decade of investment (for Ford some $2 million, not adjusted for inflation), it was hard to see any impact at all. Salvador Allende was president, and implementing a radical socialist economic policy that, whatever its merits, was anything but modern. Most of the economists that Ford and others had helped train sat on the sidelines. They'd had zero impact.

A few years later, however, nearly everything had changed. The military overthrew the Allende government in 1973, and in 1975 enlisted many of those newly trained economists (largely from the Catholic University of Chile) to establish its economic policy. They quickly made Chile Latin America's best-performing economy and fundamentally changed economic thinking in the country. Ford's efforts to establish a modern economics in Chile had had a major impact. But only after fifteen years and the emergence of a military dictatorship, neither of which anyone at Ford would have predicted or wanted.

The second example has to do with the network of private social science think tanks that Ford helped establish in Chile after the military coup of 1973. As I explained earlier, Ford's objective was to maintain critical, independent thought within a repressive regime and keep high-level social science talent in the country so it could eventually guide national policy once democracy returned. Ford spent considerable amounts of money supporting these groups for the next fifteen years, during most of which they had almost no visible impact.

That changed too. Eventually the think tanks helped the political leaders rethink their politics and strategy, played a key role in defeating

Pinochet in the 1988 plebiscite and then filled dozens of high-level positions in the democratic government that took over in 1990 (I sketched this a few pages back, and provide plenty of detail in my book, *Thinking Politics: Intellectuals and Democracy in Chile, 1973-1988*).

So Ford got the impact it wanted, and more. But, like its investment in modern economics, it took fifteen years and a fundamental change of government for that impact to occur. Those of us who were involved hoped deep down we'd get results like that. But we'd never have dared predict it. We simply took the road that looked best (and was, arguably, less traveled) and hoped.

Both cases illustrate the perils of predicting impact when objectives are abstract and long-term. Your calculus needs to be different. You need to do what's right and have a reasonable argument about how doing what's right will eventually pay off. Different people will have different views about what's right, of course. There's no remedy for that. Just try to get the right right. Then move forward and do your best without worrying too much about the when or the how of the impact. History seldom proceeds in a straight line. Making solid, lasting contributions to a good cause is often the best you can do. The rest has to work itself out. It's probably a little like raising kids.

(This sounds like something I learned in Sunday School, and maybe it is. But it's what I saw time and again while working in Latin America.)

In these two cases, though, and in much of Ford's work in Latin America back then, there is another point to make. We were playing the policy game. Our goal was to improve policy. And it turns out that the policy game, as Peter Hakim has pointed out, is like chess. You play for position rather than for victory. Most of your moves have no immediate impact. They are intended only to establish a position that will enable you to have impact later on. That's how it worked out for the Chicago Boys who dreamed of revolutionizing economic policy, and for the think tanks opposed to Pinochet who dreamed of restoring democratic government. They spent years getting into position. Then, when the stars aligned and opportunity knocked, they were ready. Check and mate.

So I'm confident that we had impact in Chile. And the limited academic analysis (why isn't there more?) tends to agree. In *Foundations of the American Century: The Ford, Carnegie, and Rockefeller Foundations in the Rise of American Power*, Inderjeet Parmar of the City University, London, offers analysis, otherwise highly polemical, of the role of foreign foundations in Chile, concluding that

> Ford's programs in Chile were ultimately profoundly successful: they generated networks of scholars linked with political and state organizations and affected the course of Chilean political and economic development.

He states further that

> In creating a network of centrist research and semipolitical organizations during the Pinochet years, Ford generated the basis of the transformation of a diverse and divided set of academic and political exiles into a powerful centrist force for Chilean reform. Once again, their pre- and postcoup investments overlapped and reinforced one another, creating an opposition cadre of scholars for political and technocratic rule in the 1990s.

That's impact.

My apologies for this lengthy digression into the nuts and bolts of giving away money. I started out talking about Peru, where our work was nearly normal, and thought it might be the right moment to give you a sense of what our type of philanthropy was like under normal conditions. Philanthropy—like trading derivatives or being an undertaker—is an uncommon occupation. Few of us know anyone who does it. I wanted to try to capture how we saw it, what we did, and what we (or at least I) learned. I find that interesting. Some may find it useful.

Now let's get back to Peru.

As I mentioned earlier, I'd inherited the education portfolio. It was largely about strengthening education research and policy analysis capacity in Peru. A year or so later they gave me the economics portfolio as well, which was part of Ford's broader effort to establish a modern economics profession in Latin America but was winding down. So I had plenty to do. I dove into the details and process of managing our grants. My job was to monitor, evaluate, comment, and recommend. In the Foundation world, that constituted business as usual. We hadn't had to rethink our strategy in Peru, the way we'd had to further south. It was, compared to working in Chile, smooth sailing.

Frankly I remember little about those grants. It was, of course, more than forty years ago. But it may also have been because they were so unexceptional compared to what I was dealing with in Chile—and later in Argentina. Any problems or challenges I ran into in Peru at that point (and in contrast to a decade later when I returned to Peru) seemed routine; not much stood out.

There was one exception. Ford had seldom, in Latin America, made grants to governments, but my predecessor had made a grant to support a research institute recently established at the ministry of education. That grant was probably six months or more from its termination date and we'd expected to renew it, but the director asked whether we could renew it right away. They needed new funds to beef up their data processing capacity so they could get some research out that would inform pending ministerial decisions. I said sure and put other work aside to process their proposal and submit it to New York. It was approved and I sent the grant letter over to the ministry. All they had to do was sign and return it to me with a request for payment, and they'd have their money.

Nothing happened. Every time I asked, they said they'd get the letter back to us right away. Still nothing happened. We'd responded immediately to their request to renew funding ahead of schedule, and yet they couldn't or wouldn't sign a letter accepting the money. A year went by. I was mystified. I got no clear explanation. The director of the program asked whether I'd ever read Kafka, which I thought that was a nice touch. He was frustrated too.

Eventually they did what they needed to do and we gave them the money. But they never explained. I was aghast. Clearly the ministry was not a reliable partner. It faced incentives it couldn't ignore but that had little to do with providing services to the citizens of Peru. Something else was going on. I began to wonder whether this was an organic feature of government ministries—that they were organized to serve politicians, bureaucrats, and public sector unions first, and that only once those groups had been satisfied could they serve the public. Whatever the answer, we had no comparative advantage in the game they were playing. We didn't even understand the rules. During the fifteen or so years of my subsequent service with Ford, I don't recall ever making another grant to a government. It didn't seem like a good use of Ford Foundation funds.

That's about as much as I have to say about my first five years with the Ford Foundation. Going in, my only expectation was that I'd get a shot at making the world a better place and work with people who were smarter than I. Both happened. But I got much more, having lived in two countries, worked in four, been held to high standards, dealt with monumental uncertainty, met a slew of extraordinary people, and learned a lot about politics (and more than I wanted about dictatorships). I'd been surprised, privileged, challenged, and blessed. Now I was off to Stanford for a sabbatical year.

Which was also a surprise. I never asked for (nor dreamed of) a sabbatical and wasn't sure how to react when they offered it—except to take it. Ford required that I submit a proposal regarding what I'd do, and I'd (after initially not having a clue) chosen the obvious: reflect on and write up Ford's experience in providing development assistance within the repressive regimes of Chile, Argentina, and Uruguay from 1973 to 1978. I had no idea what, if anything, I'd come up with. But since I'd been there and done that, it seemed like a good idea.

XV

STANFORD, SAN FRANCISCO, AND MORE

I CHOSE STANFORD (actually, the Stanford International Development Education Center-SIDEC) because it was one of three centers of excellence in comparative education that had received funding from the Ford Foundation a decade or more earlier (the others being at Harvard and Chicago). I'd gotten my degree at the Chicago center, specializing in the economics of education, and knew an economist, Martin Carnoy, who taught at the Stanford center (he'd studied economics at Chicago, by the way, but detested the Chicago Boys). So I figured I'd see what was going on at SIDEC. Stanford was a good school, after all. I'd audit a few classes, check out the California mystique, and write. And anyway I knew almost no one at Harvard.

I arrived Stanford in the fall of 1978, looking for a place to live. SIDEC's director, Hans Weiler, suggested that, instead of living in Palo Alto (boring, he said) I consider living in San Francisco and commuting to Palo Alto. I'd find that more interesting. It sounded like a good idea. I was already staying temporarily with a college friend, Bill Weiner, in San Francisco's North Beach. I'd try to find an apartment there, although it might be tough, given how fashionable that area had become. The strategy Bill recommended was to drive around the neighborhood once in the morning and once in the afternoon, with the goal of spotting a new For Rent sign the moment it went up and grabbing that apartment before someone else did. The first week I found nothing. Early the second week I noticed, on Chestnut Street halfway up Telegraph Hill, furniture and a moving van sitting in front of a building. There was no sign. I stopped and asked and was told that the guy who'd lived there had died, and that his first-floor apartment would be on the market as soon as they got it cleaned out. They gave me the name of the rental agency. I went there immediately and got it. No For Rent sign never went up. I moved in a week later.

Hans had been right. North Beach gave you Telegraph Hill with its great views and Little Italy with its great food. You could buy freshly made focaccia each morning and catch the scent of stir-fried garlic floating up from Chinatown each afternoon. There were comedy clubs and live music. People sang along to opera in coffeeshops and danced to jukeboxes in bars. The City Lights bookstore was just a few blocks away, as was the ancient cable car that ran from Fisherman's Wharf to Union Square. You could jog along the ocean. All that in the midst of San Francisco's thick gray fog and crazy steep hills. Delightful. Palo Alto couldn't compete.

I saw Stanford mostly as a break from the tension, pressure, and anxiety I'd faced during nearly half a decade of trying to do good while working, from two Ford Foundation offices, in four countries governed by military dictatorships, three of which were repressive. Now I'd put that behind me and luxuriate in the groves of academe, mingling with great minds, hanging out in the library, and writing. I'd have the luxury of leisure, of being at loose ends, of wondering what to do next and of doing it. Or not. I had a project to work on, of course. And I'd work on it. But I also had time to explore. It was a huge change of pace.

I did a few obvious things—like auditing Carnoy's graduate seminar in the economics of education, partly to refresh my stock of knowledge, but also to see how his left-of-center perspective differed from what I'd gotten at Chicago. And of course I worked on the paper I'd proposed to Ford as a condition for being granted a sabbatical year.

Just as often, though, I dabbled. Stanford (and the Bay Area more generally) seemed like a good place for that. I was curious to see what might turn up.

For example, I audited a course on organizational leadership at the Business School, taught by James March (whom I mentioned earlier), mostly because someone told me he was good. He turned out to be first-rate. Instead of lecturing, he posed questions for students to answer. Then he commented on their answers. That made it a conversation and got most students involved. He invited students to drop by his office every Friday afternoon for wine and conversation, which many of us did. His syllabus included a long list of academic articles, but I remember most his assertion that if you read *Don Quixote, War and Peace*, and *Macbeth*, you'd learn all you needed to know about leadership. Eventually he put together a couple of films making that point. March combined erudite with unpretentious, a prime example of the extraordinary scholars I'd hoped to get exposed to at Stanford. And so often stumbled across by luck.

Another example of dabbling: I'd go to the library in search of a specific book and, once in the stacks, scan the books around it to see what else I might find interesting. I came across Albert Hirschman's *Exit, Voice and Loyalty* that way—a book I'd heard of but hadn't read. I took it back to my office and read it. More than a decade later, and after corresponding with Hirschman, I'd cite that book in my own book on intellectuals and democracy in Chile. But I'm not sure I'd ever even have read Hirschman's book had I not had time to sniff around the Stanford library while on sabbatical.

I also attended an informal conversation with Robert McNamara that the Business School organized. I did it entirely because McNamara was a big name. But what I remember was not so much McNamara, who was predictably crisp and sharp. Rather it was the business students leading the discussion who were surprisingly relaxed and self-assured. This was, after all, the former president of the Ford Motor Company, former secretary of defense and current president of the World Bank. It would be hard to imagine a more accomplished and distinguished speaker. Yet they seemed at ease. They knew the rules. It looked to me like they'd grown up expecting to deal with people like him.

And I hadn't. None of us back in Eaton Rapids had been taught to expect that we might someday rub shoulders with the likes of Robert McNamara. You didn't need that skill set because it wasn't going to happen. I was struck, again, as I had been at the Chicago business school, by how different those students seemed from me, and how far their world seemed from mine.

The delicious irony was that, a few years later, I'd spend time with McNamara (he was a member of the Ford Foundation's board), chatting at board meetings, discussing the Bay of Pigs invasion over dinner in New York, taking him to meet a few Latin American dignitaries (among them, the president of Argentina), visiting a tango club in Buenos Aires, and even calling him "Bob." Pretty hard to anticipate that. He was easier to deal with than I had expected.

I also dabbled outside the university, signing up, for example, for a weekend workshop at the Esalen Institute in California's Big Sur. I mentioned earlier that Esalen was at the center of the human potential movement, a serious place for exploring the frontiers, and the overlap, of psychology and religion, and an emerging countercultural icon. That spoke to me. I had to see what it was about.

I enjoyed Esalen a lot but remember only a little. It was first of all gorgeous—120 acres of mountainside in the Big Sur, with dozens of springs, many of them gushing hot water, and all perched at the edge of the Pacific Ocean. Your first impression was of rugged, beautiful nature. The buildings were spartan, and the dining room communal. The food was healthy, presumably organic, largely vegetarian, and surprisingly tasty. The guests seemed an eclectic bunch, sharing only an interest in trying something new. The vibes were natural, spiritual, and sensual. I don't recall there being wine, or alcohol of any kind. You weren't there for luxury, nor to indulge your every whim. Esalen had an agenda. You were there to check it out.

After dinner that first evening I made my way down to the hot tubs, which were spring-fed and overlooked the ocean. I still hadn't grasped Esalen's dress code, so wore swimming trunks—and was promptly mortified because everyone else was naked. I got out of my trunks and into the nearest tub as fast as I could, trying hard to blend in with all those nude bodies. It was my first lesson in the Esalen agenda: nude was normal. You could pretty much get out of your clothes as soon as you got out of your car. That was completely new to me. I adjusted. It was easier than I'd have thought.

The next morning I woke up early to find my roommate (shared rooms were the norm) meditating alongside his bed. I was careful not to disturb him. He'd sounded like a serious guy when I met him the night before and he'd mentioned meditation and yoga. I shaved, showered, and went to breakfast, feeling I'd gotten myself into a world that was very different from the one I knew. I don't recall whether I wore clothes.

I had signed up for a two-day workshop on I know not what but that's not important since I was there basically to see what Esalen was like, just as a couple of years earlier I had wanted to see what psychotherapy was like. The workshop turned out to be interesting, but I remember little except that we were nude and stared into each other's eyes a lot. I think I got something important out of it. I just don't recall what. I do remember that one of the participants, a woman slightly older than I, struck me as extraordinarily neurotic. She went on and on about how her husband didn't appreciate her concerns or share her interest in psychology. She was pretty worked up. I felt sorry for her but even more for her husband whom I suspected she was driving crazy. At some point our workshop leader suggested that she focus less on her husband and more on herself, which sounded like good advice.

I also signed up for a Saturday evening massage, which was delivered under the stars by a lady masseuse. I knew nothing about massage, but it's hard not to like, and mine was fine. We were nude, of course. You could hear the surf. It was a little chilly. I found the lady interesting and asked for her phone number. But I never followed up. Big Sur was, I realized, a long drive from San Francisco.

The rest of the Esalen agenda I never got. That's because I never took another step. My sense is that Esalen offered an uncommonly rich collection of current, even cutting-edge, thinking and practice in psychology and spirituality, and that the workshops were samplers that showcased its mysteries and delights. You could meet extraordinary people and get introduced to extraordinary ideas. Then, if you wanted, you could go further and dig deeper. I discovered that I didn't. One weekend was enough. My own agenda was full, and I felt no particular need to soak up more psychology or religion. Had I done so, I suspect I'd have been fascinated, but I stopped. It was a road not taken.

So much for dabbling. What really happened at Stanford was that I met my future wife—Myriam Waiser (Miri). She was from Chile, my age, recently divorced, studying for her doctorate at SIDEC and working as Carnoy's teaching assistant. She had a Ford Foundation graduate fellowship that I had recommended several months before (misspelling her first name). I'd met her on a visit to Stanford half a year earlier to see how our graduate fellows (there were several) were doing, and to make arrangements for my sabbatical. Carnoy was off skiing at Tahoe and asked her to show me around, which she did. She even invited me to dinner at her apartment. I probably should have realized right then that this was no normal woman. I didn't.

Then when I arrived at campus in September I found that my office was next to hers in the basement of Cubberley Hall. The office on the other side belonged to another doctoral student, Alejandro Toledo, who later would become president of Peru. Office assignments aren't usually a big deal; this one was spectacular. So much so that I've occasionally wondered whether it really was random, or the work of some celestial being with an inspired sense of humor. Or maybe it was Miri.

I was clueless, of course. Miri was smart, cute, and nice, but I had no idea she was the woman of my dreams. It took me years to figure that out. I saw a lot of her while at Stanford, in the office and out. Her brother-in-law, Edmundo Fuenzalida, was a SIDEC professor, which meant that her sister, Lucia, was also on hand. Since I had a background in Chile, we quite naturally socialized. I remember in particular a birthday party at my apartment in San Francisco. Miri provided the cake and topped it with trick candles that continued to burn no matter how hard you blew. I kept blowing and blowing but the flame wouldn't go out. (Was she sending a message about our future?) We laughed. We danced the *cumbia*—a sensuous dance from Colombia's Caribbean coast that I'd learned while in the Peace Corps. I also remember going whale-watching with her some time later and unconsciously taking her hand as we walked upon the beach. I was surprised when I noticed what I'd done and wondered why I'd done it. Impulse? Me? I wasn't an impulsive guy. What was going on? I shrugged it off.

You'd think all that would have led to something, right? At least if I were a normal human being. There she was. It should have been a slam dunk. But nothing much happened. We didn't date. I wasn't attracted. For a long time it was another road not taken. How come?

Part of what was going on, I think, was that I had no sense of how to find a mate. I mentioned earlier that, after finishing psychotherapy in Chile, I felt I was finally ready to get married. But I needed to find the right person. And, looking back, I realize that I was extraordinarily unprepared to do that.

Not that I'd given it any thought. My default position was that the right person would appear dramatically, like a bolt of lightning or a ringing of bells. It would be obvious. Love at first sight. An unveiling. You hear stories about men who, upon seeing a woman on the street for the first time, knew immediately they would marry her, and did and lived happily ever after. Jeb Bush did that, as I recall. As did an old college friend of mine (although it was his second wife, after he'd divorced his high school sweetheart.)

I thought that was normal. I was waiting for something like that to happen. It didn't, and it was another five or six years before I saw the light, and even more before we finally got married. It never occurred to me that love could creep in on little cat feet and curl up beside you like an old friend before you even knew it was there. It did. Surprise! Thank God I noticed—eventually—and sorry it took so long. Miri was the best thing that ever happened to me. Stanford got that underway.

The other part of what was going on I think is that I'd grown up distrusting impulse (I mentioned that I was raised Lutheran, right?). Impulse was the unruly child of emotions and could—probably would—get you into trouble. You had to watch out. You kept impulse at arm's length. Much safer was sober analysis. Look at things cooly and from a distance, consider the pros and cons, and make sure you understood what was going on before you acted. That was me. I'd resist the siren call of impulse. And stay the hell out of trouble.

That view has its merits, of course, but can keep you out of things you'd be better off getting into. Call it an excess of rationality. Or maybe caution. It turns out that impulse can be your friend. You don't need to give it carte blanche, but you ought at least to give it a chance. It took me a long time to realize that. I missed signs that might have brought me to my senses sooner, and drawn me in directions I ought to have gone in. Like dating Miri.

Maybe that explains my failure to see the writing that was up there on the wall and would eventually make me very happy. But I think that just as important was something like simple blindness. I didn't know what was good for me and couldn't make sense of what was in front of me—at least when it came to love. I wasn't ready. How many of us can explain why we did or did not fall in love at a certain point in time? There's mystery there that we can only accept. You do your best with what's in front of you and live with the consequences. In that sense I was like everybody else. Those were the cards I was dealt, and that's how I played them.

I'm comforted just slightly by the story that Russell Baker, one of my favorite writers, tells in his memoir about being certain he would not marry his girlfriend, Mimi (whose given name was Miriam, by the way), whom he'd been dating off and on for several years. She just wasn't right for him. "It's not in the cards," he kept telling her. This went on for years. Then he saw the light, married her, and they lived happily ever after. Love triumphed over I don't know what. So at least I'm not alone. But on the other hand, he came to his senses a lot faster than I did. And he's a much better writer.

What I did do was go off in a completely different direction.

I began dating a woman that my college friend Bill Weiner fixed me up with. Her name was Joyce Saltalamachia and she was a Californian, Berkeley grad, law librarian, divorced, and intelligent, with a job in San Francisco, a house in Oakland, a quirky personality, and a nice sense of humor. When I picked her up outside her office for our first date, she was reading a copy of Mary Shelley's *Frankenstein*. Or maybe it was Bram Stoker's *Dracula*—I don't quite remember. Whichever, it seemed like a plus.

I liked her. But pretty quickly, and almost subconsciously, I felt that we weren't a long-term fit. Something wasn't there. I didn't know what, but it wasn't. After a few weeks I told her so. We stopped dating. Then, for reasons I don't fully understand, we started dating again. My sabbatical was coming to an end and I still hadn't met anyone who'd set the bells ringing so maybe I was expecting too much. We dated until I left for New York. Then we said goodbye. But we stayed in touch.

A year or two later she got a job in New York and, well, you can imagine the rest. I still had mixed emotions, but I guess not mixed enough. Maybe it was time to experiment. Give love a chance. I'd bought a small but nice seventh-floor loft in Tribeca with a view of the World Trade Center. I invited her to move in. She did. We'd see.

That lasted a couple of years. It was like a trial run in the business of marriage. I learned a lot. On the surface we were smart, well-educated professionals who had similar interests and agreed on lots of things. But underneath there was a differentness that I felt more than I understood.

Latin America, of course, was the big, obvious difference. I was bilingual and bicultural. Latin America was part of my personality, my career, and my life. None of that was true for her. Maybe that was the problem.

But there was something else more fundamental and harder to see. I first noticed when I realized that I had no urge to introduce her to my parents. What? Doing that simply seemed inappropriate. She didn't fall into that category. And that feeling came from my heart rather than from my head. All I did was observe it.

Worse, I found myself doubting that my mother would warm to her. I can't explain why I felt that way, but it made me uncomfortable. I'd regularly disagreed with my mother on all sorts of things, but this one was somehow different. I realized that I wanted my mother to be gut-level comfortable with the woman I got serious about, and in this case I didn't think she would. That bothered me. Maybe my Michigan roots had kicked in. When it came to a mate, I didn't want to disappoint my mother.

You can see where this was going. It was increasingly clear that we didn't have a future, and that we didn't want to talk about it. We drifted apart. We traveled a lot on business. When my boss asked whether I'd be interested in moving to Peru to head up Ford's regional office there, I said yes. It was, of course, a great professional opportunity. But it was also a way out of something that wasn't working. I spent the next four years living in Lima; she bought a co-op of her own in Manhattan's financial district and moved out. It was over. That was appropriate.

Can we learn from this? Sure. The first lesson I got was listen to your gut. The signals aren't always clear, but most of the time your gut is trying to tell you something you need to know. Pay attention. Try to figure it out. I mentioned earlier my tendency to intellectualize rather than to feel. Had I listened more to what I felt in San Francisco, I might not have embarked on that experiment in New York. Maybe I'd have been better off. I'm not sure. But my eyes, if not wide open, would at least have been open wider. That would have helped.

Another lesson is that when it comes to finding a mate, values and lifestyle matter probably more than you think. You don't have to overlap on everything, but you do have to overlap on what feels important. There is a combination of who we are, what we believe and what we do that is a kind of magic when it works for both of you. Take it seriously. If any of these are too far out of kilter, it gets tough fast. Fit matters. If it's not there, you may need to call the whole thing off. We're all a little tribal.

Finally, experiments work even when they fail. Failure, after all, is the norm. It generally precedes and exceeds success. Dating is a good example. It's a series of experiments that fail. You see what works and what doesn't. You learn. You adjust. So failure is not something you should fear. Most of the time it's good for you. Make it your friend.

Another lesson Stanford gave me about how hard it is to see what the world is sending your way was Alejandro Toledo—a guy who went from nowhere to president to jail. I've already mentioned that I'd met him at a conference in Lima while I was still a graduate student. We'd gotten together a few times since, in Santiago and in Buenos Aires while he was there doing some consulting. Now my office was next to his in the basement of Cubberley Hall. We got to know each other.

Alejandro was not just another graduate student. He was a phenomenon. He'd been born into poverty in a Quechua family of sixteen children in Northern Peru, started out shining shoes, was the first in his family to graduate from high school, made friends with a couple of Peace Corps Volunteers who helped get him into a special program for non-English speakers at the University of San Francisco, and then got a Master's from Stanford. Over the next few years he would finish his PhD, go back to Peru to teach at a business school, decide to enter politics at the top by establishing his own political party, run for president and win on his second try—becoming the country's first president of indigenous ancestry. That qualifies as phenomenal.

Alejandro was also bright, engaging, funny, and had a big smile. He loved playing soccer. You could see what had attracted those Peace Corps Volunteers. This was a guy who was smart, wanted to talk, wanted to get ahead, and wanted to explore the world beyond his immediate surroundings. But he was starting at the bottom. You wanted to help him.

What he wasn't, so far as I could see, political. There was no sign of politics in the Alejandro Toledo I got to know at Stanford. He didn't talk politics or mention ideology. I could not have labeled him as left, right, or center. I would never have predicted he'd run for the city council, let alone for the presidency. Yet later he would break into Peruvian politics with nothing—no background, connections, organization, or money—and get elected president. That was going to require an awful lot of commitment. You'd have to want it very much. I didn't see that. I have no idea why not.

Many years later Bob Myers, my former professor at Chicago and colleague at the Ford Foundation, told me of interviewing Alejandro in San Francisco in 1966 when he was nineteen years old and studying English. In response to a question about what he'd like to do in the future he said that he wanted to get a degree in economics, return to Peru, enter politics, and change the political system. So there were some signs. But Bob, who like me kept up with Alejandro over the years, never imagined him becoming president either. Neither of us saw or felt the political animal in Alejandro Toledo.

It is, by the way, at least Interesting that another Peruvian president, General Juan Velasco, did something similar—grew up in poverty in Northern Peru, started out as a shoeshine boy, and then became president. A major difference is that Velasco used the army to escape poverty and a coup d'etat to become president, while Toledo used education and a democratic election. You could argue, and I would, that making it to the top as an army General in Peru back then was easier than making it to the top as a Stanford PhD. And that becoming president via a military coup was easier than becoming president via a democratic election.

But Alejandro's biggest achievement was neither. It was making it to the top as an Indian. He was a *"cholo"*—high cheekbones, straight black hair, big nose, slightly brown skin—the glittering symbol of Peru's large and once-mighty Indian population, conquered four centuries earlier by the Spanish, and systematically repressed, excluded, and ignored ever since. People like him in Peru didn't make it to the top.

I once took Alejandro to dinner at the home of my best friends in Peru, Julio and Mayu (of the *Pensión Vargas* fame). I simply told them he was a Peruvian I'd met at Stanford. When we walked through the door, they were—to put it mildly—surprised. No one, I suspect, had ever brought anyone like him to their house for dinner. I was, of course, *"el gringo,"* so they were used to my doing the unexpected. I'd done it again. They got along fine with Alejandro.

What was more interesting, though, happened a couple of decades later when Alejandro decided to run for the presidency and asked Mayu to run with him as vice president. She turned him down—politics wasn't her game. (Later, during Toledo's administration, she also turned down an offer from finance minister and future president Pedro Pablo Kuczynski to head Peru's Central Bank.) But since she was not only a woman but also a strong leader, Alejandro's offer showed not only an ability to move in new directions, but also an ability to recognize talent. I found that encouraging. And I was always a little disappointed that I didn't get to play at least a tiny role as matchmaker in Peruvian history.

Our relationship, then, had more to do with friendship than politics. We socialized at Stanford, usually with Alejandro's longtime girlfriend, Eliane Karp, a Belgian anthropologist also studying there. When they married, I was one of two witnesses who signed the marriage license (the other was a SIDEC PhD who'd lived for a while in Peru and who a few years later jumped from the Golden Gate Bridge, the victim of schizophrenia, or something just as dreadful). Half-a-dozen years later when both of us were back in Peru we stayed in touch and occasionally got together over lunch or dinner. But there was one big exception that turned into an adventure: a trip to a high mountain valley in Northern Peru known as the Callejón de Huaylas.

We'd been discussing an Andean hike for some time, specifically a four-day, 26-mile trek that started just below Cuzco, rose to over 13,000 feet through cloud forests and Inca ruins, and then descended quite a bit lower to finish just above the magic and majesty of Machu Picchu. That hike was reported to be demanding, gorgeous, and (back then, at least) relatively free of tourists. But somehow we never got organized enough to do it. Instead we ended up going to the Callejón de Huaylas. I don't recall why.

The idea was simple and relatively innocent: do an overnight hike in the Cordillera Blanca, the 120-mile chain of snowcapped peaks (then, and perhaps still, the world's longest tropical ice-covered mountain range) that forms the east side of the Callejón de Huaylas and attracts climbers from around the world, and see the sights—of which there were reported to be many. Alejandro knew about a trail that started just above Huaráz, the provincial capital located in the middle of the Callejón. It went up over a ridge and then down the other side into a glacial valley and eventually to a village (whose name I don't remember) that had no roads at all and depended entirely on the trail to get its produce out and down to market in Huaráz. So it was a well-traveled route, in addition to being remote, spectacular and possibly perilous. We'd give it a try.

We spent the night in Huaráz, at about 9000 feet, and the next day drove up a narrow, winding road that ended at the base of Peru's highest mountain, Huascarán, which topped out at just over 22,000 feet. We passed through what had been the village of Yungay until the 1970 earthquake caused the northern side of Huascarán to collapse into an avalanche that, moving at several hundred miles per hour, wiped out the village and killed some 20,000 people. Nothing was left. A few stone walls. The remains of a church. An entire community gone. The village had been rebuilt, a mile or so away. But walking across the original town plaza made clear how precarious life could be in the high mountains, and how overwhelming the forces of nature. We took pictures, tried to feel what we ought to feel, and moved on.

We followed the road beyond Yungay to its end, left the car, put on backpacks and began to hike. The trail was narrow and rough but didn't require fancy mountaineering. The scenery was stunning—blue sky, fluffy clouds, snow-covered peaks, rugged rock outcroppings, and occasional crystal blue-to-turquoise glacial lakes. We met people coming up out of the valley that lay beyond the ridge we were climbing, sometimes with mules carrying produce, on their way to market in Huaráz. The trail went up and up and then leveled off at what must have been around 12,000 feet. The hiking was hard work but felt good.

As the afternoon wore on, the sun—and temperature—went down, and snow began to fall. We decided to make camp. I pitched our pup tent, barely big enough for three, with some difficulty in the wind. It was getting dark. I decided to make some tea using the white gas stove I carried for camping in the mountains. In order to strike a match and light the stove I needed to take off my gloves. When I went to do that, nothing happened. I couldn't remember how to take off my gloves. What? That's when I realized I had a problem. Snowflakes swirled across my face. It was cold. I stared at the fingers of one gloved hand in the waning light and tried hard to remember what it took to get that glove off. First you pulled on the index finger, right? Then you…. What had been automatic was now a puzzle. I had to figure out each step as if I were doing it for the first time. That was scary.

I got it done and the tea made but realized that I was experiencing altitude sickness. I remembered the story I'd heard years ago about Peace Corps Volunteers in Colombia (while I was there, I think) who'd hiked up a snow-covered peak near the Caribbean coast and brought along some sort of inflatable birthday toy as a surprise for one member of the group whose birthday it was. Two of them went behind some rocks, blew into the requisite tubes to inflate the inflatable and presented it to their friend, with birthday greetings. Soon they began to have trouble breathing. Later they died, apparently of pulmonary edema—a buildup of fluid in the lungs that leads to drowning—caused by their sudden ascent to high altitude, and too much exertion. Hiking in the high mountains is serious.

I was frightened. Not only was I having trouble with routine tasks like removing gloves, I'd developed a sinus headache and couldn't breathe through my nose. How bad was that? What should I do? The only remedy I could imagine was to get down to a lower altitude as quickly as possible. That would be hard in the dark and the snow. I had to decide whether to stay put or go down. It was a matter of placing a bet. I decided to stay. I could, at least, breathe through my mouth. Maybe it wouldn't get worse.

We made some kind of soupy dinner on the white gas stove and turned in. What I remember about that dark night in our tiny tent with snow coming down was discussing how *gringos* are different from Latin Americans. Most important, I said, was that they define reality differently—the *gringos* being a little more demanding about what they're willing to call real. I thought that was a great insight. They thought it was funny. The other thing I remember was Alejandro trying to teach me about the *huayno*—a popular Andean folk music. Someone camped nearby was playing *huaynos* on a *quena* (an Andean flute), and the music floated over to us on the cold, crisp air. Alejandro wanted me to understand it. I'd have to say he wasn't successful but I was glad he tried. It took my mind off death. Eventually we slept.

The next morning I woke up. Which was good news. I'd made it. In fact, my symptoms were gone. I crawled out of the tent into the sun that was coming up behind the mountains and sparkling on the thin layer of fresh white snow that covered the trail. I took a deep breath and felt good. I put my gloves on without a hitch. We made breakfast, broke camp, and tromped around a bit, oohing and aahing at the snow-capped peaks above us and at the green valley lying below, just beyond the ridge we'd climbed. Then we turned around and worked our way back down to the car. The hike was over. As you can see, I wouldn't forget it.

This was all pre-politics. After that I saw less of Alejandro and Eliane. I would move back to New York, leave the Ford Foundation, write a book at NYU, and then get married and move to Washington to join a think-tank—the Inter-American Dialogue. Alejandro would remain in Lima, take up politics, establish his own political party, and get elected president.

I wasn't around to watch his extraordinary (and to me, startling) metamorphosis. And we never got together during the five years he was president. Only later, after he stepped down, did I see him again. He invited me to speak at a meeting of former Latin American presidents that he'd organized in Sao Paulo. And when he moved to Washington to spend some time at The Brookings Institution, Myriam and I organized a welcome reception for him and Eliane at our home. All that was fun. But basically, our paths diverged.

Then the Peruvian government charged him with corruption, specifically that he'd taken millions of dollars in bribes from a Brazilian construction firm, Odebrecht, in exchange for facilitating huge contracts in Peru. He maintained he was innocent. But after the Peruvian government requested his extradition (by then he was back living in California), the U.S. government decided he was a flight risk and put him in jail while the case worked its way through the courts. The State Department then granted his extradition. He was tried, convicted and sentenced to twenty years in prison.

What a tragedy! From shoe-shine boy to Stanford PhD to Peruvian president to jail in Peru. How do you make sense of that? It's a novel waiting to be written.

Back in the 1980s when two radical terrorist groups, *Sendero*

Luminoso (Shining Path) and *Túpac Amaru* (MRTA), were convuls-
ing Peru with rural and urban violence, Mario Vargas Llosa wrote a
novel, The *Real Life of Alejandro Mayta*, about an obscure Trotskyite who
dreams of revolution, takes part in an uprising in the Andean highlands,
fails spectacularly, and ends up selling ice cream in an upscale Lima
neighborhood and living in a slum. Vargas Llosa was trying to explore,
at least in part, how politics and psychology interact—how the lure of
revolution connects with the powerful and often dark urges that lurk in
all our minds. Toledo's story would make a nice complement but would
be different because it would focus on conventional, rather than radical,
politics, and add the delights, pressures, and seductions of going from
obscurity to fame. I hope someone writes the novel. And that I get to
read it.

What is clear to me is that Alejandro Toledo managed to reach rarified political heights and that the demands and temptations at that level
are probably well beyond anything you or I have ever had to deal with.
The clouds must be pea-soup thick, the winds strong, and the maps
vague. Thunder roars and tremendous bolts of lightning come out of
nowhere. It's probably hard even to get your bearings, let along know
where to go and how to steer the ship. So if you weren't brought up like
Winston Churchill, you just have to hope that you've somehow acquired
the values, character, education, and experience—and get the colleagues,
advice, and luck—necessary to pull you safely through. I suspect not
many do.

People who make that journey—from poverty and obscurity to
wealth and/or fame—probably tap some vital inner force they neither know nor understand. Imagine the desires, emotions, doubts, and
fears—even black rage—they must deal with. How much of that is good
and how much bad? Where might it take them that they ought not to
go? Anyone who confronts that urge and takes that ride needs to realize
the risks they're running, and the difficulty of reaching the top of the
mountain unscathed. They've mounted a powerful, unruly beast. There's
no guarantee it will turn out well. They are riders on the storm.

I'm not suggesting that presidents aren't responsible for what they do or can't be expected to do a good job. It's just that some people handle the extraordinary challenges of being president better than others because they're better prepared, get better advice, or have better luck—or all three. How that will turn out for any given person is hard to predict.

What I also know is that, from 1985 to 2018, four of Peru's six elected presidents were arrested. A fifth, Alan Garcia, avoided arrest by going to his bedroom and putting a bullet through his head when the police came to his door. The sixth, Valentin Paniagua, was president for less than a year. It's not an encouraging picture.

Finally—and this takes us in a slightly different direction—Alejandro had a Ford Foundation fellowship while at Stanford and I was responsible for it. At some point, and following standard procedure, I terminated his fellowship, telling him it was time he returned to Peru. Which he did. Ford's graduate fellowship program was intended to create future national leaders and people had to go back home for that to happen. Toledo turned out to be one of just two (at least so far, in Latin America) former Ford Foundation graduate fellows who were later elected president. The other was also a Peruvian, Alberto Fujimori. Both were trained as academics. Both were political outsiders. Both ended up in jail. (In 2020, a third former Ford graduate fellow and Peruvian, Francisco Sagasti, was named—but not elected—interim president by Peru's Congress after a president was impeached and an interim president had resigned.)

What should we make of that? Probably not much. When you try to position yourself at the edge of history, as Ford often did, you're playing a worthy but uncertain game. You can only do your best, recognizing that at some point the results will be out of your hands and hard to predict. History is like that.

OK. I know I got a little off the track (again) but I'm still at Stanford. What else did I do? I wrote my paper, just as I had promised Ford I would. It turned out, in my humble opinion, to be pretty good, documenting how Ford had come up with a different approach to providing development assistance within repressive regimes, concentrating on preserving critical, independent thought rather than just packing up and leaving, or sticking to technocratic work that the dictatorship didn't find threatening. I wasn't aware of any cases in which a major foreign donor, operating on the ground inside a repressive regime came up with an alternative to those two options. And even less, had written up the experience. Documenting what we did, identifying principles and drawing lessons was new and maybe even useful—a kind of break-glass-in-case-of-autocracy for foreign donors. The paper, "Higher Education, Development Assistance and Repressive Regimes," appeared in an academic journal and then the Ford Foundation published it as a reprint. I was happy. I still like it today.

The year at Stanford was full and good. I depressurized, looked around, learned a lot, made new friends, caught up with old ones, wrote a pretty good paper, and met my future wife (although I had no idea). I sampled the mellow, laid-back, much-hyped culture of California and decided that mellow wasn't really my cup of tea but was worth sipping now and then. My sabbatical was what it ought to have been, probably more. I was blessed.

But I never saw the sabbatical as a new start. My contract was ending and I had, at the beginning of that year, no guarantee of future employment. I could only be thankful Ford had given me a sabbatical at a wonderful university. Yet I made no alternative plans. For me Stanford was always a breather between stage one and stage two of my Ford Foundation career. Something would work out. Ford was changing—McGeorge Bundy was stepping down as president and Frank Thomas was taking over—so some uncertainty was understandable. My bosses in New York were vague: "We'll see what's available when we get closer." It turned out that what was available was a short-term job working with Jim Himes, the head of the Latin American program, until the new president decided on his team. I suppose, had they hired someone else (and I heard later but can't confirm that they talked with someone else who wasn't interested), that I'd have been out of luck and looking for a job. But it seemed right that I stick with Ford, and they with me, for a while longer. We weren't done.

Then Ford offered me the job in New York and I took it. I was delighted. I'd go to New York City, with its energy, style, guts, money, and sophistication. And Ford's home office with its power, prestige, and world-class standards. I'd be there day after day, face to face. Would I like it? Could I make it? The city and job had a big-time feel that made me nervous. Mostly, though, I was excited.

Time for a quick breather. I may be getting the hang of this writing stuff. I notice now that when the going gets tough, I tend to know what to do. For example, to just back off and wait till the proper words and thoughts come to me rather than spin my wheels. And to trust my impulse when I felt the urge to replace one paragraph for another—on the theory that if I kept wanting to make that change, it probably was the right thing to do. I may be developing a sense of how to find the path. I feel a little bit like I know what to do. And I still like it.

XVI

NEW YORK CITY

"…the city makes up for its hazards and its deficiencies by supplying its citizens with massive doses of a supplementary vitamin: the sense of belonging to something unique, cosmopolitan, mighty and unparalleled."

—E.B. WHITE, *ESSAYS*

"…a town that existed in black and white, and pulsated to the great tunes of George Gershwin."

—WOODY ALLEN, *MANHATTAN*

FROM THE BEGINNING New York was for me about the power, beauty, and romance that gush from the opening bars of Gershwin's *Rhapsody in Blue*. That's because I saw Woody Allen's movie—and paean to the city—*Manhattan* a week or so after checking into the midtown hotel (in Turtle Bay, to be exact) where the Ford Foundation had rented me a room for a month while I looked for a place to live. The movie opens with the bliss of *Rhapsody in Blue* overlaid by scenes from the streets and skyline of Manhattan. It told me I was going to like it.

Pretty quickly I did. My overwhelming first impression of New York City was of riches. Some of that was money, of course, but most of it was culture. It was art, architecture, music, writing, cuisine, ethnicity, fashion, theater, history, and tradition. It was jazz and it was Bach. Ellington and Bernstein. It was Grand Central Station, Lincoln Center, Fifth Avenue, the Lower East Side, Central Park, Wall Street, the Village, Carnegie Hall, the Chrysler Building, the Brooklyn Bridge, and Chinatown. I left out Times Square. And the MOMA. And the Yankees. It was the Oyster Bar, Zabar's, and Dean & DeLuca. It was high culture and street culture, It was WASPish, Jewish, Irish, Black, and Latino. It was Pakistani taxi drivers and Korean markets. Did I mention Little Italy? Harlem? Soho? The place glittered. It was right in front of me for the taking. I'd never seen anything like it. All that came with living in New York.

There was also a raw, primitive quality. I remember on one of my first visits waking up early and hearing a garbage truck roaring and grunting down on the street like a hungry animal. I heard that sound just about every morning I awoke in New York. I got a similarly elemental feeling from Bernstein's *West Side Story*, Coppola's *The Godfather*, and Scorsese's *Taxi Driver*. And from the guy I once noticed sitting across from me on the subway with a pistol strapped to his ankle. And from running through the Fulton Fish Market (before they moved it) on a dark winter morning with shadowy figures buying and selling fish from stands in the freezing cold, fires burning in oil drums, and the Brooklyn Bridge gleaming brightly above as it filled with traffic. And from contemplating a huge iron fire escape that had fallen in a twisted heap to the sidewalk on a street that I regularly walked down in my neighborhood. New York was tough, strong, immediate, and real. Scary, sometimes. You couldn't ignore it.

As you can see, I fell in love. New York City became mine. I came to consider it my home town. It still feels that way.

One measure of the City's astonishing richness was Broadway, which to my surprise turned out to have two additional dimensions: Off-Broadway and Off-Off-Broadway.

Peter Hakim introduced me to two of the three. During a visit a few years earlier he and his wife told me they had tickets to see Richard Burton star in *Equus*, which had just opened on Broadway and was sold out for Burton's run, and suggested I go along. "Don't worry. You can buy a ticket on the street just before the curtain goes up. Someone's always got tickets to sell" Peter said. That, it turned out, was what you did when you wanted to see a sold-out Broadway show. "Fine!" I said, and it worked. I got a good orchestra seat at slightly below the original price. When we entered, though, Peter and his wife were held up. It turned out that their tickets had been for the previous evening and were no longer valid. Peter was a little sheepish. The theater people were nice and let them stand in back and watch. It was my first Broadway play. Burton was great.

Later Peter told me about Off-Off Broadway, which I had never heard of but discovered was small, low-budget, often experimental, always diverse, and typically took place below 42nd Street, mostly in the Village. Off-Off-Broadway listings appeared in the papers—I remember checking them in the *Times* and *Village Voice*. It was like searching for treasure in a flea market but with better odds. We once went to see some sort of a classic drama (a Greek tragedy like *Medea*, perhaps?) performed by students from a local drama school. It was charming and the admission was free. Later, on my own, I went to see an experimental show in Soho in which a guy with a hatchet chopped his way into a wooden box to release a naked woman. At least that's what I remember. Definitely avant-garde. Which was part of the attraction. There was plenty more.

Off-Broadway I discovered by myself. Unsurprisingly, much of it took place just off Broadway—a few blocks west of the theater district. Strictly speaking, it was a matter of theatre size, with Off-Broadway theaters being defined as having a seating capacity of between 100 and 499. Here you saw more experimental stuff that, if it did well, might make it to Broadway. And you might see two or three short pieces in a single show, as producers and writers tried to figure out what worked. I once saw a brief sketch—just two characters, a Black male student and a white female teacher. She, wanting to encourage him, told him his work was good, and he, knowing it wasn't, accused her of failing to hold him to high standards and thereby condemning him to a second-rate education. It was powerful. A year or so later that sketch became a Broadway play.

Another was a rock musical comedy I saw in the Village called *Little Shop of Horrors* that included, among other things, a man-eating plant that devoured a sadistic dentist. I told my dentist, perhaps a little slyly, that he ought to go see it, but don't recall whether he did. What was amazing, though, was discovering that I liked something so bizarre. It was the kind of surprise—and stretch—that New York offered.

Yet another was a play in the Village, perhaps at the Public Theater, starring Rip Torn and Amy Wright (who eventually became his third wife). The only thing I remember is that she looked great and was feeding him his lines. During the intermission she came out to the lobby to chat with the audience and said hello to me. It was a charming Manhattan moment.

The theater was just one example. There was so much more. I looked Andy Warhol in the eye on an East Village street corner as he flagged a cab. I saw Claudio Arrau, one of the world's great pianists (and a Chilean) in concert from a seat on stage right next to his piano at Lincoln Center. I ran into Victor Borge, perhaps my parents' favorite comedian while I was a growing up, in my dentist's office where he'd come with some kind of emergency. They made me wait (probably because of that cheeky musical I'd recommended) while they took care of him. I took my parents to see Mickey Rooney's Broadway debut in *Sugar Babies* (they were delighted). I tried out subscriptions to Carnegie Hall, the New York City Ballet, and the Metropolitan Opera. I discovered the MOMA, the Met, and the Guggenheim, along with the galleries of SoHo and Madison Avenue. I read the *New York Times*, the *New Yorker*, *New York*, and the *Village Voice*, along with several downtown papers that sprang up once Lower Manhattan became fashionable. And, of course, I enjoyed those eye-catching *New York Post* headlines you saw on subway platforms while waiting for the train (I keep remembering one headline that began the day as "William Holden Dies" and morphed by the afternoon into "Bill Holden Dies Alone"). I contemplated the zen-like twoness of the World Trade Center towers and, just a few blocks away, the ornate, fantastic lobby of the Woolworth Building. I discovered you could get wonderful freshly made smoked mozzarella shortly before noon on Saturdays at the Alleva Dairy in Little Italy. I even lunched in an automat in Midtown—probably one of the last (do any still exist?). It went on and on.

I also discovered Jewish culture, which turned out to be a big deal but crept up on me because it was everywhere rather than in any particular place. Half the people you met—I'm exaggerating—were Jewish. Yiddish appeared. I learned to *schlep* and to *kvetch*, to appreciate *mensches* and avoid *schlemiels*, and of course to *schmooze*. There was Jewish food (lox, bagels, pastrami, knishes) and Jewish jokes (my favorite is about the Jewish mother who gave her son two ties for his birthday and then, when he showed up on a visit wearing one of them said "You didn't like the other one?"). And of course there was the Jewish presence on Broadway (Irving Berlin, Rogers & Hammerstein, the Gershwin brothers, and many others). Someone told me that the key to success in New York was to "think Yiddish, dress British." I took that seriously. I tried to figure out Jewish culture. And started buying clothes at Brooks Brothers. Later I moved on to Paul Stuart and then eventually to Alan Flusser—who considered himself, reasonably I thought, the best men's tailor in the world.

More generally, there was a Jewish sensibility that I struggle to put into words but had something to do with complexity, irony, *chutzpah*, humor, and hope. It combined talent and attitude to give New York a depth and an edge that was different from any other place I'd been. It transformed and enriched.

Getting a job in New York wasn't enough, of course. You had to find a place to live—which turned out to be one of the biggest challenges a newcomer had to deal with. Living in New York was easy. Finding the right place to live was not.

That's because the place was so diverse. It was full of neighborhoods, each with different identities, histories, people, and street life. Yours might have skyscrapers, four-story townhouses, faceless apartment buildings, or historic cast-iron architecture. The streets might be teem with artists, immigrants, or people in suits. It might feel rich or poor,

Latino or Black, bohemian or conservative, old or new. You might be near Lincoln Center or Little Italy, Columbia University, or Central Park.

You might, for example, live in a big apartment building in Midtown, or in a five-story brick walkup in the Village, or in the spare bedroom of someone's loft in SoHo, or in a rent-controlled sublet in the West Sixties. Your place might be small, large (at least by Manhattan standards), noisy, quiet, bright, or dark. It might have a view of the East River, or of an elevator shaft. For any given budget you might find a place you liked, or one you didn't. No guidelines applied to everyone, except that it had to be secure (New York could be a dangerous place). To the newcomer it was bewildering. Riches usually are.

But once you managed to find a place you liked, the rest was a piece of cake. New York, I soon decided, was a much better place to live than to visit.

I knew nothing, of course, except that I wanted to live in Manhattan and to buy rather than to rent. I'd saved enough for a down-payment on something and figured, with absolutely no research, that Manhattan real estate was a good investment. That was flimsy enough. I also had no idea where in Manhattan I should live, or what difference it might make.

The Foundation had offered to pay for a service that showed newcomers like me the real estate ropes, and I took it. After absorbing their *spiel* (I told you about Yiddish), I followed several real estate agents around looking at apartments.

None of which I liked. Most were in traditional neighborhoods (Midtown, the Upper East, and Upper West Sides) which I had nothing against, but nothing for either. They were adequate but not charming. The bells didn't ring. I didn't buy.

At some point, and simply because what I was doing wasn't working, I began looking around on my own, mostly in the papers, and found an ad for an old office building way downtown that had been converted into "finished loft" apartments (whatever those were), and they were now for sale. The building—261 Broadway—was located at the edge of a neighborhood that had traditionally housed wholesale food markets and warehouses but hadn't been residential. It was called *TriBeCa*, which was short for Triangle Below Canal Street. I'd never heard of it.

I checked it out. The finished loft apartments, it turned out, were inspired by the "lofts" that had sprung up decades earlier in SoHo (short for South of Houston Street, by the way), a few blocks north—large spaces in old, semi-abandoned manufacturing and warehouse buildings with high ceilings, no interior walls, and big windows that artists with little money had turned into combined living and working space.

These were an updated version of the SoHo lofts, smaller and with proper bathrooms, kitchens, and closets, but otherwise no interior walls, and with new wood floors. They had high ceilings—sometimes ten feet—and large windows that filled them with light and added a spacious feel that worked well in Manhattan's dense urban environment. They had pretty good views. From some you could see City Hall Park and the Brooklyn Bridge; from others you could see the World Trade Center. (I was beginning to realize that views were important in New York. And high ceilings.) They also met the city's residential building codes, which the SoHo lofts generally hadn't. These were lofts for yuppies.

The building, on Broadway just below Chambers Street and across from City Hall, was a twelve-story, seventy-year-old, standard-but-nothing-special Manhattan office building. The word was that Robert Moses once had his office there. I never knew. It was, I think, the second building in Tribeca to be converted from offices to apartments, making it a pioneer and keeping prices low. The neighborhood hadn't yet become fashionable. Only low prices would attract buyers.

The neighborhood was special, although it took me a while to realize that. It was located where the island of Manhattan narrowed before terminating at the Battery, so everything came together. On the east you had the Brooklyn Bridge and the Staten Island Ferry. On the west you had the train and several ferries over to Jersey. You could walk from one side to the other—from the East River to the Hudson—in under fifteen minutes. Even better, most of Manhattan's subway lines came together near City Hall, so you could take a subway to almost anywhere—West Side, East Side, Midtown, Brooklyn, the Bronx, parts of

Queens—without having to change trains, an advantage any seasoned Manhattanite would recognize in an instant.

There was more. Chinatown and Little Italy were just a few minutes' walk, as were Wall Street, Battery Park, and ferries to Ellis Island and the Statue of Liberty. City Hall Park was right in front of you—a small but welcome oasis of leafy trees, grass, and flowers. And beyond was the grace and majesty of the Brooklyn Bridge, waiting to take you up and over the East River to the distant shore.

I always appreciated the Brooklyn Bridge. I was a runner and running on the Bridge's elevated promenade above the zooming traffic, beside the complex network of cables holding it up and over the glistening blue water, was exhilarating. You felt the way birds must feel soaring over the waves and taking in the views. Coming back was better yet, with Lower Manhattan's sumptuous skyline filling your entire field of view. Try that at night with the island ablaze head-on, the lights gleaming on the suspension cables alongside and the waves glinting darkly below. It's gorgeous. You'll see what Gershwin saw.

You could run as well around Manhattan's southern tip, through Battery Park along the water and then, starting at the World Trade Center, north and up on the abandoned West Side Elevated Highway (until they demolished it) all the way to the Village. It was a long run with great views, and quiet—your own private road floating just above the big city. Later they built a green, leafy Esplanade with some interesting sculpture along the Hudson from Battery Park up to Chambers Street, so you could run the length of that and enjoy. There was something intimate and privileged about having access to so much peace within the city's tumult.

Lower Manhattan was also filled with history and architecture. New York City had been born there, and it was briefly the capital of the United States. George Washington had been inaugurated nearby. Alexander Hamilton was buried in the graveyard of Trinity Church. Ticker-tape parades had been invented just a few blocks south on Broadway. There was Wall Street, the Tweed Courthouse, and the South Street Seaport. There was splendid architecture to gaze at (I've already mentioned the Gothic beauty of the Woolworth Building and the Le Corbusier-inspired World Trade Center). There was outdoor sculpture by Noguchi, Calder, Dubuffet, and others, including the bronze bull that symbolizes Wall Street and that everybody takes pictures of, and Koenig's extraterrestrial-looking "Sphere" at the base of the World Trade Center. And a whole lot more.

All of this, as I've said, within a few blocks. You could walk it.

I'd found my place to live. For the same price as uptown I could get larger, brighter, and more spacious, along with views and an interesting neighborhood. I bought. On the seventh floor. Small but big enough, and with a great view of the twin towers. I became a Manhattanite—and on Broadway, no less.

Moving in was like urban camping. At first it was just boxes and a mattress. Plus some second-hand office furniture I'd bought in grad-school, an old-but-charming dining room table my thesis advisor at Chicago had given me, and a couple of solid-oak end tables and a bamboo couch I'd picked up in Chile. I must have had a lamp. I could cook, sit, read, and sleep. I was fine.

Except I didn't have a refrigerator. The kitchen only had a stove, so I needed to find a refrigerator fast. I asked Peter Hakim (not only a friend but a native New Yorker) for advice:

"Peter, I've never bought a refrigerator before. Any advice?"

"Yeah" he said. "Find a place that delivers."

That was funny. And useful. It felt very New York. You asked. Then you figured it out.

Everyone in the building was new, of course, and it was easy to feel like an urban pioneer. Tribeca back then was not fashionable. It was a place nobody—at least nobody from uptown—went to. (The one exception was the actor, Robert DeNiro, whom we understood lived a few blocks away, and hoped we'd see on the street but no one I knew ever did.) For decades it had been mostly offices, warehouses, and wholesale markets—especially produce markets. There were buildings with loading docks and big metal doors. One block had housed spices and still smelled delightfully of cloves. There was a place where you could buy nuts in quantity. There were cheap overstock shops (Meshuganner Ike and Push Cart are the ones I remember). On the southern edge there was a typewriter repair shop. And a remarkably large tropical fish store (it ran all the way through the middle of a block, from one street to another) that I visited regularly just to watch the many-colored fish swim languidly in tanks while bubbles rose beside them to the surface. That fish shop was simultaneously not very New York and very New York. I took my parents there.

There were even horses. The New York Police Department had for years maintained a stable just below Canal Street, and the door always seemed to be open so you could see those big police horses stomping in their stalls and—surprise—sniff the decidedly un-New York odor of horse manure. This provided, I later I realized, a whiff of history. Horses had once been common throughout Manhattan. It used to smell that way.

What there weren't were the upscale attractions you found uptown. No movie theaters, museums, or concert halls. No high-end clothing or art. No sushi, baguettes, or cappuccino. No French food. There was just one "good" restaurant (which may have been called the Bread Shop Café; and where Meryl Streep was reported to have eaten), and one supermarket (although there was a perfectly nice Korean market with great produce, and you could always schlep over to Chinatown and get all kinds of wonderful stuff). There were neighborhood bars, of course, and unpretentious restaurants. I ate occasionally in diners and discovered their lingo. "Adam and Eve on a raft" (two poached eggs on toast) was a favorite. They were sassy, immediate, and real, like New York.

My building was a co-op rather than a condominium. That meant that instead of buying a specific apartment, you bought shares in the building, and those shares were tied to a specific apartment—which you could live in. But you didn't own that apartment, the building did. You owned shares in the building. The city of New York had granted tax advantages to that kind of legal structure—I have no idea why—so most owner-occupied residential buildings were set up that way. Notably, the coop legal structure brought a social dimension to the building that I appreciated. There was a board of directors composed of shareholders the rest of us had elected, and quite a bit of participation in the building's affairs. You met fellow residents at board meetings. We organized an annual dinner at a local restaurant.

I never ran for the board, but for a while edited the building's newsletter. That led me to play with headlines. One, for an article on water leaks, read: "Living With a Drip?" I still like it. My pride and joy was a tiny column called "Heard in the Stairwell" where I posted comments that I imagined my fellow residents making about life in our building. Once I even threw in a little T.S. Eliot:

"I am moved by fancies that are curled

Around these images and cling:

The notion of some infinitely gentle

Infinitely suffering thing."

I have no idea why I did that. It probably sounded weird in a co-op newsletter. But it was fun. And it expressed, albeit mysteriously, something I thought New York was about.

My neighbors were interesting. On my floor there was a guy who worked in British TV and whose American wife had a landscaping company. She seemed sexy, and I had the feeling he thought so too. But I was mystified by the idea of landscaping in Manhattan (roof gardens? balconies?) There was also a woman who did something in pop music (I never figured her out), a fellow who was in men's fashion, and another Brit, very friendly, who edited some sort of a business publication. His wife was into choral singing, so they'd have these get-togethers in their apartment with people leaving their shoes outside the door and inside singing and the music would flow out into the hall. It was just what you would expect from New York—almost a stereotype. And delightful.

But the surprise was next door—James Galway, perhaps the greatest and most famous flute player in the world. His girlfriend, also a flutist, owned the place, I think, and he was around a lot. They later married.

Flute music came right through the wall, and I can still hear it. I never knew whether it was him or her practicing. And I never complained. This was what living in Manhattan was supposed to be like.

A few years later she sold and they left. The guy who bought the place told me he acted in soap operas.

I hit Tribeca just when it began to change. Commercial space was being turned into residential space. Prices were still low. People were just beginning to move in. Most seemed different from traditional Upper East and Upper West Siders—certainly more adventuresome, maybe less conventional, and probably less rich, although often with good prospects. Tribeca was becoming a neighborhood of recent arrivals—urban migrants looking for a better place.

But an important part of the influx had started a couple of years earlier and was very different, composed of creative types drawn to the neighborhood's raw, loose, and disorderly character, and to the fact that it was cheaper than Soho, which had recently shifted from bohemian to chic. That generated a growing downtown, late-night club scene that I knew was out there but never participated in.

The center was the Mudd Club, which opened on White Street a year before I moved in and attracted (I found out only later) people like Keith Haring, Jean-Michel Basquiat, Allen Ginsberg, Madonna, and Jeff Koons—some of whom weren't even famous yet. Soon there were other clubs, striving for a kind of downtown chic that combined punk, new wave, cult, underground and whatever else was bubbling up, and aimed to be an alternative to uptown glitz. It was, as they say, a scene.

I completely missed this. I was never a late-night guy anyway, and the one time I tried to get into an after-midnight club I was turned away by the doorman. Obviously not the right profile. Probably not even close. Probably not even a fun guy. I went home and didn't try again. I wouldn't know or savor this particular side of Manhattan.

So my only source of information was what I read in the downtown papers, and what I saw at 6 am when I went out running: cabs, town cars, and limos lined up in front of what presumably were clubs (none of them had signs) waiting to take revelers home once they'd decided to call it a night (or more accurately, a morning).

And there were a couple of shops—clothing stores as I recall—whose business hours began after midnight. I found that charming.

It was mildly exotic—like living near a strange tribe and occasionally glimpsing their celebrations and rituals. I didn't need to get any closer. Just having them around felt enriching—that I was somehow in touch with an alternative, creative energy. It was fun, and part of why I wanted to live in Manhattan.

More visible, and accessible, was the restaurant scene which, as people with money moved into the neighborhood, became robust. It started slow, with just one or two tender shoots poking up in the culinary soil that was accumulating south of Canal Street. It would become lush.

The pioneer and trendsetter was the Odeon, a French-style brasserie established on West Broadway by the McNally brothers (Brian and Keith) about six months after I moved in, and designed to serve the late-night crowd, which it turned out to be good at. The Odeon was a sea change. Its retro, Art Deco look, lit in neon, stood out on Tribeca's dark, drab streets. Its combination of nouvelle and casual cuisine worked well for a crowd that wanted simultaneously to be cool and have fun. The place radiated comfort and class. The likes of John Belushi, Robert DeNiro, Martin Scorsese, along with all sorts of vanguard painters and gallery owners hung out there, at least according to the papers. Lorne Michaels, the executive producer of *Saturday Night Live*, and a regular, captured the feeling: "It had sophistication and it had French fries."

Since there was no doorman at the Odeon, I could get in. Which I did, occasionally. Mostly I sat at the bar drinking something with gin in it and gazed at the scene. I never saw anybody famous. But that wasn't the idea. I went for the atmosphere. The Odeon was one more way of connecting to something I felt—a quintessential Manhattan, or maybe Jazz Age, spirit that dated back at least to F. Scott Fitzgerald, was based on the island's rich and seamy history, and shouted glamor, glitter, and style. I wanted to take it in. The idea wasn't to emulate those people.

It was more about seeing and appreciating. To say "Pretty good, guys" or something like that. It was like going to a college football game. Or tromping around in Michigan's North Woods. Romantic. Occasionally exciting. Maybe inspirational. And with a touch of fairy tale.

Enough about Tribeca. It became my neighborhood, and my home. It still feels that way. Were I to move back, that's where I'd want to live. I was lucky.

<h1 style="text-align:center">XVII</h1>

<h1 style="text-align:center">FORD/NEW YORK</h1>

LET'S MOVE ON to Ford. I had a job, after all. What was that like? How did I do?

Inserting yourself into a new working environment is a little like jumping off something for the first time. You've decided to do it, but you don't really know what it'll be like or how you'll handle it. I had that feeling—supercharged by Ford/New York's aura as an establishment icon that was staffed (I was pretty sure) by smart, sophisticated professionals who wouldn't hesitate to spit me out (politely, of course) should they find me wanting. I approached the job with a measure of awe. Could I make it there…?

I have to begin with the building. The Ford Foundation's New York headquarters was spectacular. Designed by architect Kevin Roche in the 1960s and built at great cost, it combined granite, glass, and weathered steel in a look that was striking, modern, and cool. It wasn't tall—just twelve stories—but it had presence. It looked completely different from the buildings around it—as if an extraterrestrial had landed in midtown Manhattan and decided to stay. It embodied beauty and authority. It sent a clear message: "These people are special."

I loved that building. Now I'd have an office there.

Inside was the atrium—a twelve-story, one-third acre of trees, vines, shrubs, ground cover, and aquatic plants that contrasted nicely with the crowded, noisy streets outside. You entered and relaxed. There were magnolia and citrus trees, azaleas, hibiscus, Japanese camellias, and asparagus ferns. The air was balmy and slightly humid. There was a small hill. A brick pathway led to a fountain that gurgled in the center. It was peaceful and green. You expected at any moment to see deer.

Many of the offices had sliding glass walls that opened on the atrium, enabling staff to look down on the forest for inspiration, or at least tranquility, as they struggled mightily with how to give away Ford's millions. (And if they didn't measure up, they could leap.) I got one of those offices.

The office decor was understated but stylish—Honduran mahogany desks with leather-inlaid work surfaces, wool rugs set into white oak parquet floors and walls covered with Belgian linen. Some offices had lithographs by Miró, Chagall, and Picasso (I missed out on those). The place felt lush, warm, and special. As if you were at the pinnacle of something. I found it to be remarkably comfortable. I enjoyed the combination of posh and taste. But it could be intimidating. "A hell of a place" as one Foundation officer reportedly put it to Kai Bird, "to invite a community organizer from Harlem."

I dwell on the aesthetic charms of Ford's headquarters because for me they were important. The building didn't just look good. It made a statement and set a standard. This was no ordinary place and you didn't have an ordinary job. Quality was high. Demands were great. It was an honor and a privilege to work there. You were lucky and needed to recognize that. And you'd damn well better meet standards. Otherwise maybe you didn't belong. There must be lots of theories about how architecture and design affect morale and behavior—I don't know. But what I do know is that that building affected me. It told me I had to up my game.

So, on to the job.

I was a seasoned-but-still-junior staffer who knew almost no one in New York and whom almost no one in New York knew. And most of the few I knew were on their way out. McGeorge Bundy had retired. Dave Bell had been fired. Kal Silvert had died. It was a new ballgame. I worked for the director of the Latin American program, Jim Himes, whom I knew and liked (although he would soon leave to work at UNICEF). My job was to help out. But that was short-term. Ford had a new president (and the first Black president in an institution with few Black staff and few women in senior posts), Frank Thomas, who was figuring out what he wanted to do, how and with whom. Declines in the stock market had led to cuts in programs and staff. Change was in the air. Directions weren't clear. All I could do was make myself useful and hope that when the clouds parted there'd still be a place for me.

That uncertainty didn't bother me much. I'd decided by this time that I was smart enough to hold my own with these people (despite my earlier failure to impress the vice president, Dave Bell). What would probably decide my fate was hard work, good judgment, chemistry, and luck. So I figured I had a shot. And just being there was great.

The job I had involved not only helping manage the Latin American program, but also responding to queries from the new president's office about what we'd done and achieved in Latin America since starting work there a couple of decades earlier—all of that being grist for decisions about what Ford should do going forward. That had me combing through files, assembling facts, and helping my boss develop a narrative for the planning process. I learned a lot about Ford's history in Latin America and the Caribbean. It was a great exercise for someone settling into a new position.

But most of what was happening regarding Ford's future was happening above my head. I don't recall a single meeting in which anyone asked my opinion about what Ford ought to do going forward—or even one in which these topics were being discussed. The president had brought in some management consultants to help chart the future and commissioned several papers by a few of our staff and by grand poobahs in countries where we worked (which I had the impression, but don't remember why, were largely window dressing). He invited people more senior than I to discuss these things. Sometime during that year (my first in New York) a plan came together and was approved by the board. I had little to do with it. I remember nothing about it. I wasn't in the loop.

What I do remember is that I ended up with a job. Bill Carmichael was named vice president for Developing Country Programs, and he asked me to stay on to manage our work in the Caribbean to help him manage the Latin American program. I was delighted. I'd always gotten along with Bill (although the fact is I got along with virtually everyone I met at the Ford Foundation). More important, I liked working with him. He was smart, strong, articulate, challenging, and had a sense of fun. He valued the intellectual, academic, and policy perspectives that I found so attractive. He seemed to respect my opinion. I guess I saw him as a guarantee that the values, standards, and programs that had attracted me to Ford in the first place would persist, at least in Latin America and for a while. We'd disagree on some things, but that was OK. Our disagreements would likely be some combination of manageable and worthwhile. I'd learn. It felt like a good fit.

There was one memorable, and probably fateful, detail about this process that I need to mention. Frank, in charting a plan for the future, had brought in Bill Dyal as a consultant on international programs. Dyal and I (as you may remember from my chapter on the Peace Corps) already had a history. He'd been Peace Corps director in Colombia in the late 1960s, where he'd fired my boss, Joe Mitchell, from his job as regional director of Peace Corps/Antioquia. I'd objected and we'd locked horns, although we managed to be nice about it. I'd always liked Bill Dyal. He was decent and charming, and very good with people. But I'd disagreed with how he'd treated my boss. And I'd acted on my disagreement. Bill had gone on to become head of the Peace Corps in the Middle East, North Africa, and Asia, then founding director of the InterAmerican Foundation, a public institution that funded social and economic grassroots development in Latin America and the Caribbean. He'd led that outfit with great success, marked by support from a largely Republican board, bipartisan fans in Congress, and a solid reputation in Latin America. (It's worth noting that Bill Dyal was succeeded as president of the InterAmerican Foundation by Peter Bell, my first mentor in the Ford Foundation. Probably just a coincidence.)

What appeared to be going on—and this is mostly hearsay—is

that Frank was leaning toward asking Dyal to be his vice president for Developing Country Programs and told him so. And he (or someone) told Alex Heard, who chaired Ford's board and was also chancellor of Vanderbilt University. But when Heard heard, Heard objected. I don't know why, but apparently that led Frank to change course and offer the position instead to Bill Carmichael, leaving Dyal out. Carmichael was well-regarded by several members of Ford's board, so removing him was probably always a long shot. Frank may simply have decided it was a battle he didn't want to fight. Or perhaps he decided that Dyal really wasn't the right fit and so opted for Carmichael. I don't know.

Regardless, what may have been at stake were two different approaches to development: macro versus micro. The Ford Foundation of McGeorge Bundy had, at least since the mid-60s, focused on the macro, on influencing elites—particularly academic and policy elites. It aimed to work largely at the national level, developing capacity in areas it thought were crucial to social and economic development, and promoting sound policy and programs. The assumption was that good work of that kind and at that level would filter down and have a broad, positive impact on the poor. That's the program I'd been attracted to, worked in, and swore by, even though—not surprisingly—it took time to get results.

The other view, represented (it seemed) by the Foundation's new president, Frank Thomas, was that you should focus more on the micro, on action at the grass roots level, and promote change from the bottom up. "Empower the poor" might sum it up. Or maybe activism rather than academics. Bill Dyal shared that vision, so far as I could tell. And, of course, I'd happily done that kind of work in the Peace Corps.

But I didn't think the grass roots was where the Ford Foundation had its comparative advantage. Ford had figured out how to work with academic elites in developing countries, and had the money, stature and staff to do it. Few other private foundations did. And academic elites were levers—force-multipliers, even—whose actions could have a major impact on the poor, and on social and economic progress more generally. They deserved attention. Ford was positioned to tackle that kind of thing. It probably should.

I'm simplifying, of course. There was plenty of overlap and nuance. And I never remember anyone at the Foundation suggesting formally that these were opposing viewpoints, and in play. But they were in the air, at least informally among staff. One story I remember hearing—but never verified—was that when Frank Thomas made the case for his vision to the board, Bob McNamara responded with something like: "So now the Ford Foundation is going to do little things for little people?" I don't know whether McNamara really said that. It could certainly be apocryphal. But I always thought it was a great story.

Right after Frank announced his decision, Dyal and I had lunch at the Foundation's cafeteria and he told me the story (the details of which I can only hope I've gotten reasonably straight). He was a little bitter (which for him was a lot). He'd thought he'd be named vice president and then hadn't. He felt that the experience had been unpleasant and unprofessional. I don't remember what I said, but I do remember that I was pleased that he confided in me after our contretemps in Colombia a decade or more earlier. And I felt we'd patched things up. It was the only heart-to-heart I ever had with Bill Dyal.

There's an obvious question, though: What would have happened had Bill Dyal been named vice president rather than Bill Carmichael? Would Dyal have offered me a job? And if so, how different might that job have been? I don't know the answers. What I do know is that Dyal was very different from Carmichael—more attuned to work that was immediate and action-oriented, and less attuned to the academic and policy work that had been Ford's calling card outside the United States for so many years, and that Carmichael favored and I loved. Dyal was different from me as well. I doubt, for example, that he considered himself an intellectual. Personally, we were fine. I don't know how we'd have done professionally. So it was a fateful decision. I was probably lucky. I wonder whether Bill Dyal was lucky as well.

Dyal went on to become the director of the American Field Service, which organized student exchanges around the world (my brother had been an AFS exchange student in Norway) and whose office, coincidentally, was just down the street from the Ford Foundation's 43rd Street entrance. Later he served as president of St. John's College in Annapolis. Our paths didn't cross again.

So that was settled. I'd spend a few more years at the Ford Foundation. This would be my second assignment, but a lot seemed new. I'd gotten, during my first assignment, a good sense of how the Foundation operated, and solid experience in several South American countries. But I knew nothing about the Caribbean (aside from Peace Corps training in Puerto Rico) and had no idea what helping manage the Latin American program might involve. I'd just do it and see.

Someone asked whether I was worried about working in a region that was so different from the South America I'd cut my teeth on, and I said no. I was, rightly or wrongly, confident. I'd learned the basics of giving money away, and of getting the lay of the land in a new country. And my first five years with the Ford Foundation had been so fraught with adversity, change, surprise, and borderline danger that I doubted the next few would be any tougher. I'd figure it out.

The fact was that dipping into the Caribbean (please forgive the deliberate pun) was an exercise in discovery. The Caribbean was strewn with the historical residue of colonial powers: the sugar cane economy they established to serve their needs; the descendants of the African slaves they brought in to work the cane fields; the stark dissimilarity of the region's four largest countries, Haiti, Cuba, Jamaica, and the Dominican Republic—all of which colonial powers had created but not connected; the need for the small island countries to find ways to deal collectively with their much larger neighbors; and the hybrid character of Puerto Rico which, although formally a territory of the United States, struggled mightily with its cultural and political identity. Then you had Cuba, the socialist dictatorship supercharged by Castro charisma that had nearly sparked World War III a couple of decades earlier. It was an amazing collection of historical anomalies.

In fact, diversity was what set the Caribbean apart. Its countries (15, depending on how you counted, spread across 700-plus islands and—surprise—the mainlands of South and Central America) spoke at least four languages. The colonial past they shared was itself diverse. The colonizers had included Spain, England, France, and the Netherlands, and even, for a few small islands, Denmark and Sweden. Several former colonies (French Guiana, the British Virgin Islands, Martinique, Aruba and more) were still part of the countries that had colonized them. I got dizzy trying to keep all that straight.

Their cultures were sharply different as well (think calypso, compas, and the cha-cha-chá). They didn't identify much with each other. The Anglophone countries did hang together in various ways. But the three former Spanish colonies (which accounted for over half the region's population) did not. And Haiti, the Caribbean's second most populous country and first to achieve independence (from France), largely went its separate way. It was as if chance had tossed a bunch of very different people into the same neighborhood and most, except those who shared British culture, opted to have nothing to do with each other. The Caribbean was a pot in which the contents hadn't melted.

It was even more complicated. I figured I might get a sense of the region's culture and history by reading a few novels, so I picked up *A House for Mr. Binwas* by V.S. Naipaul, the only Caribbean author I'd heard of, and discovered that his grandparents had emigrated to Trinidad from India to work as indentured servants. He was documenting the cultural presence in the Caribbean of a country—India—that was halfway around the world. I saw that Indian presence most vividly a year or two later coming in from the airport in Guyana and noticing Hindu prayer flags fluttering atop houses. And I realized that *roti*, a flatbread often eaten with curry and popular in much of the West Indies, is native to India.

So the Caribbean was diverse. And very different from South America, which by comparison seemed like a bunch of large, relatively homogeneous, countries.

My strategy for getting to know this exotic place was to visit and talk. I started where Ford had mostly worked: Jamaica, Barbados, and the Dominican Republic. Then I did some exploring. I became a regular on flights to Kingston, Santo Domingo, Bridgetown, and San Juan, and an occasional on those to Port-of-Spain, Port-au-Prince and Havana. I got used to stepping off planes into sunshine and balmy air, seeing the bright blue Caribbean sparkling alongside the runway. And to spectacular beaches that were everywhere except in the capital cities of the larger islands like Jamaica and the Dominican Republic, where you pretty much had to get out of town to find beaches worth lolling on. I learned to adapt to the two dominant colonial cultures, Spanish and British, and to appreciate the African cultures underlying them. I learned to value the cheekiness of calypso, the energy of merengue, and the seriousness of reggae. I stayed in hotels with lots of tourists and tried always to walk upon the beach. I learned about dark rum (Barrelito and Barbancourt were early favorites). I stopped wearing ties—well, almost. It turned out that there were plenty of occasions in the Dominican Republic and Puerto Rico, and some elsewhere, where a tie was proper. I once met with the chief justice of the Supreme Court of Barbados at a cafe to talk about human rights and he wore a tie—tied stylishly loose. Good form, it turned out, mattered. You just had to figure out what good form was in any particular situation.

I also managed to visit several of the smaller islands, mostly on vacation. My favorite was Saint Barthelemy, which had been a Swedish colony for nearly a century (that's why the capital is named Gustavia) before becoming part of France, which it had been for another century and still was. You got there by flying into St. Martin and changing to a small propeller-driven plane that, after clearing a ridge near the island's edge, suddenly dropped straight down and landed almost with a thud—something you survived but didn't forget—before taxiing proudly to the tiny building where you disembarked (gratefully) and found a cab.

St. Barts became my getaway—a place I went to recharge. It was luxe but low-key. The food was French. The beaches were gorgeous. Some were topless. The hotels were a mix of exclusive and reasonably priced but were generally small. Nothing looked lavish. Tall buildings were frowned on, maybe even banned. You could rent a casual, open-air jeep and explore all ten square miles in a few hours. You went about your business, which was to relax.

I once arrived St. Barts from New York in early March sick of winter and work and, after checking into my hotel, collapsed on the beach to read a few pages of Hermann Hesse's *The Glass Bead Game*—also known as *Magister Ludi*. Ford trustee Rodrigo Botero had urged me to read it because it described an imaginary order of intellectuals that reminded him of us. I fell asleep and woke up an hour or so later relaxed and refreshed, with waves lapping at my feet and the afternoon sunshine winding down. The bustle and tension of New York had trickled into the sand. I'd reconnected with the sublime. I felt renewed. I went back to my hotel and put on shorts, espadrilles, and a nifty madras shirt I'd picked up at Paul Stuart in New York. I was ready for some of that French food. That's the kind of thing I got from St. Barts.

There were plenty of islands like St. Barts—small, remote and unknown to most of us but that beckoned like sirens seeking sailors. They offered beauty, quiet, and a hint of mystery. You wanted to explore them and learn their secrets. The one I keep remembering was Mustique, which was part of St. Vincent and the Grenadines but owned entirely by a private company that catered to the rich and famous, and where I figured the beach would be awash with rock stars and princesses, none of whom I'd recognize. I never got there, of course. But imagining what the place might be like was great fun.

Finally, while I'm having fun describing the Caribbean I want to say something more about beaches. By that I mean the combination of white sand, turquoise water, easy breeze, soft waves, blue sky, fluffy clouds, and bright sunshine that is so common in the Caribbean. Beaches are to the Caribbean what mountains are to Switzerland. They're the first thing foreigners think about. They're what draw tourists. They're everywhere. And they're gorgeous. Maybe most importantly they grab your attention and slow you down. They take you out of whatever you're in. They almost invite you to meditate. I never understood whether people who live in the Caribbean see it that way, but I'm certain that most of us who don't, do. And I realized that beaches, like mountains, are more about seeing than doing. You don't need to get into the water—or onto the summit—to get their benefit. Having them in front of you is enough. They were like the Great North Woods I'd grown up with in Michigan. By just being there they changed everything.

I met extraordinary people. One was Ashton Preston, vice-chancellor (i.e. president) of the University of the West Indies (UWI) in Mona, Jamaica. He turned out to be strong and smart, with a droll sense of humor. During our first meeting he told me he refused to take calls from Jamaica's prime minister (the colorful and golden-tongued Michael Manley) because he feared Manley would talk him into something he didn't want to do. I found that charming and civilized. It made Jamaica feel more like a small town where people knew each other and didn't get too impressed by rank.

Another was Rex Nettleford, who when I met him was director of UWI's Extra Mural Department (which we supported) but later became vice-chancellor of UWI himself. Rex was a former Rhodes Scholar and a serious intellectual who wrote about politics and history. He'd also founded the National Dance Theater Company of Jamaica, which helped turn traditional Jamaican music into ballet. He was a smart, creative, and motivated—a guy whom (like so many) I wish I'd gotten to know better. Rex once took me to a play and afterwards told me what was wrong with the plot and how he would have improved it. Few of the many academic leaders I met over the years would have done anything like that.

Yet another was Vaughan Lewis, who when I met him headed a research center at UWI that we supported, but later became head of the Organization of Eastern Caribbean States (OECS)—and later yet prime minister of St. Lucia. Vaughan was from a family of West Indian intellectuals (he'd been the first Black student at the London School of Economics, and his uncle, Sir Arthur Lewis, won the Nobel Prize in Economics), but had gravitated to politics. He was smart, thoughtful, and easy to talk to. What I remember most, though, was the last time I saw him, in Port of Spain, when he refused to talk.

It was the night before the United States invaded Grenada. I'd arrived that afternoon from Georgetown, Guyana, where I'd met with the head of international affairs (his title was something like that) at the Caribbean Community (CARICOM), who repeatedly interrupted our conversation to step into an adjoining office and talk via short-wave radio with people in Grenada. The saga of Grenada was underway and its leftist prime minister, Maurice Bishop, who himself had come to power via a coup, had just been executed by the People's Revolutionary Army, a hard-line Marxist party. Not surprisingly, my host at CARICOM was distressed. He apologized profusely. I said I understood.

I ran into Vaughn in the lobby of one of those big tourist hotels you find in Port of Spain (a Hilton maybe, or a Sheraton) and where I was staying. I hadn't seen him since he'd become head of the OECS and was surprised.

"Vaughn. Great seeing you. What are you doing in Port of Spain?"

"Uh, hello." he said, surprised as well. "We have an OECS meeting."

"What a mess in Grenada" I said, hoping for some insight.

"It is. I'm afraid I have to go. Nice seeing you. Goodbye."

That was our conversation. I was taken aback. We'd always talked freely. But I hadn't put two and two together, as I should have and quickly did. Vaughn was chairing a meeting of the OECS to decide whether to ask the United States for help in Grenada. No wonder he wasn't talking. Late that night they asked. Early the next morning the invasion got underway.

Heading back to New York the next day the airport in Port of Spain looked like a movie set. Military aircraft were everywhere—massive cargo planes, helicopters, fighters, and others I couldn't identify. This was what overwhelming force looked like. It was a vivid reminder of the twists and turns that history can take, and of the big decisions that small countries sometimes had to make. I'd gotten a glimpse of history. I never did discuss it with Vaughn.

So what did I (we, really) do with Ford's money in the Caribbean? We'd worked there over a couple of decades mainly in Jamaica, Barbados, and the Dominican Republic, and mainly in higher education (including, especially, support for the University of the West Indies). We'd also funded an agricultural school run by a business group in the Dominican Republic, and research by U.S. scholars on Cuba. I looked that over, continued some of it, and tried out a few new ideas (you'll remember my comments, several pages back, on deciding not to work in Haiti). I didn't do much that seemed in any way special. Or at least much that merits your attention here.

There was one big exception: Cuba. Not because we achieved all that much but because Cuba was so strange, and working there so challenging, that it stuck in my mind.

There was, of course, nothing normal about Cuba. It was a socialist dictatorship led by a charismatic revolutionary, allied with the Soviet Union, constantly at odds with the United States, and relatively unconnected with rest of the Caribbean. It was romantic—a darling of the left, Che Guevara and all that. It felt like a movie. There was nothing like it in the Caribbean, nor anywhere else in the Western Hemisphere.

I wasn't a fan of the Cuban Revolution. At best I was skeptical. Mostly I doubted. Whatever gains Fidel's charisma and guns had achieved, largely in education, health, and housing, had cost far too much in blood, tears, liberty, creativity, and economic growth. I couldn't buy it. The Bolsheviks and the Maoists had followed that path and it hadn't ended well. I'd seen my share of dictatorships—in Chile, Argentina, Uruguay, and Peru. I didn't like them. There had to be a better way.

But I was intrigued by the possibility of working in Cuba. It was a puzzle and a challenge. Could we operate successfully on that tricky (and possibly high-profile) stage? Could we do something to make things better without compromising our principles or getting into trouble, and despite the great-power rivalry raging overhead? Would they let us? I thought it was worth a try. My boss, Bill Carmichael, did too. I began casting around for a strategy.

Politics, of course, was the big constraint. The United States and Cuba had been at odds pretty much since the establishment of Cuba's socialist dictatorship a couple of decades earlier. The Bay of Pigs Invasion and the Cuban Missile Crisis had cemented enmity between the two countries. Moreover, the Ford Foundation's former president, McGeorge Bundy, and current board member Robert McNamara, had been JFK's national security advisor and secretary of defense, respectively, during both those Cuban crises. So you could imagine the Cuban government being suspicious of our motives. And the Miami-based Cuban exile community was strong, vocal, firmly against anything they thought smelled like rapprochement, and ready to attack anyone serious they suspected of even thinking about it. Finally, we had to avoid getting into trouble with the U.S. government, which had embargoed trade, restricted travel and prohibited activities that might benefit Cuba. So for us—the Ford Foundation—work on Cuba was a highly political proposition. These were treacherous, fast-moving waters.

We weren't starting from scratch. Ford had established a Cuba program years before that, although now moribund, had funded research and policy analysis on Cuba by academics in the United States—a perfectly sensible thing to do. And we had recently funded a visit to the United States by several Cuban academics organized by Riordan Roett, director of the Latin American program at the Johns Hopkins School for Advanced International Studies (SAIS). But more of the same didn't attract us much. We wondered whether we had the comparative advantage necessary to take a worthwhile next step, and what that next step might look like.

We consulted, debated, and pretty quickly decided that the best path would be to fund activities that connected professionals in Cuba with their counterparts in the United States, addressed issues that were not obviously political, and were organized outside government channels. That's a mouthful, but it meant establishing working relationships among professionals from the two countries in areas that we (Ford) knew something about—primarily the social sciences and culture. And keeping as far away as we could from either government. Doing that, we thought, might build understanding between the two countries, and be politically feasible

I met with the head of the State Department's Cuba Desk in Washington to make sure they understood what we had in mind and had no objections. They did, and they didn't. What we proposed, they said, did not violate U.S. government laws and regulations vis-a-vis Cuba, so not to worry. I was surprised. I'd expected caution and doubt but got basically a green light.

More complicated was the Cuban government. We had no idea how it might feel about what we proposed or about the Ford Foundation more generally. Would they allow us to operate without imposing restrictions we couldn't live with? We needed the freedom to choose projects and counterparts. And I needed to visit Cuba to communicate our intentions and identify appropriate people, activities, and institutions. No Ford Foundation staff member had ever paid an official visit to Cuba. I wasn't optimistic.

I made an appointment at Cuba's "Interests Section" in Washington (which operated under the aegis of the Swiss government since the United States and Cuba didn't have full diplomatic relations) to pitch our plans. To my surprise, the Cuban diplomats were receptive and, after some back and forth, reported that their superiors in Havana were too. They mentioned no restrictions. The only sticking point was my visiting Cuba, which they encouraged but suggested I do unofficially—something U.S. citizens could do fairly easily as long as they weren't engaging in tourism or commerce.

There I balked. My experience and my gut said that we needed more buy-in from the Cuban government. A formal invitation would signal that they approved in principle of our plans. It would also make it harder for them to back out should something come up. They'd have at least a little skin in the game.

They were surprised but, after more consultation, agreed. They offered to issue a formal invitation, arrange for an official visa, make hotel reservations, organize an agenda that we would agree upon in advance, and provide a car and driver. All I had to do was buy a plane ticket and pay my hotel bill once I got there. We had a deal.

I flew in from Miami on American Airways Charters, a company that organized intermittent flights to Havana and prudently maintained a low profile in the airport (no sign) so it took a while to find the check-in counter. I'd been told to check in three hours before flight time, and when I did was informed that we'd depart an hour late. The flight had been scheduled on an Air Cubana plane but the FBI, at the last minute, had advised that there were threats of trouble if an Air Cubana plane appeared on the runway so the company had chartered an Air Florida plane instead. This was Miami. A few months earlier someone had rammed a service truck into an Air Cubana plane on the runway. The company took the FBI's warning seriously.

Travel between the U.S. and Cuba seemed largely to be a family affair. The passengers tended to be elderly Cubans or Cuban-Americans, presumably visiting relatives. Few were young. Virtually none appeared to be traveling on business. I struck up a conversation with a Cuban-American from Queens who was returning (with his Puerto Rican wife) and loaded down with gifts, to his hometown and family for the first time since the 1950s. Our conversation was pleasant but uninformative. He looked more nervous than I felt. Neither of us knew what to expect.

The flight took just half an hour, most of which I spent at the window looking down. The Cuban countryside consisted of good-looking farm land (much of it sugar cane, I guessed) dotted with a few large industrial installations (dams, perhaps) that fit my stereotype of socialist countries. Havana, as we approached, looked like many Latin American cities except that its streets were nearly empty. Cars and trucks were few. There was nothing you could call traffic. It was quiet.

We landed and taxied up to the main building. All the commercial planes were Russian-built Iluyshin jets with single and double pods of engines on either side of the tail. There was one Czechoslovakian Airlines plane. And four or five glorious old biplanes that looked like something out of World War I. I was struck by the lack of color and variety in the airport buildings, and wondered whether that reflected my prejudice about the sameness that famously characterized socialist countries.

I was one of the first off the plane and breezed through passport control with a minimum of fuss. In the baggage claim area I encountered Hugo Yedra of the Ministry of Foreign Affairs, who was to be my *responsable* during the visit. Yedra was affable. He'd spent six years at the Cuban Mission to the United Nations in New York. He informed me that he knew a number of people I knew. I immediately wondered how he knew that. And then wondered whether my reaction was just my prejudice rising to the bait. But I liked him.

We cleared customs without opening my bags or even slowing

our pace. An official black Volga sedan awaited outside. Yedra told me that the car and driver would be at my disposal all week. He outlined the schedule and noted that there was still considerable unscheduled time, particularly in the evenings, that we could fill in as we saw fit. He mentioned, carefully, that while they had managed to meet most of my requests, they hadn't been able to make appointments with every official I had requested. And he asked that I take part in a *conversatorio* one evening with students and professors at the University of Havana to discuss the Ford Foundation and its programs. He said that the Ford Foundation was not much loved in Cuba and that I should not be surprised if I ran intro strong criticism. I replied that we'd been criticized by many people in many places and were used to it. He also suggested that I not work too hard and to take some time to relax and get out.

Driving in from the airport I was struck by how different things looked compared to other countries I'd visited. There wasn't much traffic. Nor many pedestrians. Buildings were mostly shades of grey. There were few billboards or signs, and those there were carried political messages like "Solidarity and Production: Our Two Chief Objectives." Not lively. When we finally passed a restaurant that had a neon sign I noticed because it was the only one I'd seen in fifteen minutes.

I'd arrived Cuba on election day. Yedra informed me that although people said there were no elections in Cuba, this was the third round in a process that began in Matanzas Province several years earlier. Cuba's experiment in participatory democracy, known as *Poder Popular*, was a process in which neighborhoods elected representatives to city councils, which in turn elected representatives to provincial councils and so on.

I was skeptical. The devil is in the details when it comes to democracy, just like anything else, and I had my doubts about the details. I wondered how the candidates were chosen, whether autonomous opposition was allowed, what the rules for campaigning looked like and whether the councils, once elected, had real power. That night the radio said that 89 percent of the population had voted, up one percent from the previous election, and asserted that the massive voter turnout demonstrated the strength and legitimacy of the Cuban social and political system. The announcer repeatedly used the term "socialist democracy" which sounded to me like something George Orwell had probably used in a novel.

The election coverage illustrated a more general aspect of the news in Cuba that I would notice every day I was there—orthodoxy. The news was tightly controlled. The government provided it, slanted it, and made sure that all slants went in the same direction. Opposing viewpoints, when mentioned, were portrayed as misguided, and their errors spelled out. I was particularly struck by how government journalists (i.e. all journalists) used language. Nouns were cloaked in carefully chosen adjectives. During my visit Solidarity was emerging as a major challenge to communist rule in Poland, and the Cuban press covered it expansively, but with phrases like "the counter-revolutionary members of the parallel union Solidarity…." Orthodoxy flowed over the news in Cuba like syrup over pancakes.

I'd seen dictatorships do this before, or at least try—Chile under Pinochet being a prime example—but the Cuban government took it much further. It blanketed you with the government's viewpoint, making it hard (and hard work) to disagree. And easy to give up and fall in line. The strategy was to overwhelm you and tire you out. That, they figured, would undermine doubts and limit dissent. They wanted you on board, or else to shut up.

It reminded me of church. Some things were sacred, and others profane. You were supposed to revere the former and condemn the latter. If you didn't and said so you got noticed, and in an unpleasant way. You were out of bounds—an infidel in the land of Fidel. That was uncomfortable. It could be dangerous. There was, after all, only one church and one orthodoxy in Cuba. You had no other place to go. So you were careful about what you said. You thought twice before you questioned the news. Or anything else.

None of this was a surprise, of course. I knew that dictatorships did those kinds of things. But it's different when they do them in front of you and to you. It becomes personal and chilling. I didn't like it. I didn't want to live that way. I realized that I cared a lot about personal freedom—especially freedom of thought and speech. I didn't want someone telling me what to think. That's part of what drove me to leave rural Michigan, go to college, and see the world, even when doing those things meant I'd probably have to discard at least a few of the beliefs I'd been raised with. I wanted to see what was out there, understand the options, and decide for myself. The Cuban government, it seemed, didn't want its people to do that.

But I'm getting ahead of myself.

We arrived at my hotel—the Havana Riviera—which had been built shortly before the revolution by mobster Meyer Lansky as the most luxurious hotel in Cuba. Though a bit tattered, it still exuded 1950s charm. You could imagine William Holden, Ginger Rogers, Nat King Cole, or Ava Gardner lounging beside the pool (all of them had). Maybe even Ernest Hemingway. It provided a whiff of history. I was glad they'd put me there.

Here, though, I ran into my first hitch. I had understood I could use my credit card in Cuba but discovered that was true only if I were on an organized tour, which I wasn't. So I'd have to pay cash. Fortunately I'd brought enough dollars to cover my expenses—barely. I'd be OK. But it was one more reminder of how different Cuba was from the other places I'd visited.

The next day in the hotel lobby I ran into the Cuban-American I'd met in the Miami airport and who'd been returning to Cuba for the first time in twenty-some years. I asked for his first impressions. He said the place looked fairly good; it just needed a little paint—"a couple of million dollars worth."

Then began a week of meetings. Mostly with people and institutions that we (or they) thought Ford might develop activities with, plus others they simply thought I ought to meet. They represented the future of our program there, if we had one. They were why I'd come.

The Cubans started me out with their pride and joy—science. They'd put a lot of chips on developing research and training in science and technology, more perhaps on a per capita basis than any other country in Latin America. They wanted us to notice, scheduling meetings at the Cuban Academy of Sciences and the Center for Scientific Studies and Research. I got the message and was impressed. The people running these institutions were bright and serious. I liked them and figured they were doing good work. Science shone brightly in Cuba.

But since Ford didn't work in the hard sciences, the chances of our supporting activity in those fields were slim to none. Our pride and joy was the social sciences, which they hadn't mentioned. When I asked they said there was also a social science institute that focused on history and archeology—which seemed to me like the least controversial of the social sciences. Later I was informed that that institute also did work on economics, cultural anthropology, and psychology. No one mentioned political science or sociology. I was not invited to visit.

The next day I visited the Ministry of Public Health, where there was a real possibility we might fund a project. In New York I'd already spoken with people at Columbia University (including a Chilean friend, Giorgio Solimano, who was on the faculty there) regarding support for research on Cuban policies aimed at reducing the impact of infant mortality due to diarrheal diseases. Ford had funded this kind of thing elsewhere, so doing something similar in Cuba was a logical next step. It would also achieve our goal of helping professionals from the two countries work together. And it was far enough from politics to keep us out of trouble.

The researchers at Columbia had been talking with the folks in Cuba, and plans were well-advanced. The Cubans' one concern was making sure that any formal agreement be with Columbia University, rather than with the Ford Foundation—which was our requirement as well, so no problem. This would get done. Later, when a reporter from the *New York Times* called to ask about the project, I described it as a "serious opportunity to document Cuba's experience in delivering health-care services and thereby enhancing world understanding of the Cuban approach to development." Which it was. It became the center-piece of our Cuba program over the next several years.

So it went. I met with many impressive people, including Ricardo Alarcón, vice-minister of foreign affairs, Pastor Vega, director of the

Cuban Film Institute and Mariano Rodriguez, director of the *Casa de las Americas*. I had lunch with Wayne Smith, chief of the U.S. Mission in Havana, who suggested that the average standard of living in Cuba was lower than in 1958, despite the enormous economic aid it had received from the USSR. (He also asked that I leave him the copy of the Sunday *New York Times* I'd brought with me, since he otherwise couldn't get it. I did.) These meetings were a privilege and a pleasure, but I see no reason to burden you with the details.

I do want to mention a couple of people who stood out.

By far the most interesting was Eugenio Rodriguez Balari, the director of the (improbably named) Institute for Internal Demand. I'd met him earlier in New York and had been impressed by his intelligence and creativity. Balari's outfit was responsible for determining the demand for consumer goods in Cuba, and therefore, indirectly, for determining what kind and how many goods would be produced (or imported). He'd taken that mandate quite a ways, publishing a weekly newspaper called *Opina*, which included articles on fashion, music, sports, and even political commentary, and that made it an oasis of style and personal expression in a country that emphasized equality and uniformity. It may have been the most popular publication in the country. Balari had recently been asked to establish a center for clothing design, and to launch a line of clothes bearing the Opina trademark—just like the designer clothing in the United States. He showed me photos of shirts with an Opina label on the pocket—and then stood so I could see the Opina label on his pants. Balari seemed on his way to becoming the Ralph Lauren of Cuba, or at least as close as you could get to that in a thoroughly socialist economy.

He was also planning a TV program that would air on weekends and be, in his words, a television version of the newspaper. The program was to include subtle and carefully done political criticism. Clearly Balari was at the center of a powerful public opinion operation. He may have been one of Cuba's most influential people.

We also talked politics over glasses of Armenian brandy. He saw the Reagan administration's approach to Cuba as anachronistic and bankrupt. All the damage that could be done to Cuba had been done, he said, and maintaining the blockade only strengthened Cuba's resolve to resist and generated support abroad for Cuba as the victim of a much larger country. He said that Cuba would like to deal with the United States on the basis of ideas rather than threats, and that doing so would be much harder for Cuba than dealing with the blockade. (I heard pretty much the same argument from several Cuban officials).

I wondered aloud whether the Cuban model would work in countries that didn't have a *patrón* like the Soviet Union to bankroll their policies. He responded that the Soviet Union had treated Cuba very well, making demands neither in domestic nor foreign policy. Cuba, he said, had a "mature" relationship with the Soviet Union that involved full independence. Its decision to intervene in Angola, for example, was taken with no prior consultation with the Soviet Union. I found that interesting. But he didn't really address my observation about the importance of having someone beyond your shores paying the bills. I sensed that this was a sore subject.

What I didn't ask was how a guy so intelligent and creative navigated a society so narrow and repressive. My impression was that he'd signed on early to the Cuban Revolution and was a true believer. He'd invested a lot and had been given a lot of power and responsibility in return. So maybe he'd just decided not to look beyond the fences. I could understand that. As with a holy order, you take the vows and accept the limits. But I wondered how, when he woke up in the middle of the night, he thought about those tradeoffs. And I suspected that, should restrictions be relaxed, he'd be leading the charge to change.

Another of the extraordinaries was Manuel Moreno Fraginals, perhaps Cuba's most distinguished historian, with whom I had dinner in Old Havana one evening along with his wife, Beatríz, who was an architect. Manolo (his nickname) was not part of the official schedule. I'd met him earlier in the Dominican Republic and we'd agreed to meet in Havana, should I manage to visit. We ate at the Bodeguita del Medio, the place Hemingway made famous years before. Manolo was intelligent, clear-thinking, and not at all doctrinaire. He gave me good advice, pointing out that every institution in Cuba is a government institution and there was no getting away from that. Therefore, we should focus on people of top quality who could be trusted to exercise sound judgment whatever their political views. After dinner we spent a marvelous hour touring Old Havana, with Manolo describing the history and his wife the architecture. I didn't ask him the tough questions either, perhaps because I sensed he had no illusions about what he was dealing with and had decided for reasons that were personal rather than political to stay put. (A decade or so later, Manolo and his wife would emigrate to Miami.)

A couple of more general observations about Cuba back then.

First was the limited emphasis on style in clothes. During my week in Havana, I did not see a single stylishly dressed woman. Many of the clothes in stores were imports from places like Bulgaria; some were locally produced. All were remarkably uninteresting. The result was a pervasive drabness. I chatted briefly with an obviously sophisticated woman while at the Institute of Internal Demand, who lamented the absence of stylish clothes. I offered to give her the Style section from the Sunday *Times* I'd brought along. (I figured Wayne Smith could do without that part of the paper.)

Second were the small but ubiquitous mechanisms of social control I kept noticing. For example, persons entering the elevator in my hotel were routinely asked to show their registration card. If you didn't have one, you couldn't go upstairs. The authorities justified this on the grounds that it protected against robbery and prostitution, which they said were potential problems. That was probably true, but it was also a convenient way of restricting association among individuals. The use of control mechanisms in the name of efficiency, order, and protecting people from danger seemed common. (My elevator operator also asked that I leave her the copy of *The New Yorker* I had tucked under my arm, which I was pleased to do.)

Finally, I was struck by the government's relentless emphasis on seriousness, hard work, and the common good. The streets were full of signs saying things like "Defense and Production: The Duty of the People" and "The Power of the People: That's Real Power." Completely absent were signs promoting food and drink—or, more generally, extolling the virtues of fun. I don't remember ever seeing a bar. Or a dance hall. Or a bingo parlor. Or anything remotely frivolous. Nor do I remember anyone telling a joke.

That was curious, and unlike any other country I'd ever been in. I wondered how people felt about it. It seemed to me like a kind of secular Calvinism, and not all that different from the world view I'd been exposed to via my Lutheran upbringing, and later my courses in American Thought & Language at MSU. And that I'd rebelled against a bit (although it's pretty hard to get genuinely past those things). The unremitting soberness of Havana bothered me.

On my final night I was invited to the home of Pablo Armando Fernandez, one of Cuba's best-known writers. This wasn't on the official schedule (I'd turned down, reluctantly, an official evening at the *Tropicana* nightclub). My contacts in New York had put me in touch with Pablo, and he'd invited a bunch of writer and artist friends to come by and drink rum and sip bitter Cuban coffee in rocking chairs on the front porch of his old Spanish-style house. It was casual and pleasant. Not surprisingly, they asked for my impressions of Havana. I replied that I found the government's persistent emphasis on seriousness, hard work, and the common good to be admirable, but at some level curiously non-Latin. I wondered what had happened to exuberance, frivolity, and fun, and whether the people of Cuba ever committed any sins. My remarks drew some uneasy chuckles. They didn't seem to want to say much but did assure me that there were sinners in Cuba, perhaps even a few in our midst. Looking back on my conversations, this was one of the few topics on which the Cubans I spoke with did not have pat answers.

That evening ended with my first and only bus ride in Havana. Since I was off the official schedule I was without my car and driver, so a poet, a playwright, and I set off on foot for the bus stop. We boarded a huge bus that tossed us about as it sped over bumps and around curves. I realized quickly that the trick was to keep your knees bent and both hands on the railings—a lot like riding the subway in New York, and about as much fun. The bus dropped me near my hotel.

The next morning I went jogging along the *malecón*, which was strewn with men fishing so I had to be careful not to trip over their lines. I jogged to the Hotel Nacional, past the monument commemorating the sinking of the battleship *Maine* some eighty years before, which, not unreasonably, blamed the "imperialists" for the incident. There I found a large group of people, mostly in street clothes, practicing military maneuvers. Fatigue-clad soldiers were teaching civilians the elements of crawling on their stomachs, charging with bayonets, and other techniques of close-in fighting. I was impressed by the sight of Cuban citizens on a Sunday morning in front of Havana Bay practicing military maneuvers that could only be intended to protect them from an invasion by their big neighbor to the north. I thought of Central Park on that same morning, where joggers and bicycle riders would be celebrating a day of rest and relaxation. And I remembered how warm and friendly virtually every Cuban I had met this past week had been.

My flight back that afternoon was on a Russian-made Iluyshin jet belonging to Cubana Airlines that, I was informed when I checked in, would leave at 1 pm, an hour earlier than scheduled. It left at 12:45. This was the first time I'd ever been on a flight that left before its scheduled departure time. The plane rose swiftly out of the thick, damp mist of Cuban orthodoxy and into the Caribbean sunshine. Arrival in Miami was uneventful. No one tried to ram us on the runway.

That was my first visit to Cuba. There were more—including one with Ernie Bartell, director of the University of Notre Dame's Helen Kellogg Institute for International Studies. Eventually I managed even to take in the show at the Tropicana (although, frankly, going to a show like that all by yourself is more perfunctory than exhilarating). We funded, over the next few years, a modest set of exchanges between Cuban and U.S. institutions in areas that they and we were comfortable with, including not only research on infant mortality but forays into contemporary art and traditional music (think cha cha chá). I wouldn't argue that any of these were big breakthroughs. They constituted small, non-governmental advances in relations between the two countries. You take steps like these because they seem to go in the right direction. And you hope that sooner or later they'll make a difference. But most of the time you never know.

The achievement that most warmed my heart was funding a few short-term stays by Cuban economists at economics departments in U.S. universities (including Notre Dame, my old football nemesis). I had fond hopes that by doing so we might chip away at conventional economic thinking in Cuba, which was old-school socialist and almost completely impervious to the virtues of markets, prices, efficiency, and growth. It was the only genuinely subversive impulse I remember having. I have no reason to think that those visits had any impact on Cuban economic policy (or thinking). What was interesting, though, was reaching agreement on how to select the economists to go off and study. We wanted to do this ourselves, but figured, perhaps unfairly, that the Cubans wouldn't let us—and would only want to send the most doctrinaire economists off to U.S. universities. I brought this up, as I recall, with the rector of the University of Habana who, after some thought, said something like "You guys pick 'em." I was relieved. We did.

Two other incidents related to our work in Cuba were genuinely memorable. The first was a phone call I got in New York from a prominent conservative leader—a woman whom I didn't know (and whose name I don't remember) but had seen quoted in the press. She was very unhappy to hear that the Ford Foundation was working in Cuba and wanted me to know that. My impression was that she didn't really know anything about what we were doing but had been asked by the anti-Castro network to send us a message, and she did. I don't remember how I replied. What I do remember was feeling uneasy. Quite uneasy, actually. How'd she get my name? I was apparently on the radar of anti-Castro groups in Miami, and that wasn't a great place to be. They didn't always pull their punches. What might come next? Fortunately, nothing did. But it was one more learning experience. The beautiful, idealistic webs we spun at the Ford Foundation could look very different to people on the ground. We needed to keep that in mind.

The second near-indelible memory was of being asked at a Ford Foundation board meeting, with no previous warning, to explain what we were doing in Cuba. The query came from Dorothy Marshall, a vice chancellor of the University of Massachusetts whom I had met and liked. This was just as we were fine-tuning our strategy, but before we'd done much. She must have gotten word.

I thought my boss, Bill Carmichael, would answer Dorothy's question. Instead (and alas) he turned to me. I usually attended board meetings but always sat in the back and had never said a word. Now I'd have to speak on what I thought was one of the most politically sensitive programs we had anywhere in the world. And I hadn't prepared. Robert McNamara, who had his own history with Cuba, was sitting there listening. I was petrified.

Fortunately (and to my surprise) I managed to reach into my mind and bring up the memo I'd written a few weeks earlier laying out the parameters we'd agreed upon for our work in Cuba. My words came slowly, as I struggled to remember what I'd written. But they came and seemed coherent. I was glad I'd spent so much time writing that damn memo. I got through it. There was some discussion. Dorothy seemed satisfied. I don't remember whether McNamara said anything. I was relieved. It was like going before a firing squad and they didn't shoot.

That's enough about the Caribbean. It was great and rich and I learned a lot. But I did other things as well while in New York, mainly managing Ford's regional program, which consisted of grants for activities that extended beyond the jurisdictions of any of our three field offices in Latin America. These were few but interesting, and included support for:

- an effort to develop a region-wide human rights program (the Inter-American Institute of Human Rights, in Costa Rica)—which turned out to be harder and take longer than we'd expected;
- the Latin America program at the Smithsonian Institution, which had been established several years earlier by former Ford Foundation staffer Abe Lowenthal.
- Americas Watch, the Latin American branch of what

eventually became known as Human Rights Watch (and shared the Nobel Peace Prize in 1997);

- the Washington Office on Latin America (WOLA)—that a group of church leaders had established in the 1970s to conduct research and advocacy on human rights in the Americas; and
- a brand-new think tank on international affairs in Latin America called the Inter-American Dialogue, that several highly respected leaders were setting up in Washington.

(There may have been others; it was four decades ago.)

They turned out to be quite a group. All went on to become leading voices on Latin American affairs. All continue to operate as of this writing. And all exemplify the long-term, policy-intensive, institution-building strategy that dominated Ford's thinking back then. Managing that work thrust me into a world of regional policy analysis I'd not previously had much contact with. It was interesting, and a nice step ahead career-wise.

But more interesting was the fact that very few of those regional grants happened because I possessed extraordinary vision or professional judgment. What's truer is that I was part of an organization that was well-positioned to do certain kinds of things. Ford had staked out a terrain—policy work on Latin American affairs that targeted elites, emphasized human rights and sought to influence government policy— and had the vision, staff, contacts, prestige, and money to operate effectively on that terrain. It was, for that kind of work and at that point in time, a kind of philanthropic juggernaut. That fact thrust me into rarified networks I'd not otherwise have gotten into, introduced me to people I'd not otherwise have met and enabled me to support work I'd not otherwise have been able to support. Ford set me up. That was a privilege and, of course, why I'd wanted to work there in the first place. And why I tried to do my best. But I was a cog in the Ford Foundation machine. A happy and lucky cog. Much of whatever I managed to do was more Ford than me. You need to recognize those things.

Ford's support to get the Inter-American Dialogue up and running also, it turned out, set me up for the afterlife (meaning, of course, life after the Ford Foundation) and illustrates the privilege that flowed naturally from working there. The Dialogue was established substantially by two extraordinary people—Abe Lowenthal and Peter Bell—both of whom I'd met previously thanks to the Ford Foundation, and one of whom (Bell) had been my first boss and mentor (Another prime mover behind the Dialogue was Sol Linowitz, former head of Xerox and U.S. Ambassador to the OAS, who had no background with the Ford Foundation.) Bell later became co-chair of the Dialogue and a long-time board member. Lowenthal became the Dialogue's first director and hired Peter Hakim (my former colleague at Ford's office in Chile) as his number two. Later Hakim became the Dialogue's director and, once I'd left Ford and spent a couple of years at New York University writing a book, offered me a job. These were people I'd known and worked with for years; now I'd get a job at the think tank they'd built. I'd work there for the next two decades.

Some of that, I'm willing to believe, was because I'd done pretty good work. But some, perhaps a lot, was because I'd done that pretty good work at the Ford Foundation, where people like Lowenthal, Bell, and Hakim could see it, get to know me, and decide whether I could make it on their team. Had I done good work elsewhere, I doubt I'd have even been on their radar. Ford plugged me into a distinguished professional network. That made moving on a whole lot easier. And rewarding.

The Dialogue was distinctive as well in its Latin American and Caribbean character. Half its membership and board came from the region and included major political and business leaders such as former secretary general of the Organization of American States Galo Plaza, former secretary general of the United Nations Javier Perez de Cueller, and future president of Brazil Fernando Henrique Cardoso. It was a distinguished, influential group.

Two more examples of Ford's network effect: On my way to the Dialogue's first big meeting in Washington in 1982, I stepped into a tiny elevator in the Smithsonian's Castle Building and found two people already there, one of whom introduced himself as David Rockefeller and made pleasant conversation as we rose to the fourth floor. At that meeting I also met Gabriel Valdés, a former foreign minister of Chile who would later play an important role in the country's return to democracy. Those were mere introductions, but over the next couple of decades I'd do projects with both, and become almost chummy with Valdés, who was a chummy guy if you were on the right side of him. Ford got all that rolling.

The other thing I did in New York was recruit. I knew nothing about recruiting, of course. I did know, firsthand, how tough working in a Ford field office could be. And how impressive virtually all my colleagues in the Santiago and Lima offices had been. And I'd noticed that many of my colleagues at Ford were graduates of Princeton's Woodrow Wilson School of Public and International Affairs (three of six in the Chile office when I started there), so I figured that might tell me something. (On the other hand, the Wilson School had turned me down when I'd applied a decade or more earlier, so obviously their judgment wasn't perfect.) That was as much as I knew. Over time I came to realize that finding people who had the right stuff to work at the Ford Foundation was extremely important—perhaps the most important thing I did while I was in New York. (The Woodrow Wilson School, by the way, was recently renamed the Princeton School of Public and International Affairs, in recognition of Wilson's racist views.)

I learned a lot from my boss, Bill Carmichael. He had strong opinions about the kinds of people we needed and where to find them. I'd characterize his starting point as "ordinary people need not apply." Working at Ford was demanding—intellectually, psychologically, and ethically. You had to be up to it. Not many were.

That was the single most important lesson I learned about recruiting, and one I came to embrace and apply. If the Ford Foundation was to do extraordinary work, it had to recruit extraordinary people. That was a reality. There was no way around it. You had to find those people. In fact (and this is me talking), if you didn't find an extraordinary person you were probably better off leaving a position open until you did. Average simply wouldn't do.

The question, of course, was how to define extraordinary. My answer, which emerged from listening to Bill, talking with our Human Resources people and from trying my hand, was some combination of intelligence, education, motivation, and character—each of which had to be extraordinary. Three out of four wasn't enough—in fact, three out of four was a crapshoot. Our staff would have to deal with extraordinary people and extraordinary problems. They needed to check all four boxes. They also needed to be fluent in Spanish (or Portuguese for the Brazil office) and have already had significant living experience in Latin America. We expected them to hit the ground running.

That was a lot, but they were out there. The trick was finding them. Putting an ad in the paper wouldn't do it. The best way to find people like that was to consult networks—people who were at the top of fields we worked in and whose judgment we trusted. Since much of our work back then was academic or policy-related, that largely meant consulting professors at first-rate universities—the Ivy League, Oxbridge, Chicago, Berkeley, and Stanford. They had extraordinary students who'd gotten extraordinary educations. Some of those would meet our needs. We seldom looked elsewhere.

This sounds elitist and was. We were an elite institution looking for elite staffers. It probably wasn't all that different from recruiting fighter pilots or neurosurgeons. You had to find the right people, there weren't many and time was short. So we mostly looked where we thought the chances of success were greatest. In our case people who'd managed to get into and out of first-rate universities were good bets. We started there.

Finding highly intelligent, well-educated people with experience in Latin America wasn't all that difficult. What was harder was finding people with the right motivation and character. We needed people who cared deeply about the kind of work we did, and who wouldn't wilt under the demands and stress that often came with it. They had to have commitment, backbone, and people skills. And they had to want to work for us. We tried to avoid careerists. Sorting that out was more art than science. You started by reading CVs and talking with references. Then you talked with the candidate. Then you asked yourself how you felt. I came to think I was pretty good at reading people, and figuring out whether they had what we needed. (Decades later while at the Inter-American Dialogue, I once hired someone after just reading a CV, checking references, and doing a ten-minute telephone interview. I sensed right away that this person had what it took. She did and did well.)

Three anecdotes:

- We interviewed an impressive candidate to head up our office in Mexico City, Bob Pastor, who had a Harvard PhD, high-level White House experience, and a record of significant academic and policy achievement on Latin America. I already knew and liked him. Clearly, he could handle the job, but we worried about his motivation. He seemed committed to a broader diplomatic/political career; we needed more of a team player. We decided not to make him an offer.

- We interviewed a candidate, Michael Shifter, for a program officer's position in our Lima office. I thought he was per-fect—smart, well-educated, and experienced—a summa cum laude graduate of Oberlin and ABD in sociology from Harvard who'd worked for several years at the Inter-American Foundation. I was certain, after our interview, that he had the motivation and character we needed (and delighted to discover that he was also a pretty good stand-up comic). But one of my New York colleagues wasn't convinced, and that meant we couldn't move forward. I was dismayed. The guy was too good to lose. So I backed off a bit, consulted more references and brought him back in for another round of interviews. My doubting colleague still objected. I backed off again, consulted even more references and brought him in for a third round of interviews. Maybe there was even a fourth round, I don't remember. Poor Michael. (He recalls colleague Anne Kubisch grabbing him in the lobby and saying "You're almost there.

Don't blow it!") Eventually, though, my doubting colleague folded and we were able to offer Michael the job. He went on to become a first-rate program officer (working with me in the Lima office). Years later he joined the Inter-American Dialogue, where he eventually became president (and my boss!) and served with great distinction. Pushing through the objections and finding a way to get Michael hired had been the right thing to do. I did that entirely because I was convinced he had the combination of intelligence, education, experience, drive, and temperament we needed—the right stuff.

- Much later, during my final months with the Ford Foundation, and after a new regime had taken over, we interviewed a candidate for a position in the Lima office who had just finished his PhD (at UCLA, perhaps). I didn't think his intelligence was extraordinary, but liked his motivation and thought he was our strongest candidate. His references were good, if not great. Still, something bothered me about his character—something I couldn't put my finger on. That plus less-than-stellar intelligence said second-tier to me. I intended to express my doubts when we gathered in New York to discuss his candidacy. But my colleagues were so uniformly enthusiastic about the guy and so ready to hire him, I decided not to push back. I was leaving the Ford Foundation and they were staying. They should have the kinds of people they were comfortable with. I held my tongue. We offered him the job. He took it. A few weeks later while in New York for orientation he called to say that he was having trouble completing a task I had assigned him. I told him it was normal to feel that way. Working at Ford was demanding. You had to take it step by step. I made some suggestions and said not to worry, that he'd get the hang of it. He thanked me. A day or so later he leaped from his hotel window to his death. I felt terrible. I'd sensed a problem with this fellow but had failed to speak up. I should have. Later we discovered that he was being treated for depression, something neither he nor his references had mentioned. We also discovered that, although he'd told us he was single, he had a wife and child in California. Clearly, he had serious problems. We never should have subjected him to the pressure that was pretty much standard with our jobs. It was the only suicide I ever heard of at the Ford Foundation.

Here I want to say a bit more about Bill Carmichael, with whom I would work closely in one way or another for nearly a decade. He was quick, well-spoken, incisive, brilliant at making a case, energetic, positive—a prime example of the extraordinary people you often ran into in Bundy's Ford Foundation. He'd been an undergraduate at Yale, Rhodes Scholar at Oxford, and done a PhD at Princeton. He'd been director of the undergraduate program at Princeton's Woodrow Wilson School of Public and International Affairs, Dean of Cornell's Business School, head of the Ford Foundation's office in Brazil, and director of its program in Latin America and the Caribbean, which was when I met him. He was a risen star. I was a junior staffer looking to learn.

I was particularly attracted to Bill's idealism. He wanted to make the world a better place, as did I, and knew more than I about how to do it. And he brought to that task energy, lucidity, and charm.

I was also attracted by his intelligence. Bill was smarter and quicker than I was. I mentioned earlier that I liked going up against first-rate minds. It's like skiing challenging terrain or hiking a tough trail. You find out what and how much you can handle. You learn who you are. You grow. Bill offered that.

I was especially struck by Bill's insistence that things are seldom as they seem, and that the most intractable problems can be solved, or at least managed, by liberally applying intelligence and hard work. That was something I needed to hear. Work at the Ford Foundation thrust me into plenty of unfamiliar terrain, and too often my default was to accept rather than to challenge. Bill didn't accept well. His instinct was to challenge. He was determined to get things done.

Working with Bill was demanding—like stepping into a fast-moving stream. You were pretty sure it was going to be interesting, exciting and worthwhile. But you didn't know how it would turn out. And you had to find your footing. Bill liked to push and test; you needed a firm base from which to respond. Once you'd gotten that, and shown you could add some value, you'd probably be OK. You might even get to help navigate. Without it your days were numbered.

Bill was also jovial, carrying you along with easy dialogue on all sorts of topics. He enjoyed debate and was a master at making his case. You could disagree but you probably wouldn't win. He'd tell you, with a smile, precisely where you were wrong, making you feel respected but corrected (although not necessarily convinced). He liked a good joke—and especially a good pun. At times he could be glib, and it was great fun to catch him when he said something that, if you looked at it carefully, didn't hold water. But he was always thoughtful. You might disagree, but you wouldn't ignore. His combination of smarts and *chutzpah* (the WASP variety, to be sure) was a great match for me at that point in my career.

Bill was also adventuresome. Earlier I mentioned his suggestion, which I managed to fend off, while visiting Cuba that we make an unscheduled and unapproved visit to the Isle of Youth. With Lima office colleague Grid Hall, we did a hike one weekend way up in the Cajón del Maipo in Chile that put Bill knee-deep in a fast and icy mountain stream wearing sneakers. And we spent a couple of midsummer days in the heart of Tierra del Fuego sampling the charms of Argentina's southernmost city, Ushuaia, on the Beagle Channel just 700 miles north of Antarctica. That was a business trip—the chairman of the Ford Foundation's board, Alex Heard, and his wife were going to visit following the board's first-ever meeting in Latin America a month or so hence and we had to reconnoiter the area. Duty called.

We also once shared a rollicking dinner in Haiti's capital, Port-au-Prince, with Connecticut Senator Chris Dodd and his Cuban-American girlfriend, whom we ran into at the celebrated Hotel Olofsson—which had been the inspiration for the Hotel Trianon in Graham Greene's novel *The Comedians* and for years attracted celebrity guests, such as Jacqueline Kennedy Onassis and Mick Jagger. Dodd had been a Peace Corps Volunteer in the Dominican Republic, next door, so had things to say about Haiti. And I'm sure we talked about U.S. politics, although I remember nothing. What I know is that we had a good time. Upon returning to the Olofsson, we encountered the Japanese photographer who'd taken up with the widow of the New Yorker who'd run the place for years, and who insisted we pose for group pictures. We smiled brightly at the camera. I've always wondered what happened to those photos.

Years later Bill resigned from the Foundation for reasons I've never really understood, although I have my theories. What did seem clear was that he had too many people reporting to him, and so faced a lot of pressure—perhaps too much. I had the feeling it wore him down. And I had long had the feeling that Bill's exceptional talent and motivation had, for whatever reason, never been properly harnessed and channeled. It was an unfortunate ending.

When Bill resigned, I thanked him in a letter and tried to capture his uncommon ability to deal with difficult situations:

> Somebody said that "Talent does what it can, and genius does what it must." I've always thought that phrase applied especially well to you. Thanks for your enormous contribution to the social sciences, to human rights and to clear thinking.... Thanks for making it fun.

Bill responded—on his last day at the Foundation—with a warm thank-you enclosing a message he'd recently gotten in a fortune cookie: "Keep your feet on the ground even though your friends flatter you." He observed "I am not at all sure that some of your observations are deserved but I am certain that the learning process has been a joint one, and that the values and standards we have both tried to reflect have been mutually informed."

My five-plus years at Ford's headquarters in New York were challenging and diverse—a nice complement to the nearly six years I'd spent on the ground in South America. I got unparalleled exposure to the Caribbean, learned something about management, met all sorts of extraordinary people, including several of Ford's stellar board members, and got a sense of how the top of a large institution like Ford operated. It was a serious education in more than just philanthropy. Most importantly, I came to think that I could operate successfully at that level and with those kinds of people—no small step for a kid from rural Michigan.

But five years was enough. You couldn't stay in one job much longer at Ford. I needed to move on. The question was where. I still didn't feel I was done with the Ford Foundation. And I certainly wasn't done with Latin America.

Several years earlier Bill Carmichael, had asked whether I was interested in becoming a "representative" i.e. heading up our field office in Lima, and I'd said no. That was a gut reaction. I was still learning plenty and didn't feel a need to move up, nor ready to take on more responsibility. Now that same job was coming open again, and Bill asked again whether I was interested. This time I said yes. I'd probably gotten what I was going to get out of the New York job. It was time for new challenges. And on a personal level, my relationship with my live-in girlfriend, Joyce, was coming to an end. I needed change there too. I was ready. My gut said it was time.

XVIII

FORD/PERU (AGAIN)

RUNNING THE OFFICE

So I'D MOVE back to Peru and become the "Representative" at what by then had become Ford's office for Spanish-speaking South America—including not only Peru, but also the countries that formerly were managed from the office in Santiago (Chile, Argentina, and Uruguay) and from the office in Bogotá, Colombia (which we'd recently closed). All were places I already knew. The big difference was that now I'd be the boss.

It turned out I was wrong. The big difference would be bigger and different. But it would take a while for me to realize that.

I got my first inkling of how different it might be a few months before heading to Peru when I found myself on the New York-Washington shuttle sitting next to well-known (and Pulitzer Prize-winning) humorist Art Buchwald. I didn't recognize him, of course, but he, no shrinking violet, introduced himself and started a conversation. What I remember is that he talked at length about Teddy Kennedy—that he was drinking too much and generally in a bad place and that it was a real shame. Buchwald, it seemed, just had to talk. I was happy to listen. It was part of the shuttle experience: you saw, and sometimes sat next to, people who were famous and interesting. (Once I sat next to a guy who was widely expected to run for governor of New York--Lew Lehrman, I think. He ignored me.)

Then he asked about me and when I told him I was going to go off to run the Ford Foundation's office in Peru he gave me a serious look: "Do you have kidnapping insurance?" I didn't and told him so. He expressed dismay. I thanked him for his concern. Then I began to wonder. Did he know something I didn't? Did I need kidnapping insurance? Was I getting myself into something I hadn't anticipated? Probably not. I already knew Peru, after all. Buchwald didn't. I decided not to worry.

What was true was that now I'd be the boss. I'd become a "Rep," a position that represented a personal pinnacle—certainly the most I could aspire to at the Ford Foundation. I remember thinking—drawing on the romantic vision of the Ford Foundation as a kind of Camelot that I'd gotten way back when I was in the Peace Corps—it was like making prince or maybe bishop. That seemed pretentious and probably was. I never told anyone. But I felt it and it was fun.

I arrived in Peru just in time for Alan García's inauguration as the country's 53rd president, which I watched on TV from my room at the Country Club Hotel—my favorite in Lima. García was larger than life. He'd been president of Peru's most cohesive political party, the American Popular Revolutionary Alliance (APRA) which, despite its size, age, and energy, had never won a presidential election. He was South America's youngest head of state and presided over Peru's first peaceful transition from one democratically elected president to another in nearly four decades. He painted a beautiful picture, and promised he'd deliver. Some called him the "JFK of Latin America." I admired his energy, eloquence, and appeal to national unity. My second stint in Peru was going to be interesting.

It was. But it was also a disaster. Alan García turned out to be a textbook example of populism run wild, and possibly the worst president in the contemporary history of Peru. Beauty and joy rolled off his tongue, but he hadn't a clue about what to do. He was more about magical realism than governance. Peru became a mess.

Economics was a big part of the problem. García adopted a

"heterodox" economic policy that included defaulting on part of the national debt, running huge budget deficits, and nationalizing private banks. For a couple of years, he avoided disaster. Then the money ran out, investment dried up, and the economy fell apart. The country was racked by hyperinflation (reaching 7500 percent in 1990), widespread strikes, and growing shortages of basic products like sugar, cooking oil, flour, and milk. Poverty grew. Much of that was García's fault.

He also had the bad luck to be president just as two recently established guerrilla groups—the fundamentalist Maoist *Sendero Luminoso* (Shining Path) and the much smaller Marxist *Movimiento Revolucionario Túpac Amaru* (MRTA)—were kicking into high gear. This turned out to be a big deal. The terrorists were vicious, determined and gaining ground. They regularly dynamited electrical towers in the hills above Lima (more than a thousand by 1989), leaving large parts of the city without power. They assassinated government officials, mostly in rural areas, by shooting them or slitting their throats. They kidnapped. They issued death threats. Sometimes they hung dogs from trees. They were barbaric.

García didn't cause any of that, but neither did he deal with it. The government had no plan. The country seemed adrift. Rumors flew. There was talk of a coup, and even a civil war.

But none of that happened the first couple of years so for a while we were fine. And those were good years. I had a first-rate staff, most of whom I'd helped recruit and all of whom ranked high on the four criteria I mentioned earlier (intelligence, education, motivation, and character). All went on to distinguished careers (except Grid Hall who would die of AIDS within a few years). Two, Steve Cox and Ray Offenheiser, eventually became Ford Foundation Reps (in Mexico and Bangladesh) and Ray went on to become head of Oxfam America. Michael Shifter (as I've mentioned) became president of the Inter-American Dialogue. Cynthia Sanborn remained in Peru and had a long and productive academic career at the Universidad del Pacifico (where she produced, with several colleagues, a history of the Ford Foundation in South America). Jane Thery later held a number of executive positions at the OAS. Christine Pendzich became an environmental specialist at USAID and at several non-governmental organizations. Pablo de la Flor went on to hold a series of private sector positions in Peru along with a couple of vice-ministerships. Jeanine Anderson became a leader on women's issues in Peruvian higher education. It was a stellar group that met or exceeded my expectations.

We continued to practice what had been Ford's bread and butter in Latin America since it first started working there: research and policy analysis in the social sciences. What had changed was that we'd left behind the goal of developing academic disciplines and added work on topics like human rights, women's studies, governance, and international relations. Most of these were relatively new as academic or policy pursuits in the countries where we worked, so it was particularly rewarding to help get those topics on agendas, and to connect national specialists to international networks. Our agenda mixed old with new, seemed timely and was achievable. There were plenty of good people out there to work with. And we covered a lot of territory—Colombia, Argentina, and Chile—in addition to Peru. We spent a lot for time on airplanes.

And life in Lima was comfortable. I'd found, courtesy of my friend, Julio Vargas, an apartment in a small, upscale complex that a friend of his had just finished building in the foothills above central Lima and therefore above the worst of the cold winter mist. The place was quiet, spacious, and stylish. It had a lovely pool and sauna—perfect for relaxing after a hard day's work. The architect who'd designed the complex took me to see it and explained why he'd done what he'd done. Then my friend Mayu Hume introduced me to a wonderful housekeeper— Alicia—who (with her dog, "Braunie") took charge of keeping the place neat and clean. Alicia's cooking was superb, but more impressive was her enterprising character. She once organized a surprise birthday party for me, inviting colleagues from the office and managing to keep it a secret until guests began arriving. Another time she made a well-used pair of shoes disappear for a couple of weeks and then presented them to me, completely reconditioned and stained in a different color. Alicia did what she thought ought to be done. She reminded me of my mother.

Life in Lima was also lively. I got to know some first-rate academic and policy leaders, among them Father Felipe McGregor (rector of the Catholic University), Julio Cotler (perhaps Peru's leading public intellectual), Richard Webb (twice president of the Central Bank), Roberto Dañino (later prime minister), and Eduardo Ferrero (a future foreign minister). There were more, some of whom I'd stay in touch with for several decades. I also got to know the U.S. ambassador, Alex Watson, who lived across from our office in an elegant residence with a tennis court and occasionally invited me to come in early for tennis and breakfast with him and his wife before crossing the street to start work. Once again Ford had plugged me into a network of talented high achievers. Once again I was privileged.

One highlight of a those first few years in Lima was helping organize the first-ever meeting in Latin America of the Ford Foundation's board. We invited members to visit each of the three field offices (in Brazil, Peru, and Mexico) prior to the meeting to meet grantees and see what we were about. And since our field office—Lima—worked in the most countries, we hosted visits for board members not only to Lima, but also to Santiago and Buenos Aires. That was a lot of work. I was nervous, of course. Hosting board members was always a mix of excitement and fear. I looked forward to meeting such special people but worried I wouldn't impress them. Or that something would simply go wrong.

I have two vivid memories from the Buenos Aires segment, which included half a dozen board members, among them Ford's president, Frank Thomas. Both memories, perhaps not surprisingly, involved Bob McNamara. The first was a meeting with Argentina's president, Raúl Alfonsin. The meeting was scheduled for mid-morning at the Casa Rosada—Argentina's equivalent of the White House—and I'd hired a van to take us there. When the board members gathered in the hotel lobby, I noticed that McNamara wasn't wearing a tie. That worried me. This was Latin America. And the president of Argentina. You did not show up without a tie. All the other board members (and I of course) were wearing ties. Bob was talking a mile a minute as he often did. None of the other board members appeared to be concerned. I wondered what to do. Saying anything to him about his lack of a tie seemed presumptuous. Who was I to tell the former president of the Ford Motor Company, secretary of defense, and president of the World Bank how to dress? I struggled for some principle that would show me what to do. Finally I decided to keep my mouth shut. He'd met with plenty of heads of state over the years and knew what the hell to do, right? The van pulled up to the *Casa* Rosada and we all got out. Bob, still talking, calmly reached into his jacket, pulled out a tie, and put it on. All was well. We went inside and met with the president.

The other memorable moment happened that evening, as we were gathering in the hotel lobby to head out for dinner. I'd left the evening open, so that board members and their spouses could make their own decisions regarding what to do. I was standing with a couple of board members, including Frank Thomas, who said something like "Let's get out of here before McNamara shows up." (He and Bob had their differences.) Almost immediately, McNamara stuck his head between the two of us and said "You guys got dinner plans?" That settled that. I took them to my favorite *asadero* for some great Argentine beef.

The most important thing that happened to me during my second stint in Lima, though, had nothing to do with Peru, and everything to do with my love life. I mentioned earlier that leaving New York meant leaving behind my live-in girlfriend and effectively ending our relationship. That was painful and took a couple of years but was the right thing to do. What happened next was a surprise. My gut took over. One day I simply knew that I needed to find Miri—the Chilean woman I'd met at Stanford several years earlier and should have fallen in love with but somehow didn't. This was not something I consciously decided. It just came to me. But instead of the ringing of bells I'd long (and romantically) thought would tell me when I'd found the right woman, there appeared in my mind a low-key, mysterious message: Find Miri.

So I did. Miri was back in Chile working as a consultant on education policy, and living in *Providencia*—a Santiago neighborhood that had long been fashionable and residential but was turning commercial. I had her address. While on a business trip I went by and rang her bell. She came to the door.

"Hi," I said. "I was in town and thought I'd say hello."

Right. That was lame. We hadn't seen each other in maybe five years. Either I didn't know what I was doing, or I couldn't own up to it. She looked astonished. But—fortunately—she didn't close the door.

"Would you like to go out to dinner?" I said.

"Yes," she said.

We did. That was more than thirty years ago. Today we have two grandchildren. I'm very lucky.

Now I see I was just plain wrong to expect that ringing bells would tell me when the woman of my dreams appeared. The only bell that rang was Miri's doorbell. And I rang it. What happened instead was different and lower-key: I did what felt right and stopped worrying about bells. I opened myself to the unpredictable. Love crept in.

I suppose the lesson here is that sometimes your gut is right. But how do you know when? I don't know. In this case I just knew I should do that. It was clear. Maybe some kind of clarity is what you should look for. When it all seems to add up, do it. The odds are in your favor.

It took a while, though—like five or six years. Miri lived in Chile; I lived in Peru. The flying time from Lima to Santiago was three-and-a-half hours and I traveled there at most once a month so our courtship was sporadic and unconventional. And I didn't have a plan. I was simply responding to my gut, putting one foot in front of the other. Something felt right. We'd see.

The process had its charms. We started by just going out to dinner when I was in town. That was fun. Food in Chile was simple but great (I particularly liked the cheese, avocados, nectarines, artichokes, *empanadas de pino*, sausage, *pan amasado*, and olives—along with the wine, if you count wine as food, which I do). Seafood was some of the best in the world, ranging from sea bass to sea urchins (well, maybe you should forget about the sea urchins), with just about everything in between, including oysters, prawns, flounder, hake, abalone, salmon, tuna, clams, conch, conger eel, and several kinds of crab. And did I mention the seaweed omelettes? I became a big fan of *machas a la parmesana, corvina la plancha*, and *gambas al pil-pil*, accompanied by chilled sauvignon blanc, which in Chile was delicious. (Chile's red wines were even better, particularly the cabernet sauvignon and the carménère.) There was much more. We ate. We talked. We started getting to know each other.

That turned into a big deal. I came to see and appreciate Miri. I realized she was strong, smart, warm, principled, and fun. She cared deeply about values and about family. She went out and did things, rather than waiting to be shown or told. She had an admirable commitment to proper behavior— "*la buena educación*"—as they say in Chile. Details and appearances were important. You did things right and didn't cut corners. She had a nice sense of style. She liked movies, art, and the theater. She'd probably read more good novels than I had—and spoke more languages. She was a first-rate cook. She had a wonderful daughter named Milena, who had just started school. She also had the memory of an elephant, and the keenest sense of smell of anyone I'd ever met who didn't have four legs and a tail. This was a special person.

And despite our national-origin differences I noticed we shared a lot. We both came from close-knit, decidedly middle-class families. We both wanted to make the world a better place. We had graduate degrees. We were bilingual. We'd lived in, and were comfortable with, each other's country and culture. We liked kids, nature, cooking, books, walks, gossip, and politics. We enjoyed socializing, but not too much. We both liked dogs. I'd not thought much about compatibility before—what it meant and how it might feel—but suddenly there it was, staring me in the face. I began to pay attention.

I remember especially a lunch that Miri prepared for me and my former Ford Foundation colleague Gary Horlick, by then a Washington lawyer, who was in Chile on business. It was a lesson in good taste. The table was set simply but beautifully. The food looked—and tasted—great. Everything was perfect but nothing was elaborate. Miri, I realized, was more about style and standards than about luxury. I liked that. Taste was more important than money.

We also began socializing with Miri's sister (Lucía) and brother-in-law (Edmundo) who lived upstairs and whom, of course, I knew from Stanford. Lucía was a well-known artist and Edmundo was a legal scholar turned sociologist who'd taught at the Institute of Development Studies at the University of Sussex. We had plenty to talk about. I was edging into the family.

Things got seriouser and seriouser. Our monthly rendezvous took on some emotion. Miri picked me up a few times at the airport in her little Renault with Chopin's *Nocturnes* (a favorite of mine) pealing from the car stereo. Great messaging.

You can see where this was going. The process was a little like walking step-by-step into the ocean on a beautiful summer day. I got in over my head but it felt so good I couldn't stop. I had to learn how to swim.

We began spending an occasional weekend at Miri's parents' apartment on the beach in Viña del Mar. I'd fly down to Santiago on Friday afternoon instead of on Sunday (Air France had a lovely Friday flight from Lima that offered champagne and occasional free upgrades to first-class) and we'd head for *la playa* which on a good day was under two hours by car. We developed a routine: pick up groceries at the supermarket, drop our stuff at the apartment, water the poor geraniums clinging to life on the balcony (her parents didn't use the place much), and then go out to eat. Dinner might include a pisco sour (me—Miri barely drank), sea bass sautéed in butter and garlic, french fries, the wonderful avocado, celery, walnut, and lemon salad I've only seen in Chile, and for dessert maybe *torta de lúcuma* or a fruit compote. And some sauvignon blanc, of course. That set us up for the weekend.

The next morning I'd get up early and run on Viña's long and expansive waterfront, marveling at the birds scouring the beach for food (gulls galore of course but also sandpipers, petrels, cormorants, and others I couldn't identify) and enjoying the crisp seaweed-and-saltwater air. The run was especially exhilarating in the winter, when the air was cold, the people few, and the waves coming up from Patagonia crashed icily on the beach.

We'd have a simple breakfast—local *pan amasado* with butter, jam, avocado, cheese, fruit, and coffee. We'd read the papers. We'd talk. Maybe we'd go for a walk. Later Miri would prepare a sumptuous lunch and I'd help—mostly by making the gin-and-tonics. The food was always delicious. We'd follow lunch with a nap. That evening we might go out for dinner. These were self-indulgent weekends. We knew no one in Viña so talked only with each other. We moved slowly but steadily like the tides.

One of those beach escapes (not to Viña, however) marked a big step up in our relationship. It was summer in the southern hemisphere—probably January—so the sky was blue, the sun was hot, and the air was dry. My brother, Gary, and his family were visiting from Boston. We'd spent several days in Peru and then went down to Chile where I'd rented a place in Cachagua, a smaller and trendier beach resort than Viña, with two miles of beach and a small island offshore filled with penguins, pelicans, and comorants—and that attracted politicians, particularly from the Christian Democratic Party (Chile was very tribal back then, even at the beach). We spent some time with Alejandro Foxley, a good friend who was about to become minister of finance in the newly elected Aylwin government, and to whom I mischievously presented a University of Chicago T-shirt in honor of his new responsibilities. (He'd be replacing the "Chicago Boys" who'd run the economy for nearly fifteen years.) Another friend, Gabriel Valdés, a former foreign minister who'd been a leading figure in Chile's return to democracy, invited us over to his place for drinks with the family. It was all very nice.

A few days later I took my brother and his family to the airport. Then I drove into Santiago, picked up Miri and we went back out to Cachagua for a week. We did almost nothing except cook, read, and walk upon the beach. But something happened. Something big, or fundamental, or similarly momentous. We were no longer just dating. This was no longer a casual relationship. We were in love. We were probably going to get married. After Cachagua it was just a matter of time and logistics.

What really got my attention, though, was that no one asked my permission. Our impending union was a fait accompli. I didn't decide, I discovered.

Now let's go back to life in Peru. I mentioned that the first couple of years of the García administration had been OK, but then the country fell apart. Bad economic policy combined with inspired terrorism produced a debacle. It's hard to capture how it felt—a mix of surprise, surreal and scary. Some days we had electricity, some we didn't. The same was true for water. Inflation got so high we had to raise local staff salaries each month. The terrorists (*Sendero Luminoso* and *MRTA*) stepped up their attacks. The things they did were savage and horrifying, and pervaded the daily news. We didn't like talking about them. But we wondered whether they might happen to us. Why not kidnap someone who worked for the world's largest private foundation? Or at least toss a bomb in their direction? We reinforced the door of our third-floor office and posted an armed guard.

The government didn't seem to have a plan. Rumors flew. There was talk of a coup—even a civil war. Life became so strange I began taking notes on what I saw, hoping that would help me figure things out. Here are just four entries from my notes, verbatim:

Terrorist killed El Comercio journalist Barbara D'Schilie and chief of FAO-supported Vicuña-breeding program on 31 May in Huancavelica. Staff had apparently received threats over several months as part of effort to interrupt foreign aid to development programs targeted at the peasants of the area. She was killed by crushing her skull, presumably with a rock.

The last remaining elected mayor in the province of Leonicio Prado, village of Altavista, was assassinated yesterday by two young men and a woman while having lunch. The men opened fire, wounding him several times. Then the woman finished him off with a shot in the head. A military post is located a few blocks away. They were unable to find any suspects.

15 June: Ford Foundation has been mentioned in a magazine that focuses on Amazon issues. An editorial states that some people allege that we have decided to fund Vargas Llosa in his presidential bid. It says that our support is being kept secret.

16 June: A mayor of the village of Las Palmas, whose predecessor was assassinated, resigned after terrorists killed his daughter by placing a grenade in her mouth.

This was scary. I learned also that Peru was one of just four countries in the world where the U.S. State Department had authorized danger pay (one level above hardship pay) for its staff. The others were Lebanon, Guatemala, and El Salvador. And at a dinner party I sat next to a medical doctor who, when I told him I was with the Ford Foundation, asked whether I had a bodyguard and was taken aback when I told him I didn't. That kind of thing wore on me.

I suppose I should have seen at least some of it coming. My good friend Julio Vargas, an *Aprista* who had accepted a vice minister's post (in I don't remember which ministry), told me early on: "We're going to screw this up." It was a matter-of-fact appraisal, something Julio was good at. I guess he had a premonition. And Alejandro Toledo, who would become president more than a decade later, told me that García suffered from manic-depressive disorder (or something like that) and took lithium to control it. That should have set off at least a few warning flags. It didn't.

In fact, I recall running into Rodrigo Botero, a member of the Ford Foundation's board and former minister of finance of Colombia, on a Manhattan street-corner several months after García took office (it's amazing how often those things happened) and, in response to his query, telling him I was impressed by García. He smiled, perhaps a little indulgently, and said he wished he could share my optimism.

But things got worse and I got worried. Even if the security risk were small, it was hard to assess and clearly could change fast. The chances of something bad happening may not have been high, but the consequences might be huge. Imagine if one of our staff, or their family, were threatened, attacked, kidnapped, or worse. How would we feel? Were those consequences too negative to justify the level of risk we were facing? (Thinking this through seemed like a straightforward application of the Bayesian statistics I'd studied at the Chicago Business School—those tools turned out to be useful.)

I also realized that, even if our current staff were willing to tough it out, we were going to have a hard time recruiting anyone new—particularly the talented high-achievers we sought and prided ourselves on getting. No one enjoys coming home to darkness, no water, and cold food. Or to confronting daily in the press and in office chitchat the blood-chilling terrorism of the Shining Path. Especially no one with a family. The professional demands we placed on our staff were hard enough. We shouldn't ask them to come and live in what had become a hardship post—or worse. Most of the best would refuse.

I began telling my boss, Bill Carmichael, that we needed to take seriously the possibility that something bad could happen to our staff or their families, and consider alternative arrangements—specifically, moving our New York-appointed staff to another country and letting them fly in and out of Peru as needed. That would, for the most part, get them out of the line of fire. They, and we, would breathe easier. And I suggested we simply go back to Chile, where we'd maintained our (very privileged) legal status after closing the office a few years before and could quickly and easily set up shop.

I didn't get much uptake. I was the bearer of bad news that Bill could hardly have wanted to hear. My impression was that he was dealing with a bunch of problems (he would, in fact, be forced to resign a year or so later), and didn't think this one was urgent enough to invest precious time in. And since he'd recommended, several years earlier, that we make Lima our regional office, backtracking wasn't going to be easy. He'd like to put that off if he could.

I couldn't and decided to go on the record. I wrote Bill a four-page confidential memo, with a copy to his deputy, John Gerhart, laying out conditions in Lima, my concerns, and steps we might consider. I wanted it to be clear that I had sounded the alarm. That's how worried I was. Doing that had the merit of formalizing what I'd been saying informally and forcing higher-ups in New York to take a position. They could decide I was right and do something. Or they could decide I was wrong and do nothing (except maybe wonder about my judgment, which I'm sure they did). But they'd share responsibility for whatever happened. I didn't want that responsibility entirely on me.

For more than a year they did nothing. And (fortunately) nothing bad happened to us in Lima. Then, once Bill had resigned and a new team was in place, they decided we really did have a problem and needed to get our staff out of Lima right away. But they weren't ready to commit to Chile, so instead relocated everyone to New York while they thought it over. After another year or so they decided that Chile was the right move, reopened the office there and put staff in. All of that took time, cost money, and disrupted the lives of the staff members involved. It could have been avoided had I managed to convince my colleagues in New York early on to take the step they eventually took. I wondered what, if anything, I might have done differently.

Some time after we pulled staff out of Lima, our third-floor office was struck by what appeared to be a grenade. It happened around 9 p.m., so one was hurt. My colleague Michael Shifter reported that, when he came in the next morning and began to review the damage, including a huge hole in his office chair, one of our secretaries, Angie Hirata, dismissed it as just a "*bombita*" (little bomb).

We never knew who did it or why.

Dealing with Peru's turmoil was probably the toughest challenge I faced during my seventeen years with the Ford Foundation. It was the only time I felt close to disaster, and the only time I was genuinely scared. And it was one of the few times I disagreed seriously with the people above me.

It also marked a step toward the end of my tenure at Ford. The Ford Foundation, and specifically its culture, was transforming itself. I wasn't sure what direction it was taking, but it no longer seemed the glittering "City on a Hill" that had captured my imagination back when I was in the Peace Corps. The place I'd long thought of as my own—and that felt almost like family—was changing.

And I'd changed as well. I'd probably learned as much and grown as much as I could. I was probably done with giving away money. It was probably time to leave.

There was nothing wrong with that. Things change. The proper response was to be clear-eyed and thankful. I'd had a good run and gotten a lot. Ford had helped me address all three of the big urges I had while growing up. It put me into Latin America and the Caribbean for seventeen years. It gave me real money to help make the world a better place. And it helped me establish professional and personal relationships with some of Latin America's leading intellectuals. I needed to smile, appreciate, and move on. That's basically what I did, although I did it with a pang of sorrow.

And in fact I'd begun thinking a year or two earlier that it might be time to leave, not because the Foundation was changing but because I wasn't. I worried I was no longer growing professionally. I began sounding out trusted friends, specifically Peter Bell and Abe Lowenthal, regarding how to think about moving on. (As I recall, Abe suggested I try to become one of those thousand points of light that President Bush mentioned in his speeches—which I found helpful but maybe a little vague.) I didn't have a plan but thought perhaps I should. At some point, after Bill resigned and the new administration took over, I informed the people in New York I was planning to leave the Foundation once I completed my current assignment. I was already on that track. It was time.

What's notable, though, is that a little later, once the new regime announced a reorganization and created the position of director for Latin America, I couldn't resist applying. Looking back, it seems like a dumb thing to do. But at the time the temptation was just too great. Ford had been my professional life. It had held me to high standards, introduced me to extraordinary people and gave me the opportunity to make a difference in a part of the world I loved. You don't give that up easily.

I needed to, however, and fortunately they gave the job to someone else—whom I congratulated right away. I would have been the wrong choice. Ford was no longer my place. I'd lived my dream for seventeen years. Now it was time to think post-Ford. I could see that but still had to adjust. I had no idea where I would go.

Then Ford, ever generous, offered me a golden handshake: a year or more at a place of my choice to do some writing while I figured out what to do next. That was perfect—and one more example of the privilege I enjoyed while working at the Ford Foundation. I needed time to sort out my thoughts and chart a new path. I probably had things to say that ought to be said. If so, it made sense for Ford to fund me while I said them. I'd write a proposal and be off.

But what would I propose? The whole idea was to write something worth reading. Ford wasn't going to fund me just to hang out and think. During my previous sabbatical I'd written an article on how the Ford Foundation had responded to repressive governments in South America's Southern Cone during the mid-1970s, I was proud of my article and it had been published in an academic journal (and reprinted by the Ford Foundation). Now what?

Here Abe Lowenthal was extraordinarily helpful, pointing out that I had privileged access to the people and events behind Chile's recent transition to democracy and was probably the only person who'd manage to sit down and write it up properly. So I should. And it would have to be a book.

That made sense. That's what I proposed. That's what Ford funded.

I spoke with Chris Mitchell, the head of New York University's Center for Latin American and Caribbean Studies, who kindly offered me an appointment as a visiting scholar, complete with office and access to NYU's library. So I had a plan, a place, and money. And my new office would be within walking distance—a long, healthy walk through the artsy streets of SoHo—of my co-op in Tribeca. I was ready to go.

Except there was one big problem: I'd never written a book and had no idea how to do it. Deciding to write a book doesn't produce a book, after all. For me the act of writing a book was mysterious, even audacious. What exactly did you do? I remembered a wonderfully ironic observation long ago by a high school friend of mine, Jay Shirley:

"I'm selling my car. Nobody's buying it, but I'm selling it."

There's wisdom there. Declaring isn't enough. You have to make it happen.

I started asking around, and three people helped a lot. Gary Sick, a colleague at the Ford Foundation who'd worked at the National Security Council with Zbig Brzezinski during the Carter administration and had written a well-received book on the 1979 Iranian Revolution (*All Fall Down: America's Tragic Encounter with Iran*), walked me through his book-writing experience and in the process demystified it. That was helpful. I could see a path. Guillermo O'Donnell, a distinguished Argentine political scientist who'd done ground-breaking work on transitions from authoritarian rule, and whom I'd met because we supported the private think-tank, CEDES (*Centro de Estudios de Estado y Sociedad*), that he'd co-founded in Buenos Aires, helped me sort through an otherwise bewildering set of issues. And Abe Lowenthal, over lunch at the Ford Foundation's tenth-floor dining room, gave me concise advice: ask a single good question and make the book your answer. I did that and it worked. Getting that core question clear made all the difference. (Mine turned out to be something like "How is it that an extraordinary group of intellectuals helped engineer a successful transition to democracy in Chile?"). I was on track. Abe, by the way, also helped me at the end of the process, once I had a finished manuscript, by putting me in touch with the editor of the Johns Hopkins University Press, Henry Tom, who pretty quickly offered me a contract. I barely knew that the Johns Hopkins University Press existed, and would never have thought, or known how, to knock on their door. Once again I'd benefited from the talented and well-connected network of colleagues and friends I'd developed during those years at the Ford Foundation.

So that's the Ford Foundation. Seventeen years. The most important and most moving years of my professional career. It was a great adventure. A dream come true. I'm glad I did it and glad I left. Ford helped me address two of the three big urges I'd grown up with: getting out of rural Michigan and making the world a better place. I'd exceeded my expectations for both. And it moved me well along toward the third—becoming an intellectual—by introducing me to Latin America's world-class intellectuals. Now I'd work full-time on that one. I went off to NYU.

XIX

NEW YORK UNIVERSITY

WRITING A BOOK, FINDING A JOB, GETTING MARRIED

"It must be considered that there is nothing more difficult to carry out, nor more doubtful of success, nor more dangerous to handle, than to initiate a new order of things."

—Niccolo Machiavaelli,

The Prince, 1513

I ARRIVED AT New York University formally committed to writing a book and informally committed to getting married. Plus I had to find a job. I figured I could do all three. But I doubted I could do all three at once. And I was nervous.

I started with the book. I didn't really know how to write a book, or whether I had what it took. But I was committed to, and getting paid for, doing it. So I'd give it my best.

I'd already settled on the core question, so my next step was to spend several months in Chile interviewing seventy or so intellectuals and politicians, collecting and reviewing a large pile of books and documents, and sifting through my memories. Then I sat down in my little office at NYU and asked how should I begin. And then I began. I didn't have much of an outline. Mostly I grappled with what I'd seen and collected

356

and tried to make something good appear. The surprise was that usually it did. Slowly. The process was difficult but somehow reliable. Almost always something respectable—maybe even beautiful—would emerge. A narrative took shape. I was delighted.

I learned at least a couple of things.

I found that for any given section I needed first to load the relevant facts into my mind and let them process a while before I could write. It was like cooking in that I had to assemble the ingredients before I could make the dish. But it was unlike cooking in that I didn't have a recipe. I was deciding on the fly how much of each ingredient to use, how to combine them and how to cook them. Once I did that, a narrative would take shape. I'd write it down.

I also learned that sometimes you have worthwhile things to say even when it seems as if you don't. Most afternoons I'd get tired of struggling with ideas and words—it just wasn't happening—and decide to stop for the day. But I discovered that, if I kept at it, the sentences would often begin to come out almost by themselves and in pretty good shape. They appeared to have a life of their own. A process was going on in my mind that I could neither see nor feel, but that, if I were patient, would bear fruit.

The result, after two years, was *Thinking Politics: Intellectuals and Democracy in Chile, 1973-1988*, a real book that got published and got good reviews. That was fine, and what I'd hoped for. The surprise was how much I liked it. I always thought I'd approve of what I'd written once I'd written it, but I hadn't expected to have what I'd written warm my heart. It did and still does.

Which makes me wonder why.

Part of what was going on, I think, was that I was satisfying one of the biggest urges I had while growing up: to become an intellectual. All that time I'd spent in the ivory tower had paid off. I remembered the scholarly literature and traditions I'd been exposed to and was impressed by at Michigan State, Duke, Chicago, and Stanford, and thinking maybe now, at NYU, I'd finally earned a place in—or at least near—those hallowed ranks. I'd written a real academic book. I'd established my bona fides. I'd become an intellectual.

Another part was less intellectual and more emotional. Many of the people I wrote about were friends, or at least close acquaintances. Some I'd even helped support in their work by steering Ford Foundation money toward their institutions. We had debated, despaired, and dreamed, over coffee, cocktails, lunch, and dinner, and even at the beach, during more than fifteen years. They'd made history—little by little and for the most part unexpectedly. I'd watched and helped a bit. I needed to write that up. It was part of me.

And part, I think, was that I'd finally done some heavy-duty writing. That brought my recently discovered urge to write into the sunlight where I could see it. I liked the sound of what I said: the words, the phrases, the esthetic thrill of coming up with a good sentence. All of that spoke to me. I began to appreciate the craft of writing. And to think maybe I could do it.

But how much of this is delusion? Writers, let's remember, tend to bare their heart or their soul or their feelings when they write, so often a lot's at stake personally. Your book is your baby. Of course it's beautiful. How could you not love it? I worry maybe that's what's going on with me.

My bottom line, though, was and still is that I wrote a good book—at least good enough. I took on an important topic, analyzed it rigorously, wrote it up clearly, and drew serious conclusions for the academic literature. I met my personal standards—which is a good place to start. And I'm pretty sure I met many of the standards I was exposed to in graduate school and later in my work with social scientists in Latin America. Even today when I dip into it, I smile. You don't need much more than that.

Getting married took longer. Maybe I was just afraid. It was, after all, my first time, and marriage was a big responsibility (serious and life-long, I'd been brought up to believe). I knew deep down I was going to do it. But I didn't want to mess it up.

The logistics were complicated. I had eighteen months of funding at NYU to write the book (which, it turned out, wasn't enough) and after that, nothing. I assumed I'd find work somewhere, but what or where was unclear. Getting married in the midst of that and bringing wife and daughter to the United States to live, getting the requisite visas, finding a place in Manhattan large enough for the three of us, enrolling Milena in school, getting that book written (was I up to it?), and looking for a job seemed formidable. And Miri would need to find work. I worried especially about Miri's daughter, Milena. Adapting to a new country, language, and culture would be tough enough for her; it would be tougher if she got settled and made friends in New York and then had to move elsewhere a year or so later once I'd found my next job. What to do? My instinct was to take one step at a time, so first I'd get that book written and out of the way. Which I did.

The upside of holding off was that our courtship extended to New York. Miri would visit for a week or so and we would explore Manhattan. That was largely about the theater, museums, and restaurants. And about street life, mostly below 14th Street (I'd become a downtown guy) including long gastronomic walks through Little Italy and Chinatown (the pasta, olives, and fresh mozzarella; the greenmarkets and dim sum; those ducks—Peking, presumably—hanging upside down in shop windows!).

On several occasions Miri brought Milena, who was maybe six or seven, and we got to watch her reactions to the Big City. She insisted on sleeping beside the window from which she could see the World Trade Center looming like some kind of extraterrestrial over Lower Manhattan. Once during a serious snowstorm I took her out to hunt for boots and we (she in sneakers) trudged through the Village with wind and snow pelting our faces. We didn't buy any boots but had a great time braving the near-blizzard. Finally we took the subway back to Tribeca and made snow angels in a little park near the base of the World Trade Center before heading back to the apartment, where Miri had judiciously stayed in and warm, and prepared a tasty dinner.

We also wrote lots of letters—always in Spanish and always filled with love. These were here's-what's-on-my mind-and-I miss-you-very-much letters which, read today, seem simultaneously intimate and humdrum. I talked a lot about the city, the weather, what I was cooking, the music I was listening to (almost entirely classical, apparently), the movies I was seeing and the progress I was or wasn't making on my book. There was nothing extraordinary about that stuff except it was my life and I was trying to share it. That seemed important. I was opening my heart.

Some examples (translated, of course):

I miss you very much. It's like a wound.

It's been a pleasant, relaxing day filled with newspapers, art and music. I'm moved by the pleasure I get from doing nothing. I'm a tragic mix of the protestant ethic and indolence.

I send you the freshness of rain, the beauty of autumn and the warmth of a down jacket.

It's snowing. The snow started after midnight and has continued, gathering strength and covering the city with a thick, white blanket. The air is full of big snowflakes carried diagonally, and even horizontally, by the wind to the street. Some rise [with the wind] and then fall. From inside the air seems full of cotton pieces falling implacably over the city, making me feel happy and peaceful. It reminds me of my youth in Michigan, with huge snowstorms that fall from a mysteriously gray sky, cover the woods and suspend normal life, replacing it with a new and peaceful landscape. I want to put on my boots, coat, hat and gloves, and walk. On the last day of winter we've received the first snowstorm of the winter. What a relief!....I miss you even more in the snow.

A tasty kiss from the lonely cook.

Once, just before going to Paris to do some consulting, I wrote her a playful letter mixing Spanish with French ("Je t'aime mucho.")

And I was moved to send Miri a poem I'd composed decades earlier while an undergraduate at Michigan State, imagining (I can only presume) the girl of my dreams. Here it is:

It has long been my wont to praise
A figure from within a dream,
The sparkle of a tumbling mountain stream
The warmth of a thousand sunlit days.

All and each inside her stays
And cast a glow till it would seem
That everything around her gleam
Reflecting her appealing ways.

Nature ne'er so perfect cast
Impulsiveness imbued with grace
Action fraught with quick release
From clichés since long past

A mischievous smile on her face
And underneath a calming peace.

Not bad, I think. And romantic. Today it seems prescient—as if I could see what I wanted back then and just had to wait until I found it. Decades later, when I reminded Miri I'd sent her that poem, she replied with the mischievous smile mentioned in the next-to-last line above: "How many other women did you send that to?" "None" I said. "At least none that I remember."

Our extended courtship also included camping in southern Chile. I mentioned earlier that the south of Chile is spectacular—like Switzerland but longer (a thousand miles!) and with active volcanos, fjords, and an ocean (the Pacific). Twice we camped down there—on a remote Indian reservation up in the mountains just beyond a couple of snow-covered volcanos (Llaima and Lonquimay) and on the shore of Lake Icalma. I'd found out about the place from Andrew Wallace, the Ford Foundation's office manager in Santiago. He and his family had camped there for years. It was way off the beaten path. We got there by driving eight or ten hours south from Santiago to Curacautín and then taking a sometimes one-lane, sometimes dirt road that, near our destination, had us bumping along a train track that ran through a dark, narrow mountain tunnel—exciting on a good day. The road was marginally passable in the summer; you'd have needed real courage to try it in the winter.

The place was gorgeous, dominated by rugged mountains, blue glacial lakes (whose water we routinely drank) lofty *araucaria* (AKA monkey-puzzle or *pehuen*) trees that can live for more than a thousand years, and a jumble of sparkling brooks. The night sky was especially splendid. There was no ambient light so the stars glittered like diamonds spread out against the absolutely black sky. Beautiful didn't really capture it. Awe-inspiring was closer.

The place was also remote, at least back then. There were no villages nearby, or stores. No cottages on the lake. There was no electricity. We never saw another tourist. We slept in a tent I'd lugged from the U.S., cooked on a wood fire we built beside the tent, and stored our perishable food in plastic bags in an icy mountain stream that flowed nearby (which Milena dubbed our "Jeffreygerator"). That worked. We packed in pretty much everything, except water which was everywhere—and goat meat which local families were happy to sell and grill for us a few steps from our campsite on an iron skewer they stuck in the ground, angled over the coals and turned slowly. As the outer meat cooked they rubbed it with salt and cut off pieces with a large knife. We ate the hot, juicy meat standing up beside the fire and washed it down with cheap red wine. It was superb. At a roadside stand on our way into the mountains we'd picked up boxes of near-ripe tomatoes and nectarines to eat during our stay. And on a tip from Andrew Wallace, we'd brought flour, yeast, and shortening and gave it to a local woman, Doña Juanita, to make fresh bread which she delivered to our tent every couple of mornings, warm.

Once we bought a chicken from her and roasted it on the fire but it was so dry and tough we ate little.

The Indian families living on the reservation (Mapuche or Pehuenche—I was never sure)—were poor. They raised some livestock (I mentioned the goats and chickens) and harvested the seeds of the araucaria trees (which, like pine nuts, were edible). There must have been a few other crops. But it was hard to see how they made it. We were thankful they let us camp on the reservation. And treated us so kindly.

There wasn't much to do in Icalma and that was plenty. We hiked, swam, talked, cooked, and slept. We oohed and aahed a lot with Milena. We followed trails to see where they led, waded into streams to see how it felt, and poked around forests to see what was there. We also read. I brought whatever editions of the *New York Times* I'd found at a Santiago kiosk, back issues of the *New Yorker* and maybe a novel—cerebral reads for primordial surroundings. But reading was incidental. Icalma was mostly about remoteness, nature, and unremitting beauty.

That was three decades ago. I understand that now the government has put in a proper road, making Icalma easier to get to. And that people, presumably outsiders, have bought land near the reservation and built cottages. Today you can rent a place to stay in Icalma on Airbnb. It must have changed—attracting tourists and maybe even offering electricity. We were lucky we went when we did.

Those were all upsides. The downside of holding off getting married was that we held off getting married. It was taking forever and Miri felt we were marking time. She asked whether she would be writing me letters for the rest of her life. I responded as best I could: "You're not going to be 85 years old and still writing me letters. I treasure your courage and passionate patience. Together we'll solve this puzzle." As you will see, we did.

I was, of course, still living in New York, trying to finish the book and realizing I should start looking for a job. My funding was running out. NYU (Chris Mitchell, really) kindly said I could stay the extra months I needed to get the book done. I filed for unemployment and did some consulting for the World Bank (I mentioned in an earlier chapter the trip to Paris). That kept me afloat. But I needed to get a real job.

What's curious is that I didn't really look for a job. Deep down I think I figured something would turn up. Something that flowed naturally from the work I'd done before. That wasn't very responsible. But when I look back at what I did and didn't do, that's how it looks. The gods would come up with something.

What's even more curious is that they did. Peter Hakim was now working at the Inter-American Dialogue, the Washington think-tank I mentioned earlier. He asked whether I'd be willing to design an education program that the Dialogue could try to raise money for.

I was surprised. I had a PhD in education, of course, and had been originally hired by the Ford Foundation to work on education. But I had steadily moved out of education and into other program areas, like economics, international affairs, and governance. I had left education behind—psychologically and professionally—and did not expect to go back. Moreover, education hadn't taken off as a policy concern in Latin America. The region's traditional model of educational development—in place since the 1960s—focused almost exclusively on expanding enrollment, and paid little attention to quality, equity, or efficiency. Nobody was challenging that model. Education (unlike economics) was a policy backwater in most of the region. So I told Peter I'd be happy to try to come up with an education program, but that I didn't think there was any future in it.

I worked up a draft and ran it by my friend, José Joaquín Brunner, an education specialist, former Ford Foundation graduate fellow, one of Chile's leading public intellectuals, and one of the smartest people I'd ever met. He shared a document he'd been helping develop for the United Nations (later published by UNESCO's office in Latin America as "Educación y Conocimiento: eje de la transformación productiva con la equidad") and made some suggestions. I reworked the draft.

Then I sent it to Peter. We went back and forth for a couple of months before settling on a final version. He began shopping it around to donors and, to my surprise, got funding from the governments of

Canada (IDRC), Sweden (SAREC), and the United States (USAID) for a one-year project that I would direct.

So now I had a job in Washington. There was only funding for twelve months, but I figured that was enough. I'd either turn the project into a long-term program or find another job. The odds seemed good. I'd do it.

It's important to recognize, though, how connected getting that job was to the seventeen years I'd spent with the Ford Foundation. I was going to work at an institution—the Inter-American Dialogue—that had been founded by two former Ford Foundation staffers (Abe Lowenthal and Peter Bell) and with a Ford grant that I'd put together a decade earlier. I would direct a project that a former Ford colleague—Peter Hakim—had suggested, helped design and raised money for, and that a former Ford graduate fellow—José Joaquín Brunner—had helped strengthen. None of the money came from the Ford Foundation. Most of the connections that led to the job did.

We got married, finally, with family and friends on a beautiful spring day at Miri's sister's home in Santiago in a civil ceremony that my Jesuit friend, Patricio Cariola, donned priestly garb to bless and that my art buddy, Pepe Zalaquett, vouched for by signing the government document that needed signing. The atmosphere was festive and pleasant. There were flowers. There was Mendelssohn's "Wedding March." There was me breaking a glass with my right foot as per Jewish tradition. There was chilled Chilean *champán*. Once we'd been pronounced man and wife, I thanked everyone and announced that Miri and I recognized that marriages didn't always last forever and so had agreed to limit our initial commitment to fifty years. After that we'd sit down and see how things were going. So far, we're on track. Our wedding took place fifteen years after we first met in California. It was the best decision of my life.

That evening we drove out to Viña del Mar for one last weekend at Miri's parents' apartment on the beach. Miri says that was our honeymoon. I say that's when it began.

All that remained was to move to Washington. I was already there, having sold my Manhattan co-op and taken a short-term rental. And well before the wedding Miri and Milena had come up for a week or two to help look for the missing piece in our plan—a house. We knew little about Washington but were convinced we wanted to live in the city rather than in the suburbs.

Miri's take on this was simple: "I don't want to feel isolated." Making the adjustment from Chile to the United States would be hard enough. She'd need to connect and that would be tougher to do if we were in the suburbs. Mine was based on experience: "I don't want to commute." I'd been traveling to Washington on business for years and liked the place but had almost never ventured beyond the city limits. Why start now? And it was Washington—historical, political, and cosmopolitan. Our kind of place. Of course we'd live in the city.

What we didn't know was that Washington was in deep trouble—nearly bankrupt and with a mayor who'd been convicted of drug possession. Homebuyers were leery. Many thought the city's government was dysfunctional. Congress would soon create a Financial Control Board to oversee the city's spending. The suburbs looked like a better bet. Fortunately, none of that influenced our thinking. Washington's woes kept prices down and that was good for us.

We ruled out Georgetown pretty quickly (we needed a back yard for Miri's dog, Manchi, and back yards were expensive in Georgetown). And we missed out on a house in Woodley Park when the owner (who'd gone off to marry Ted Kennedy) decided, before we could make an offer, to rent it out instead of selling it. But we saw plenty of houses and got a sense of the market. Miri and Milena went back to Chile, leaving me with a pretty good idea of what would work.

I went out with our realtor just about every day and saw lots of places that I didn't like or were too expensive. Nothing clicked. Then we got lucky. One morning I got a call from our realtor:

"A family in Spring Valley just cut the price of their house below what their realtor recommended. I haven't seen it, but let's go take a look."

We did, that afternoon. Spring Valley was expensive. I hadn't thought we could afford a house there. But this one turned out to be perfect—big enough, nice enough, affordable, and with a back yard any dog would love. That evening I called Miri and got a green light. The next morning I offered $10,000 below the new price. The owner took it. Our realtor, when we closed the deal, said: "Congratulations on stealing a house."

I hoped that was true. The house certainly exceeded my expectations. But I wondered whether she said that to everybody.

We were almost there. I had my belongings delivered, hired a guy my neighbor recommended to do some painting, and moved in. My parents came out from Michigan and made a few suggestions. I had my decorator in New York—Jamie Drake—come down and put together a plan. I bought some stuff. The place took shape. We'd be fine. After the wedding Miri packed up her belongings, had them shipped, and we flew together to Washington with Milena and their dog, Manchi. I opened the front door and carried Miri across the threshold. Milena and the dog followed. We had a house. I had a job. Manchi had his back yard. We enrolled Milena in the Horace Mann Elementary School, just a few blocks away. Our life in Washington had begun.

XX

WASHINGTON

THE INTER-AMERICAN DIALOGUE
THE POLICY GAME

I ALWAYS THOUGHT I'd end up in Washington. Few jobs anywhere combined what I did—Latin America, public policy, and international development—and most were in universities, which I'd ruled out because I didn't see myself as an academic. Most of the rest were in Washington. Plus I had good contacts there. Washington seemed not only logical, but inevitable.

But going from the Ford Foundation to the Inter-American Dialogue was a major change—almost the flip side of philanthropy. I went from patron to supplicant. From giving money away to raising it. From having people knock on my door to having to knock on people's doors. From judging proposals to having mine judged. I took a pay cut. I had no job security.

Which was good. I'd worried, during my final years at the Ford Foundation, that I'd stopped growing. Now I was in a different institution doing different things, none of which I'd done much of at Ford. It was almost a different culture. I had to come up with proposals and convince donors to fund them. I had to write papers and give talks. I had to design a program that would resonate with policy-makers in Latin America. I had to create and convince. That ought to help me grow.

I think as well that I was trying to see how I would do outside the protective shell of the Ford Foundation—where having all that money to give away could lull you into thinking you were pretty good. I'd worked at Ford for seventeen years. It was time to leave the nest and see whether I could fly.

I suppose I should have worried more about taking on so much that was new, but I didn't. I figured I could tap the skills I'd picked up in graduate school at Duke and Chicago, and during nearly two decades of funding policy work at the Ford Foundation. I had the training, some of the experience and knew many of the people. I was probably smart enough. And I knew Latin America. It seemed like a natural next step. Plus I was genuinely interested in doing this kind of work.

Just as important, I was where I wanted to be. The Inter-American Dialogue was small back then—maybe seven or eight people. It was non-governmental, non-partisan, and non-bureaucratic. Its bread and butter was policy analysis and debate. It brought together some of the region's top political leaders, policy analysts and intellectuals. It didn't have much money but it was respected and connected. It was, so far as I could see, the best think tank working on Latin America and the Caribbean in the country. People I knew and admired—Enrique Iglesias, Alejandro Foxley, Rodrigo Botero, Abe Lowenthal, and Peter Bell, for example—were playing key roles. And my friend and former colleague Peter Hakim had just been promoted to president. So I don't want to overemphasize the amount of change I faced in moving to the Inter-American Dialogue. I was still dealing with many of the extraordinary people I'd met while at Ford. It was pretty much the same mafia.

I think partly what was happening was that my long-standing attraction to the best was kicking in again. I had, since high school, felt drawn almost mysteriously to people and institutions that signified quality. That irresistible sparkle had led me to the University of Chicago, and then to the Ford Foundation. Now it was leading me to the Inter-American Dialogue. I was responding to the siren call of talent.

Plus the work—analysis and debate on education policy—would address two other urges I'd had since high school. I'd get the chance to make the world a better place, and to do work that was pretty clearly intellectual. It was the kind of work I'd been aiming at and preparing for since I left rural Michigan. It felt right. And it was, let's remember, the only path that was clearly in front of me. I'd sign on, do my best and hope it worked out.

So I stepped, carefully and hopefully, into the world of think tanks.

A few words on what think tanks do. Mostly it's about policy—about identifying key problems, developing policy options and marketing them to policy-makers, policy-influencers, and the public, all with the goal of making things better. You have to establish an agenda, come up with good policy ideas, and sell them. That's it in a nutshell, I think. (Andrew Selee lays this out nicely in his book *What Should Think Tanks Do?*)

Doing that, of course, takes time. And impact is uncertain. People who know more about it than I make that clear. Fred Bergsten of the Peterson Institute of International Economics argues that "Think Tank work at its finest [involves] ten years from inception of idea to implementation of idea…" and Leslie Gelb of the Council on Foreign Relations observes that [Influence is] "…highly episodic, arbitrary and difficult to predict." (All of these are cited in Selee's book.)

My experience supports those cautions. Getting people—even smart, sophisticated people—to recognize problems and good ideas is harder than you'd think. I recall, for example, chatting with a former president of Chile, and being amazed by his assumption that education was doing just fine—which it clearly wasn't. You can't, I discovered, assume that politicians know all they should.

Influencing policy is even harder. You hope for impact but can't demand it. Even if you get it, you may not know you did, or be able to prove it. And it may take decades. There's an element of faith in the think tank business. Sounding the alarm, making the case, and pointing the way is all you can do for sure. You need to do those well.

Here I think it's worth pointing out the kind of uphill battle we were taking on. Improving education in Latin America was a tall order. In fact, you could easily argue that we were on a fool's errand, trying to reform policy in the face of ministries that were change-resistant, teachers unions that were all-powerful, and political leaders who, because they sent their kids to private schools, didn't directly experience the failings of the public system. The minister of education of El Salvador, Darlyn Meza, probably captured our plight (and spirit) when she presented us, more than a decade later, with a bronze statue of Don Quixote recognizing our "tireless work in promoting education reform in Latin America." She was on to something. Think tanks try to make things happen that haven't happened. That takes a certain amount of faith. Like Don Quixote, we needed to dream and push and see what we could accomplish.

And I was acutely aware that we had a short time horizon. Funding for the project would run out in twelve months. I had to produce and fast. Plus I had to start lining up funding for year two and (fingers crossed) maybe even year three. Or else find another job. There was a sense of urgency.

But then what? I didn't really know. I'm reminded of a framed cartoon someone gave me when, during my freshman year at Michigan State, I was elected president of my dorm floor. The cartoon showed a bunch of nebbish-looking characters facing someone who was obviously their leader and who was asking a confidante: "Now that they're organized, what the hell do we do?" That was our dilemma. All we knew was that we wanted to make education better in Latin America. We didn't know how to do it.

That question—what to do—may be the most distinctive aspect of my foray into think-tanking at the Inter-American Dialogue. When I started, there was no education program—no objectives, no structure, no activities. That was unlike my previous jobs (in the Peace Corps, for example, or at the Ford Foundation), where what to do had pretty much been established before I got there. At the Dialogue what to do was up to me. I was going to have to figure it out.

We started by doing what you do when you don't know what to do: we analyzed. We commissioned a series of country studies by national experts and mulled them over. That enabled us to establish an initial diagnosis—and, as you might imagine, an argument for additional funding. We quickly made the case to our original funders for a second year of support and got it. Then we added funding from the GE Fund and the Tinker Foundation. I also started talking with the Inter-American Development Bank (IADB) about bigger bucks. We were off!

I say "we" but that first year it was mostly me—with encouragement, merciless criticism, and helpful advice from my boss, Peter Hakim. As our funding grew, however, we joined forces with a think tank in Chile, CINDE (the Development Research Corporation), led by Osvaldo Sunkel, one of Latin America's most respected development economists. And we recruited my good friend, and superb Chilean social scientist, José Joaquin Brunner, to be co-director. We gave ourselves a name—the Partnership for Educational Revitalization in the Americas (PREAL). Then we established a Task Force on Education, Equity and Economic Competitiveness in the Americas, chaired by Senator José Octavio Bordón of Argentina, a former governor of the province of Mendoza who a few years earlier had nearly won a presidential election, and John R. Petty, former chair and CEO of the Marine Midland Bank. Both were members of the Inter-American Dialogue, of course.

Then we had our first big hiccup: Brunner resigned to become a minister in the government of Eduardo Frei. CINDE replaced him with Marcela Gajardo, a highly regarded education policy analyst, also from Chile, whom I'd known for years. Marcela was smart, strong, and creative. She brought not only long experience in education policy, but also a greater sensitivity to national leaders—and especially to government leaders—than I had. She and I co-directed PREAL, happily and productively, for the next fifteen years.

Perhaps the most important point to be made regarding those first (and even subsequent) years of my think tank work is that I had to raise money. Without it I wouldn't have a program. So I was not only keenly attuned to developing an agenda, analyzing policy, and building relationships with education specialists in Latin America, but also to figuring out which donors might fund our work and how I might convince them to pony up the money. I had to sell.

That added a dimension. Fortunately, the seventeen years I'd spent giving away money at the Ford Foundation had given me a sense of how donors think and what they need. I'd been in their shoes, after all. And my boss, Peter Hakim, was crucial. He'd already spent several years raising money for the Dialogue and had developed a remarkable sense of strategy. One principle I particularly remember was something like "Give 'em what they want." That wasn't a call to misrepresent, but rather to recognize that donors have their own programmatic and bureaucratic guidelines and in fact want to give money away because doing that well will assure their success (and their salary!). So you should, within the limits of your own objectives, do your best to accommodate them. You can probably find common ground. Try.

I ran into this problem early on while completing negotiations with the Inter-American Development Bank for much-needed major support. Peter and I were in Lima kicking off a big conference on the government of Alberto Fujimori. I got an urgent fax from the Bank demanding answers by the next day to a dozen or more highly bureaucratic questions. I was disgusted, but Peter said do it, so I did, staying up much of the night answering their damned questions. We got the money.

I also recalled something my friend Abe Lowenthal, who'd played a key role in founding three think tanks—among them the Inter-American Dialogue—told me long ago about donors. Their problem is that they have money they must give away. Your job is to help solve their problem. If you can do that, they will not only give you the money you need, but be genuinely grateful to you for helping them do their job well. Abe's pearl of wisdom was a great help in thinking about how to raise money, and one more way in which the extraordinary people I'd met during all those years at the Ford Foundation smoothed my path once I'd left.

And we may have caught a wave. Latin American governments had made real progress in economic (and particularly macroeconomic) policy over the previous decade and were beginning to turn their attention to other policy areas. Education was a logical priority. But the debate focused principally on getting more kids into school, and paid little attention to the quality, or equity, of the education those kids were getting. Policy elites—politicians, analysts and intellectuals—were beginning to ask new and different questions about education. We were gearing up to provide answers.

To my surprise, things went swimmingly almost from the start.

We managed quickly to land major funding—more than a million dollars—from the Inter-American Development Bank (IADB) for a six-country effort to develop a process of discussion and debate on key education policy issues. We also developed a project with a group led by David Rockefeller (the Chairman's International Advisory Council of the Americas Society) and the Latin American Business Council-CEAL regarding how the Latin American business community might promote better education. I put that project together with David's daughter, Peggy Dulany, who, it turned out, had a MA in education from Harvard University. That project established the vision and contacts we needed to develop, with funding later on from the AVINA Foundation, a major program on business and education over the next several years.

We began to have an identity and maybe even a presence. It was a solid start.

Two years later, as the IADB support was winding down, we got five-year core funding from USAID. Here we benefited both from good timing and from connections. The United States had just committed, at the 1994 Summit of the Americas in Miami, to "improve the quality and equity of education in Latin America and the Caribbean by promoting better education policy." That was what we were already trying to do, so why should they look any further? We met with Mark Schneider, USAID's director for Latin America. I already knew Mark. He'd helped me vet someone I'd hired while at the Ford Foundation several years earlier, and we'd both been Peace Corps volunteers (a year or two later Mark would be appointed Director of the Peace Corps). Peter knew him as well, probably better, than I did. My impression is that Mark, and USAID more generally, thought that PREAL's base at the Inter-American Dialogue set it up to reach and influence leaders—business, political, academic, government, and religious—who were crucial to improving education policy. We had the visibility, the prestige, and the connections. That made us a good bet. We got the money.

That set PREAL up for nearly two decades. USAID liked our work and had more than enough money to fund it. They became our mainstay. It's hard to overstate how important that ongoing core support was. Most programs need it. Few donors provide it. We were very lucky. USAID's support enabled us to operate without the constant fear of running out of cash and to develop a medium-term strategy—which in the policy business is crucial. We established a small office in Chile, and began funding work by specialists in many other countries. And we raised even more money, from the AVINA Foundation, the World Bank, and others. Since no other think tank working on Latin America focused on education PREAL had a huge advantage. We were the only game in town. (I particularly remember Peter's observation that "PREAL is the big guy on the block" and Osvaldo Sunkel's rejoinder that "PREAL is the only guy on the block.") PREAL became the Inter-American Dialogue's largest program. I was, of course, delighted but also amazed. I'd never imagined raising so much money.

I want to point out, since it's a natural concern for any institution receiving government funding, that USAID never pressured us in any way regarding politics. Their one request was that we give Central America special attention in our work, since that's where, in Latin America, most of their education program was concentrated. We were happy to do that. The only other issue that came up was a blanket and highly bureaucratic requirement that all programs receiving USAID funding must display the USAID logo and say in writing up front something like "From the people of the United States." We objected fiercely to both, on the grounds that political independence and a multi-national character were crucial to PREAL's success. We managed to get a formal exemption from those requirements. Otherwise, politics never came up.

On the other hand, the staff at USAID seemed to live on another planet. I liked them—don't get me wrong—but was struck by how different they were from us and from the colleagues I'd had at the Ford Foundation. Few spoke Spanish. Some had no experience at all in Latin

America. Very few specialized in education policy. None were connected to the network of Latin American education policy specialists we dealt with, nor even to the first-rate education policy staff at the World Bank, or the Inter-American Development Bank, whose offices were just a few blocks away. Their professional contacts seemed to reside almost entirely among staff at the private consulting firms that were scattered, mostly, around Washington (popularly known as the "beltway bandits") and that they financed. They seemed like a separate professional community.

One experience, early on, brought home to me how different that ecosystem was. Our liaison at USAID asked that we consider using some of our USAID money to fund a Latin American add-on to a global project on education statistics that USAID had funded at one of its consulting firms. We decided to do it. The project was straightforward, looked positive, and wouldn't cost much—although it was borderline in terms of our objectives. And, more importantly, USAID had asked that we do it. They were our major funder. We wanted to keep them happy.

So we signed a contract with the consulting firm for a clear set of deliverables to be completed by a specific date. Time went by, the date arrived, and the deliverables did not. The consulting firm requested a no-cost extension that would double the amount of time it would take to get the job done. We granted their request. The new date arrived. Still no deliverables. Then the consulting firm informed us that producing what they had agreed to produce would cost twice what they had said it would cost—and we had agreed to provide—so we'd have to pay them twice as much. I was aghast. In our world you didn't—and couldn't—behave that way. It was flat-out unprofessional and irresponsible. Your donors would cut you off. So I said no. Pretty quickly I got a call from our USAID liaison saying that the consulting firm had called him to say we were "nickel-and-diming" them. He asked that we at least reconsider. I was even more aghast. But I was also pragmatic. We needed to keep USAID happy and could afford to spend the extra money. The only real downside was that it violated our principles. We did it. I found it painful. Clearly the world of government funding was different from the world we operated in. We vowed never again to do business with USAID's consulting firms. We didn't.

(I need to point out that we ran into a similar problem when we opted to fund a project at UNESCO's Latin American office in Santiago, Chile. It was a total failure. We concluded that we did not know how to deal productively with large, government-funded bureaucracies—and would not do so again.)

More generally, I had the feeling that USAID had in some sense lost its way. It was highly bureaucratic (we were warned, for example, that if we didn't spend all the money we'd been given by the end of the fiscal year, they might take it back). Its staff were not required to show much analytical skill, nor given much power. They were required to hew closely and literally to bureaucratic requirements and objectives. If they didn't, their careers were in jeopardy. Our USAID liaison referred occasionally to the "know-nothings" upstairs. The contrast with the Ford Foundation I had worked in, and the world of Washington think tanks I was getting to know, was stark. There, talent was sought and valued. At USAID, talent seemed secondary; what really counted was bureaucracy. I suspected that youngsters just starting out at USAID would have a hard time getting the mentors and experience they'd need to grow. I was glad I hadn't started out there. All of that's based, I realize, on my contact with just a small slice of the USAID bureaucracy at a particular point in time. But it's what I saw and felt.

On the other hand, it's also true that USAID supported us handsomely for nearly two decades, enabling us to develop a strong program that operated throughout Latin America and had (we're pretty sure) a major impact on education thinking and at least some impact on policy. USAID made a good decision and stuck with it. They deserve credit. (Although I can't help wondering how much of that decision happened simply because the director for Latin America—Mark Schneider—knew Peter and me, and figured we were a good bet.)

And I always had the feeling that those consulting firms—the "beltway bandits" that depended mostly on USAID for funding—were camped outside USAID's door like a pack of hungry wolves, howling about the money we were getting, and trying to find a way to snatch it.

So we got the money. What did we do?

Basically, we experimented. We had proposed that USAID fund a number of things that seemed promising, and we did them all. But we didn't really know at the outset which of them might work. Sometimes that made us nervous. My standard line when we considered a new and unproven activity (the education report cards were a good example) was "*Estamos experimentando*" ("We're experimenting"). That didn't bother me much, but occasionally (and appropriately) it bothered Marcela, and she was quick to poke fun: "Well, Jeffrey, this is another experiment, right? That makes it OK?" That was fine, and probably what ought to happen when you aim high and try things that haven't been done before. We laughed a lot.

I don't mean to suggest that we were just throwing darts at the wall. Marcela (and José Joaquin before her) had long participated in the debates on education policy and reform in Latin America. They knew the people and the issues. I did too, although not as well as they. We also learned a lot from the emerging global literature on education reform (which was robust), as well as from the experience of countries outside Latin America (Finland was all the rage back then). But we didn't start with a clear policy agenda we were dying to transmit. It was more about putting two and two together and seeing where that took us. And quite apart from figuring out what ought to be done, we had to devise a marketing strategy. We were trying to influence policy, after all. How would we communicate and promote whatever analyses and policy recommendations we came up with?

This was important because marketing was a key part of our comparative advantage. Our base at the Inter-American Dialogue gave us access to a network of leaders who were visible and respected in their own countries, and often at the regional level as well. When they talked, people listened. We needed to take advantage of that asset and we did, recruiting (in addition to Bordón and Petty) leaders like Enrique Iglesias, president of the Inter-American Development Bank, Patricio Aylwin, former president of Chile, Nicanor Restrepo, president of Suramericana de Inversiones in Colombia (which, back then, was responsible for several percentage points of Colombia's GDP), Roberto "Bobby" Murray Meza, a top business leader from El Salvador, Jonathan Coles, a Venezuelan business leader and dean of the country's most prestigious business school, Jacqueline Malagón, former minister of education of the Dominican Republic and many others to guide and endorse our work. There were plenty more. Very few think tanks had access to people like that.

These people were interesting. When I met him, Restrepo was also president of the Latin American Business Council-CEAL (a network of Latin America's top business leaders) and had been governor of the province of Antioquia, where he'd put together a peace agreement with the FARC—a major guerrilla organization. He was a strong advocate of corporate social responsibility and had played a key role in establishing a nationwide network of Colombian business leaders committed to improving education. (He subsequently helped PREAL establish a similar network in Central America.) Restrepo was one the most unassuming leaders I'd ever met. Once I failed to recognize him at a conference in Miami because he was wearing jeans, a t-shirt, and a windbreaker; I thought he was a maintenance worker. After retiring, he spent several years in Paris pursuing a doctorate in history. I was privileged—and delighted—to spend quality time with him. When he died, I wrote an obituary for the Dialogue's web page.

Jackie Malagón stood out for her tireless commitment to education reform. Once she invited me to go with her to a small town well outside the capital city of Santo Domingo to hear the minister of education (her successor) give a speech. As we rode in the back seat of her SUV (with a driver and an armed security guard up front), I noticed she had a cell phone in each hand. "Jackie" I said "I've never seen anyone with two cell phones." "Oh," she replied, "I used to have three but my psychiatrist made me give one up."

More generally, we found the movers and shakers easy to deal with. They seemed genuinely interested in education and were generous with their time. They wanted to know what we thought ought to be done. My regret is that we didn't spend time talking seriously with them about how actually to make happen the changes we were proposing—the getting from here to there. They knew their countries well and would I'm sure have had interesting opinions. But we didn't ask. Our focus was on what do. We left getting it done to politicians and government leaders.

We built the PREAL program step by step. I mentioned earlier that initially we concentrated on figuring out what was going on. That began to pay off. Pretty quickly we realized there was a big problem: governments were spending lots of money on education but most kids—especially the poor—weren't learning much. People didn't realize that. We thought they should. We decided that our first step should be to sound the alarm.

Here we were inspired by the U.S. experience. In 1983 the National Commission on Excellence in Education had published *A Nation at Risk: The Imperative for Educational Reform* which argued that U.S. schools were failing, and sparked alarm in public opinion and a surge in efforts to improve education. We figured we should do something like that for Latin America.

We did, producing a big report on education that outlined serious failings in the region's school systems and made four policy recommendations that pretty much became PREAL's core message for the next decade:

- Set standards—especially learning standards—for the education system and measure progress toward meeting them.
- Give schools and local communities more control over, and responsibility for, education.
- Strengthen the teaching profession by raising salaries, reforming training and making teachers more accountable to the communities they serve.
- Invest more money per student in preschool, primary and secondary education.

The report, entitled *A Future at Stake*, was signed by our (highly respected) regionwide Task Force on Education, Equity and Economic Competitiveness, and published in Spanish, Portuguese, and English. It made a splash, I think, and put us on the policy map. Pretty quickly we decided to produce more reports, but to turn them into "report cards"— a concept that seemed especially appropriate for work on education.

The Education Report Cards became PREAL's flagship—the best-known and most visible thing we did. Most were presented and endorsed by a Task Force and issued in the language of the countries it tracked. Each was pitched to a non-specialist audience—parents, politicians, business leaders, media. Each graded the region's schools on specific criterion like enrollments, test scores, keeping kids in school, equity, accountability, teacher quality, and investment. Each criterion was given a letter grade (A to F) along with an arrow (up, down or flat) to indicate progress. Grades were generally low—mostly C's and D's, no A's, maybe one B, and at least one F (in equity). Schools clearly weren't doing well.

We issued several report cards for Latin America, followed by several for Central America. Later, at the request of our partners, we began producing report cards for specific countries. In Colombia, we even sponsored five at the municipal level. The report cards seemed to be a hit. They were easy to understand. Leaders liked them. They got mentioned in the press. (Once while riding the N4 bus in Washington I noticed a woman sitting across from me reading one of PREAL's Report Cards. I was delighted, of course. I resisted the urge to introduce myself.)

Producing the report cards was a group effort but, crucially, very much under the direction of our colleague in Washington, Tamara Ortega Goodspeed, who did a heroic job of working with our national partners to pull together data and analysis, synthesize results and come up with a simple statement of findings. Report cards were hard to do well. You couldn't just analyze. You had to get the message right and communicate it effectively. Tammy figured that out and was great at showing others how to do it.

Hiring Tammy, by the way, came right out of my Ford Foundation playbook. She'd been a summa at Yale and had an MPA from Princeton's

Woodrow Wilson School. She checked all the boxes—intelligence, education, motivation, and character—that I'd learned produced first-rate staff. And—a big plus—Tammy also became one of my most effective critics. She'd read my drafts and tell me mercilessly what I'd gotten wrong. My gut reaction was usually "Oh c'mon Tammy—I worked hard on this and it's good." Then I'd usually decide she was right. Tammy was a great editor. She made my stuff better. One more argument for surrounding yourself with talented staff.

More generally, we tried always to hire only the best people to work at PREAL. Patricia Arregui, for example, had directed one of Peru's top think tanks, GRADE, before coming on board. Many others—Ana María de Andraca, Denise Vaillant, Santiago Cueto, Pedro Ravela, Alejandro Ganimian, Katherina Hruskovec, and many others—either already had distinguished careers or were youngsters clearly on their way up. Working with such first-rate people was remarkably rewarding. They were crucial to any success PREAL had.

We didn't always get our hiring right. That happened mostly when we hired someone we weren't totally sold on because we were in a hurry, or felt we had to keep a donor happy. I won't go into detail, but those experiences simply reaffirmed the principle I'd learned at the Ford Foundation: If you hire people you have doubts about just because a position has to be filled, there's a good chance you'll regret it. Most of the time you're better off waiting.

Another principle that was key for us: become a collective effort by education professionals from across Latin America rather than a top-down initiative by a group of experts based in Washington. We aimed to establish a "hemispheric partnership"—a kind of region-wide network—working on education policy. All our activities—data gathering, policy analysis, debate, outreach—were done in collaboration with analysts and leaders based in their own countries. We didn't, in fact, do much of anything in Washington (an observation that, every time I made it, prompted my boss, Peter Hakim, to roll his eyes in mock frustration—"Boy that's for sure. You guys never do anything.").

Our program extended well beyond report cards and ran for nearly two decades, but I'm not going into detail. This is a memoir and not a history (you can find more at *www.preal.online*). I offer only a list:

- Multi-country task forces on education reform.
- Expert working groups on specific policy areas (four).
- Policy and Best Practices briefs that pointed the way to improvement (well over a hundred).
- Study tours that enabled community leaders and teachers to visit innovative education programs in other countries.
- National-level business-education partnerships.
- A research competition.
- A web page that housed our policy briefs, report cards, and a blog.

What I find most striking about all of this is how long it held my attention. For more than fifteen years PREAL became most of what I did, and all I needed to do. It kept me interested. It kept me happy. I never dreamed of moving on to something else.

When, for example, I got a feeler from the World Bank regarding the post of director of education for Latin America, I decided not to apply. It would have been a significant step up—more money and more job security (presuming, of course, that I could get hired and then make it in an unfamiliar bureaucracy). But it was clear to me that I should stick with what I was doing. I had commitments to staff and to donors. The work was challenging. I wasn't done.

How come?

Part of the explanation, I think, is that instead of funding people to do policy analysis, writing, and debate (as I'd done for seventeen years at Ford), now I was doing those things myself. I'd moved to the front lines. I liked it there.

Another part is that education policy in Latin America was fascinating—a complex intellectual puzzle that begged solving. Here you had a huge government program—public education—that was crucial to economic growth, poverty reduction, and democratic governance, but was doing poorly in just about every country. Spending was high. Test scores were low. Reform wasn't happening. I needed to figure that out.

But yet another part—probably the biggest—was that I was following the script that my parents and I had written back when I was a kid: get out of rural Michigan, become an intellectual, and make the world a better place. That was what I was supposed to do. That was what I was doing. I didn't need anything more.

Was that bad? Did I lack vision? Was I living out my parents' dreams rather than coming up with my own? Was I becoming a stick-in-the-mud?

I never felt that way. Most of us start (and are pretty much stuck) with what our parents give us. We navigate from there. Maybe we buy it. Maybe we rebel. But you're only raised one way. You have to work with it. My parents loaded me up with values and the urge to excel. I bought that, but the details were mine. They could never have imagined the things I did after graduating from college. The Peace Corps, the Ford Foundation, and PREAL were all examples. I was doing it my way. I liked it. I felt no need to move on.

The biggest surprise, I suppose, was that I was working on education at all. Back when I was at the Ford Foundation, I'd decided that my work on education was over. I'd gone on to other topics and didn't expect to go back. But Peter Hakim had changed that by asking me to develop a program on education at the Dialogue. I did, and now I was becoming something of an authority. My PREAL colleagues and I had looked at the research, thought it through and come up with answers. I edited several books, published more than a dozen papers and gave more than a hundred talks. Much of that I did in Latin America and in Spanish. I'd gotten fascinated.

That gave me the opportunity, at some level, to speak truth to power. I mentioned, in an earlier chapter, my conversations about education policy with two future presidents of Colombia. More generally, and routinely, at events organized by PREAL or by others, I spoke to a broad variety of national leaders—political, academic, business, governmental—and so had at least a chance to influence their views on education policy. For someone who grew up thinking he was supposed to make the world a better place, telling people like that how to make education better was a dream come true.

Some examples that I keep remembering:

The Latin American chapter of the global federation of teachers' trade unions (Education International) invited me to speak at one of their meetings in Latin America. In my presentation I suggested that teachers' unions were not playing a positive role in raising the achievement levels of poor students in the region. The audience seemed a little uneasy with my analysis. They didn't say much. They didn't invite me back.

The Council on Foreign Relations asked me to write a paper on education in Latin America, then invited me to give a talk at their offices on East 68th Street in Manhattan. When I entered, there was a modest sign announcing the two people speaking at events that evening: George Soros and Jeffrey Puryear. The talk went well. Al Fishlow, a Senior Fellow at the Council whom I knew fairly well because he was a member of the Inter-American Dialogue, introduced me and commented. I was delighted to get that topic on the radar of that (presumably) influential group. I just wish I'd gotten a picture of the sign.

When the World Bank invited the minister of education of Finland to speak at its headquarters in Washington (back then Finland was the darling of the global education policy community because it had the highest student test scores in the world), I was invited to comment on her presentation. I was delighted, of course. My two questions were: 1) How did Finland manage to recruit teachers from the top 25% of the talent pool, while Latin America only managed to recruit them from the bottom 25%?; and 2) How come teachers' unions didn't seem to be a problem in Finland, while they were a major problem in Latin America, resisting efforts to raise standards for entry into the profession, opposing efforts to evaluate teacher performance, and threatening to shut down entire national school systems with strikes? All I remember about the discussion is that it was spirited.

And once I flew down to Guayaquil, Ecuador to attend a meeting of former Latin American presidents organized by my friend and former president of Peru, Alejandro Toledo (this was, of course, before the Peruvian government charged him with bribery and money laundering). When I arrived at the hotel the clerk told me I had no reservation. I said I was there for the meeting of former Latin American presidents. After consulting, he informed me that that group was meeting the following week. I'd confused the dates. So I checked into the hotel and then rebooked my reservation for the first flight out in the morning—which turned out to be the same plane and the same crew. When I boarded, they looked a little surprised. I grinned sheepishly and mumbled something about making a mistake. I had the feeling they'd seen this before.

There were many more.

Over more than a decade, then, PREAL repeatedly organized, or spoke at, events in nearly every country in Latin America. It sounded the alarm regarding education, urged countries to give it more attention, monitored progress and made numerous policy recommendations. It put issues on the table that had not been there, and pressed countries to address them. I won't go into more detail, but I do want to say something about impact, since that's the holy grail of think tanks, and what we thought we were about. Did we have any?

We're pretty sure we did, but it's hard to prove. I mentioned earlier that measuring impact in the policy business is fraught with uncertainty. Policy change is seldom direct. Mostly it takes shape in the minds of leaders and behind closed doors. You'll probably never know for sure whether what you said, wrote or did convinced a country's president to propose new education policy, and the legislature to pass it, and the media to applaud it and the teachers' union to accept it. There's a kind of mystery to influencing policy that you just have to accept.

On the other hand, decision-makers get their ideas from somewhere. They respond not only to ideology and pressure but also to information, arguments, and ideas. A program that can consistently command their attention and provide credible analysis and policy recommendations has a serious chance of influencing their views, and eventually their actions. That's what think tanks are all about.

So what I can say about PREAL's impact is far from being definitive, but is certainly suggestive. Maybe it's just the tip of the iceberg. Here are four clear accomplishments we think set us up to have impact:

First. PREAL became visible. It established a strong presence in Latin American education policy circles. Its short, well-written documents—in Spanish and Portuguese—reached not just education specialists but opinion leaders more generally and got cited in the press. Its events drew leading policy analysts and political figures. Its website got traffic. PREAL became a brand name.

Second, PREAL became credible. International organizations—the World Bank, the Inter-American Development Bank, UNESCO, and the Organization of American States—participated in PREAL's activities and invited PREAL to participate in theirs. Political leaders and government officials spoke at PREAL's events. PREAL provided input to the Summit of the Americas process. We got invited to speak at meetings of the Latin American Business Council, the World Economic Forum, Education International (the global federation of teachers' unions I mentioned earlier), and the Council on Foreign Relations. When PREAL talked, people listened.

Third, PREAL became productive. It generated well over 150 publications during its first ten years, organized numerous conferences and seminars in countries throughout the region, and developed a diverse set of programs that included not only Task Forces and Report Cards, but also business-education partnerships, working groups on key policy issues, a research competition, study tours for teachers and principals, and ad hoc "coaching" of ministerial officials in policy reform. It did that with just seven full-time staff.

Fourth, PREAL became connected. It established networks that included government, political, academic, and business leaders throughout Latin America and, occasionally, the United States, Canada, and Europe. PREAL built relationships that made it easier to share information, experience and policy ideas.

And what we do know is that at least some change happened. Education moved up on the priority list of governments across Latin America, often to the top tier. Leaders began to pay more attention and ask more questions. The terms of debate shifted away from quantity and towards quality. There was less talk about spending and enrollments, and more about learning and equity. The issue of accountability—who is responsible for student success or failure—began to be discussed, pretty much for the first time.

Policy also changed. Public spending on education as a percent of GDP rose by roughly half between 1990 and 2006. Nearly all countries established national student achievement tests, which gave them reasonable measures of quality. Many began participating in international achievement tests, like the Trends in International Mathematics and Science Study (TIMSS) and the Programme for International Students Assessment (PISA). For the first time, several countries established national learning standards. Many also began experimenting with new approaches to teacher management. Several began implementing accountability reforms, such as school level outcomes reporting, and merit pay for teachers. More generally there was a clear and growing interest in identifying promising policies and giving them a try. And the business community began asking serious questions about education and establishing national programs to promote better education policy.

Most of this was new. All of it was in line with what PREAL recommended for well over a decade. In a very few cases leaders explicitly credited PREAL with sparking their decisions. The ministers of education of Central America, for example, resolved to launch a regional project on education standards, citing specifically PREAL's first report card on education in Latin America (A Future at Stake) and several other PREAL documents (that initiative did not prosper, unfortunately). More generally, though, we had to be content with noting that some, perhaps many, of the changes we recommended were taking place. That was positive. It's probably about as much as most think tanks can expect.

What I'm sure of is that PREAL nudged the conventional wisdom on education policy in Latin America in a positive direction. We convinced some, perhaps many, that there were serious problems with public education, and that just getting more kids into school wasn't going to solve them. We urged leaders to pay more attention to learning and to equity.

We made the case for systemic change rather than just piecemeal projects. We urged countries to establish learning standards and national student achievement tests. We argued that business leaders should promote education reform. We planted seeds. Some, perhaps many, have taken root.

And—something we hadn't anticipated—several PREAL collaborators went on to become ministers or vice ministers of education, or to hold other high-level government or political positions. One, Ricardo Maduro of Honduras, was even elected president. And one PREAL staffer, Michael Lisman, ended up running the very USAID education unit that funded PREAL in the first place. The logical question is whether their experience with PREAL had any impact on what they did later on. I don't remember asking any of them. And they might not know. Or maybe they'd rather not say. I'm reminded of something a wise friend told me long ago: "You can accomplish a lot if you don't insist on getting credit for it." I was never tempted to ask those folks whether they did any of the things we recommended. I was just thankful they'd given us their time and attention. And happy to hope we'd had a positive impact.

What PREAL didn't do much of was take on the question of getting from here to there. To be sure, it involved and targeted political leaders in its work. And it pointed out that some of the major obstacles to improving education were political rather than technical. By doing so it hoped that those leaders might be moved to devise political strategies for improving education policy. That was important. But it was about as far as we went.

And politics was a major impediment to education reform. Public education in Latin America was dominated by the providers: ministries and teachers unions, both of whom had enormous power. The clients of public education, mostly poor parents who couldn't afford private schools, had very little power. Many were just thankful that their kids were getting more schooling than they did. They had little or no information about the quality of education their kids were getting and no levers to influence education policy. Teachers could strike; parents could not. It was a tough environment.

Ricardo Maduro brought that home at a meeting with PREAL's senior staff in his office in Tegucigalpa shortly after being elected president of Honduras: "for a president...education reform is a net-negative political enterprise. It has high political costs and it produces nothing." I'm paraphrasing, but his cold appraisal of the realities of education reform was clear and strikes me as solid. Politicians had few incentives to fight for serious education reform. It was a Sisyphean endeavor.

So while I'm fairly sure that PREAL changed thinking about education, I'm less sure that it changed much policy, at least in the short term.

On other hand, let's remember my observations several chapters back about the Ford Foundation's impact on policy in Chile over nearly three decades:

> ...the policy game, as Peter Hakim has pointed out, is like chess. You play for position rather than for victory. Most of your moves have no immediate impact. They are intended only to establish a position that will enable you to have impact later on. That's how it worked out for the Chicago Boys who dreamed of revolutionizing economic policy, and for the think tanks opposed to Pinochet who dreamed of restoring democratic government. They spent years getting into position. Then, when the stars aligned and opportunity knocked, they were ready. Check and mate.

PREAL was playing the policy game. There was no reliable way to predict impact. It might take a while, but it might happen. If you couldn't deal with that level of uncertainty, you were in the wrong game.

So that's PREAL—the last and longest stage in my professional career. I did several other things while at the Inter-American Dialogue, most notably establishing a broader social policy program. But those were small by comparison, and never had as much influence as PREAL. So I'm not going into them. Let's move on to the next stage. I retired.

This has been a hard chapter to write. Maybe I shouldn't be surprised. Jill Ker Conway, after writing her second memoir, *True North*, pointed out that she ended it just as she took up her position as president of Smith College. She did not write (then, at least) about her experience as a college president because "…you have to be at least twenty years away from what you write about to have the necessary detachment."

I'd say she's right. I stopped working at the Dialogue just over ten years ago, and I may not yet have the proper perspective. When I shared the first version of this chapter with my good friend Peter Hakim, he said it read like a grant proposal. He was right. It was too academic and perfunctory. There was too little me. So I rewrote it. It's still pretty wonky, but I don't think it's realistic to wait another ten years. So here it is. It could have been worse. Sometimes you just have to move forward.

XXI

THINKING IT OVER

WHICH TAKES US back to where we began: A kid from rural Michigan wants to get out, become an intellectual, and make the world a better place. He works at that for more than four decades. Then he retires and decides he also wants to try his hand at real writing. So he does. How'd all that go?

Pretty well, I think.

I certainly got out. I left Michigan upon graduating from college and returned only to visit. I lived in five cities in the United States and four in Latin America. I visited just about every Latin American and Caribbean country, plus maybe a dozen countries elsewhere. That's out.

I also became an intellectual, at least by my lights. I got a PhD, published several academic articles, wrote an academic book, and lectured at numerous universities (including a couple that had turned me down for admission decades earlier). I wrote lots of policy papers and gave dozens of talks. I felt like an intellectual. I hung out with quite a few. That was more than I expected. It was plenty.

Did I make the world a better place? I think so, but it's harder to demonstrate. I certainly tried. I did the kinds of things you might choose if you wanted to make the world a better place: rural community development in the Peace Corps, social and economic policy at the Ford Foundation, and education reform at the Inter-American Dialogue. I did them reasonably well, I think. And I've documented in these pages what look like positive impacts. But making the world a better place is pretty ambitious, especially when you target social policy and social change, as I did. So impact is always going to be slow, elusive, and even mysterious. That's the game I was in. I'm satisfied—delighted, really—with how far I seem to have gotten. And surprised.

And how'd that "try his hand at real writing" thing turn out? "Wonderful" is the word that comes to mind. An adventure. One of the most rewarding things I've ever done. Even if nobody reads this memoir, I'm happy. (Hard to believe, I know.)

How come? I think partly because I was satisfying an urge I'd had since college but put aside while satisfying all those other urges I've been talking about here. Serious writing was always at the end of the line. Finally I got to it and discovered I liked it.

What did I like about writing? Some of it's the craft. The idea of not just saying what's on my mind, but saying it in a way that's clear, maybe charming, or even beautiful. I'm moved by the idea of writing well. It's a puzzle I want to solve. That led me to take a look at what writers write about writing. And now I read with different eyes. I notice the strategies writers use, like establishing a voice, drawing the reader in, managing detail, substituting dialogue for description, employing emotion, and shifting perspective. More than once I've reacted to something I was reading by saying (to myself, of course) "Wow! Look what she just did." I see that stuff now. I didn't before. It's rewarding. And fun.

Another part of it is figuring out what deserves to be said. A good writer helps people see things that are worth seeing but they might not see on their own. That's valuable. And a responsibility. At some level I suppose it's like the little boy showing his mom the pretty stone he found on the beach. But in this case, it's more challenging and, I think, meets a real need.

Yet another part is that this kind of writing—a memoir—comes from the heart. It's about making sense of myself. Putting my past into words made me see things that I hadn't seen clearly before, or only half understood. Sense is what they began to make. Writing, as I mentioned a while back, is discovering.

What's interesting is that even though writing is almost always hard I still want to do it. I get enormous pleasure when I manage to write well—or at least feel like I have. That's a good in itself. Maybe I could have been a professional writer. I don't know. I find the idea enticing. But I'll never know. It was one more road not taken.

My final thought is about how lucky I've been.

It's tempting, if you've lived a relatively happy life, to focus on how your hard work and good judgment made that happen. And there's always something to that. But I am struck by how much of it, at least in my case, was luck. I didn't get to where I got all by myself.

My luck started at birth—in the United States as World War II was ending and just before the postwar economic boom got underway. We weren't rich, but neither were we poor. My father had a pretty good job and would soon get one that was better. Unparalleled prosperity and opportunity were peeping over the horizon. Primary and secondary school were free, good enough, and included friends and fun. Teen-agers like me could, if they worked part-time, buy a used car—a precious and enthralling kind of liberation. There was a modern, affordable university nearby, ready to show the world to anyone who walked through the gate. I had resources and options. None of the poor *campesinos* I met while I was a Peace Corps volunteer in Colombia had that kind of luck. Nor did most of the rest of the world.

And I was born into a family that, although not long on money, was long on love, standards, and discipline. I was surrounded by people—parents, grandparents, aunts, and uncles—who worked hard, cared about right and wrong, and tried, as the old song goes, to keep on the sunny side of life. They gave me their time and made me feel like I mattered. Family, it turns out, is destiny for most of us—defining what's out there, what's possible, what's good, and what's bad. The values and expectations those folks instilled in me became a kind of operating system that made it easier to navigate the unfamiliar waters I'd venture into later on. How lucky was that?

The key departure, I think, was going to college. That got me out of rural Michigan and into the wide world. It exposed me to new ideas and new people. It presented me with paths I would not have found on my own. I got charmed. There was no going back.

But how is it I went to college at all, while most of the kids I grew up with didn't? Intelligence probably played a part. But more important I think was that I got born into a family that told me I was going to college and did everything necessary to make it happen. Not everybody did. I was lucky.

After that I started making at least some of my luck, by working hard and aiming high. I chose, for example, to do graduate work at the University of Chicago even though I had no particular interest in the field (comparative education) that I'd applied to, and had gotten a fellowship in. I wanted to be exposed to the best minds and that's where they were so that's where I went. It was as simple as that.

And then, once I realized what a special institution the Ford Foundation was, it became the place where I had to work. I applied nowhere else. Somewhere Somerset Maugham observed that "if you refuse anything but the best, you very often get it." There's probably something to that.

But there was also lots of luck. Growing up I had no interest in Latin America and only signed up for Peace Corps/Colombia because something else didn't work out. That led me to spend the rest of my career working on and in Latin America. I came across the Ford Foundation by chance, when one of their staff in Bogotá, Ralph Harbison, spoke to my Peace Corps training group. Working there then became my goal. And when they finally hired me, I had the extraordinary good fortune to have as my first boss and mentor Peter Bell, one of Ford's most talented staff members. And how lucky was I to meet Miri, my future wife, at Stanford? And then to find her still willing to listen to me several years later when I finally realized she was for me? I could go on, but you get the point. I've had incredible luck.

I suppose I might have done even better. Gone higher in the world of philanthropy or think tanks, for example. Maybe. But I didn't. The fact is that my inner compass, if that's what it was, never pointed in that direction. I was almost always happy doing what I was already doing.

And trying to do it well. That was hard enough. It was worthwhile enough. I didn't need more.

And I wonder what "going higher" might have cost. I've seen plenty of people who, upon opting to sample the seductive, rarefied air at the top, struggle with other parts of their lives. Would I have had to neglect my personal life? Might I have ended up not getting married, or not being a good dad? Would I have spent less time exploring art with Pepe Zalaquett in Santiago and New York? Read fewer novels? Missed those glorious hikes in the Andes? Skied less? Not been moved to write this book? Nobody knows, of course. But it's important to keep those questions in sight. Not much is free. Probably nothing.

So I'm satisfied, gratified, and happy. And thankful. That's enough. My bottom line, I guess, is aim high, but don't be greedy. Try to be humble (it's hard). Be sure each step you take is as good as possible. Make things better. Appreciate. All of that sounds more than a little Lutheran, of course.

But by now you know me.

THE END

AFTERWORD

I've covered a diverse and often unconnected set of topics and places in this memoir—which mirrors my life. Readers wanting to dig deeper into a few might consider the following:

- Bruce Catton. *Waiting for the Morning Train*. New York: Doubleday and Company, 1972.
- Bruce Catton. *Michigan: A Bicentennial History*. New York: W. W. Norton & Company, 1976.
- Jerry Dennis. *The Living Great Lakes: Searching for the Heart of the Inland Seas*. New York: Thomas Dunne Books, 2003.
- Laura Ingalls Wilder. *The Little House in the Big Woods*. New York: Harper & Brothers, 1932.
- Mildred Armstrong Kalish. *Little Heathens*. New York: Bantam Dell, 2007.
- Moritz Thomsen. *Living Poor: A Peace Corps Chronicle*. Seattle: University of Washington Press, 1968.
- John W. Boyer. *The University of Chicago, A History*. Chicago: The University of Chicago Press, 2015.
- Michael Reid. *Forgotten Continent. The Battle for Latin America's Soul*. New Haven: Yale University Press, 2007.
- Dwight Macdonald. *The Ford Foundation: The Men and the Millions*. Routledge, 1988.
- Kai Bird. *The Color of Truth: McGeorge Bundy and William Bundy, Brothers in Arms*. Simon & Schuster, 1998.
- Richard Magat. *The Ford Foundation at Work. Philanthropic Choices, Methods and Styles*. New York: Plenum Press,1979.
- Abraham F. Lowenthal and Martin Weinstein. *Kalman Silvert*.

Engaging Latin America, Building Democracy. Boulder: Lynne Rienner Publishers, 2016.

- Jeffrey M. Puryear. "Higher Education, Development Assistance and Repressive Regimes" *Studies in Comparative and International Development* XVII, No. 2. 1982. Reprinted by the Ford Foundation, February, 1983.
- Jeffrey M. Puryear. *Thinking Politics: Intellectuals and Democracy in Chile, 1973-1988.* Baltimore: The Johns Hopkins University Press, 1994.
- Tom Wolfe. *The Painted Word.* New York: Farrar, Straus & Giroux, 1975.
- Patricia Hidalgo and Constanza Toro. *Idealista Sin Ilusiones: Conversaciones con José Zalaquett.* Santiago: Lolita Editores, 2017.

www.ingramcontent.com/pod-product-compliance
Lightning Source LLC
Chambersburg PA
CBHW061549120626

46550CB00004B/1419

* 9 7 9 8 9 9 2 1 7 4 1 2 0 *